CARL SCHURZ
From a bust by J. O. Schweizer

THE

FORTY-EIGHTERS

POLITICAL REFUGEES
OF THE
GERMAN REVOLUTION
OF
1848

Edited by A. E. ZUCKER

NEW YORK

COLUMBIA UNIVERSITY PRESS

1950

Dedicated to the Memory of

VEIT VALENTIN

Scholar and Liberal

Historian of the German Revolution

of 1848

PREFACE

THERE has never been a book written on the Forty-eighters, the group of German idealists who fought to establish a liberal and unified Germany and then came to the United States as refugees from the reaction. As the centenary of the Revolution approached, a number of us who had been working in this field felt that the men and the event should be commemorated. After some preliminary planning the present writers met at the headquarters of the Carl Schurz Memorial Foundation in Philadelphia on February 7, 1948, and outlined the various chapters. The result is the present book.

All of us collaborators owe a great debt to Veit Valentin, author of the definitive work on the German Revolution of 1848 and refugee from the Hitler regime. We therefore dedicate the volume to this fine scholar whom death took from us January 12, 1947.

The present generation has witnessed revolutions in Russia, Italy, and Germany. The German Revolution of 1848 stands in direct contrast to these more recent upheavals through its regrettable lack of success and through the humanitarian spirit of the leaders which contributed to its failure. The following paragraph from Valentin's *1848* is very illuminating regarding the character of the Forty-eighters.

The German Revolution of 1848 erected no guillotines and held no extraordinary courts of a purely political nature. No one except Prince Metternich was banished; there was no confiscation of fortunes, no holding-up of salaries, no refusal of pensions. No one in Germany thought that in order to combat the past, its representatives must be made personally defenceless and economically impotent. Outwardly it was nothing more than a purely political reversal, borne aloft by representatives of pure humanitarianism; a humane revolution is necessarily a semi-revolution. This was probably the deepest error of the men of 1848.

The positive side of this picture is presented by President George N. Shuster in his address at a commemoration of the Forty-eighters held in the Library of Congress on May 12, 1948:

From one point of view the impact of the Forty-eighters on the trend of events was manifestly not very great. There were relatively few of these men and women, nor were they ever kneaded into a compact group. You cannot speak of the Forty-eighters as you might of the Boston Irish, or the Puritans, or the Virginians. But seen from another point of view their story seems of almost breath-taking significance. Whether they were temperate and magnanimous, or irate and uncompromising, they were always men of ideas. Service to the spirit of humanity was to them a sacred trust. They had been reared in the best tradition of their native land, and so, though they might indeed be greenhorns, as the phrase went, they were also proud and tested refugees. They had wanted desperately to release the German soul from the dozens of little princely curio cabinets in which it had been confined and variously labeled. They had sought the unity in which there is strength, but also the inviolate personal separateness which we call freedom. It was therefore difficult for them ever to forget that they had failed, but it was also impossible for them not to remember that they had tried—that their battle had been for everything that confers stature and nobility upon the race.

A fairly objective evaluation of this particular group of immigrants may be obtained from the *Dictionary of American Biography*, a work compiled by leading American historians in the decade around 1930. The editors considered 385 men and women born in Germany or Austria sufficiently distinguished in their various fields to deserve a place among our great. The distribution of the dates of arrival of these immigrants shows plainly that the decade after 1848 (a period of a numerous, but not the most numerous, German immigration) brought so disproportionately many persons of distinction that this group obviously merits attention:

17th Century	8	1836–1845	38	1876–1885	26
18th Century	57	1846–1855	103	1886–1895	17
1800–1825	21	1856–1865	42	1896–1907	6
1826–1835	30	1866–1875	37		

The definition of the term "Forty-eighter" offers some difficulties. For the purposes of this book we have chosen to define him as "one who came to the United States from German-speaking territory as a result of his participation in the Revolution of 1848." This excludes hundreds of thousands who emigrated for economic reasons. It also does not include political refugees from earlier periods of political repression who were exponents of the same ideals, both in Germany and in the United States, although in the telling of the story it has not been possible to overlook such men as Francis Lieber, Gustave Koerner, Friedrich Muench, or Johann Bernhard Stallo.

When in Henrik Ibsen's *An Enemy of the People* the politician Peter Stockmann holds out to his brother, Dr. Thomas Stockmann, the possibility of a return to his post and his salary provided only that he will recant his scientific findings, Dr. Stockmann characterizes this meanness of soul by the very worst epithet he can think of: "You plebeian!" Contrariwise, Ibsen, after having lived six years in Bergen, pays this town the highest compliment by calling it "a city with no plebeians." After having become pretty well acquainted with the Forty-eighters, I can say that among their number there were some muddle-headed fellows like Dr. Stockmann, but no plebeians.

It is a pleasure at this point to acknowledge our gratitude to the Carl Schurz Memorial Foundation for friendly support of our work, to Dr. Guy A. Cardwell and Dr. Dieter Cunz of the University of Maryland for a critical reading of the manuscript, and to Miss Kate Lewis, secretary of the Foreign Language Department, for understanding help with the details of the text.

A. E. ZUCKER

University of Maryland
September 7, 1948

INTRODUCTION

O N AN October day in 1682 the ship *Concord* bobbed up
and down against the western bank of the Delaware River
in Penn's Sylvania. A group of Crefelders, self-exiled from their
Rhineland homes, gathered their chattels and stepped ashore to
find new homes in the areas which now form the continental
United States. They were the vanguard of the tens of thousands
of their countrymen who came to Pennsylvania before the middle of the eighteenth century. Their descendants are the Pennsylvania Germans, popularly called the "Pennsylvania Dutch."

Fore more than two centuries this group has maintained a
distinct, almost separate existence. Tenaciously they have held
to the German dialect which they brought with them; it has
survived to this day with comparatively few English admixtures
and completely free from later European influences. In like
manner they have retained their customs and lore to a degree
which amazes students of social phenomena. Yet they are as
American as the covered wagon, an empire-building vehicle
which they themselves built on the banks of the Conestoga
creek which drains the fields they till.

The intense ethnocentric culture of these devoutly religious
people, who similar to the Quakers wear or wore their distinctive
dress, prevented them from making common cause with any of
the Germanic groups which emigrated during the nineteenth
century. In some quarters there is an aloofness approaching
hostility to the later comers.

More than a century and a half intervened from the time of
the arrival of the first Germans in Pennsylvania until the wave
of Germanic immigrants which we call the Forty-eighters. The
high tide of the Palatinate exodus to America was fully a hundred years before 1848. And yet, on infinity's yardstick, the span
of years which separates the various waves of refugees from re-

ligious persecution in 1682, 1710, 1727–1755, the political refugees of 1830, 1848, 1870, or immigrants for economic reasons of many other years, dates which mark the miseries of Europe, all of these must someday merge into one when students begin to assess the part played by Germanic peoples in the settlement and development of our country.

For the sake of the record it is well that we, in our time, attempt to evaluate the distinct contributions which they have given. Each group has made, and it is probable that new groups will continue to make, unique contributions to the multicolored quilt of American life. Each group encountered difficulties in the processes of adjustment and assimilation; each one produced its heroes and scoundrels; each was subjected to undue praise and unwarranted maligning.

It may be pointed out that the Germans have always been the largest non-English speaking group in America and that their experiences as a minority are typical of all other non-English speaking groups now attempting to earn for themselves the un-hyphenated title, American. No one sheds his nationality with the same ease that he removes a garment, and no one assumes a new loyalty as readily as he dons a new suit of clothes. There is always the matter of backgrounds—a matter of history. In this volume a group of scholars attempt to write that history and to survey, in a century's perspective, the gains both to the United States through the German immigration of 1848 and to these newcomers through their adoption into our community.

Perhaps in a similar manner we may hope that the day is not far off when other groups such as the Poles, Greeks, Italians, Scandinavians, Slavs, and Hebrews will record their experiences in the complex process of Americanization. When these contributions are offered we suspect that we shall find a remarkable degree of conformity to a pattern. As in the cases of the various Germanic groups, we may find first a sequence of economic, religious, or political upheavals in the Old World; then a period of hapless wandering lighted by the hope of a new-world Canaan. There is sure to be a period of disillusion during the early years on American soil, brought on by a contrast of the ideal with the harsh realities facing the immigrant; then a period of severe trial while conflicting cultures brush against each other, full of distrust and nostalgia as distance lends enchantment to the old-world setting; then a new conflict between generations as offspring adopt American ideals through education and social controls. The final triumph must wait for a few generations to come and go. Then, in perhaps one century, as from 1848 to 1948, they all merge as Americans.

ARTHUR D. GRAEFF

Robesonia, Pennsylvania
July 15, 1948

CONTENTS

ILLUSTRATIONS

THE AUTHORS

ARTHUR D. GRAEFF, Ph.D. (University of Pennsylvania). Author of: *Conrad Weiser, Pennsylvania Peacemaker; The History of Pennsylvania; Industrial Berks County, 1748–1948; It Happened in Pennsylvania; Lebanon County through the Centuries, an Appreciation; The Relations of the Pennsylvania Germans and the British Authorities.* Contributing author to *The Pennsylvania Germans.*

CARL JOACHIM FRIEDRICH, Ph.D. (Heidelberg, 1925). Professor of Government, Harvard. Author: *Responsible Bureaucracy; The Politica of Johannes Althusius; Constitutional Government and Politics; Foreign Policy in the Making; Constitutional Government and Democracy; Radiobroadcasting and Higher Education; The New Belief in the Common Man; Inevitable Peace* (1948). Dr. Friedrich has served as Governmental Affairs Adviser to the U.S. Commander-in-Chief and Military Governor, in Germany.

OSCAR HANDLIN, Assistant professor of the social sciences and a member of the departments of history and of social relations, Harvard. Author: *Boston's Immigrants, Commonwealth, This Was America;* also numerous articles in the fields of American economic and social history.

AUGUSTUS JOHN PRAHL, Ph.D. (Johns Hopkins, 1933). Professor of Foreign Languages, University of Maryland. Author of: *Gerstaecker and the Problems of His Time.* Contributor to *Modern Language Notes, Modern Language Quarterly, Comparative Literature News-Letter, German Quarterly, American-German Review.*

HILDEGARD BINDER JOHNSON, Ph.D. (University of Berlin, 1933). Assistant professor of Geography, Macalester College. Two Grants-in-Aid from the Social Science Research Council to study German immigration to the Middle West. Specialty: Historical Geography and German immigration. Articles in *Rural Sociology, Pennsylvania Magazine of History and Biography, American Journal of Sociology, Agricultural History, Iowa Journal of History and Politics, Minnesota History,* and *American-German Review.*

FRANK X. BRAUN, Ph.D. (Michigan, 1940). Instructor in German, University of Michigan (since 1945). Author of: *Kulturelle Ziele im*

Werk Gustav Frenssens (Ann Arbor, 1946); *English Grammar for Language Students* (Ann Arbor, 1947); also articles in *Germanic Review*, *Monatshefte*, and *Papers of the Bibliographical Society of America*, dealing with German literature and German-Americans.

LAWRENCE S. THOMPSON, Ph.D. (University of North Carolina, 1936). Director of Libraries, University of Kentucky; Fellow, American Scandinavian Foundation; special agent for the Federal Bureau of Investigation; contributor to library science, bibliographical, philological, and critical journals. Translator of Albert Predeek's *History of Libraries in Great Britain and North America* (ALA, 1947). Arranged library exhibits to commemorate Forty-eighters.

EITEL WOLF DOBERT. Instructor in Foreign Languages, University of Maryland. Author of: *Ein Nazi entdeckt Frankreich; Europa, Stirb und Werde;* and *Convert to Freedom.*

ELLA LONN, for many years professor of History at Goucher College. Author of: *Reconstruction in Louisiana after 1868, Desertion during the Civil War, Salt as a Factor in the Confederacy, The Colonial Agents of the Southern Colonies,* and a forthcoming book on foreigners in the U. S. Army and Navy. President of the Southern Historical Association (1946).

BAYARD QUINCY MORGAN, Ph.D. (Leipzig, 1907). Professor of German and department head at Stanford since 1934. Bibliographer, editor, translator, and reviewer, and author of numerous articles and a variety of textbooks. Chief work: *A Critical Bibliography of German Literature in English Translation, 1481–1935.* Also, *Carl Schurz, 1829–1906. A Great German-American,* published in Germany; now out of print.

A. E. ZUCKER, Ph.D. (Pennsylvania, 1917). Head of Foreign Language Department, University of Maryland. Author: *Robert Reitzel; The Chinese Theater; Ibsen, the Master Builder.* Translator: *The Redentin Easter Play.* Contributor to various journals and the DAB on Americana Germanica.

THE FORTY-EIGHTERS

Chapter One

THE EUROPEAN
BACKGROUND

By Carl J. Friedrich

WHEN, on the third of September, 1948, a joint American and German ceremony was held in the rebuilt *Paulskirche* at Frankfurt to recall the life and to honor the memory of Carl Schurz, it was, indeed, a symbolic "return of the native." As one sat in the severely simple yet beautifully proportioned circular assembly hall listening to the eternal music of Bach, one could not help reflecting upon the extraordinary turn of events of the last hundred years. Schurz, the liberal, who had been driven by the failure of the Revolution of 1848 to go overseas and become an American, was now overshadowing Bismarck, the reactionary, who had been brought by the same event to despise freedom and democracy. When one rereads the official German historians of the Empire—the Treitschkes, Sybels, Onckens, and their school—one is struck by their complacent acceptance of the success philosophy of "blood and iron," and of "unity and power." In commenting upon the political background of the Forty-eighters, Hermann Oncken wrote in 1911: "In the year 1848–9 a negligible minority had failed in an attempt to impose an artificial republic on the German people. The attempt failed because the German people were not constituted democratically in either their inner or outer life and they could not achieve national statehood without a military-monarchial leadership." This revealing passage from a leading German historian, when viewed in 1948 from a vantage point in the Frankfurt rubble (which testifies to the outcome of that way of achieving national unity), is a striking misstatement of the background of the Forty-eighters. The significance of this passage is enhanced by the fact that in the preceding paragraph Oncken had quoted Carl Schurz's letter to Malvida von Meysenburg in which the budding young American speaks of reading in the book of reality and of experiencing an inner revolution as a result. But it may well be doubted whether the personal evolution of Carl Schurz from an "ideological German democrat" to a "realistic American democrat" suffices to justify the official German historian's version of the meaning of the year 1848. For, in addition to such youngsters as Carl Schurz, many seasoned and experienced politicians participated in the movement of that year. The facts as now known to us do not support such a contention. However, these men did often lack the cynical sort of realism that would have enabled them to assess accurately to what degree the actual possessors of military and financial power were determined to suppress that which they could not lead: the democratic movement of the German people.

It is this revolutionary *European* background, as symbolized in Carl Schurz, which has given the Forty-eighters their distinctive character in the long steady stream of immigrants from Germany to the United States. As far as American life is concerned, there was nothing peculiar or extraordinary which would mark 1848 as a year of special grace. As some of the chapters in this volume will show, many immigrants of the preceding and following years are associated with the Forty-eighters, although they had no particular connection with, nor interest in, the revolutionary movement of that year. However, it is true that the United States watched with especial sympathy and friendliness the efforts of the revolutionary movement in Germany. The American government was the only major government which saw fit to send greetings to the Parliament at Frankfurt. The American press followed with great interest the fortunes of this hoped-for recruit to the forward march of democracy and deeply regretted the movement's failure and collapse.

The course of the Revolution focused on three centers: Austria, and particularly Vienna; Prussia and Berlin; and finally

Baden and the southwest. The last of these centers had always been close to movements in France; French liberal and radical ideas had found a more receptive audience in that part of Germany than anywhere else in Europe. But the centers of real power were Berlin and Vienna. From the latter, dominated by the aging Metternich, the policy of reaction had received its impetus and direction.

No sooner had the Revolution raised its head than Metternich resigned. His power had been more apparent than real after the death of Emperor Francis; now it was a hollow shell. In the years before 1848 Metternich's government had been saved from collapsing of its own weight by the absence of any real opposition and, once such an opposition did appear, the government toppled. Parliamentary institutions in the form of a *Reichstag* were granted on March 13. But at Vienna the spectre appeared of an immediate breakdown of the entire Hapsburg empire. The Hungarians, Czechs, Italians, and Southern Slavs all demanded autonomy and self-administration. As a consequence, the task of maintaining the state seemed quite incompatible with revolutionary aspirations. Nationalism here worked centrifugally, rather than reinforcing unity as in France or Germany.

At Berlin, King Frederick William IV, a mystic and confused autocrat, at first tried to appease the revolutionary elements by conceding a united diet (*Landtag*) on March 14, but this effort failed and open street fighting ensued (March 18). Although the troops were victorious, the king was deeply shaken and ordered the withdrawal of the royal troops from Berlin. The revolutionaries thereupon seized control of the situation and the king was obliged to acknowledge the legitimacy of the revolutionaries by honoring their dead. A constitution to be drawn up by the people's representatives was promised. At the same time the king identified himself with German aspirations and announced that Prussia had become a part of a united German people which he would be prepared to lead.

The triumph of the revolutionary forces in Berlin and Vienna laid the basis for the election of a national assembly after an attempt of the radicals in the southwest to stage a bloody upheaval of the masses had petered out miserably. The elected national assembly gathered at Frankfurt on May 18, 1848; it met at the *Paulskirche* and proceeded to organize a provisional government for the whole of Germany, to hold office while the Parliament drafted the constitution. John of Austria was made temporary regent, but he failed to establish a real government since he could not secure control of the troops of the several states and was at the mercy of the foreign policies of Austria and Prussia. It is clear that the dispersion of governmental authority in Germany handicapped the revolutionary forces; the dual task of unity and freedom proved too much.

By fall of 1848 the reactionary forces were on the march both in Vienna and Berlin. A new revolt in Austria was bloodily suppressed and a number of leaders, including the radical democrat Robert Blum, were executed. On December 2 the weak Emperor Ferdinand resigned and his nephew Francis Joseph appointed Prince Schwarzenberg, a man of blood and iron, to carry forward the tradition of Metternich. Similarly, at Berlin, the efforts of the Parliament to achieve genuine constitutional democracy were thwarted by military strength, and an authoritarian constitution was imposed on December 5. These reactionary developments in the two key centers of political power had taken place with the Regent and Frankfurt *Parlament* unable to do anything about it.

From May 18 until late autumn the Parliament was engaged in a sophisticated debate upon constitutional principles representative of the best which European thought had produced in this field. But the debates really hid an irresolvable division in the assembly: How to unite the German nation, including its Austrian component, without including the non-German elements under the Hapsburg monarchy. This had to be done when no adequate resources of power were available to the democratic movement with which to dislodge the Hapsburg monarchy from its control of the Austrian government. (This problem brings to mind the task which the United Europe movement is facing today in regard to Britain and her overseas Commonwealth of Nations.) Had a majority in the Frankfurt *Parlament* been willing to exclude Austria entirely from a united Germany, they might have succeeded in establishing a German state, by acting with great dispatch. But the Germans, like most unpolitical people, have often shown a fatal lack of a sense of timing. They did not appreciate at Frankfurt in 1848 (any more than they did at Bonn in 1948) that any constitution right away, in July, was better than the best constitution six months later. Thus the revolutionary spark was squandered and dissipated, instead of being fanned into a greater blaze. Probably nothing short of a trial and dethronement of the princes and princelings of Germany would have accomplished this feat. For such an undertaking both the will and the power were lacking. Had the will been there, the Parliament might have started by organizing a national army, as Cromwell had done. But somehow these lofty spirits had no passion to destroy that which stood in their way; they did not seem to know their enemies.

The Revolution of 1848 was, of course, an all-European event. Its first outbreak occurred in France on February 25, 1848, and spread rapidly in various directions, attacking the established monarchical order in Belgium, Austria, Italy, and other countries. It also became a factor in the Separatist War in Switzerland which led to the federal reform and unification of the ancient Swiss Confederacy. Everywhere it signalized the more radical expression of bourgeois sentiment with its insistence that the new preserves of the upper classes must be abolished. These were the retreats that the privileged elements of bygone feudal society had re-erected for themselves in the shadow of the thrones of the Restoration Age, following the French revolution. The revolutionary spark found much inflammable material in the various principalities of the German Union, which had been held together for the past generation by the skillful reactionary diplomacy of Count Metternich and his Prussian rivals and sympathizers. But what infinitely complicated the German revolutionary movement, gave it its peculiar color, and brought about its tragic culmination, was that in Germany the problem of establishing a constitutional and popular government—a republic, as the time called it—was linked to the problem of uniting the German people in a genuine organized community.

Throughout its long and tortuous history, the democratic movement has borne a close and natural relationship to national and patriotic, even nationalistic sentiments. The rationalist and revolutionary ardor of the Jacobins of the great French revolutions was ever balanced and nourished by their passionate love for France and her *mission civilisatrice*. It was this ardent patriotism which could be used and subverted by the first Napoleon when he harnessed the French revolutionary masses to his imperial chariot. The same thing occurred a hundred years earlier in the English revolution when Cromwell time and again appeared in the role of the savior of his nation and the defender of its sacred soil against the Spaniard. In the United States, also, it was the most active revolutionaries who inclined towards the most ardent patriotism. It was men like Sam Adams, who, feeling distinctly the American individuality, were the most outspoken republicans and closest to the common people.

It would have been strange, indeed, if the German democrats and revolutionary radicals of 1848 had lacked national sentiment. There were, however, special reasons for their cherishing both national and democratic enthusiasm. Ever since the struggle against Napoleon had been won by an appeal to the idea of national freedom and self-determination, popular self-government had appeared to many a devoted nationalist as the only practicable way to national unity. Only democracy seemed capable of overcoming the deeply rooted vested interests of the many dynasties and their local bureaucracies and of subordinating them to a higher common interest. What we are witnessing today in India, as the princely states are being absorbed, provides a close parallel to the German (and also the Italian) problem of the mid-nineteenth century. What is perhaps more pertinent is that this strongly felt connection between democracy and unity continues today, a hundred years later, to animate the policy of the German Social Democratic Party. The German Socialists' puzzled antagonism to an American policy which seeks to democratize Germany by encouraging such extreme separatist ele-

DR. JOHANN JACOBY
From *Kladderadatsch*, November 12, 1848

A physician from Koenigsberg, Dr. Jacoby was a member of a delegation received by King Frederick William IV on October 31, 1848. The king accepted their written petition and turned toward the door. Jacoby asked whether he would not listen to what the members of the deputation had to say. The king replied with a curt "No." Then Jacoby spoke the famous words: "That is the misfortune of kings—they never care to hear the truth." The king rebuked him indignantly, but thousands of Berlin citizens honored Jacoby with a torchlight procession.

ments as the Bavarian reactionaries has been unrelenting. Yet, when these historical antecedents are kept in mind, it seems natural enough that these separatist elements should be closely tied to monarchical reactionaries.

Underneath the bourgeois sentiments of liberal nationalism, there appeared in these revolutionary upheavals throughout Europe another and yet more radical force: the industrial proletariat. The so-called March Revolutions in Baden, Berlin, and Vienna, all carried the proletariat to the barricades, thus anticipating a revolution which did not come to fruition until seventy years later in Russia. In 1848 these revolutions were drowned in blood. The pronounced hostility of the proletariat to property and all that goes with it as proclaimed most dramatically in the Communist Manifesto (1848) eventually so terrified the *Buergertum* that it retreated and surrendered to conservative and reactionary elements. Caesarism in France, monarchism in Germany and elsewhere became the order of the day in the years following the uprisings.

It should be clear from the foregoing brief remarks that, intellectually speaking, three aspects dominated the scene from which the Forty-eighters and their immediate followers in '49, '50 and '51 fled into the freedom of the United States. These were: (1) liberty, (2) democracy, and (3) national unity. With regard to each of these ideals, Europe had developed a rich and varied tradition. A great literature, philosophical, historical, and poetical, had grown up and shaped an intellectual environment such as might arouse the allegiance of any man of imagination and idealism. Germany was not only no exception to this, it had witnessed an unusually rich spiritual flowering during the very period when France was absorbed in the violence of revolutionary controversy. To name merely the most illustrious, in philosophy there were Kant, Fichte, Herder, Schelling and Hegel; in history Moser, Niebuhr, and Savigny; in poetry Lessing, Goethe, Schiller, and Hölderlin. These distinguished men had created a setting for a national rebirth so beautiful that it gave rise to the complimentary epithet of "the nation of thinkers and poets."

It would be narrow-minded and Beckmesserish indeed, to try
to "grade" these lofty spirits according to their greater or lesser
enthusiasm for one or another of the ideals of liberty, democracy,
and national unity. This path has unfortunately been trodden
too often by the wartime propagandists who have picked over
the works of these men. These propagandists have searched for
sentences that could, when torn from the context, support their
puny, if not downright malicious, contentions that the German
people have forever groveled at the feet of those who would
kick them around. No open-minded reader of the works of any
of these men could help experiencing a great lift, a freeing of
the mind from the dross of the dogmatic and the authoritarian.
It was so felt by foreigners of the calibre of Emerson and Cole-
ridge, of Madame de Stael and Shelley. It was much more in-
tensely felt by the younger generation born after the turn of the
nineteenth century and who reached maturity during the decades following the wars of liberation. The finer spirits suffered
deeply from the atmosphere of stuffy reaction which pervaded
the public life of Germany after Count Metternich had clamped
down upon the young enthusiasts of the *Burschenschaften* and instituted his policy of persecution of professors and students alike.
In these latter days, with the spirit of liberalism on the wane, a
number of noteworthy efforts have been made to depict Metternich as a great conservative statesman, and this has led to a
perhaps juster appreciation of his historial role. But when one
seeks to recapture the European background of the Forty-
eighters, one must realize that Metternich was a symbol of
abomination, comparable to Hitler in our own days. Throughout the centuries the Austrian, like the Prussian, has contributed
important leadership to the authoritarian and militaristic element
in German history, while the spirit of freedom and enlightenment has found its most vigorous and gifted champions in the
smaller states of the west. Suabia and Thuringia, Franconia and
the free cities have all contributed a substantially larger share to
the intellectual ferment of freedom and democracy. They produced the majority of the men of genius just mentioned.

It is a striking fact, and one deeply appreciated by men like

Schurz, that in Germany liberty and democracy, national unity and cosmopolitan spirit had a purely spiritual and even highly theoretical quality. The lack of the nourishing roots of concrete experience in everyday life gave these ideals a radical and un-compromising intensity which caused those men who cherished them to be incapacitated for effective, practical action. The high-flown idealism of these liberal radicals could never have compromised with such sordid realities as the British colonial empire or the slavery of the Southern states of America. Its very perfectionism was a great danger to its vitality; it readily turned into reactionary despair, or cynical defeatism and misanthropy. Some of the great thinkers themselves demonstrated this inherent weakness. Hegel, in his youth the believer in progress and revo-lution, turned into the narrow-minded admirer of the Prussian bureaucracy who wrote the *Philosophy of Right*. However, con-trary to a widespread impression, the result was that the German intelligentsia turned against and away from Hegel, and by the year 1848 he was ignored, especially as far as his later and re-actionary ideas were concerned.

The truth is that one must take a broad view in assessing an intellectual background and tradition. Britain and America have had their intellectual reactionaries and snobs. Furthermore, the apologists for and believers in democracy too often forget the questionable, even vicious side of democracy that grants ex-cessive power to the masses. As I have pointed out in *The New Belief in the Common Man*, such a belief can be and deserves to be maintained, but its greatest enemies are those who so exaggerate the role of the common man, who so overestimate the rational faculties of man that failure is inevitable. Romantic philosophers were prone to do that very thing, and to seek refuge in a fanciful return to some past era such as the Middle Ages. But there were always the others, those stouter spirits who retained their faith in the common man, in liberty and democracy. To many of these America became the symbol of the new life. The realities of this new life, beyond the corrupting influences of an aging civilization, remained a beacon of hope, even of confidence. Goethe's famous line: "Amerika, du hast es besser. . ." is only

the trite reiteration of the vista with which Faust's endless search
for the good life ends: "Solch ein Gewimmel moecht' ich sehn',
mit freiem Volk auf freier Erde stehn" (Aye! Such a throng I
fain would see, stand on free soil among a people free!). Faust,
the restless searcher for happiness, at last arrives at the recognition of the freedom that comes from work; he is reclaiming land
for new settlements, in short, pioneering. Is it too much to say
that this famous passage offers the key to the deepest layers of
feeling in many of the Forty-eighters? From *Sturm und Drang*
through *Burschenschaft* and revolutionary *Verein* they went forward to share the freedom that was and is America.

The continuing influence of Goethe and the German idealistic
philosophers, as represented by the Forty-eighters, can be seen
in the Middle West by the St. Louis Movement in Philosophy
to which Goethe's *Faust* appealed particularly. The deep link
between the final views of Faust and the outlook of the settlers
in America was constantly stressed by Denton J. Snider, a prominent writer in the movement. Snider wrote:

Faust becomes the settler, the frontiersman on a vast ocean of savagery,
he becomes the American, transforming a wild continent into the hab-
itable abode of rational men. Often we have said, much oftener have
we thought, that this Second Part of *Faust* in many portions seems an
American Book, or rather the *Mythus* of America, in its settlement and
conquest, as well as in its spiritual significance. That old Europe has
not fully appreciated the book, cannot perhaps; but here we can see
the mythical forms turning to living facts before our eyes.

Thoughts such as those just cited open up the fascinating topic
of what picture lived in the mind of the Forty-eighter when he
embarked for the United States. Some twenty years earlier the
great Niebuhr had said to young Lieber as he was taking leave
to go to America: "Bleiben Sie ein Deutscher." Lieber both did
and did not; the Forty-eighter went further. Judging from the
many memoirs, one is able to conclude that the distinctive approach of the Forty-eighter (after he was convinced that the
Revolution was a failure) was precisely this: he had no intention
of remaining a German. His greater political passion, and his
very attachment to liberty and democracy, made him more

consciously ready to change and become another man. This prevailing mood seems to contrast with the national ardor which motivated these men in their desire to bring about a political order for all of Germany. Indeed, we find a hidden rift in quite a few of their personalities. After all, Goethe's sentiment was rooted in his broad humanity, his all-embracing cosmopolitanism. But the Forty-eighter, eager as he was for establishing national unity, was yet more fervently a liberal and a democrat.

America, in the eyes of the Forty-eighters, was first and foremost a successful constitutional democracy. In this they reflected American opinion itself. Travelers during the first half of the nineteenth century repeatedly noted the expectancy with which every foreign visitor was queried about America's *institutions*. Upon these free institutions, the pride of the country and of its inhabitants was built. For more than fifty years, these institutions had now provided an effective framework for continued progress and expansion. Books like de Tocqueville's *Democracy in America*, while sharply critical of some of the more sordid aspects of popular government, yet in sum preserved the hopeful outlook; voices like that of Dickens were few and crying in the wilderness.

Besides this sober and rational aspect, the romantic sentiment continued to play its role. Seume's famous poem about the "noble savage" who did not know the "varnished politeness" of old Europe continued to reverberate in the hearts of Germans with a romantic penchant. The melodious lines of Lenau, the sentimental count, echoed the feeling for the savage who is overwhelmed by civilization. His ballad of the three Indians, father and two sons, who decide to commit suicide by hurling themselves in their canoe down Niagara Falls, after cursing the white men's invasion of their freedom, was hardly likely to attract the romantic to America. Yet, when combined with such accounts as those of Count Chateaubriand, they might heighten the sense of adventure and hope.

Chateaubriand's "A Night among the Savages of America" does indeed express the attraction of America to the thwarted freedom-lover.

Everyone boasts of liberty, and hardly anyone has a just idea of it. . . .
Released from the tyrannical yoke of society, I comprehended the
charms of that natural independence, far surpassing all the pleasures
of which civilized man can have any idea. I comprehended why . . .
several Europeans had become savages. . . . It is incredible to what
state of littleness nations and their highly boasted institutions were reduced in my eyes. . . . Benevolent savages, who so hospitably entertained me, . . . may you long enjoy your precious independence in
those delightful solitudes.

This sort of romantic interpretation of freedom as solitude, independence, uniqueness, is even more succinctly portrayed in
Chateaubriand's anecdote of his encounter with Philip de Cocq.
After recounting his conversation with Cocq, who describes himself as happy only since he became a savage, Chateaubriand
exclaims: "His soul, free from the conflict of social passions, appeared to me, in the language of the savages with whom he
dwelt, calm as the field of battle after the warriors had smoked
together the calumet of peace." The slums of fast-growing New
York bore little relation to such an idyl, but it still lived in the
caravan of covered wagons moving West.

The high-flown utopianism of much reformist sentiment in
Europe could thus continue to imagine the American world as
extremely malleable and a promising soil for the most radical
experimentation. It had been so conceived by Owen and Fourier
and their enthusiastic followers. Looking back at their experiments, we naturally see them as small enclaves of a spirit violently at variance with the prevailing trends. But to the European contemporary of Thoreau and Emerson it was not at all
clear what were going to be the victorious forces in America; he
could readily share Thoreau's dislike for the railroads as disturb-
ers of a rustic freedom, yet fail to anticipate the Granger movement and the Interstate Commerce Commission.

The brief previous remark regarding the role of the proletariat
requires some further elaboration at this point. Emerson, when
first commenting upon the Revolution of 1848 in his *Journal*,
noted: "This revolution has a feature new to history, that of
socialism." This was, of course, particularly true of France, but

socialism played its role in Germany, too. The reader of Carl Schurz's *Reminiscences* knows, of course, that the March Revolutions in Berlin, Vienna, and elsewhere had had a distinctly proletarian flavor. The "democratic" stress was put forward by the radicals who were more concerned with popular, than with constitutional, government. Schurz himself met Karl Marx in the sessions of the Democratic Club at Cologne; he attributes Marx's failure to attract a following less to his doctrine than to his disagreeable personality.

In any case, the popular radicals with more or less of a socialist outlook and point of view certainly were the element most cordially disliked by the resurgent reactionaries. Governmental persecution singled them out particularly, and, since at that time no restrictive immigration laws interfered with the coming to America of radicals of every description, it is right to consider these doctrines an important element in the background of many a Forty-eighter. Communist settlements had already been numerous in the United States. Concord had its Fruitlands, and Indiana its New Hope in the Owenite vein. It is no accident that Emerson speaks of Fourier and other socialists as the mythologues of his age; America seemed the ideal haven of every kind of social experimentation. The failure of most of these activities, and the triumphant progress of industrial capitalism in the United States in the second half of the nineteenth century, has tended to obscure the very real role which anti-capitalist strands of thought and purpose played in attracting opposition elements to our shores during the first half, indeed, throughout the nineteenth century.

Socialism had of course had a fairly long history in European thought. The Levellers in England in the seventeenth century as well as Blanqui and his followers during the French Revolution had high-lighted a type of communal utopianism which had also found expression in writings of a more highfalutin kind, such as Thomas More's *Utopia* and James Harrington's *Oceana*. But the ancient longing for social equality, with its roots in the Old Testament as well as the New, had recently been given fresh poignancy and a wider appeal by the development of the factory system characteristic of the new industrial society. The unscrupulous exploitation of ever larger sections of the population by the owners of capital had stimulated the imagination of men with broad human sympathies into considering wholly novel modes of social organization. The richest crop of such speculation had been reaped in France during the half century preceding the Revolution of 1848. Simon, Fourier, and Proudhon are only the most outstanding among a large and growing circle of people who proposed comprehensive plans for the reorganization of society along socialist lines. These thoughts, plans, and dreams found a considerable echo among the intellectuals of the German revolutionary movement. But all of this earlier work was challenged as unrealistic and impractical by two men filled with the materialist spirit of the new positivist science: Karl Marx and Friedrich Engels. In the Communist Manifesto they called upon the workers of all the world to unite and throw off their chains, because they were demonstrably the chosen of destiny: a close scientific analysis of the past and the present economic organization would prove the proletariat to be preordained to become the ruling class through conquest of the state and establishment of complete control over its economy and the means of production.

Looking back to the United States of 1848, which was quintessentially a capitalist and a free enterprise economy in a fuller sense than any European one, especially when contrasted to the paternalistic and bureaucratic German states, one may wonder why anyone should have considered the United States as a good place to which to go. A plausible answer may be that American freedom must have seemed to offer enough leeway for new experiments, such as those mentioned. Also, the full significance of what was in the making in America was perhaps not appreciated either. In any case, the class struggle was more definitely recognized by *The Federalist* than by most European apologists for the established order.

Carl Schurz has left only some rather general indications of what he had in his mind as a picture of America: "a new world, a free world, a world of great ideas and purposes." In a special study on the process by which Schurz became an American, Chester V. Easum has gathered further material which leads him to conclude that

viewed in the light of these letters, his move to America appears to have been that of one who was a republican in opinion, to be sure, but still a German republican in feeling. Maintaining, as was natural, the strong bond of sympathy between himself and his revolutionary associates, he wished for them a success for which he was willing to work in America; and in the earning of the enjoyment of which, if it should come, he expected to return and have a share.

Yet, the later growth of his personality suggests that Carl Schurz was an American before he ever set foot on the soil of the United States. The nationalistic trends in the writing of American history in recent years have tended to obscure the fact that in the first half of the nineteenth century the United States was distinctly cosmopolitan in outlook and point of view. Its leading spirits, men like Emerson and Thoreau, would have rebelled at the narrow provincialism of a later day. In a very real sense, Carl Schurz and his future fellow citizens were children of the same spirit: the spirit of freedom, democracy, and constitutionalism, as manifest in the French and American revolutions.

Looking back at Carl Schurz's *Reminiscences* from the vantage point of 1948, nothing strikes the sympathetic reader more forcefully than the secure *kleinbuergerlich* (*petit bourgeois*) atmosphere of his background and upbringing. The Rhineland, always close to and deeply affected by French ideas, was as ready to acknowledge *liberté, egalité, fraternité* as were most Frenchmen. It may confound students delving into the deeper layers of human motivation of our bitter age that so ardent a revolutionary temperament as that of Carl Schurz should have sprung from the affectionate and secure family circle described in the *Reminiscences*. How ready Schurz was to play a constructive and cooperative role is clearly shown by his career in America. Would he, had he remained in Germany, have become a loyal subject of the Prussian king? Would he have hailed the founding of Bismarck's empire? Or would he have carried forward the revolutionary program? There is no clear answer to such questions to be found in his own writings or letters. But his rather conservative political leanings in the United States would suggest that had he remained in Germany he would have been a loyal subject and reconciled with the established regime. Yet we know that in 1868 he passed over in silence Bismarck's hint that, like Friedrich Kapp and a few other Forty-eighters, he should return to Germany; he merely remarked that the American Republic was highly congenial to him. In his happy acceptance of the outward forms of American democracy, Carl Schurz proved to be the highly typical child of the bourgeois age, its rationalism, its optimism, and its progressivism. These peculiar ingredients of nineteenth century liberalism were ideally adapted for the American scene and fitted it well. The progress of America was virtually inevitable, given the vast potentialities of a continent awaiting technological exploitations. Human relationships were bound to permit wide latitude for divergent viewpoints in a place where the earning of a living was possible for all who wanted to work, and even quite a few who did not, like the bard of democracy, Walt Whitman. Rationality could be a reliable guide indeed where irrational forces of blood and soil, of faith and superstition were reduced to dim memories of the "old country," and to the intermittent relaxation of an occasional Sunday morning. The knocking at the gate by the industrial proletariat which terrified the bourgeoisie into reaction all over Europe after 1848 was only dimly heard in the United States. Emerson knew of it, and so did other forward-looking men. But neither Emerson nor the others sensed the clarion call of the Communist Manifesto, published that same year. Nor did Carl Schurz, for the *Reminiscences* tell us nothing about his attitude on the doctrine Marx stood for, but comment only on the latter's conceit and domineering temper. The Socialist and Communist movement was not unique in its world-wide cosmopolitanism; the bourgeoisie of France and Germany had ever cherished cosmopolitan ideals as much as any other Europeans. The narrow nationalism of the second half of the nineteenth century, with its accompanying doctrine of a fanatical *mystique nationale*, as preached by Maurice Barrès, Moeller van den Bruck, or the expounders of Fascism in its various forms, was as alien to the rising bourgeoisie as the feudal reaction they were fighting. There is a curious yet distinctive flavor about this patriotism of the Jacobins and their brothers-in-arms two generations later: This patriotism remains ever ready to embrace the world, at least all the world of Europe, past and present. This cosmopolitanism was a humanist heritage. As yet, most educated men were brought up in this great tradition. Periclean Athens and Republican Rome were seen as universal teachers of a creed that included all nations.

It stands to reason that this cosmopolitanism should at once have aided those who believed in it to achieve more smoothly the transition from Europe to America, and have given them a more truly American capacity for participation in the new community of their choosing. Nativism was then, as now, a potent force in America, and a natural one. The unhappy term "one hundred percent American" had not yet been invented, but the underlying bigotry was endemic in American society. Where the leveling impact of a pioneer existence had tended to obliterate all the usual distinctions, it was to be expected that even so primitive a criterion as the fact that someone's parents and grandparents had been born in the country was to be seized upon as a sign of superior endowment. Indeed, the rampant rationalism of the age could almost be said to have called forth such a corrective as the Ku Klux Klan, as if it were the vengeance of the darker divinities of the earth. Yet nativism in all its forms is clearly designed to corrupt the true spirit of America, simply because nativism substitutes artificial signs for the true moral excellence which American nativity demands.

The special endowment which the Forty-eighters possessed was precisely this faith in humanity. Kant, Schiller, Goethe are not only free of narrow nationalism, but they are apt to instill in their more devoted adherents a passionate belief in the universality of man's ethical calling. Whether it be the categorical imperative, or the Song of Joy (Lied der Freude), or Goethe's "Noble be man, helpful and kind. . ." they were all expressions of the same spirit of the revolutions of 1776 and thereafter which had led to the founding of America. It was a simple matter for the Forty-eighter to adopt the Declaration of Independence as his credo, though he might read its opening sentences with more ardor than the recital of the misdeeds of George III.

The full measure of this broad sweep of cosmopolitanism has never been taken. No one has ever fully assessed the extent to which cosmopolitanism has served to fertilize the American mind, as its fields were watered by successive waves of Europeans filled with this spirit. So brilliant and so profound a student of American literature as L. V. Parrington, in his *Main Currents in American Thought*, fails us on this important score. (Some readers may be surprised to learn that Parrington gives only passing mention to Carl Schurz, in spite of the latter's *Reminiscences;* Schurz was not in the national vein which provided Parrington's framework.) The past generation, seeking to distill some kind of American soul, would of necessity treat this ingredient of cosmopolitanism as extraneous, even destructive. But the truth of the matter is that the cosmopolitanism of America's heritage has, in this very generation, commenced to spread over the earth. In the course of the Second World War, Europe's universalist tradition has been revived by a liberating America at a moment when that tradition was all but trampled under foot by the legions of a militant supernationalism which had nothing but contempt for the internationalist, whether bourgeois or proletarian. It is, therefore, easier to appreciate the significance of the Forty-eighter's cosmopolitan outlook in 1948 than during the earlier part of this century.

One other ingredient of the Forty-eighter's background deserves to be mentioned, and that is his religious views. The typical Forty-eighter was a freethinker, if not an atheist. He was a humanist in the more militant sense in that he was opposed to conventional religious views concerning man's otherworldly commitments. America, unlike most of Europe, was then, as it is now, the land of the many churches. The doctrines of these many churches represent many different outlooks and viewpoints. Yet, their common recognition of Christianity combines the most diverse dogmas and to many of their adherents these dogmas are of little consequence, if they are known to them at all. For people accustomed to this state of affairs, it is difficult to appreciate the bitterness of people who had experienced religion as the intellectual weapon of a clergy closely allied with the reactionary forces of the bureaucracy, the army, and the vested landed interests. Thus, the Forty-eighter, regardless of whether he remained aloof from all organized religion or whether he came to share the faith of one of America's many churches, must have experienced a deep sense of liberation when he witnessed America's firm insistence on the separation of church and state. For a religious community freed of the formalism of an ecclesiastical bureaucracy and gladly sharing each member's fortunes and misfortunes is certainly a far cry from what most of these men had combated in Germany, whether they were Catholics or Protestants.

In this connection, it may be interesting to recall the migration to America of a substantial number of orthodox Lutherans (*Altlutheraner*) who came to the United States after King Frederick William III had combined by royal fiat the Lutheran and Calvinist creeds in a new "Evangelical" compromise. To explore the romantic and mystic antecedents of this act of royal absolutism would lead much too far afield. It is mentioned here to show that the more dyed-in-the-wool conservatism of these *Altlutheraner* had found refuge in America as readily as had the conservative Catholics who left Puritan England two hundred years earlier. But everyone knows that these conservative refugees pulled less weight in the building of America than the religious radicals. If in the seventeenth century men of this type were nonconformists of various hues, and in the eighteenth they were drunk in the Faith in Reason as represented by Thomas Paine, it is only natural that in the nineteenth century they should have reflected the positivism and materialism which, as a creed, contrasts so strangely with the idealism and sacrificial devotion of their adherents.

But another and contrasting feature of the religious back-

ground was the development of liberal Catholicism, as represented by men like Count de Montalembert. High-ranking in
the revolutionary leadership at Frankfurt were ardent liberal
constitutionalists of the type of August Reichensperger. Reichensperger himself was a native of Mainz, the main city of Hesse
in which so much revolutionary tradition has remained alive
ever since 1789. The *Pius Verein*, centered here, projected forward the separation of church and state which became a main
plank of liberal Catholicism, especially in Protestant-dominated
Prussia. The basic principles of their petitions to the Frankfurt
Parliament are revealing: (1) civil and political rights are independent of a man's religious faith, (2) all religious denominations enjoy equal freedom and protection, (3) each denomination is, in its ecclesiastical and religious affairs, . . . independent
[of the state], (4) the state will never and under no pretext in-
terfere in the ecclesiastical and religious affairs of any denomination; and so on. These principles clearly foreshadow both the
Kulturkampf of the seventies, and the Catholic (Centre) party as
a mainstay of liberal constitutionalism down to our own day.
Principles such as these were definitely in keeping with American precepts and traditions. Catholic elements coming to the
United States with such ideas naturally had little difficulty in
fitting into their new environment.

The German immigrants before 1848 had shown little interest
in politics and those of later decades were to show even less. But
the true Forty-eighter was a "political being" and it is therefore
not surprising that he should have participated vigorously in the
political life of his new-found community. Later chapters of this
book will offer considerable evidence of this trait of the Forty-
eighter. But in a discussion of the European background the
matter is primarily of interest to the extent that a glance at this
background helps one in understanding why the Forty-eighter
tended to adopt the position he did. It is, of course, well-known
that he inclined toward the Republican party, that he was predisposed toward abolition of slavery, often in a rather radical
and combative manner, that he was the champion of the Union

(even though a few fought in the Confederate armies), and that he cherished good government, especially in respect to the civil service. This latter principle is clearly a reflection of the old German belief in a sound and incorruptible officialdom, and is curious in view of the Forty-eighters' hostility towards bureaucracy. But, torn between the Scylla of patronage and the Charybdis of bureaucracy, the German is clearly predisposed toward the latter and the Forty-eighter was no exception. Though often a good Republican, or even a good Democrat, the Forty-eighter continued to be ill at ease in the rough and tumble of party politics. Even Carl Schurz, though much the most successful, made it quite clear that he never acquired the love of party, and all its attendant virtues and vices of good fellowship, loyalty, intolerance, and influence.

It is a curious and perplexing feature of many a European (and German) biography that the minor adjustments of personal conduct, which are involved in "playing the game" in politics and social life, have given rise to sharp inner conflicts and tensions. There seems to be a persistent inclination for the Continental European to incapacitate himself for effective political action of a constructive kind by upholding a moral perfectionism which is perhaps best epitomized in the Kant essay "Concerning an Alleged Right to Lie," in which the view is expounded that nothing may be told but the truth. It is pretty generally admitted, at least by the closer students of the practices of political parties in a democracy, that no social life among ordinary mortals could be maintained by following this maxim. Forty-eighters, like other Europeans, had a tendency to resent this fact so bitterly that when it proved to be inescapable, they forthwith inclined either to withdraw from the dirty game of politics, or to adopt a cynical and misanthropic view. I believe that this is the reason why so many of these men turned from their progressive outlook to rather conservative, if not actually reactionary, opinion. Of course, part of this tendency may be assigned to the mere fact that they grew old. It rarely happens that political idealists, maintaining a balanced outlook, continue to fight for the ideals of their younger manhood and at the same time participate fully and actively in the community's affairs; such a practical idealist was, for example, George William Curtis, who was as interested a champion of civil service reform as Carl Schurz.

However, very few failed fully to become Americans. Even while they followed with a measure of pride the unification of Germany under the Iron Chancellor, they rarely showed any inclination to return to Germany to participate in its newly won constitutional life, or to aid her in becoming a democracy. Neither their cosmopolitanism, nor their German nationalism nor yet their democratic idealism proved strong enough to plunge them back into German politics. This, it would seem, is the measure of their political passion, or lack of it. They had become Americans, but as such they felt neither a right nor a duty to reform Germany. Unlike men such as Max Brauer in our own day, they were ready to leave Germany to her own resources. What Germany and Europe thus lost politically, America gained. The foregoing reveals the fundamental weakness of the democratic and revolutionary cause, even among these leading exponents.

In discussing the European background of the Forty-eighters, we have stressed the broad ideological and cultural elements, rather than the specific events of the Revolutionary year. For, apart from the difficulty of portraying so far-flung and colorful an event within so short a space, such a presentation would emphasize the differences in background of the various rival groups. As Alfred Whitehead, in *Science and the Modern World*, has pointed out regarding the study of philosophy, a view equally valid for the history of ideas generally, it is the common assumptions, rather than the explicitly defended positions, which give to the thought of an epoch its peculiar flavor. Personal freedom, constitutionalism, cosmopolitanism, and the nation as the natural foundation of political society—these, combined with a firm belief in the progress of mankind and in the superiority of Western civilization as the leader in this progress, all contributed to the background of the Forty-eighter. America firmly shared these progressive ideas, and hence reinforced the liberal *Weltanschauung* of the Germans who arrived as refugees, ready to become Americans. Their European background soon merged with the new foreground of the United States.

The great liberal German historian Friedrich Meinecke has summed up the year 1848 in the following words:

The year 1848 was a year of contrary effects. It stirred up everything that was alive in state, society and church, whether it was old or new in origin. It somehow gave light and room for everything to unfold in keeping with its innate strength.

Fortunately for America, unfortunately for Germany, many of the human beings of greatest vitality left, to find in the United States a new arena for their lifework. They thus testified to the increasing strength of the American facet of Western culture. When the native returned to Germany in 1948, he was transfigured and enhanced by the American community of which he had become an integral part.

Chapter Two

THE AMERICAN
SCENE

By Oscar Handlin

THOSE Germans who, in 1848 and after, left the Old World to come to the United States found themselves projected into a turbulent scene. Disappointed in the outcome of their struggle to reform the Fatherland, these refugees saw all about them a universe being reshaped. In the ten-year period in which the bulk of the exiles arrived, fundamental economic changes modified the productive system and left in their wake deeply troubling social, intellectual, and political problems that a whole generation would struggle to solve.

In the decade after 1845 the full effects of a drastic revolution in transportation made themselves felt throughout the American continent. The system of canals had by then already been completed and the outlines of the railway network were already sketched. But the available facilities continued to grow, and at an ever faster rate. Railroad mileage mounted from less than five to more than eighteen thousand between 1845 and 1855, and in the next five years almost doubled itself again. Meanwhile the use of steam increased enormously the volume of traffic that could flow along the inland and coastal waterways; nearly every river and lake was made to serve thriving business. And all the while, scores of new vessels, clippers and steam, as well as the older ships, carried goods in a rising tide across the oceans and into the great seaports.

All these developments contributed to the integration of the American economy. They drew the scattered regions of the Union into a single market unit within which commodities could freely flow. The increased volume of sales and of production made possible more division of labor and the introduction of new time and labor saving techniques. These were the conditions of a rise in efficiency and of an impressive expansion in the productive system.

Further stimulus came from the astounding growth in population which in these years seemed to double itself every two decades; the seventeen million souls of 1840 by 1860 numbered fully thirty-one million. No small part of the increment came by immigration, for the Forty-eighters were by no means the only newcomers to reach these shores. The ten-year span beginning 1846 alone saw close to three million arrivals from Ireland, Germany, Scandinavia, and other parts of Europe.

Most of these new Americans had been peasants in the Old World. Here they supplied the manpower for a new industrialism that had already struck roots in the northeastern states. With their help primitive mills dependent upon water power were turned into giant factories powered by steam. Full-grown cities suddenly sprang up where before there had been rural villages or rolling farm land; Lowell, Lawrence, Fall River, Syracuse, Paterson were only the most prominent among dozens of others. At the same time, the same fresh hands began to uncover the subsurface riches of the continent—in California, gold, and in Pennsylvania the more precious black gold that was coal. All in all, by 1860, fully one-sixth of the people in the United States lived by manufacturing; and the products of their labor were worth almost two billion dollars each year.

It was not surprising, in the light of these developments, to find that a much larger proportion of Americans than ever before lived in urbanized localities. On the eve of the Civil War more than 16 per cent of the nation resided in towns of eight thousand or more. And by then quite a few cities had reached truly metropolitan proportions; Boston, New York, Philadelphia, Baltimore, and New Orleans were over the hundred thousand mark.

To keep the residents of these places fed and supplied called

for a corresponding expansion of the nation's agriculture. The
call was answered by the continued conquest of the frontier.
Hundreds of thousands of acres were brought under fresh cultivation while the outposts of settlement moved well across the
Mississippi through Kansas, Nebraska, Iowa, Wisconsin, and
Minnesota. With the introduction of new machinery and new
settlers, the volume of production leaped upward; new records
were set for wheat and corn, for hogs and sheep. There was
enough to supply all Americans, and a surplus for foreign trade
as well.

Agricultural prosperity touched not the great West alone but
also the South where staple crops brought wealth and confidence. Bags of rice and casks of sugar, above all bales of tobacco
and of cotton, mounted ever higher on the wharves of Charleston, Mobile, and New Orleans. If production of the crop first-
named tended to slacken somewhat after 1850, that last-named
more than made up for it; the number of bales of cotton almost
doubled ever decade. These growing piles were the symbols of
the prosperity of a whole region and of the planters who were
its masters. They were also symbols of the fixity of the plantation system and of a hardening acceptance of slavery, once regarded by Southerners as merely a temporary institution.

In every part of the nation, the dominant condition of life was
rapid change. That was a condition under which no person, no
group could stand still. These transformations which affected
every aspect of existence in the United States were not neutral
in character. They operated to the advantage of some people
and to the detriment of others. Inevitably men reacted in terms
of the effect upon their personal lives; and inevitably, as they
put their reactions into action, they found it useful to establish
alliances with other men whose interests were the same. But
such groupings—merchants and artisans, laborers and indus-
trialists, planters and farmers—were by no means rigidly cir-
cumscribed. For the basic changes in the economy made for
constant mobility, moved individuals from class to class, and

sometimes suddenly altered the interests of large segments of the population.

Whatever the specific lines along which they acted, all these people found ample opportunities for expressing themselves and for influencing the policies of their governments; for this was a period when, throughout the Union, participation in the determination of what the state should do was open to ever-larger masses of people. In the West, in the newly settled regions, any social or economic distinctions were difficult to perpetuate; all comers grasped and retained a certain minimal power. In the older districts of the Northeast, earlier agitation in the 1830's had largely wiped away the remnants of political privilege. Property qualifications for voting and for holding public office had disappeared or had become negligible, and control of the government had been dispersed in many hands. In the South, too, the same democratic influences were at work; the last serious aristocratic relics were eliminated in Virginia in 1850 and in North Carolina six years later. The planters still constituted a powerful force just as did the merchants above the Mason-Dixon line; but in neither case could a wealthy minority count on having its own way. Other groups, the small farmers and artisans, for example, were conscious of their own interests and also of the difference between those interests and those of the masters of plantation and countinghouse.

Diffusion of the right to use the instruments of politics was accompanied by a steady spread of the ability to make use of those tools. There was a noteworthy development of educational facilities that widened the scope of opportunities for all American citizens. A higher rate of literacy enabled people to become familiar with public issues, to react intelligently, and to participate in a wide range of cultural activities.

Improvement of the schools came at every level of instruction. Those states which had formerly boasted of systems of public education now made the regulations for compulsory attendance really effective. Elementary schools were now more adequate in numbers and were regulated by state boards of education instead of by the laxer local authorities. Higher education was, as

yet, available only to a more select group. But there was a notice-
able increase in the number of academies, while some two hundred and fifty colleges, including seventeen state universities,
offered education at the highest level. Perhaps the most significant phenomenon, however, was the appearance of a succession
of teacher-training institutes that ultimately lifted the quality of
all instruction.

Education was moreover by no means confined to the schools.
Everywhere there sprang up less formal, but no less effective,
media for transmitting culture to the mass of Americans. By
1850 almost three thousand periodicals of every kind circulated
throughout the country and penetrated into every American
home. The daily newspaper reached a high point of technical
and editorial development; by now it cost so little to produce a
journal that survival could be assured with the support of quite
a small group. Every point of view could therefore receive expression through its own organ. The large cities often had a
dozen or more journals, some selling for only a penny, and many
in languages other than English. In the field of journalism the
politically conscious Forty-eighters found a fine opportunity for
leadership among citizens of German descent.

But one did not even have to be able to read to be able to
learn. To listen was often enough. For in these years the lecture
platform became a great educational influence in hundreds of
towns, large and small. Famous American and European speakers and writers toured the nation, bringing a new kind of intellectual experience to large and attentive audiences. The most
highly organized form of the lecture was the lyceum, which
regularly offered a wide range of instructive courses; but there
were also innumerable series, sponsored by local groups, that
added to the variety of such offerings.

Many of these educational developments depended upon the
extraordinary growth of communications that drew together all
parts of the Union. The railroads had an obvious function in
this respect; and so did the telegraph and the cheap postage
which came to the American scene at about the same time. All
these ties enabled like-minded people from every part of the na-

tion to make contact with each other; they provided the means for the emergence of a host of national associations, some dedicated to a single purpose, some fraternal, but all vehicles for more effective group action.

No doubt almost all the busy people who found time to join lodges and political parties, to attend lectures, and to read newspapers would have explained their activities by the desire to improve themselves. In the expectation of improvement were concentrated the most significant hopes and aspirations of this period. Nor was the conception of improvement limited simply to an immediate, personal sense. That concept took in also the broad, general confidence that man was capable of indefinite progress, that his condition on earth could advance ever closer to perfection.

The Americans of these years were so certain of that universal premise that they derived from it an invariable corollary. If their society was not as yet perfect—as obviously it was not—then what held it back was not any deficiency in the qualities of human beings, but rather some weaknesses in institutions, survivals of a backward past, which retarded the development that was otherwise sure to come. The task of the citizen was so to alter those institutions as to permit men fully to cultivate themselves. Forty-eighters, as we shall see, were ready, not to say impatient, for changes.

The citizen of the United States looking about him thought there was a need for change. Moreover, he could find plentiful evidence of the beneficent effects of the changes that had already come into being. Extension of the boundaries of his country, populous cities and flourishing farms where a little while before had been empty wilderness, above all, a host of inventions that made goods abundantly available, all these made an identical argument: every change was for the better.

These changes, the most obvious to the casual onlooker, were —it was true—in the realm of material things. But basic to the thought of this period was also a deep religious sentiment. If these Americans sometimes seemed godless to outsiders, it was not because religion played a small part in their lives, but rather because its role was not the same as that to which Europeans were accustomed; they had never experienced the reactionary pressure of a state church.

American preachers emphasized ethical practice rather than dogma; with them religion, like other American activities, was regarded as an instrument of progress, that luminescent goal toward which all the energies of the country were directed.

Progress as an ideal was truly universal in its acceptance. But it did not at all follow that there was complete agreement among Americans when it came to putting the ideal into practice. Proposals which seemed crystal-clear in the abstract became vague and shadowy when reduced to the concrete. For in these matters not ideas alone were involved; every measure affected the interests of men, and while the ideas were alike, the interests were not.

There was also the question of pace. Even when great masses of people believed in the ultimate desirability of a proposal, they sometimes could not agree on the speed with which it was to be put into effect. And it was not unusual to find that the cautious, worried as to the effect upon vested rights, split violently from the impatient, eager for reform at any price.

The most radical would tolerate no compromise with the past at all. From time to time, groups of zealots, small in numbers but loud in proclaiming their panaceas, demanded that the change come at once and all at once. Some enthusiasts phrased this demand, or rather expressed this confidence, in a religious mode. A widespread millennial conviction, now and then, drew together earnest groups of men who ordered their whole lives by the expectation that the promises for redemption through a Second Coming were soon to be fulfilled. The band which waited with William Miller for a quick end to the terrestrial world were no doubt extremists; but they nevertheless reflected a point of view not at all incongruous to the society in which they lived. Others interpreted the day of redemption in secular terms and searched hopefully for economic clues as to how it was to be hastened. These people were often influenced by the ideas of European utopian socialists. But the attempt to put those ideas into practice was grounded in American conditions. The well-known experiment of the New England intellectuals at Brook Farm had just come to an end, as had the great majority of phalanxes which had attempted to put flesh on the optimistic theories of Charles Fourier. Similarly the radical proposals of some Forty-eighters, discussed in a later chapter, had a background of European thought but dealt with the role of the United States in a changing world.

Most Americans regarded the more extreme experiments in social reconstruction with a mixture of amusement and sympathy. The settled citizen did not hesitate to reject the radicalism that involved a total break with custom, but he nevertheless had a deep sympathy for the objectives toward which the zealots worked. In more limited ways, through more moderate measures, many earnest people strove to reach the same goals. They embraced one or another of the many-hued reform movements that now sprang up, contributing time and money to the amelioration of the condition of society.

For some reformers, the way lay through assistance to the unfortunate. The poor, the bad, the insane, the orphaned, and the ill were no longer to be counted helpless victims of an overpowering fate, useless, and worthy only of being shut out of the way. These were now reckoned human beings capable, by human means, of being redeemed and rendered useful members of their communities. Devoted men and women set themselves the task of correcting the criminal and of teaching the blind, of helping all such people, somehow crippled, to take a dignified place in society. In the same spirit Forty-eighters naturally enough turned their attention to aid for exploited immigrants.

Other evils too evoked similar attention. What once had been the personal vices of individuals, in the growing cities became offenses to the whole society. Intemperance thus had been an unpleasant but a tolerable habit on the lonely farms of the early nineteenth century. In the towns it was a serious menace. When the attempt to curb the use of spirituous liquors by voluntary abstinence failed, there were strong efforts to halt it by the action of the state. At first the reformers called simply for provisions for licensing and regulating. But in the 1850's the struggle shifted to the issue of whether the government, after the pattern of the Maine Law, should prohibit the sale of intoxicants entirely.

The same impulse went into the efforts to make sure that one day of rest would be guaranteed to every person. The Sabbatarian movement attempted to secure the sanctity of Sunday by state action and, incidentally, brought to the surface some of the old Puritan fervor. But at the root of this drive was the fundamental desire to reaffirm some of the elements of human dignity being obscured in the new society. Newcomers, unfamiliar with the modes of American reform would find Sabbatarianism and Temperance puzzling; to Americans, these movements were aspects of a single reform process.

Most citizens deemed the improvement of education the key to all other reforms. Education could elevate man and prepare him to develop all his capacities to the fullest. Much had been gained by 1845, but much more was still to be gained. Under the leadership of Horace Mann and Henry Barnard, the struggle continued through these years. The reformers held forth the ideal of a public school that would be free, secular, and universal. Toward that end they sought state supervision and support of local efforts in the interests of maintaining standards and securing a trained staff of teachers. They wished also to free the schools of religious and denominational control—a desire also shared by the Forty-eighters.

These aspirations were only the brightest stars in the galaxy of reform. The year 1848, for instance, saw a signal turning point in the struggle for women's rights; a feminist declaration of independence at Seneca Falls then set the goals for the emancipation of the sex from the legal and social discrimination that kept it inferior in status. Many leading Forty-eighters joined in this reform movement, while others retained a Continental view regarding woman's place in society.

When these new departures touched upon issues that involved the fundamental economic structure of the nation, they aroused a great deal of uncertainty and often provoked bitter quarrels.

In a changing world, people whose position was fluctuating, some for better, others for worse, looked to the state for direction and aid, and sought to use the machinery of government for their own ends.

Sometimes reform meant a realignment of old standards. So, the artisans and working people in general resented the anachronistic laws for imprisonment for debt and struggled successfully in these years to have them repealed. Quite another group was concerned in an analogous question, the reform of the bankruptcy laws which often seemed to hamper the operations of the trading community.

In every realm in which the activity of the government affected the economy, men worked to make sure that the effects would serve their ends. Inevitably that precipitated conflicts of interests. Sometimes such clashes involved clear-cut group divisions. In the case of the ten-hour law for corporations, for example, it was primarily a matter of the employers of labor against their employees.

But sometimes the question at issue influenced the whole society and touched off complicated reactions so that diverse groups were compelled to combine and to accommodate clashing points of view. Banking regulation thus evoked a wide diversity of opinion. Farmers, especially farmers in debt, wanted cheap money. Artisans who suffered from the uncertainty of the circulating medium wanted sound money based on specie. Manufacturers also favored sound money, but they wished it tied to loose credit. Merchants, on the other hand, felt it essential to have both sound money and a sound credit structure. Planters had agricultural interests but, at the same time, were also often investors in banks. From these diverse perspectives, people for their own ends espoused various solutions: that the government should perform banking functions directly or through banks that would act as its agents; that the banks be purely private, chartered, or free; that bank notes be issued without limit, or be based on specie, or be restricted in some other way. In this particular struggle Carl Schurz came to play an important part.

Many of the turbulent forces involved in reform converged about the issue of slavery. On this question there had once been the appearance of unanimity throughout the country. Earlier in the century almost everyone, North and South, had agreed that such servitude was a necessary evil but one that would gradually correct itself as the slave trade came to a halt and as masters steadily set free the Blacks already here. Some Americans at one time wished to go even further and, through colonization, sought to deport the freed slaves to Africa. But, in any case, few then would have ventured to predict that slavery would remain a permanent feature of American life.

After 1820 the situation changed. In the next quarter-century, the opening of new lands to plantation culture from Alabama westward, the expansion of the textile industry in Old and New England, and the general adoption of the cotton gin fixed the peculiar institution more firmly in the economic life of the South. The slave rose in value as the demand for his labor increased, and the prospect that the four million who worked the Southern fields in 1860 would eventually be emancipated grew ever slimmer.

At the same time, the existence of the slave system within their own society year by year became more offensive to many Northerners imbued with the reform spirit. This was the greatest indignity of all, for it denied to large groups of people the most elementary of human qualities and certainly stood in the way of progress for the whole nation. Abolitionism gained greatly in strength after 1830 both in the West, where it developed as an aspect of revivalist religion, and in the East, where it grew as an aspect of rationalistic and humanitarian reform. There were divisions of opinion as to degree and means, as to whether the end of slavery should be attained gradually or immediately, whether with compensation or not. But there was no serious questioning of the ultimate judgment that the Negro's bondage was an offensive evil—some would have said a sin.

There was also a large measure of agreement over certain practical consequences of the question. Slavery might for the time being remain in the South under whatever conditions it could, but there was to be no extension of the institution and it was not to be aided directly by federal power.

The rise of abolitionist spirit in the North provoked a counter-reaction in the South. The slaveholders now found it more difficult to agree to the proposition that they were victims of a necessary evil. Attacked as wicked sinners, they found it necessary to defend themselves by justifying the institution as such, by arguing, first that it was divinely sanctioned, and secondly that it was inherently good. The proslavery theorizers, on the first ground, searched the Bible and ancient history for justificatory precedents. On the second, the defenders of the *status quo* produced a significant line of argument to demonstrate that Negroes were inherently inferior, really inhuman, and could enter modern civilization only as slaves. Sometimes such reasoning turned the most extreme against the whole complex of humanitarian reform.

These developments produced a hardening of spirit on the part of both Northerners and Southerners, a rigidity of thinking that made for unwillingness to compromise. Everywhere men became afraid to yield even on minor points lest they thus endanger their whole position.

The perils of that situation emerged in the long series of crises that followed the end of the war with Mexico. As a result of the Treaty of Guadelupe Hidalgo which closed that conflict, the United States acquired immense tracts of new territory, the disposition of which would be fateful in determining the future government of the country. No one doubted that those areas were to become integral parts of the United States. That meant that these regions would be ruled as territories by the federal government for a while and then, when adequately settled, would be admitted to the Union as states, equal in rights with the old states.

The first question was whether these lands should be open to settlement as free or slave territories. The answer would determine the quality and the source of the people who came to live in the area. The same answer ultimately would also determine whether the states formed there would be free or slave, and that in turn would decide whether control of Congress would lie in the hands of the free or the slave states. That these were the ineluctable consequences quickly became clear to the lawmakers pressed with the necessity of acting in 1848. They knew too that the coalitions which had formed about the slavery issue had by then acquired so much cohesion that this decision would influence every other facet of national policy.

For the time, however, unifying forces were still strong enough to throttle any threat to the integrity of the Republic. There were, of course, even in 1850 extremists unwilling to compromise: In the South, Calhoun realized that the basic forces working against his section would not be stayed unless a fundamental amendment altered the Constitutional basis of power; in the North, the Garrisonians were unwilling any longer to tolerate the "covenant with Hell" embodied in the Constitution. But far more numerous were the Americans who realized that the whole structure of the social order, the balance of trade among the sections, and the place of the nation in the world, all were threatened by this disruptive issue; and such people pressed for compromise. The merchants of the North and the great planters of the South in particular worked for some adjustment of the various divergent points of view.

The compromise of 1850 seemed to mark the limits of concession which the two parties were willing to make. An effort was made to appease the antislavery faction by abolition of the slave trade within the limits of the District of Columbia and by admission of California as a free state, which, however, amounted to no more than recognition of a *fait accompli*. On the other hand, slavery itself remained legal in the federal capital and the Fugitive Slave Law was strengthened as a sop to the Southerners.

As for the most nettlesome problem of all, the status of slavery in the territories, that was evaded. In appearance the compromise provided for a kind of self-determination; each new state was left free to determine in its own constitution whether it would recognize the South's peculiar institution or not. But the immediate problem was whether slavery would be protected while the area was still a territory, for that would determine whether the settlers would be free-state or slave-state men. And that decision was left to the discretion of the federal judiciary where, it was vainly hoped, the question would be removed from the realm of partisan politics.

Those hopes were illusory. In the next few years enforcement of the Fugitive Slave Law spread bitterness through the North. And the solution for the territories proved no solution at all. The Kansas-Nebraska Act of 1854 may have been the outgrowth of Stephen A. Douglas's personal ambitions for the Presidency or it may have been an unforseen consequence of the attempt to get support for a railroad from Chicago to the West or, still another possibility, an outcome of local political rivalries. But whatever its origins, the law destroyed the modicum of peace achieved four years earlier. By repealing the Missouri Compromise of 1820 this measure cast doubt upon the validity of all compromises. The Kansas-Nebraska Act put into law the principle of squatters' sovereignty by which the fate of the territory would be determined by the faction which got its men there quickest. This opened the field for the violent competition that went with settlement in Kansas and made way for the savage hatreds of the struggle for "bleeding Kansas."

To cap the climax, a judgment of the Supreme Court of the United States in 1857 removed the foundation of Constitutional legality for the whole system of compromise so laboriously erected by the moderates. The Dred Scott Decision, which denied to Congress the power to exclude slavery from the territories, threw the whole question back into the realm of politics.

The political parties of this era reflected the disturbing influence of such disruptive issues. These organizations had developed as coalitions after 1824. They drew together diverse interests and classes from diverse sections, for limited common goals. In the 1830's and 1840's these coalitions had not always cohered on matters of local politics, but they had held together nationally. In those two decades the most important attacks upon the *status quo* on ideological and class grounds had been delivered through the organization of "third parties." The Whigs and the Democrats would, on occasion, cooperate with one or another of these groups but never to an extent that destroyed their own national unity.

After 1848, however, the two major parties began to crumble under the shock of successive issues on which the national coalitions could not hold. The long state of crisis over the slavery issue tended to crystalize all reform impulses about that central core and played into the hands of the third-party leaders. As the old parties showed themselves increasingly incapable of coping with the crisis, dissidents gained in power and influence.

At first the Liberty and the Free Soil parties in the North tended to join forces with the Democratic party which was out of power nationally. But after 1850 the reformers began to draw strength also from the Whig party, the members of which could not subscribe to the role of their leaders in compromising with slavery. After 1852 when the Whigs lost power nationally, that tendency continued, and the coalition of insurgent Whigs, abolitionists, and reformers of other kinds drew together in a series of working arrangements from which ultimately emerged the Republican party with which, as later chapters will show, almost all Forty-eighters aligned themselves.

Meanwhile in the South the plantation Whigs grew ever more alienated from their old party and deserted in droves to the Democrats who now emerged as the stanchest defenders of slavery. In the election of 1856 the essential social and sectional lines were already drawn.

In that year there also appeared on the ballot a third party which immediately proved a tremendous disappointment to its supporters. The American party had emerged suddenly in the local elections of 1854 when it gained control of several states and also secured the balance of power in the federal Congress. For a little while it seemed well on the way to dominance in national politics. Yet in 1856, with a former President, Millard Fillmore, at the head of its ticket, it finished an ignominious third and quickly disappeared from the American political scene.

This quick rise and decline was revealing as to the impact of the American party on the political scene. For this was no ordinary political organization. It was rather the political arm of a secret fraternal society, the Order of the Star-Spangled Banner —Know-Nothings, they were commonly called. The Order had grown slowly after 1850 and its burst of popular support in 1854 had surprised even its own members. It decayed when it came into the open because it could work out no meaningful platform. Once the various groups in the party got together they found that they had nothing in common.

At least three different elements were involved in the Order. In New England it consisted of reformers and abolitionists, men dissatisfied with the stand of the old parties on slavery, men who saw as the chief obstacles to the achievement of their aims the opposition of the Irish-Catholic immigrants, who seemed conservative in politics. These Know-Nothings ultimately became members of the Republican party.

In the middle states the American party drew its support from people who wished to take a neutral stand on the slavery issue and who saw in the nativist slogans a way of avoiding the difficulties that would certainly come from confronting insoluble problems, from facing irrepressible conflicts. Finally, in the South, the Know-Nothings drew largely upon the support of proslavery people who regarded Germans as abolitionists.

The fact that these dissimilar elements came to the party for different, indeed for contradictory reasons, explains its quick demise. It also accounts for the nature of the nativism that the party professed. The Know-Nothings were not anti-foreign simply out of xenophobia or out of anti-Catholicism, although some such elements were involved. Anti-immigrant feeling was rather an instinctive rallying point around which a nation in distress could temporarily draw together.

Hostility to foreigners was, for the Know-Nothings, a means toward an end rather than an end in itself. Significantly, the American party at no time sought to enact any restrictions upon immigration. Furthermore, the movement, when it had power, put into effect only the mildest measures curtailing the political privileges of the foreign-born. The famous Massachusetts Two-Year Amendment for instance (passed in 1859 after the Know-

Nothings had already become Republicans) simply established a waiting period before voting.

The character of American nativism in this period was important in determining the reception of the Forty-eighters, as of other immigrants. Newcomers were universally welcomed as valuable additions to the forces that would help build up the country. Such an attitude and the general tolerance it embodied was, indeed, the natural outcome of the pervasive American optimism. The belief in progress nurtured a sense of confidence that there was room for all in the New World. Apart from the Know-Nothing movement, nativism, on the occasions when it showed itself, arose over specific issues—the school question in New York and Philadelphia, the water supply in Boston.

Moreover, in the United States, a favored place was reserved for all the refugees from political oppression. The people of this period felt that reform and progress would not be limited to the boundaries of the United States. These principles, it was believed, would spread through the whole world, and first of all to

Europe. Americans regarded with deep understanding the revolutionary efforts to overthrow the decadent monarchies of the Old World and to imitate the democracy of the United States. They had therefore hailed the revolutions of 1848 and had shown their sympathetic approval of the struggles with concrete assistance in money, men, and diplomatic support. Those who fled in the aftermath came as heroes, temporarily defeated, and were received as valuable additions to the elements of American life. In the turbulent years that were about to lead to a mortal conflict which few really envisaged, these new citizens were good to have in the United States.

Chapter Three

ADJUSTMENT TO THE UNITED STATES

By Hildegard Binder Johnson

W HAT did the Forty-eighter look like as he landed in New York, Philadelphia, or New Orleans? A composite picture would show him a relatively young man of good physique developed by gymnastics. He affected student costume or imitated the style of the romantic hero of the Revolution, Friedrich Hecker, by wearing a broad-brimmed hat, a shirt open at the neck, and a loosely tied scarf. He had long, wavy hair and, in particular contrast to the American fashion of clean-shaven faces, a moustache or even a full beard. He was set off from the mass of immigrants, the peasants and craftsmen, by delicate hands that showed no signs of physical labor. In some cases, if he had been a member of the Frankfurt *Parlament*, his dress was of rather formal cut and of elegant material, sometimes velvet, but by now rather shiny since his wardrobe was very meagre.

He stepped on land eagerly with no family trailing behind him to slow his pace or much luggage to detain him at the custom's inspection. His departure from his homeland had not been carefully planned, for often it had been taken just a few steps ahead of the police or, in some cases, straight after an escape from prison. Furthermore, his journey had not been direct, but prolonged by sojourns in Switzerland, France, or England, where he had eaten the bitter bread of the stranger, always waiting for a better turn of political events in Germany. Even to America he had not come as a settler but as one ever ready to return to his homeland to aid in the Revolution which would be more successful the next time. He had no household goods nor much wearing apparel, but generally just one satchel bulging with books and papers. There were manuscript sheets of a diary or of poems entitled, "Farewell to My Fatherland" or "Dream on the Ocean," and perhaps the beginnings of a political essay. By way of books he was apt to have the revolutionary poets who had inspired him to risk his life for freedom, Freiligrath or Herwegh, rather than an old family Bible. While many of his fellow immigrants gathered in family groups around chests and trunks which had to be opened for inspection and then shipped to an inland destination, the Forty-eighter was free to move on. He did so with confidence and felt much less baffled by the new environment than his fellow passengers who, aside from the recent journey, had spent all their lives in some small German town or village. He had lived in Paris, Geneva, or London as an exile or had previously traveled abroad in his student days. He knew Italian, Hungarian, or French revolutionaries in person or through correspondence. Even if he spoke little English, he had studied Latin and French, and thus foreign languages seemed no unsurmountable barrier to him. Friends came to the pier to meet him or he had the address of comrades who had participated with him in the great movement. He had read about the United States, whose Declaration of Independence had often been quoted whenever a free and united Germany was being planned. He was not afraid. On the contrary, he had great expectations and felt that he had a mission. His political past entitled him to respect and a hearing. Although his ideas of what to do next were not very precise and probably none too practical, yet he was certain that he would be doing something.

There were of course exceptions to the "typical" Forty-eighter. Friedrich Hecker was thirty-seven years old. He had come in 1848 and then returned to Germany when the Baden uprising once more gave promise of success. After the second failure he set out for the United States with his family and had a definite destination, namely his farm near Belleville, Illinois. Carl Schurz too was married though only twenty-three years of age; his wife had some means which enabled him to devote the

FRIEDRICH HECKER
From a contemporary print
Nestor of the Germans; Fighter for Freedom and Justice; for Unity; for Freedom;
against Slavery; against Sanctimonious Hypocrites

first years to the study of the English language and of American life in general. Most of the Forty-eighters who came to Iowa were family men from Schleswig-Holstein drawn there by the reports of their countrymen successfully settled in Scott County. Broadly speaking, however, the Forty-eighters form an exception to the general rule of family or group immigration during the middle decades of the nineteenth century.

Any estimate of the number of Forty-eighters who emigrated to the United States is at best a guess. The chief German authority on the period, Veit Valentin, does not attempt to give any figures. The late Marcus Hansen, the most thorough American investigator of European emigration across the Atlantic during the nineteenth century, estimates "a few thousand." He finds that the number of revolutionaries who remained in Germany despite adverse circumstances is far greater than that of the *émigrés*. The largest single fighting unit was the revolutionary army in Baden under the leadership of Hecker and Struve in April, 1848, and it numbered at most six thousand men. There was of course fighting at other places and many men were forced to flee because of their writings or even opinions. Perhaps an estimate of between three and four thousand political emigrants to the United States would be ample to include all the leaders as well as lesser followers.

A more or less accurate count of Forty-eighters on American soil is likewise made difficult for various reasons. The task would be simplified if they had come in groups, but the fact is that they came generally as individuals and their arrivals coincided with a great wave of German immigration for economic reasons during the decade of 1846 to 1856. In the stream of roughly three-quarters of a million who arrived during those years, the few thousand political refugees represent a mere trickle. All figures given for those years are subject to controversial interpretations; for example, port officials made no distinction regarding a first and second arrival. Quite a number, among them Friedrich Hecker, Caspar Butz, Carl Stifel, Carl Luedeking, and Heinrich Huhn, arrived in this country and returned to Germany before their final settling in the United States in the course of the fifties.

Some, as for example Gottfried Kinkel, Julius Froebel, or Eduard Pelz, came as what would now be called "visitors," arriving for a limited period with a definite mission. Others again returned to live in Germany after a decade or more of life in the United States, for example, Friedrich Kapp, Carl Daenzer, Theodor Olshausen, or General "Peter Joe" Osterhaus of Civil War fame. Finally there is the difficulty of defining the term "Forty-eighter"; for example, Mathias Rohlfs and Wilhelm Pfaender, later distinguished liberals in the Middle West, arrived in this country as political refugees some months before the Revolution had actually broken out. In their political attitude before emigration and in the spirit they displayed during a lifetime in this country, they are "Forty-eighters" just as much as Albert Wolff who languished in a German prison until 1852 or Franz Sigel, Dr. Ernst Schmidt, and Ernst Anton Zuendt who arrived in 1852, 1856, and 1857, respectively.

The student of immigration finds the census records on file in the National Archives in Washington very useful source material concerning the number and location of the foreign-born in the United States. He finds them listed there, under townships or city wards, with data on name, age, profession, country of birth, and so on. My investigation of numerous Midwestern census records showed that approximately nine out of ten German immigrants between 1848 and 1854 came from west of the Elbe River, that is from the very regions which were the scenes of memorable revolutionary events. But among the hundreds of thousands who gave Baden, Wuerttemberg, the Rhineland, the Palatinate, Hesse, or Bavaria as their countries of birth the young revolutionary who might have been easily recognized on the pier is almost hopelessly lost in the records ten years later.

The column "profession" may offer a clue that can lead to the identification of Forty-eighters, since very often they were the teachers, physicians, lawyers, editors, or "professors of music" in the German settlements. If the profession is listed as "turner," there is no doubt, as the members of the gymnastic societies had been ardent supporters of the Revolution. Some Forty-eighters, I suspect, tend to elude identification under the designations of "clerk," "merchant," "brewer," or "farmer." However, a few Forty-eighters who became farmers (nick-named "Latin farmers" because of their classical training) can be spotted by such classifications as "farmer and physician" or "farmer and teacher." In the census report of Scott County, Iowa, for 1860, Nicholas J. Rusch is listed as "farmer and lieutenant-governor of Iowa"; his is a somewhat exceptional case of a revolutionary *émigré* becoming a successful farmer, as is revealed by the listing of seven farm laborers, two domestic servants, and two millwrights on the Rusch estate.

Friedrich Kapp, a Forty-eighter who in 1867 was appointed immigration commissioner in New York, tells of a remarkable meeting on the Texas prairies that is very revealing regarding the life of the educated *émigré* who tried to realize the idyllic dream of freedom and happiness in a log cabin on the frontier. Kapp happened to stop at the hut of a man who had been described to him by a neighbor as a former German university student, quiet and hard-working, but no longer interested in books. The hut was bare of all comforts. Unwashed dishes on the table indicated that the owner was only temporarily absent; faded photographs on the wall showed groups of Heidelberg students among whom Kapp recognized himself in student costume and with long flowing locks. He realized that he had found a long-lost friend of whose very existence he had been unaware for a decade. After an hour's wait he saw his friend return and then the two held a memorable reunion. To Kapp's questions the friend replied that, after eight years in free America, he was not in position to say that he had found the longed-for happiness. He was rich in land but poor in every other respect. "I am not exactly happy, but not unhappy either, for I live free and unfettered. I am independent of everyone except my oxen and the weather. No one hinders me in my plans and projects except the lack of money. No one prevents me from expressing my revolutionary sentiments except the absence of an audience." He related that for some time his interest in political events in Europe had continued, but with the final collapse of hopes for a liberal Germany it had faded under the pressing problems of the daily struggle for existence. He did not even bother to write letters, and his inkwell was quite dried up. He asked Kapp to stay for the evening since a few German friends were going to drop in. This session turned out to be a pitiful affair, with an attempt to revive old Heidelberg customs. The potation was ghastly punch mixed with a dubious whisky, the songs sounded most incongruous from the lips of the ill-clad men of the frontier, and the conversation turned out to be most trivial. One of the former German officials even said, "Our life here might be quite tolerable if only we had a bowling alley."!

There are some examples of Forty-eighters who set out to realize the ideal of "free men on free soil," but who found their way to professions more suited to their training after they had failed as farmers; examples are Carl Rotteck in Iowa, Jens Stibolt in Missouri, and Hans Balatka in Wisconsin, of whom the former two became newspaper editors and the last named a distinguished musical director in Milwaukee. It was the immigration of the thirties that furnished most examples of "Latin farmers," particularly the Hilgards, Engelmanns, and Gustave Koerner. These owners of well-managed estates in the vicinity of Belleville, Illinois, had come to the United States with not inconsiderable capital; they were in fact gentlemen farmers, inasmuch as they derived their incomes from professional work rather than from farming.

An illustration of the attachment to romantic illusions regarding America on the part of the European is found in a letter written by Friedrich Hecker to a friend on the eve of his second departure for America in August, 1849: "With true longing I gaze across the ocean to the far west and to my forest solitude. . . . I am so dreadfully tired of this police state and shall praise the day when I can take my axe again and clear the woodland." In reality Hecker had bought an improved farm of three hundred acres with a spacious brick house three miles southeast of Lebanon, Illinois, close enough to Belleville to permit him to make frequent visits there at the homes of his intellectual friends. Hecker was certainly not the typical pioneer farmer. But to indicate that there were exceptions to practically every generalization one might make about Forty-eighters: there was a successful farming community at New Holstein, Wisconsin, founded by Rudolf Puchner and Dr. Carl Mieding—to be sure the only instance of such an enterprise carried out by Forty-eighters.

The vast majority of Forty-eighters settled in the cities. Here the artisan had the advantage over the university-trained, particularly if the immigrant, as was mostly the case, did not know English. The blacksmith, wagonmaker, butcher, carpenter—to mention a few typically urban occupations—could make a living with a very small English vocabulary even if he did not live in a German ward or have the advantage of working for an American employer. But a physician either had to live in a town with a German population large enough to support him or he had to know the language of his American patients. The lawyer was worse off, for he had to learn the laws of the land in addition to English. Teachers could sometimes find positions in German private schools or as tutors in German families. But the financial status of the schools was usually precarious, and there was severe competition, since intellectuals with every sort of training offered their services in the educational field. The German language newspaper seemed to offer the best opportunity to earn money and to continue with political and literary interests. But the editor who wanted to inform his German readers had to inform himself first, usually through the English press or in political meetings with English speakers. While hundreds of thousands of non-English immigrants have gotten along fairly well without learning English, the Forty-eighters with their superior educational background, their interest in politics, and their desire to make their opinions known had first of all to learn English.

Naturally many retained a decided German accent. In the Iowa campaign of 1859 the "sweet German accent" of Nicholas Rusch, the Republican nominee for lieutenant-governor, became a campaign issue. However, though Rusch had this handicap, he wrote English very well. Incidents like Emil Rothe's inability to reply in English to the challenges of his opponent Carl Schurz at a campaign meeting in St. Paul, Minnesota, in 1860, appear to have been rare. On the whole the Forty-eighters learned English quickly and very well. A by no means unusual feat was that of Hans Reimer Claussen of Davenport who, two years sfter landing in America, translated *Beadle's Collection of Iowa State Laws*. Carl Schurz and Eduard Salomon were admitted to the bar a short time after their arrival in this country. Competency in English before coming to the United States was quite exceptional as is evidenced by the fact that biographical sketches of Konrad Krez, an attorney in Sheboygan, Wisconsin, always make special mention of his knowledge of English which enabled him to begin immediately his American career as a lawyer.

The Forty-eighters had many characteristics which set them apart; yet they also retained some of the traits of Germans and immigrants. With the mass of Germans, among whom many were hostile or indifferent to their liberal aims and ardent convictions, the Forty-eighters shared an aversion to certain aspects of the new American environment. Forty-eighters, along with good Catholics and orthodox Lutherans, often took it upon themselves to criticize the frequently corrupt administrations of American cities, the "vanity" of American women and their aversion to hard work and large families, the "mechanical methods" in American schools, "Yankee avarice," or the dullness of American life. The last-named grievance, frequently voiced by Europeans of all nationalities, arose from the lack of "romantic" elements in this pioneer country where so many features seemed to call for this very thing. American art was found by them to be imitative of old world models, literature followed the fashion of English novelists or poets, in the field of music there was no typical American production, and, in fact, very little practice of this art so dear to the German. Courtship was bare of profound sentiment so different from the European fashion that a lover of the type of Goethe's Werther would appear simply as a fool. There was no particular attachment to native soil (in fact, the word "fatherland" was only a recent coinage in English introduced by Byron) and the American could without pangs exchange the Hudson for the Missouri, Virginia for Texas. Freedom was cherished by the American and he was always ready to fight or die for it, but even this ideal had no particular poetic nimbus about it. By way of contrast one can find among the Forty-eighters dozens of poets who glorify freedom and sing sad songs of *Heimweh*.

As immigrants the Forty-eighters were affected by the most important trend in American history during the nineteenth century, the Westward movement. They did not clear woods and build loghouses, but they too sought opportunities, and young cities furnished them. Horace Greeley's call, "Go west, young man, go west!" was a call of promise to the Forty-eighters just as much as to the farmer who sought free land. It appealed to their desire for freedom and action, their love of nature, their spirit of romance and adventure. New York, Baltimore, Boston, and Philadelphia were very different from Frankfurt, Karlsruhe, Köln, and Stuttgart. St. Louis, Chicago, Milwaukee, and Cincinnati were much more so. After addressing the *Parlament* in the Paulskirche in Frankfurt, a political orator was apt to find surroundings more congenial in Faneuil Hall in Boston than in Ulrich's block in Chicago or Albany Hall in Milwaukee.

Some incidents which befell the city-bred German in the West make amusing reading and probably were amusing to the victim himself when he wrote his memoirs many years later. At the time, however, it was not amusing to sleep under leaking roofs, to eat a monotonous fare of corn-meal soup prepared by the cook among six bachelors rooming together, to have unexpected Indian visitors in the barn where the cherished piano from Germany had been stored for lack of space in the log cabin, or to earn a living by playing dramas in smoke-filled halls without scenery, stage, or actresses. Great tragedies like the flood of St. Louis, the cholera in the Mississippi valley, the Sioux war of 1862 which practically wiped out New Ulm, Minnesota, and the Chicago fire had to be met with indomitable spirit. Thus the Forty-eighters who had renounced the blessings of civilization and left the culture and comfort of populated cities behind them were in a sense also pioneers.

Most of them arrived during the period when the rivers of the Mississippi basin still were the important arteries of traffic. St.

Louis, four times the size of Chicago in 1840, was for the following three decades the greatest point of distribution west of the
Alleghenies. Transportation affected the pattern of distribution
of German immigrants just as it did that of most settlers in the
West. The Forty-eighters traveled like the others, from New
York to Albany, via the Erie Canal to Buffalo, by boat to Cleveland and thence across the lakes to Detroit, Milwaukee, Chicago;
or they disembarked at Sandusky, Ohio, to go by rail to Cincinnati, and then down the Ohio River to St. Louis. Some arrived in New Orleans and traveled up the Mississippi river,
always stopping in St. Louis. From this point they could go to
German settlements in the Missouri river counties, or cross over
to Illinois to Belleville or Quincy. The greater number took another steamboat at St. Louis and went further up the river.
They settled along its west bank in Keokuk, Burlington, Muscatine, Buffalo, Davenport, Clinton-Lyons, Dubuque, Guttenberg,
and a few found their way up to Minnesota. When in 1857 the
Turner Settlement Association of Cincinnati was looking for a
good location for the German settlement they wished to found,
it was the Minnesota River that guided them to the spot that
became the site of New Ulm.

All the cities mentioned naturally took on a German flavor
with their *Turner* halls, German newspapers, singing and theatrical societies, and beer gardens. The extreme example was
Guttenberg, which permitted only German residents and thus
became a remarkably homogeneous town, with practically all
its *Turner* enthusiasts members of the new Republican party.
Today Guttenberg is a quaint, sleepy village, because it failed
to attract later German immigration.

The Forty-eighters, like most immigrants, preferred to settle
in a town or region where fellow countrymen or friends had gone
before them. Many reached their future homes through quite
accidental circumstances. Hence the Forty-eighters who lived in
the East and in the West of the United States showed fewer differences than did Easterners and Westerners among the native-
born, due to the fact that the educational and political background of the Forty-eighters was very homogeneous, their mobil-

ity great, and their cohesion as a group considerable. In this chapter their activity in the Middle West is stressed not because their role in the East should be thought of as insignificant, but because their impact in the West coincided with the early growth of cities and therefore impressed itself in the annals of the young communities more noticeably than in those of the established cities in the East. It will appear that many whose names occur only in local historical records fought untiringly for the same causes which made others nationally famous. The selection of certain cities for more detailed treatment does not imply that these were the only communities where Forty-eighters played a significant part. Space does not permit an enumeration of all the localities where Forty-eighters are recorded, nor does it permit an exhaustive treatment of their activities in even the five cities that I have selected. I shall illustrate the leadership which the Forty-eighters brought to their new home towns by case histories, rather than by generalizations concerning an entire region.

Since Milwaukee has long enjoyed the reputation of being the most German community in the nation, it seems logical to treat it first. This city had been the center of reception and distribution for German settlers in Wisconsin ever since the state began to attract them in vast numbers. However, the influence of the Forty-eighters was not so marked here as one might expect. For one thing, by 1850 the three militant German ideologies, Catholicism, Lutheranism, and liberalism, were already firmly established in Wisconsin. The first Catholic bishop of German tongue in the United States, Johann Martin Henni, had arrived in Milwaukee in 1844. The Wisconsin Lutheran Synod was organized in 1850. German liberals had founded the "German Democratic Association" in the fall of 1844 for the purpose of political enlightenment among Germans and the promotion of unity in politics. Somewhat feebly the spirit of 1848 expressed itself in the organization of the *Drei-Cents-Verein* in June of that year. Members of this society paid three cents weekly to support the German Revolution and by this means collected only the trifling sum of $21.64 which they sent abroad to Hecker in the spring of 1849. Outstanding among German liberals who had come before 1848 were Dr. Franz Huebschmann, a member of the Milwaukee schoolboard in 1843, and Moritz Schoeffler. Huebschmann was instrumental as a member of the constitutional convention of 1846 in obtaining for foreigners the right to vote after one year's residence. Schoeffler, an outspoken free-thinker, founded the first German newspaper of Milwaukee, the long-lived *Wisconsin Banner*, in 1844; it was Democratic as were also the two other German papers founded in the ensuing decade. That these men supported the antislavery cause and still remained in the Democratic party helps explain the weak role played by Wisconsin Germans in politics, where even the liberals were divided in their party affiliations. When the Republican party of the state was founded in Madison in March, 1854, Milwaukee sent no official delegates. One Forty-eighter, Christian Esselen, the editor of the journal *Atlantis*, was among the three Germans from Milwaukee who attended the convention at Madison on their own initiative. One year later Carl Roeser, a Forty-eighter from Manitowoc, was defeated as Republican candidate for state treasurer by his German-born Democratic opponent. Schurz's defeat as Republican candidate for lieutenant-governor in 1857 is the best-known illustration of lack of Forty-eighter success in Wisconsin party politics.

The ties of the foreign-born to the Democratic party had become so strong among the Germans of Wisconsin that all attempts of Forty-eighters to bring them into the Republican party proved futile; another factor was the nativist agitation on the part of American Republicans which repelled the immigrants. A Forty-eighter, Bernhard Domschke, made a valiant effort to supply Milwaukee with a Republican newspaper but the fact that it appeared first as *Corsair*, then *Atlas*, and finally as *Herold* shows that it was no success and left the editor in continuous financial difficulties. Wisconsin even had a Forty-eighter, Emil Rothe of Watertown, who fought for the Democratic party as late as 1860. The German vote in Wisconsin remained split until 1873 when there arose an issue on which Catholics, Lutherans, liberals, and agnostics voted their convictions as one man—to defeat the Graham Liquor Law.

Wisconsin, the German state *par excellence*, never sent a German-born Senator to Washington. Nomination of German-born citizens for the positions of state, county, township, or city treasurer was the customary sop thrown to German voters. Aside from Schurz, only Edward Salomon was nominated for lieutenant-governor. Salomon, one of four brothers three of whom had been active in the revolution, was elected and then succeeded Governor Harvey into office after the latter's death in April, 1862. This Forty-eighter proved to be a good governor; he suppressed draft riots, kept the state university open during the war, and is said to have avoided carefully any special favoritism toward German interests. Milwaukee elected its first German-born mayor in 1884. The historian Ernest Bruncken assesses the influence of the Germans in Wisconsin, as well as in Milwaukee, as "politically nil," and Domschke, the contemporary, declared that there was only one outstanding man among the fourteen German members of the Wisconsin legislature, while the rest were "mere ciphers."

The second reason for the weak political impact of the Forty-eighters was their outspoken agnosticism, which offended the church-going Germans. Largely because of the reactionary attitude of the German state church, the *Turner* and the Forty-eighters in general had become anticlericals, freethinkers of the aggressive sort who set up free schools in opposition to parochial schools. These groups rather than the church circles developed the colorful social and cultural life centering about German music and the German theatre which caused some writers to refer to Milwaukee as *Deutsch-Athen*.

Two Forty-eighters, Eduard Schultz and Fritz Anneke, began instruction in gymnastics in March, 1850, and founded the first *Turnverein*. A second *Turnverein* was organized in 1852 and one year later, upon August Willich's suggestion, the *Soziale Turnverein*. One of the few clergymen among the Forty-eighters, Eduard Schroeter, who had been exiled on account of his opposition to the state church, founded the first *freie Gemeinde* ("free congregation," a sort of ethical culture society) in New York, and in 1851 established another in Milwaukee. Within a year *freie Gemeinden* abounded in eastern Wisconsin. On October 1, 1853, the *Bund freier Menschen* was founded in Milwaukee comprising all freethinking Germans of Wisconsin. Twenty-three societies formed this league of non-church-going idealists including the *freie Gemeinden* of Sauk City, Burlington, Mequon, Plymouth, Paynesville, Polk, Richfield, Rhine, Cedarburg, Germantown, as well as such organizations as the *Humoristischer Frauenverein* of Milwaukee, the Society of Humanists, the Sons of Freedom, and the Sons of Hermann. These radical groups did not consist of Forty-eighters only, but the latter were the leaders. Their violent attacks on religion, directed particularly against the Catholic Church, did not serve to win churchgoers for the cause of liberalism, especially since the clergy in turn pictured the *Turner* and similar groups in sulphurous language.

The feverish activity of the freethinkers in Wisconsin can be described as a sort of boyish excess on the part of the Forty-eighters that did not outlast the early fifties. Most of these societies in the small towns were short-lived. A few, however, developed a surprising staying power, chiefly due to Schroeter's passionate devotion to free thought. He was president of the National League of Free Congregations and for many years speaker of the *freie Gemeinde* in Sauk City; this group after one hundred years still maintains a spacious meeting hall surrounded by well-kept grounds and buries its members in the near-by freethinkers' cemetery. Another long-lived freethinking German community was Thiensville in Ozaukee County about fifteen miles north of Milwaukee. It was only after the First World War that the first church was established in Thiensville which neighboring communities nicknamed "Little Paris" or "The Godforsaken Village." In Milwaukee too, the *freie Gemeinde* still maintains its building and issues a monthly "Voice of Freedom." It was because of their interest in the education of youth that these societies managed to survive the passing of the first generation. The constitution of the freethinkers' society of Milwaukee lists the teaching of youth as its "special duty." At the annual National

Conference of Freethinkers in 1871 members expressed a demand for a textbook for the Sunday schools of *Turner* and freethinkers. The *freie Gemeinde* of Milwaukee commissioned a Swiss pedagogue, H. M. Kottinger, to write the book and likewise subsidized the publication. The *Leitfaden fuer den Unterricht in den Sonntags-Schulen freier Gemeinden*, a textbook for instruction in Sunday schools of free congregations, is a fascinating catechism of humanitarianism. The *Leitfaden* was adopted by German freethinker societies from Philadelphia to San Francisco and was still used in *Turner* Sunday schools at the turn of the century. Kottinger found valuable collaborators in the persons of the minister of the Unitarian Church of Milwaukee and Peter Engelmann.

The latter was the most distinguished schoolman among the Forty-eighters. For a short time he worked as a farmhand, then became tutor in a private home, and in 1851 founded the German-English Academy in Milwaukee. He believed in learning by doing and employed visual education and vocational training decades before the introduction of these methods in American schools. He was a freethinker and natural scientist, and above all a teacher who impressed his character on generations of pupils not confined to the German population. For twenty-four years he directed the German-English Academy which served as a model for other German private schools. Because of the reputation of the Academy, Engelmann's school was selected by the National German-American Teachers' League in 1878 to serve as German-American Teachers Seminary. A Forty-eighter, Carl Adolph Douai of Boston, was the chief promoter of the idea. The lower grades of Engelmann's school were used for practice teaching. The North American Turner League transferred its Normal School for teachers of physical training to Milwaukee in 1875, where it flourished to a much greater degree than in the previous locations, New York and Chicago.

There were numerous examples of progressive pedagogy in addition to Engelmann's Academy, as for example, Mathilde Giesler-Anneke's school for girls in Milwaukee (attended by the daughters of American as well as German families), the Westside

High School in Milwaukee, Dietrich Puls's private school in Mayville, and August Wittmann's German-American high school in Manitowoc. Theodor Bernhard of Watertown campaigned for free textbooks and his city was the first to introduce this reform. Also in Watertown a kindergarten was established, probably the first in this country; the founder was Margarethe Schurz, wife of the famous Forty-eighter. Shortly thereafter Engelmann added a kindergarten to his school. Thus in the field of education the contributions of the Forty-eighters in Wisconsin were considerable.

The spirit of the schools founded by Forty-eighters was that of freedom, which can be illustrated from the principles set down by Friedrich Knapp for the school he founded in Baltimore in 1853:

Everyone, the state as well as the church, the communities as well as the government, tries to control and influence schools and teachers. The Knapp school emphatically refuses any such influence; freely and independently it will strive to realize its aims and bid farewell to the dead, memory-stuffing procedure of the past while holding with Pestalozzi that teaching and training must be suited to the nature of the child and that the school must be revamped into a training institution. It must always be the main purpose of the school to develop naturally the abilities and talents present in each person.

A famous alumnus of this school is Henry Louis Mencken, whose untrammeled individualism is a testimonial to Knapp's methods. In the first volume of his autobiographical works, *Happy Days*, Mencken reminisces characteristically on his introduction to

F. Knapp's Institute, a seminary that catered to the boys and girls of the Baltimore bourgeoisie for more than sixty years. It was already beginning, in 1886, to feel the competition of the public schools, but Professor Knapp was not alarmed, for he believed firmly, and often predicted, that the public schools would collapse soon or late under the weight of their own inherent and incurable infamy. They were fit, he argued freely, only for dealing with boys too stupid, too lazy, too sassy or too dirty to be admitted to such academies as his own, and it was their well-deserved destiny to be shut down eventually by the police, if not by actual public violence. As for sending girls to them, he simply could not imagine it; as well shame and degrade the poor little angels by cutting off their pigtails or putting them into pants.

Otherwise the professor was a very mild and even amiable man, and much more diligent at praise than at blame. He was a Suabian who had come to Baltimore in 1850, and he still wore, nearly forty years afterward, the classical uniform of a German schoolmaster—a long-tailed coat of black alpaca, a boiled shirt with somewhat fringey cuffs, and a white lawn necktie. The front of his coat was dusty with chalk, and his hands were so caked with it that he had to blow it off every time he took snuff. He was of small stature but large diameter, and wore closely-clipped mutton-chop whiskers. . . .

The professor viewed the pedagogical art with great pride, and was a man of some eminence in the town. He was on easy terms with the Mayor, General Ferdinand C. Latrobe, who once got us an hour's release from learning by dropping in from the City Hall across the street to harangue us darkly on civic virtue. The old professor, in the days when I knew him, had begun to restrict his personal teaching to a few extra abstruse subjects, e.g., fractions, but he always lined up all the boys for inspection in the morning, and he led both boys and girls in the singing that opened every day's session. For this last purpose all hands crowded into the largest classroom. The professor conducted with his violin, and his daughter Bertha helped out at a parlor organ. The songs, as I recall them, were chiefly German favorites of his youth —*Goldene Abend Sonne, Winter, Ade!, Fuchs, du hast die Gans gestolen, Hurrah, Hurrah, Hurra-la-la-la-la!*, and so on. Most of the pupils knew very little German, though they were taught it fiercely, but they all managed to sing the songs.

As I have said, the institute had already begun to wither around the edges when I first knew it. In 1879 (so I gather from a faded announcement in an old Baltimore directory) it had had a teaching staff of twelve savants, and offered instruction in French, Latin, and Hebrew, not to mention German and English, but by my time the staff had evaporated down to six or seven, and French and Latin had been abandoned.

Musical societies were organized in Milwaukee before 1850. During the fifties they developed so rapidly that contemporaries ranked the city second only to New York as a musical center. Hans Balatka, a Forty-eighter from Bohemia, deserves most of the credit for the achievements of the *Milwaukee Musikverein*, founded in 1850. Balatka was not a creative musician, but rather a skillful organizer and good conductor who developed to a high degree the excellent amateur talent which abounded in Milwaukee after 1848. With this talent Balatka was able to perform Haydn's *Creation* and Lortzing's operas during the first three seasons. Christoph Bach, who trained professional players for orchestra, was probably the greater musician; the overtures which he composed were performed in London, Berlin, Vienna, and St. Petersburg during his lifetime. After his musical organization had become firmly established in Milwaukee, Balatka became director of the Philharmonic Society in Chicago, but he continued to conduct performances in Milwaukee and remained for fifty years associated with its musical life. The Academy of Music, a concert hall built by the *Musikverein*, serves as a permanent and dignified center for the city's musical activities. The cultural superiority of Milwaukee over Chicago, despite the latter's far larger German population, can be explained by the fact that in Milwaukee the Germans lived as a more compact group. Consequently the Chicago Germans often found it expedient to draw on Milwaukee for musical or dramatic talent.

Amateur theatricals flourished in Milwaukee before the arrival of the Forty-eighters, but the serious interest of these men led to better performances and, in the sixties, to the founding of a professional stage which presented German classics and modern plays with great distinction. In the field of literature the most accomplished writers, the poets Konrad Krez and Edmund Maerklin, were Forty-eighters.

It has been possible here to mention only a few examples of the activities of the Forty-eighters, but they serve to show that it was this group which supplied the intellectual ferment and the leadership in cultural matters.

In Chicago, the Forty-eighters played their most important role in politics. In 1860, every fifth person in the city was German-born, a smaller proportion of the total population than in Milwaukee. While the German population was at first fairly concentrated, it soon became scattered over the entire city. This was a drawback for the development of cultural life, particularly after the fire of 1871 destroyed the social center of liberal Germans, the German House on Indiana Avenue and Welles Street.

But German political efforts under the leadership of Forty-eighters during the fifties and early sixties were united and not weakened by dissentions as was the case in Milwaukee.

The Germans of Chicago were active as a group as early as 1843 when they held a mass meeting in honor of Gustave Koerner from Belleville, who had urged in the legislature of Illinois the completion of the Illinois-Michigan Canal, a project close to the hearts of Chicago citizens. During the fifties a number of politically able Forty-eighters came to Chicago. Caspar Butz arrived in 1854 and found employment first in a hardware store and later on in a bank. George Schneider became editor of the *Illinois Staatszeitung*, which under his editorship soon became the leading German daily newspaper of the Northwest. Schneider in the course of time brought to his staff four other Forty-eighters: George Hillgaertner, Lorenz Brentano, Hermann Raster, and Wilhelm Rapp. Other politically active Forty-eighters were Dr. Ernst Schmidt, popularly known as *"der rote Schmidt"* both on account of his red beard and his socialist views, and Ernst Pruessing. These men and their followers found a leader in one of Chicago's older and most colorful German citizens, Francis A. Hoffmann. Hoffmann, who had arrived before 1848, had been trained for the ministry but became a banker. He was elected alderman in Chicago and lieutenant-governor of Illinois during the Civil War. It was due to Hoffmann's humor and tact that the first public German protest meeting in the West against the restriction of the rights of the foreign-born was not thwarted through an annoying accident.

This is the story: On March 4, 1854, the Kansas-Nebraska Bill was passed in the Senate together with the Clayton Amendment which granted the right of voting in the new territories only to citizens of the United States. Among those who had voted for it was Senator Douglas, who had received full support from the Germans of Chicago. Naturally the bitterness of the Germans was directed particularly against him. The protest meeting, with Hoffmann presiding, had hardly gotten under way when suddenly the lights went out and the meeting threatened to break up. Hoffmann held the audience by solemnly quoting Biblical passages with humorous effect until once more there was light! In the course of his speech he then proclaimed the readiness of his group to bolt the established parties: "So far, but no farther! We will not be subdued by the cry of party, party! The choice is easily made between freedom and party, between liberty and slavery, between right and wrong." The unanimous resolutions pronounced the bill "particularly inimical to the German pioneers of the West," and Senator Douglas was called upon "to resign his seat in the Senate immediately." To make their feelings unmistakably clear, the protestants formed a procession through the night carrying an effigy of Senator Douglas with the inscription, "The Benedict Arnold of 1854," which they burned on Court House Square.

Thus German Republicanism in Chicago began, one might say, with éclat. It soon made itself felt distinctly; one notable local success was the election of Francis Hoffmann as lieutenant-governor in 1860. Gustave Koerner, who had been elected lieutenant-governor on the Democratic ticket in 1852, went over to the Republican party. Most German newspapers of Illinois followed the *Staatszeitung* of Chicago into the Republican camp. The Germans of Illinois sent Schneider and Koerner to the National Republican Convention in Philadelphia and supported Frémont in 1856. While in some parts of the country there was animosity between the earlier immigrants who called the Forty-eighters the "Greens," and were in turn nicknamed the "Grays" (which in German carries the connotation of "old fossil"), in Illinois the two groups cooperated harmoniously in the Republican party. The chief motive that brought the Germans, largely under the leadership of the Forty-eighters, into the new party was the attitude of these freedom-loving men on the question of slavery.

The unity of German Republicanism in Chicago came to an end when the more ardent antislavery members became dissatisfied with the conduct of the war and Lincoln's emancipation policy. Radical abolitionists were certain that John C. Frémont, the Presidential candidate of 1856, would take stronger measures to eradicate slavery from American soil. The Frémont campaign of 1864 reveals a clear regional division among the Forty-eighters. Despite the fact that Karl Heinzen's *Pionier,* the most radical paper edited by a Forty-eighter, appeared in Boston, the numerical strength of German radical Republicanism in 1864 lay in Chicago and St. Louis. The antislavery Germans of Missouri —Emil Preetorius, Theodor Ohlshausen, Friedrich Muench, and Karl Krekel among them—joined forces with Pruessing, Schmidt, and Butz in Chicago against the renomination of Lincoln. The Forty-eighters of Minnesota, Iowa, and Wisconsin, along with those of the East, on the whole remained loyal to the President. Details of this story on a national plane are told in a later chapter.

During the seventies, socialism became a political factor in Chicago and the most prominent leader in the movement was the well-known Forty-eighter, Dr. Ernst Schmidt. In 1859 he ran for mayor of Chicago on a Socialist city ticket and received about 12,000 votes out of 28,000, largely because of the personal popularity of this philanthropic physician. A characteristic anecdote about him is told by Friedrich Hecker who, when he called on Lincoln at the time of the inauguration was asked by the President: "What became of that long, red-haired Dutchman, Dr. Schmidt? Almost every Dutchman has been in here asking for a job; why doesn't he come in?" Dr. Schmidt's altruism and sense of justice induced him in 1886 to head the committee for the defense of the Haymarket Riot anarchists; though public feeling was violently aroused against these alleged bomb-throwers, Dr. Schmidt's courageous stand by no means ruined him professionally—as his friends had warned him that it would do. It was a German-born governor of Illinois, John Peter Altgeld, who did all in his power to correct a miscarriage of justice by pardoning the three victims who had been given life sentences; Altgeld of course belonged to a later generation, but there is a great affinity between his spirit and that of the Forty-eighters.

As indicated above, the cultural activities of the Forty-eighters in Chicago were similar to those in Milwaukee though less distinguished. A fact worth noting is that the second generations of the Butz, Rapp, Raster, and Schmidt families furnished Chicago with solid and influential citizens. The last-named and most radical, Dr. Schmidt, had four sons, all of whom established themselves as professional men: two as physicians, one as pharmacist, and one as architect. Dr. Otto L. Schmidt is perhaps the most distinguished, not only as a medical man and member of the Board of Education, but also as one-time president of the Chicago Historical Society, the German-American Historical Society, and the Mississippi Valley Historical Association.

The Forty-eighters, who arrived in St. Louis found themselves in an environment different from that in Milwaukee or Chicago but similar to the one in Cincinnati, a somewhat comparable German community, inasmuch as there was already present a considerable intellectual nucleus. But while in Cincinnati there ensued acrimonious rivalry between the "Greens" and the "Grays," the fusion of the two elements in St. Louis was harmonious and cooperative. As early as 1844 Paul Follenius, younger brother of the Harvard professor and abolitionist Carl Follen, had founded his journal, *Die Waage*, and Wilhelm Weber's *Anzeiger des Westens* dated back even to the thirties. Other German papers flourished in near-by St. Charles and Hermann, both strong German settlements. The ideals advocated in these papers were those close to the hearts of the Forty-eighters: liberalism, freedom for the slaves, and anticlericalism.

This background explains the enthusiasm with which the news of the Revolution of 1848 was received in St. Louis. A mass meeting was held in the Court House on April 15; Dr. George Engelmann, the noted botanist, presided, and amidst great enthusiasm resolutions were adopted, which soon enjoyed wide circulation in Germany as "Message of the Germans of St. Louis to the German people." Furthermore, a "republican committee" was elected to get in touch with the leaders in Germany, to collect funds, and to make propaganda for a free Germany. Upon the vote of the city council, a meeting of all citizens was called about ten days later to celebrate the republican uprisings in the various European countries. The Germans climaxed it with a torchlight procession in which two thousand marchers participated. Everything possible was done by St. Louis citizens to show their sympathy with the liberal movement in Germany. When in January, 1849, the hero of the Baden Revolution, Friedrich Hecker, arrived in St. Louis, in the course of his American speaking tour, an immense banquet was held at which a thousand dollars were raised for the cause. The much smaller population of Belleville, Illinois, contributed six hundred dollars to the fund, according to Koerner's *Memoirs*. He adds that "American citizens took as much interest in this commotion and in the contributions as the Germans did." The St. Louis citizens, along with almost the entire American nation (with the exception of the South!), likewise gave an enthusiastic and generous reception to Kossuth, the hero of the Hungarian Revolution.

No profession seems to have been more congenial to the Forty-eighter than journalism. St. Louis and the older German settlements in its vicinity exemplify their talent for and inclination toward newspaper work. The number of short-lived though politically influential German papers is too large to enumerate; two important examples can serve to illustrate the point. Three Forty-eighters, Heinrich Boernstein, Carl Bernays, and Carl Daenzer, served as editors of the *Anzeiger des Westens*. About 1850 this originally Democratic paper became an antislavery organ and, some years before the Civil War, outspokenly Republican. In 1857 the *Westliche Post* was founded as a Republican paper and increased vastly in circulation under the excellent editorship of a leader of the Revolution in North Germany, Theodor Olshausen. Other Forty-eighters associated in the course of years with either of these long-lived papers were Carl Schurz, Emil Preetorius, Georg Hillgaertner, Heinrich Binder, Daniel Hertle, and Wilhelm Stengel; Friedrich Hecker, Carl Luedeking, Johann Rittig and others of this group were frequent contributors. These newspapers served also as channels through which American public opinion reached the German immigrants by means of the numerous translations of important articles from the English-language press, local and national. The student of the St. Louis newspapers of around 1864 finds a somewhat paradoxical situation: the leading English Republican paper is the *Mis-*

souri Democrat, the leading Democratic paper the *St. Louis Republic*, the *Anzeiger* supported Lincoln, the *Westliche Post* wished to replace him by Frémont, and the *Missouri Radikale*—founded especially for the support of Frémont—became a Lincoln supporter.

Missouri of course was a slave state, but the economic interests of the citizens were sharply divided. Of the roughly 100,000 slaves owned by 1,200,000 whites, only about 120 were to be found in St. Louis, a city of 200,000 inhabitants. The German farmers settled along the Missouri River, worked their farms themselves, and naturally considered slave labor as cheap competition; furthermore, their European background and their humanitarian feelings made them opponents of slavery. In the tense situation prevailing in such a border region, mob violence was not infrequent. Friedrich Muench, an early settler in Warren County and an outspoken antislavery man, tells in his memoirs of the days just after the outbreak of the War:

I myself was the most hated man in our region. In a meeting held not far from my home it was decided to kill me, to burn down my home, and to expel my family by force. Some of my nearby and more distant friends offered me protection, but I had no desire either to flee from my threatened farm nor to become a burden to others, and thus I remained in my home.

Of Muench's four sons, two joined the home guards and two Sigel's regiment; these and similar uniformed and armed German organizations were formed for the protection of the antislavery groups and they proved effective in saving Missouri for the Union. In forming public opinion among the Germans in this region the part played by the Forty-eighters is not separable from that of the liberals among the earlier settlers, particularly Friedrich Muench and Gustave Koerner; similarly, the two groups stood shoulder to shoulder in the fighting that came with the outbreak of the War. The part played by the *Turner* in helping to preserve Missouri for the Union will be described in the next chapter.

We find an estimate of the influence of the Forty-eighters as journalists in an address by Edmund J. James, a former president of the University of Illinois, who had known some of them personally. Dr. James spoke at the memorial services to Carl Schurz at the Auditorium in Chicago, June 3, 1906. The first paragraph places the immigration of 1848 in a world perspective and the others refer to one aspect of their influence:

The migration of the men of '48 cannot, of course, be likened in its moral and economic effects to the migration of the Huguenots from France, or the Moors from Spain, or the Scotch covenanters from the hills of Scotland, for the fugitives were neither so numerous absolutely, nor did they form so large a percentage of the population, of the education and the strength of Germany as did their counterparts just mentioned. But, although in their migration the loss to their native country was not so great, and perhaps the gain to the country of their adoption was not so large, relatively speaking, yet the coming of these men was no mean loss to Germany and no mean gain to America. . . .

In the first place, owing to the enormous dimensions which German immigration took on in the years following the political events after 1848, a very considerable percentage of the population of this country became German, either of the first or second generation. These later immigrants did not come primarily from the political causes which brought the men of '48. They were seeking not so much freedom from a political bondage which had become irksome, as opportunity to better their economic and financial condition. It was of the highest importance to this country, in its immediate and remote development, that this immense mass of German immigrants of the middle and lower classes, so far as education was concerned, should have the right kind of leadership, should have men of their own blood, men of their own language, men of their own traditions to point the way in which they might travel in becoming integral parts of this great composite people to which we give the name American. It was fortunate for them and fortunate for us that these men of 1848, men of intelligence, of education, of power, of outlook, of idealism, should have so far grown into our conditions and studied our problems that they could furnish that kind of leadership to the German element which was most advantageous for it and for the other elements in this great complex of the nations.

We were approaching the crisis in our national history when we were to determine whether this nation was still to continue half slave and half free, or whether it was to continue at all or not. Speaking as one whose ancestry unto the fifth and sixth generations have been born and died on American soil, speaking as one whose genealogical roots run deep into the Southland and far into the North, I believe that if the struggle had been left to what might be called the purely American elements as they existed in the '50's in the United States, the outcome might have been different from what it was. We who love to compromise, that characteristic of the Anglo-Saxon, might have tried to worry on under some kind of system by which slavery should have increased in power and strength without weakening the vigor and might of the free states,—of course, an absolutely hopeless proposition. Or we might have consented to a possible dissolution of the Union, which would have been a great misfortune, entailing upon our children and children's children untold and undreamed of miseries. But the men of '48 who had come into leadership of this great and ever increasing throng of German-Americans were men not bound down by any of those traditions which held us in chains. They knew nothing of the Missouri compromise or the Nebraska bill or any other of the numerous devices by which we tried to break the force of the oncoming storm. They were men who had suffered in behalf of liberty; they were men who had staked their entire careers on the side of freedom in the great struggle between privilege and democracy; they were prophets; they were seers; they were idealists; they saw or thought they saw what was right, and they planted themselves firmly and distinctly on that side with no hesitation and no wavering. They rallied to a man to the standard of the Union and of freedom.

The influence of the forty-eighters at this great and critical time of our national life was, to my mind, decisive. They turned the balance of power in favor of union and liberty. And if sometimes they were obstinate and difficult material, this very defect was perhaps an outgrowth of their virtues. They might not have been the tower of strength they were for the Union cause if they had not had the very defects which sometimes irritated and tried us.

Davenport, Iowa, merits special treatment because in this community Forty-eighters controlled the German life of the city for at least one generation. A few families from Schleswig-Holstein had settled there earlier, and their reports were instrumental in attracting large numbers of political refugees from the same German region. Thus the German immigration to Davenport during the fifties brought about the most homogeneous settlement of Forty-eighters in the United States. With few exceptions all were of the upper middle class, well educated and liberal. Among these settlers were quite a number of men who had been elected leaders in the uprising for freedom, and naturally enough they once more became leaders in the new community. Of a deputation of five men chosen by the Schleswig-Holstein Parliament in 1848 to represent their interests before the King of Denmark, three later came to Davenport: Hans Reimer Claussen, Theodor Olshausen, and Theodor Guelich. This is one very striking example out of hundreds showing how Germany lost men of energy and independence of spirit through continual political repression.

Claussen, through assiduous study of the English language and of American law, soon became a distinguished attorney and, after some years, state senator. Likewise he proved himself a recognized political leader of great astuteness. He initiated a move that finally led to the success of the German Republicans at the Chicago Convention of 1860, an event to be treated fully in a later chapter. While the German Republicans early in that election year generally favored the selection of William H. Seward as Presidential nominee, they observed with alarm that Edward Bates of Missouri was enjoying an increasing popularity that caused many metropolitan editorial writers to consider his chances as the best. This candidate was odious to the immigrants because of his close association with the Know-Nothing movement. In a meeting of the German Republican Club of Davenport on March 7, 1860, Claussen sponsored a resolution against the nomination of Bates and sent it to the editors of German Republican papers. The result was that in Cincinnati, St. Louis, Milwaukee, and other cities similar resolutions were passed against Bates. Later events proved that Claussen had gauged correctly the weakness and strength of the German vote: it was not powerful enough to determine the choice of the Party, yet it could serve to eliminate those candidates who were least acceptable.

Many of the institutions in Davenport were of course the usual ones sponsored by the Forty-eighters. There was the energetic press directed by the doughty liberal editors, Guelich and Ohlshausen; a symbol of the outspoken antislavery attitude of the *Davenport Demokrat* (of course, staunchly Republican as were practically all Davenport Germans) was the appearance of the paper with a margin of black mourning on the day of the death of John Brown! Davenport also had one of the strongest *Turner* societies in the country with gymnastics, lectures, library facilities, musical events, and theatricals—for many years the German theatre, organized in 1855, was the only one in the community and was enjoyed by Americans and Germans alike. The greatest musical event in the history of Davenport occurred in 1898 when all German-American singing societies held their conclave there providing an entire week of Beethoven, Schumann, and Schubert. The freethinker spirit impelled them to found a non-church school, a private undertaking that survived for two generations.

The prohibition struggle forms a sad chapter, perhaps especially dismal in Iowa because of the relatively small urban population. The stories of the searches by officious sheriffs with needless shootings and killings read like a local rehearsal of what was to happen on the national stage during the "noble experiment." Ironically enough it was the "free" Republican party that came under the influence of the prohibition lobby and because of the loyalty of most Germans to this party they were ineffective in combating sumptuary legislation. Yet, the spirit of the Forty-eighters, who worshiped the Declaration of Independence, including Jefferson's very individualistic phrase about the right to "pursuit of happiness," is perhaps evident in a provision of the law of 1858 which permitted "light wines and beer" while it deprived the Irish of their whisky; in the eighties, total statewide prohibition was forced on Iowa with Draconian penalties for those who did not circumvent it successfully.

Thus it is reported that the brewery of Mathias Frahm, a native of Schleswig who came to Davenport in 1848, was never closed. He had been a cooper's apprentice in his youth and after his arrival in Iowa he founded a brewery which through hard work and sober application he developed into the largest of the 118 in Iowa. The idealism he felt for his calling caused him to send his son to Munich and Wuerzburg for thorough study of the brewer's art. In his will he left $10,000 to the "Free German School" with the provision that his grandson and namesake be educated there in a liberal *Weltanschauung;* should the youngster, however, become a preacher or priest, he was to be totally disinherited!

The solid culture of the Forty-eighters in Davenport has endured. Visible evidence can be found in the stately mansions erected by the grandparents of the present owners. The descendants still cherish linens, china, and furniture brought from Germany a hundred years ago. Many of them still speak German and have traveled abroad. They enjoy the respect of their fellow townsmen as is shown by the fact that both the son and the grandson of the leading Forty-eighter, Hans Reimer Claussen, have been elected for several terms as mayors of Davenport.

Somewhat exceptional, but all the more interesting, is the settlement at New Ulm, Minnesota, founded in the middle fifties. In this enterprise Forty-eighters appear as genuine pioneers, since, at the time, New Ulm was farthest west on the Minnesota frontier. The moving spirit of the undertaking was Wilhelm Pfaender whose adventurous and altruistic career is worth noting.

Pfaender was born July 6, 1826, in Heilbronn in Wuerttemberg as the son of a poor laborer. Since the boy's health seemed too feeble to enable him to work as an artisan, he was apprenticed to a merchant. In order to improve his physique, he became interested in gymnastics and in 1844 he helped found the *Turner* society in Heilbronn. In the following year he moved to Ulm where he likewise was active in *Turner* circles. The political repression directed particularly against the *Turner* drove him to emigration in 1848 and in the course of the year he arrived in Cincinnati. At first he had a hard struggle for mere existence, as did many other immigrants who had no funds, knew no English, and were physically unable to endure hard labor. After some time he found employment in a factory and later as a waiter. When Hecker came to Cincinnati and urged the founding of a *Turner* society, Pfaender became one of the original members. Because he knew well how immigrant labor was being exploited, he conceived the idea of a settlement of workers and freethinkers in the Northwest where good soil and lumber was abundant, where each family could have its garden plot, and where a socialistic society by means of public ownership could flourish, free from the evils of unemployment and want. Together with another Forty-eighter, Jacob Nix from Cleveland, he proposed the project at the annual national convention of *Turner* societies in Buffalo in 1855. The Eastern societies declined to support it, but Western groups, particularly the *Turner* of Cincinnati, were ready to lend financial support. Pfaender was elected to draft the charter of the *Settlement Society of the Socialistic Turner League*, and he was likewise chosen a member of the committee of three to select a suitable site. After considerable search a good location was found on the Minnesota River. A society of German workingmen from Chicago had made the first settlement there; it was their aim to escape the uncertainties of the labor market by establishing themselves as a community on cheap land along the frontier. They sold their land to the *Turner* and the two projects were merged. Funds for the purchase price were raised by the sale of 800 shares of stock at $15 a share; an additional $3,000 was given by the Cincinnati *Turnverein* for the purchase of supplies to tide the settlers over the first winter. Pfaender directed the affairs of the colony and worked his own farm. In 1859 he was elected to the Minnesota State Legislature and on the outbreak of the War he joined the Union Army as commander of a battery of artillery, distinguishing himself at the Battle of Shiloh. When news reached him that New Ulm had been partially destroyed in an Indian uprising, he hurried to St. Paul where he found his family as refugees but fortunately unharmed. Here he joined a newly formed Minnesota cavalry regiment and was made lieutenant colonel in charge of the border defense at Fort Ridgeley. In December, 1865, he returned to his farm, exchanging the sword for the plowshare. In 1869 he was elected to the state senate and at the conclusion of his term he returned to New Ulm where he was chosen mayor of the town. In 1875 he was elected state treasurer for a four-year period, after which he settled down to a quiet life in the midst of his family in New Ulm.

As an experiment in community ownership New Ulm shared the fate of hundreds of other "utopias" established in this country—the group soon found it expedient to fall in step with free enterprise. The *Settlement Association* transferred the administration of the colony to New Ulm in 1858, when the number of residents had risen to over four hundred, and about a year later the Association was dissolved—needless to say, the shareholders received no other reward except the proverbial one of virtue. After some time the community-owned mills were sold to private owners. The *New Ulm Pionier* was started as a community project, "independent of everybody, neutral on no point" with the slogan "free soil, free men, free labor, free press," but the salaried editors met with so many difficulties in obtaining the necessary paper and other supplies from the community that they purchased the newspaper in 1859. The school committee transferred ownership of the school property to the public school district of New Ulm. From the sale of some land owned by the *Association* an endowment fund for teachers' salaries and textbooks was established for the public school—under condition that no religious instruction be offered there. Several acres of land were set aside for the benefit of a fire department, a hospital, and public swimming facilities. The founders laid out the town on generous lines with wide streets and ample building lots, so that today (1949) with a population of 9,900 there is everywhere still considerable spaciousness.

During the first years the settlers experienced grim frontier hardships, including near starvation—some farmers were driven by hunger to dig up seed potatoes they had planted. But the climax of pioneer suffering came in 1862 when Indians from a reservation eight miles away attacked New Ulm and surrounding farms and settlements. These Sioux massacres were as savage as those in the Mohawk or Ohio Valleys during the border warfare in the eighteenth century. Families in the outlying farms were treacherously attacked by seemingly friendly Indians; men, women, and children were slaughtered outright or tortured to death. New Ulm received some warning, and under the leadership of Jacob Nix preparations for defense were made; unfortunately these were hampered by the fact that just previously a large number of able-bodied men had enlisted in the Union Army. The first attack, in the course of which the Indians penetrated into the middle of the town, was repulsed after a desperate struggle. The next day some reinforcements arrived and the barricades were improved. Approximately a week after the first attack, a second one followed which lasted for two days, where-upon the Indians withdrew. At the direction of the government New Ulm was then abandoned and the inhabitants transferred in a train of one hundred and fifty wagons to points farther east, some of them to St. Paul. Losses to New Ulm are reported as eight killed, seventy wounded, and some hundred and fifty houses burned by the Sioux.

One of the aims of the founders of New Ulm had been to establish a community where the liberal principles of the *Turner* could be followed by German immigrants, unhampered by inter-ference from Know-Nothing mobs or by restrictions through Blue Laws. Such a congenial atmosphere was realized in this town with its population more than 80 percent German. It is interesting to note therefore what sort of social conditions obtained in the community.

It has already been indicated that in various ways New Ulm adapted itself to the American system, but naturally the German and particularly the *Turner* background endured. It affected the public school to the extent that the German language as well as gymnastics formed part of the curriculum. The *Turnhalle* functioned as the social center of the town with the usual gymnastic, musical, and theatrical activities; there were also frequent public lectures by liberals or freethinkers. A public library was established early with a nucleus of one hundred books donated for that purpose by Friedrich Kapp, a distinguished Forty-eighter living in New York. Two German papers flourished, and among the editors were Forty-eighters. As the population increased, numerous Germans with religious affiliations erected both a Protestant and a Catholic church. The memoirs of the Catholic priest, Father Berghold, reveal a pleasingly tolerant attitude on the part of the freethinkers, who were decidedly in the majority. He notes that, while the New Ulmers "did not bother much about religion," these freethinkers never showed any hostility toward him or his flock. When the church was partially destroyed by a storm, the local brewer came to the priest and, despite their difference on religious matters, offered the use of one of his buildings. Numerous other freethinkers met with the genial Father occasionally for a glass of beer in the club house. It came to be an unwritten law that the six-member school board in New Ulm should consist of two freethinkers, two Catholics, and two Protestants.

In addition to their leadership in the field of journalism, the Forty-eighters lent their pens to the effort of guiding immigrants to the best localities and of protecting them from conscienceless exploitation. Domschke, Ohlshausen, and Rohlfs translated the official immigration pamphlets of a number of Midwestern states and added valuable information of specific interest to the prospective foreign immigrant. Other Forty-eighters—Kapp, Domschke, Froebel, and Douai—were contributors to a journal of information for immigrants published in Goettingen, Germany, the *Atlantische Studien*, where through factual and concise reports they strove to correct a too pessimistic view regarding the fate of the German settler in the United States. Such an attitude had become fairly widespread in Germany by 1855, because of the many reports of immigrants who had had the most disillusioning experiences with the false promises of agents, fraudulent sales of land that did not exist, or abandonment midway to their destination by settlement societies to whom they had paid their money. Earlier in the century a catchword had been *der Europamuede*, the person weary of Europe and presumably eager to go to America. In 1855 there appeared a devastating criticism of conditions in the New World, Ferdinand Kuernberger's *Der Amerikamuede*, about as flattering to the United States as had been Dickens's *Martin Chuzzlewit*. In presenting a true picture of American conditions, in pointing out pitfalls for immigrants and how to avoid them, as well as in exposing the "runners" and "agents" who preyed on the immigrants, Friedrich Kapp's work is outstanding. As Commissioner of Immigration he investigated and reported in detail numerous scandalous cases, such as that of the *Leibnitz* from Hamburg on which, because of unsanitary conditions, 183 out of 917 emigrants died in the course of the passage, or that of the *James Foster, Jr.*, from Liverpool on which the emigrants were practically starved. His reports received wide publicity in the press of Europe and of the United States and contributed materially to an improvement of conditions.

Aside from loss of human life resulting from the hardships of travel under miserable conditions, there was another, less tragic, waste involved in the uprooting of hundreds of well-educated men and their transplantation to a strange environment. While the energetic and adaptable ones are now listed in the *Dictionary of American Biography* because of their distinguished careers in politics, in the army, in business, or in the professions, numerous others were sad failures, though they had been young men of great promise at home. Such were the impoverished musician who eked out a living by giving music lessons to the children of equally poor parents, the professor who functioned as factotum on the staff of one short-lived newspaper after the other, the sculptor who earned his bread by carving cigar-store Indians, the painter who expended his art on *Bockbier* signs, the actor who was forever organizing new troups and new tours that all ended in failures, or the mild-mannered old man who earned pocket-money by playing at the village dances on Saturday night. "Many became cigar makers, others house painters, many more saloonkeepers or bartenders, and sometimes an ex-officer would fight with a former legal luminary for the chance to get a job as janitor."

In concluding this discussion of the adjustment of Forty-eighters to American life it may be in place to take note of a criticism expressed by an English scholar, John A. Hawgood, in *The Tragedy of German-America*. This book is a trenchant, stimulating study, much better than its title—the failure of the immigrants to remain German instead of becoming Americans should be called a very fortunate outcome rather than a tragedy. The author has some very fine things to say of the Forty-eighters as the outstanding group among the German immigrants, men of liberal principles, of leadership in the crusade against slavery, and of astuteness in the field of politics. He finds, however, that after the Civil War period theirs "became a tragic case of arrested development."

It is true that many Forty-eighters foregathered in *Ratskeller*, the walls of which were decorated with German verses painted in Gothic letters and hung with portraits of the heroes of the Revolution. They sang old student songs and talked of old causes. They subscribed to a German paper founded by a friend decades earlier, when they might have been reading the English daily of their town. They venerated that poet of freedom, Schiller, and in several American cities erected a monument to his memory. They admonished their children to cherish the German language and German culture. All of this could just as readily be called a quite natural conservatism in men of fifty, for few men at that age acquire new ideals, heroes, or habits. If in the last decades of the nineteenth century, as Professor Hawgood claims, the general run of German-Americans still cherished the German culture of the middle of the century, perhaps even in diluted form, the fault is decidedly theirs and not that of their elders, for they should have progressed toward new goals even as the Forty-eighters did in their youth. The traits Professor Hawgood labels "arrested development" are but a common human weakness comparable to the "old-school-tie spirit" prevalent in his country among certain groups. Moreover, the matter labeled *Deutschtum* by Professor Hawgood is something subject to constant interactions between various groups in this country and far from so simple as he represents it. The common American attitude has in the last fifty years definitely changed toward some of the items involved. The physical training advocated by the *Turner* was something new in America; it was, partly through the urging of German groups, introduced into our schools and then modified into or replaced by basketball and other competitive sports. The orchestral music which such Forty-eighters as Balatka in Milwaukee and Carl Bergmann in New York cultivated at first in German circles has become a regular institution in all metropolitan centers. The Sunday outings into the woods, so cherished by the *Turner* and often so offensive to their fellow citizens, are not so different from the current American Sunday family picnic. Certainly sabbatarianism, considered in many communities a hundred years ago as "American" in contrast to "foreign" ways, has been relaxed. And since 1933 the majority of Americans no longer differ with the German-Americans in respect to the wisdom of prohibition. In some respects our whole country has moved away from earlier, partly "frontier," conditions to the customs and mores of an older culture such as Europe, including Germany, had established by the middle of the nineteenth century. In bringing this about all the ingredients of the American "Melting Pot" had a share, including the Germans, and along with them, as the most intellectually stimulating, the political refugees of 1848.

Chapter Four

THE TURNER

By Augustus J. Prahl

A HUNDRED years after their first beginnings, *Turnvereine* are still active in cities all over this country. When in May, 1948, their centennial was celebrated in St. Louis, President Truman sent a congratulatory letter in which he said, "Early in their history the Turners had become an important factor in American Life. Their contributions have been many and outstanding. Their encouragement of physical education and recreation generally has been a contribution of incalculable value."

As is the case with so much in European culture, the *Turner* ideal harks back to the Greeks. The word itself is Germanic of course, the same root as English "to turn," evidently derived from exercises that consisted of circular movements. In German schools where classical literature was studied, the Greek ideal of the development of the body along with the mind naturally had a great appeal. The Greek poet Pindar in his odes glorified athletic prowess, and the Turner motto, *Mens sana in corpore sano,* was adopted from the Roman author Juvenal. In the latter part of the eighteenth century a German teacher by the name of Johann Guts Muths developed a system of gymnastics on the Greek model and published a manual on the subject in 1793. But the real founder of the movement is Friedrich Jahn, who combined the practice of physical training with the inculcation of ideals of a free and self-respecting citizenship. He began his teaching in 1811, at the time when Napoleon had conquered and occupied Germany. On a field outside Berlin young men received instruction from Jahn, a giant of a man with a long flowing beard, who was soon affectionately known throughout Germany as *Turnvater* Jahn. All over the country *Turner* groups were organized with large memberships of energetic and politically conscious young men, many of them university students.

Jahn's endeavors to strengthen and liberalize German youth was part of a larger program of national reorganization planned and fostered by Baron vom Stein, Alexander and Wilhelm von Humboldt, and numerous of the leading intellects in Germany, such as the poets Ludwig Uhland and Heinrich von Kleist. Through speeches, pamphlets, poems, dramas, and songs, they imbued the common citizen with a feeling of national consciousness and of the importance of the individual in the life of the nation; in other words, they awakened in the citizen an appreciation of democratic freedom through their efforts at an "education of the people." Jahn wrote on this subject, which was of course something startlingly new in autocratic, paternalistic Prussia: "The education of the people aims to realize the ideal of an all-around human being, citizen, and member of society in each individual; gymnastics are one means toward a complete education of the people." Such enthusiasm was all very well while Napoleon oppressed the land and the Prussian king promised his people a constitution, but when Napoleon was crushed the king forgot all about the constitution, and the Metternich regime suppressed everything liberal including, in 1819, *Turner* societies, an interdict not lifted until 1842.

The *Turner* movement had about it a nimbus of poetry and many romantic aspects of university student life that Longfellow and numerous other Americans had enjoyed while abroad; many of the Forty-eighters had belonged to both groups before coming to America. In the following pages some illustrations are offered of poems that served to inspire the Revolution, verses that formed part of the poetic freight brought to their new home by the immigrants. Lyrics such as these along with hundreds of others, many of them written by *Turner* in this country, give the flavor of the contests in song or in poetry carried on at *Turner* festivities. The number of poets among the Forty-eighters is vast and their output ranges from dull imitation to some inspired lines well worth preserving. Obviously translation causes them to lose a great deal of the original verve, but their ideas can be conveyed even in somewhat lame English. A good illustration of the theme underlying all of them is an epigram written in this country by Carl Heinrich Schnauffer, fighter in the Baden Revolution and later editor of the antislavery *Baltimore Wecker;* in the three years he lived in this country before his death at the age of thirty-two, Schnauffer was twice the winner in a national *Turner* poetry contest. By means of a felicitously chosen metaphor Schnauffer conveys a message of courage for any group anywhere oppressed by a tyrannical government:

> Freedom is a diamond pure,
> Not glass to break or shatter,
> Though oft the folk with hand unsure
> May let it drop—what matter?

One of Germany's earliest political poets is Ludwig Uhland, a man of firm character who spoke his mind directly. When the German rulers failed to keep their promises of granting constitutional government after the Napoleonic Wars, he wrote a number of poems that immediately found a nation-wide echo. The following verses are from two poems written in 1816 and 1817:

> Speak first, ye princes here assembled,
>   Have you forgot that day of fight,
> When beaten to your knees you trembled
>   And bowed before a higher might?
> To save your fame the people rallied,
>   They proved them loyal to the core,
> Therefore 'tis yours, who still have dallied,
>   To grant them now what once you swore.
>
> There is no prince so high in station,
>   So high-elect none formed of clay,
> That when for freedom thirsts a nation,
>   A royal hand its thirst can stay.
> Is one alone with greedy fingers
>   The riches of all rights to grasp,
> While, for a dole, the people lingers
>   Till slow the royal fist unclasp?

Instead of heeding the demand of the people voiced particularly in student fraternities (*Burschenschaften*) and *Turner* clubs,

the German authorities by the notorious Karlsbad Decrees of
1819 suppressed these organizations. How the students felt about
this act of repression can be seen from the following poem by
Adolf Binzer published in Jena, 1819. The beautiful melody of
this song, long a favorite among German students, is employed
by Brahms as one of the themes in his *Academic Festival Overture*.
Incidentally, this poem illustrates the "devout" spirit in the
Turner slogan: *Frisch, fromm, froh, frei* (bold, devout, gay, free).

We had built us an house
So stately in form,
Where we trusted in God
Through trouble and storm.

We lived there so snugly,
United and free;
No chance for the Tempter,
So loyal were we.

The lying, the spying
Informer's jack-boot,
With slanders and curses,
Trod down the green shoot.

What God in us planted
The world took unkind;
Good folk feared our motto
"One heart and one mind."

Who thought to condemn it
Deceived himself sore:
Love's mould may be shattered,
Love's self never-more!

The mould, it is shattered,
In fragments is broke,
But what the spies sniff at
Is but vapour and smoke.

The band, it is severed—
'Twas black, red, and gold—
And God, in His wisdom,
Looked down to behold!

> The house may be ruined—
> Who fears storms that lower?
> Our spirit lives on in us,
> And God's our strong tower!

One of the favorite *Turner* poets, Hoffmann von Fallersleben, wrote along with much other liberal verse, "The Eternal Revolutionary," a delightful lampoon on the censorship during the Metternich period of "persecution of demagogues.

> Put the Springtide into prison,
> For a demagogue is she!
> From the long long thrall of Winter
> She would dare to set us free;
> Wake us from the long night's darkness,
> Bid our slumbering eyes to see.
> Put the Springtide into prison,
> For a demagogue is she!
>
> Put the Springtide into prison,
> For she sets the world astir;
> Waters murmur, woodlands whisper;
> Things of feather, things of fur,
> And the heart of man within him
> Thrill in unison with her.
> Put the Springtide into prison,
> For she sets the world astir!
>
> Put the Springtide into prison,
> Keep King Winter on the throne,
> For she is but a usurper,
> He "legitimate" alone.
> Springtide whispers "revolution,"
> Let her for her crime atone—
> Put the Springtide into prison,
> Keep King Winter on the throne.

The chief problem discussed by the *Parlament* of 1848 and 1849 at Frankfurt was the form the new German government should take and, if it was to be an empire, who should be chosen as emperor. A popular broadside gives a people's view on the question (as sung by a hurdy-gurdy man):

> Who shall our German Kaiser be?
> Prince Reuss-Greiz-Schleiz-Lobenstein, *he?*

Perhaps the Prince of Birkenfeld?
Or Windischgraetz, now hero held?
　O no! O no! We all agree,
　Some other shall our Kaiser be!. . .

Who shall our German Kaiser be?
A prince from Elbe or Rhine maybe?
Perhaps a prince from Leuchtenberg,
Munich, Hanover, Wuertemberg?
　O no! O no! We all agree,
　Not one of these shall Kaiser be!

Who shall our German Kaiser be?
Too small are Hesse and Saxony?
An Austrian of Hapsburg kin?
A Hohenzollern from Berlin?
　O no! O no! We all agree,
　Still mightier shall our Kaiser be!

Now tell us true, who shall it be?
Whose hand shall stablish Germany?
Whose brow deserves the dignity?
Perchance the People's sovereignty?
　Ah, there again we all agree,
　The People shall our Kaiser be!

Count Moritz von Strachwitz, aristocratic by birth as well as
in his poetry, expressed the feelings of a self-respecting German
during the forties in a forceful sonnet, "The God of Freedom":

Ere God the Eternal's work on earth was done
His breath informed that child of Heaven, man's Soul,
Engend'ring courage like a burning coal,
Courage like flame, to fight till the end be won.
God said: "Thou shalt not like a coward run
In flight before the press of teen and dole;
Mid clouds of war that darkly round thee roll
Thou shalt bestride the coursers of the sun.
Thou shalt not sue the Almighty on bended knee,
Look upward to yon azure vault sublime,
Before the God of Freedom stand thou free.
Him crawling in the dust I may not see,
Him whom I made, the heir to dateless Time;
Only the Free Heaven's arduous steep can climb."

Very typical of *Turner* lyrics is the "Marching Song of the Revolutionaries." Nothing is known of the author—except that he was undoubtedly inspired by the "Marseillaise":

> Forward, forward, band of brothers!
>   Forward boldly to the fight!
> Where's the fool with scorn who smothers
>   Liberty, our sacred right?
> For the best that life can lend us,
>   For our darling Fatherland,
> Stand we ready to defend us,
>   Pledge we head and heart and hand.
>   Forward! Forward!
> With God for Fatherland.
>
> Backward, backward never gazing,
>   Let us leave what leave we must;
> Destiny's bright star is blazing,
>   A new world rises from the dust.
> Foolish hopes and women's weeping
>   Have our hearts too long unmanned.
> Up, the future's in our keeping,
>   Make it good with sword in hand,
>   Forward! Forward!
> With God for Fatherland.
>
> "Men are brothers, free and equal"
>   Gleams the motto on our shield.
> Only cowards fear the sequel
>   While they still have arms to wield.
> Life or death, let either beckon,
>   We'll go forward hand in hand;
> Life and death as nought we reckon,
>   If we free the Fatherland.
>   Forward! Forward!
> With God for Fatherland.

The revolutionaries chose the old German colors, black, red, gold—in 1919 they were again used for the flag of the Republic. *Turnvater* Jahn explained them to his disciples as signifying "out of the black night of slavery through bloody strife to the golden dawn of freedom." A popular poem published as a broadsheet in Mannheim in March, 1848, gives a similar interpretation:

Black, Red and Gold, these are the colors
We Germans proudly bear on high;
Black, Red and Gold, these are the colors
For which in fight we gladly die.

The Black betokens death to tyrants
Who laughing nailed us to the tree;
And Red's the blood we poured as offering
For Justice and for Liberty.

But Gold is freedom's blossoming
That men, their duty done, may see;
So fly on highways and on by-ways
The sacred German colors three.

Black, Red and Gold, these are the colors
Fill every German eye with pride;
Black, Red and Gold, with that fair harvest
Teems all the German countryside.

As our first chapter reports, the Revolution scored some initial successes and in the flush of victory in Vienna (the emperor had agreed to abolish the censorship) a song was written by Dr. L. A. Franzl glorifying the part the students had played in the revolt:

Lo, who be these so proud in bearing?
　　The bayonets flash, the flags fly free.
They come with silver trumpets blaring,
　　The University!

The daylight hour at last is breaking
　　Our hopes and prayers have yearned to see;
'Tis your young hearts to light awaking,
　　O University!

When Kaiser Joseph came in thunder
　　To bind the tongue's sweet liberty,
Who dared to burst the bonds asunder?
　　The University!

Our tongues wake with the lark to singing;
　　O hear their dithyrambic glee!

Heart calls, and heart sends answer ringing,
 All hail, the University!

Where spirits of the dead are beckoning,
 The dead who died for freedom, see—
With the first victim paid her reckoning
 The University!

And when our sons in reverence finger
 Each glorious page in history,
On thy name, writ in gold, they'll linger,
 Our University!

The most violent revolutionary poet was Georg Herwegh, who urged the Germans to obtain their rights by fighting for them. He had great influence in arousing the people to take up arms, calling on them to beat even graveyard crosses into swords:

Cross from tomb and temple tearing
Beat to blades for freemen's bearing,
 God in Heaven will allow.
Truce to song! Let all the singing
Iron be on anvil ringing!
 Steel is your redeemer now!

Oak and pine wood ask the nation,
In a green interrogation,
 "Must we grow o'er freedom's grave?"
Nay, for freedom is undying,
And we, Hell itself defying,
 Our Eurydice shall save!

Freedom first! Let no man falter,
Lead no maid to marriage altar,
 Sow no seed and reap no corn;
Till it see in gladsome gazing
Freedom's sun in Heaven blazing
 To no cradle babe be born.

The failure of the Revolution ended in bitter disappointment and disillusion, which is nowhere more wistfully portrayed than in Robert Prutz's "By Night"—with a surprise ending:

Now fades the sun's last ray,
Tall shadows bring the night,

The little stars shine out
  In points of twinkling light.

Down from the starry vault,
  And over hill and glen,
Freedom, on pinions soft,
  Sweeps through the haunts of men.

She visits all their homes,
  She knocks at all their doors,
In every sleeper's ear
  A whispered prayer she pours.

And all, both old and young,
  Her burning kisses stir;
She has a light caress
  E'en for the prisoner.

She tries the blade's keen edge,
  Sees if the powder's dry;
As the sands in the hour-glass fall
  She counts with jealous eye;

Till the sleepers, hearts aglow,
  Dream but a single dream,
Of chargers that whinny and rear,
  Of swords that flash and gleam;

Till, laughing behind his bars,
  His sides the prisoner shakes;
Till, shivering in his palace,
  A white-faced man—awakes!

Though written before 1848, Nikolaus Lenau's "Emigrant's Song" expressed the melancholy feelings of political refugees of that later period, as can be seen from many a song on the theme of *Heimweh* written in America:

For the last time thy name I greet,
O fallen so low, my Fatherland,
Who stoop'st to kiss a despot's feet,
In dull obedience to command.

Thine arms may rock a child to rest
For thou hast gifts that children heed;

And love-sick youth may call thee blest;
But where is freedom, the strong man's need?

The hunter in the wilds forlorn
Takes sudden cover, 'neath the press
Of panic-driven hoof and horn;
And gasps, the danger past, no less.

Even so, my Fatherland, dost thou
Start when thy master's step draws near,
And, as he passes, cringe and bow
And hold thy breath in craven fear.

Oh speed, thou ship, like clouds that scud,
There, where the fires of God burn free,
And bridge the gulf, O roaring flood,
The gulf 'twixt me and liberty.

O thou new world, and Freedom's world,
Against whose fertile, flowery strand
The tyrant's wrath in vain is hurled,
In thee I greet my Fatherland!

Before quoting the "Farewell to Hecker," it is of interest to cite a pen picture of this most popular hero of the Revolution sketched by Heinrich Laube, an historian of the Revolution of 1848. He contrasts Hecker with the scholarly, ascetic Struve whom he calls "the monk of the German Republic":

Quite different is Hecker and nearer to the plain man, the sensual man. He is a meat-eater and a full-blooded, healthy man. There is directness here, when he comes forward, shakes his long brown hair from his face and begins to speak in a strong baritone voice. One instantly realises that a man is speaking who does not come from the office, nor from studying the *Contrat Social*, but from a circle of robust individuals, who desire a thorough change in the life of the state. . . . "The day of movable goods and chattels has come," he used to say, and nothing is immovable any longer, neither capital nor property, once firm as a rock. . . . His attack is poetical and not really socialistic; it springs from quite a human impulse, not from the insistent conditions imposed by dogma. . . . He appears good-natured, negligent, a rollicking student, as it were. He reminds students times without number how long he has held his seat in the Baden Assembly, and by that is shown, apart from everything else, his stimulating influence on the young men of Western Germany. These form quite a different sort of revolutionary youth from the so-called young revolutionaries of the North, particularly of Berlin. To the youth of the West and South-west the will and the way to appreciate these abstract logicians and their conclusions are strange. They refuse to give out their hearts to them, and the coldness of mere formal inference is deeply repugnant to them. . . . So he stands between the prosaic school-master Struve and the heartless logicians of the North, a solitary figure without further tie than the bond forged by a common enemy, a representative of the natural Revolution.

Numerous poems were written about Hecker, some of them distributed as broadsides showing his picture in the romantic garb he affected (even today in Germany a type of broad-brimmed felt hat goes by the name, *Heckerhut*). The following stanzas are by G. Sulzer:

> Hecker, farewell! How sore the spirit labors!
>   The words are wrung like blood from a stricken heart;
> Peace art thou seeking far from friends and neighbors,
>   Leaving for us the longing and the smart.
> Thy loyal friends will nurse for thee their sorrow.
>   Man's treachery our leader from us stole;
> And yet 'tis they who should our pity borrow,
>   The traitors with the canker in their soul!
>
> What here remains for those whom thou art leaving,
>   Thou the sole anchor of our hopes and prayers?
> Wilt thou escape the net the Prussian's weaving
>   Round us with lies, false promises and snares?
> Hope is there still, our day is not yet over;
>   Changeless the sun pursues his ancient way,
> And if at eve the clouds his brightness cover,
>   Splendid he'll rise to hail the new-born day. . . .
>
> Now fare thee well! Our hopes go with thee roaming;
>   Fortune attend thee o'er the ocean's swell;
> We shall stand fast, for all the Prussian's foaming—
>   Lo! at his feet yawns wide the mouth of hell.
> Take for a pledge this happy expectation,
>   Nurse it with joy on far Columbia's strand;
> Soon brothers all, we'll build one German nation,
>   Then, O our loved one, back to thine own land!

An example showing that the glowing idealism of the Forty-eighters expressed in vibrant language could prove infectious is found in the concluding paragraphs of the speech on Carl Schurz by President James of which some other paragraphs were quoted in the preceding chapter:

I remember well when as a boy at school in that memorable year 1870–71 I was preparing a debate upon the question whether the United States ought to sympathize with France or with Germany in the great struggle then going on. In preparing for this debate I first ran across some speeches by Carl Schurz. They impressed me as few speeches that I had ever read or heard had impressed me; and when, five years later, I heard Carl Schurz for the first time address an American audience upon the political issues of the day, I received an outlook, an enlightenment, if you please, and a moral uplift of such a distinct character that I have always looked back to that dingy hall in Cambridgeport as one of the most important and sacred places on the face of the earth.

There I heard discussed for the first time in a convincing way the duty which a man owes to his country, to himself and to his God as above, beyond, and of a different kind from that which he owes to his party. And the clarion note which Schurz sounded on that occasion, which he had sounded long before and which he kept on sounding as long as he lived, is one which it behooves every democracy to heed. For only in absolute fidelity to the highest standards of honesty, uprightness and straightforwardness can we ever hope to realize that government of the people and by the people and for the people which is the ideal toward which democracy must ever strive.

The first *Turner* in the United States were not Forty-eighters, but earlier political refugees. Carl Follen and Francis Lieber, two of the most influential German scholars to settle in this country, were active also in introducing gymnastics in the United States. Follen was called to teach German literature at Harvard and there, in May of 1826, he organized a gymnasium after the model of Jahn. Dr. J. C. Warren, professor in the Harvard Medical School, founded Tremont Gymnasium in Boston with the idea of calling Jahn as director; but since he could not raise sufficient funds the post was offered in 1825 to Dr. Lieber, who later became famous as the erudite encyclopedist and political scientist. Another German political refugee, Dr. Carl Beck, was

appointed teacher of Latin in Round Hill School (founded by
George Bancroft), where he also developed a gymnasium and
translated Jahn's *Deutsche Turnkunst*. But it was only after 1848
that the great development of the *Turner* as societies of German
immigrants came about through the vast numbers of liberals
who came to this country. Along with a democratic form of government, freedom of speech and of press, these liberals were delighted to find here freedom to organize *Turner* societies.

The first *Turnverein* in America was founded in Cincinnati,
very directly under the influence of the popular hero of the
Revolution in Baden, Friedrich Hecker. He came to Cincinnati
in the fall of 1848 where he was received enthusiastically by the
Germans, who were of course very sympathetic to the cause of
freedom in Germany since many were themselves recent or
earlier victims of repression in their homeland. If the German
governments regarded the *Turner* groups as dangerous centers of
the movement for liberation, what would be more natural than
to establish *Turnvereine* in the United States where President Polk
had sent a congratulatory message to the Frankfurt *Parlament*
and thousands were eager to help a German revolution to success.

On October 22, 1848, Hecker arrived in Cincinnati and was
greeted by a torchlight procession. On the following day he conferred with several recent immigrants and former *Turner* about
the feasibility of founding an organization there; in the course
of a month the project was established and the practice of gymnastics begun. At first the *Turner* carried on their exercises in an
open lot, but because of the numerous and not too friendly
crowds of spectators that always collected to view the "outland-
ish" spectacle, they were forced to surround their field with a
high board fence. With rapidly increasing membership the society was able within a year's time to erect a suitable gymnasium.
At the dedication ceremony Wilhelm Pfaender, mentioned in
the preceding chapter as the founder of New Ulm, was the
speaker; the *Turner* singing society rendered musical numbers;
and a competition in gymnastics was held at which the winners
were awarded prizes supplied by ladies. On a wall amidst deco-
ration was the alliterative slogan of the *Turner: Frisch, fromm,*

froh, frei. Before long the club began to issue a monthly *Turn-zeitung* which set forth in prose and verse the ideals of the organization.

The purpose of the *Turner* was described as "Cultivation of rational training, both intellectual and physical, in order that the members may become energetic, patriotic citizens of the Republic, who could and would represent and protect common human liberty by word and deed." To realize this aim gymnastic exercises were regularly held, a musical section was sponsored, and "mental gymnastics" were furthered by means of lectures and a library. On Sundays, hiking tours into the country were organized and, to circumvent Sunday liquor laws, a bar was set up in the club house.

It was in this period when frontier conditions were passing that the church engaged in a struggle to hold its monopoly of the Sabbath against business or transportation activities or, perhaps more sternly, against relaxation not in conformity with puritanical Sabbath observance. Professor Arthur C. Cole, writing about Illinois, where the situation was of course similar to that in Cincinnati, describes the violent issue of that day:

The tendency toward democratic Sunday amusement gained headway in the towns and cities. This was especially true of the German element which in the summer months repaired to nearby picnic grounds or Sunday gardens and spent the day in merrymaking. To the Germans of Chicago, who associated with the sabbath not only the idea of religious worship but also the festive holiday atmosphere, the gayety of their Sunday gardens at Cottage Grove or of the Holstein picnic grounds three miles out on the Milwaukee road seemed an inalienable right. On the same principle the Belleville Germans assumed certain privileges in the parades of their military company and of their "gymnastic infidel company" that annoyed their fellow-citizens. The North-western Sabbath Convention of 1854 therefore declared that "the vast influx of immigrants joining us from foreign and despotic countries, who have learned in their native land to hate the established religion and the Sabbath law as part of it, calls on us for special prayer and labor in behalf of this portion of our population, to reclaim them from this fatal error." Such reclamation, however, made little progress; the socially-minded westerner, indeed, found an appeal in this new gospel of the joy of life that could not be offset by his own evangels. When,

therefore, the German's right to his peculiar form of Sunday observance
was threatened, sturdy champions among the native elements of the
population came to his aid.

In various parts of the country there occurred numerous
clashes such as the following. On a beautiful spring day in 1856
the Cincinnati *Turner* held a picnic on the Kentucky side of the
Ohio, near Covington. Boys aged ten to fourteen who had followed the *Turner's* march from Covington molested the group
by shouting unpleasant epithets, throwing stones, and, finally,
one rowdy snatched a glass of beer out of the hand of one of the
Turner. This was evidently more than good-nature could bear
and the exasperated *Turner* slapped the boy's face. The boy drew
a pistol, evidently to no harm, and then ran back to Covington
to spread the report that the "Dutchmen" were about to kill
ten or twelve boys. About five in the afternoon the picnic group,
unaware of the indignation aroused in the town, started on their
homeward march with a band and the Stars and Stripes in
the van.

On the outskirts of Covington they were met by a group of
indignant men who began to attack them with stones. One of
them seized hold of a *Turner*, who naturally resisted, and others
came to his aid. The fight waxed hot and both sides hurled
rocks and finally fired pistol shots. In the course of the action
the marshall and a deputy marshall both received bullet wounds
in the arm. The *Turner* marched through Covington and Newport with an attacking mob on either side. Finally they reached
the ferry landing where they intended to cross over to Cincinnati. Meanwhile the fire alarm bells in Covington were sounded
and the mob of attackers increased in numbers. The *Turner* lined
up before the wharf facing the crowd, who renewed their attack
to which they replied with some pistol shots. The excitement
grew in intensity and Mayor Fearons of Covington called on
the U. S. troops in the near-by garrison to attack the Germans;
the commanding officer refused, however, as he could act only
on orders from Washington. The disciplined *Turner*, some of
them armed with rifles and bayonets, preserved their ranks and
stood their ground, calmly obeying the orders of their com-

mander. The police made great efforts to put an end to the
conflict and the mayors of Covington and Newport demanded
that the *Turner* surrender their weapons and submit themselves
to the civil authorities. The mob shouted that they would not
desist until all arms had been surrendered.

At this moment the ferry boat arrived, but Mayor Fearons
would not permit it to land. To the renewed demand for surrender of arms, the captain of the *Turner* replied that he had no
objection to this if it could be done with safety, but, in the face
of the threatening mob, arms were required for self-defense; if
the civil authorities felt that some individuals had offended
against the law, no resistance would be offered to legal arrest.
The police then arrested four of the *Turner*.

This did not satisfy the excited crowd, egged on by shouts of:
"Go and finish 'em! Where are you Kentucky fellows?" The
officials were powerless against the mob which grew more violent
every moment. The *Turner* then decided to march to the Newport *Turner* hall and reached it amidst a further hail of rocks.
Meanwhile Judge Johann Berhardt Stallo, an old and influential German resident of Cincinnati, had arrived on the scene.
He told the local authorities that so long as they could not control
the crowd the *Turner* would not disarm, they would however
remain in their hall during the night and place themselves at
the disposition of the courts in the morning. Thirty-one *Turner*
were indicted for felony and released under $2,000 bail; this
sum of $62,000 was furnished by two German businessmen and
the trial dragged on through several sessions of the circuit court.
Thanks largely to the very able defense of Judge Stallo, all were
finally acquitted.

The Turner had other violent clashes, particularly with Know-
Nothing mobs—the first one in Hoboken on May 26, 1851. The
enmity of this group was directed also against the Irish who
thus at times became the allies of the Germans. The Know-
Nothing men did not want any foreigners to vote and they therefore attacked those who approached the voting places. Incidents
of this sort occurred in Cincinnati with bloody fighting and even
with the burning of the ballot boxes of a German ward by a

mob that suddenly swooped down on the polling place. Sometimes, for example in Baltimore, the acts of terrorism were of a more harmless variety, as when the "Blood Tub" rowdies secured tubs of blood from a slaughterhouse, spilled it over the hapless foreigner who had the temerity to approach a polling place, and thus sent him home in a condition that was certain to cause keen alarm to his family; a more recognized practice was the stabbing of voters with an awl. The success of these nativists was considerable; for example, it is reported concerning a Baltimore city election:

The election took place on October 8, 1856, the candidates being Thomas Swann, Know-Nothing, and Thomas Clinton Wright, Democrat. It was attended by bloodshed and disorder wholly unprecedented in the annals of this or any other American city. In the vicinity of Lexington Market, and in the public squares surrounding the Washington Monument, pitched battles were fought, in which muskets were used freely, and cannon even brought into the streets—which the authorities made no attempt to quell as they had made no provision to prevent—which lasted without interruption for hours and finally only terminated with nightfall, and in which actually more men were killed than fell on the American side on the field of Palo Alto. The result of the election, if it may be so called, was the almost entire disfranchisement of all naturalized citizens who were nearly everywhere driven from the polls, and the consequent elevation of Mr. Swann to the mayorality by a majority of 1,567 votes.

The Know-Nothing oath prohibited members from ever voting "for any man for any office in the gift of the people unless he be an *American-born* citizen, in favor of Americans ruling America." It is therefore not surprising that some of the *Turner* wished to live in a community where they would be free from mob attacks, which was one of the motives that led to the founding of the settlement at New Ulm described in the previous chapter.

An undisturbed *Turner* picnic, described in the words of the secretary of the *Verein*, shows the normal character of these gatherings:

On May 17, 1851, the Boston *Turnverein* in conjunction with the Singing Society made an excursion out into the country. This picnic of the *Turner* and singers was, according to the unanimous opinion of all present, one of the most beautiful festivals ever celebrated by our fellow-countrymen from Boston. It was a celebration of spring and a festival of brotherhood. The flag of the *Turner* was on that occasion unfurled for the first time.

The group went to Jamaica Plain and made themselves at home in the woods. For the opening, the Singing Society sang a few pleasing songs whereupon our oldest member (in German "moss-covered head"), Dr. Fuester, formerly chaplain of the Vienna academic legion (a revolutionary fighting unit), who came to Boston in November, 1849, delivered the speech quoted below. This was followed by an exhibition of gymnastics, in which also the singers participated though it made them feel pretty stiff the next day. Then came the dinner under the open sky. There were inspiring speeches by Mr. Schroeder, speaker of the New York Free Congregation and our guest for a few days, our own member Mr. Wagner, and Mr. Reiter, conductor of the Singing Society. The speech of Dr. Fuester particularly was received with great enthusiasm.

What impression the blue ether and the glorious sun shining through the tips of the oak trees made upon me, what memories and what hopes crossed my mind at the sight of the charming green of the forest only a German heart can fathom. With the same pleasure I viewed the company in whose faces gay happiness was mirrored.

The chief speaker began with the quotation from Shakespeare,

> The man that hath no music in himself,
> Nor is not moved with concord of sweet sounds,
> Is fit for treasons, strategems, and spoils——

and continued by calling on the *Turner* to cling to their ideals of freedom for which many of their comrades had sacrificed their lives in the Revolution. He was pleased once more to be called "moss-covered head," the same nickname the students of Vienna had accorded him when he accompanied them in their fight for a free Austria.

Just as in Cincinnati and Boston, *Turnvereine* were organized in New York, Newark, Philadelphia, Baltimore, Peoria, Indianapolis, Milwaukee, St. Louis, and numerous other cities in 1848 or shortly after. These organizations were generally sponsored not merely by *Turner* as such, but by leading spirits in the Revolution, such as Gustav Struve in New York, August Willich in

Milwaukee, and Karl Heinzen in Boston. Like the Irish and other immigrant groups, the *Turner* organized militia companies, adopted uniforms, and enjoyed marching in parades; there were likewise non-*Turner* companies that adopted such names as German Huzzars, the Steuben Fusileers, or the Jefferson Guards. At times there was something quite Philistine about the importance attached to uniforms, as for example in Baltimore when a quarrel as to just what type of straw hat the *Turner* were to wear with their gray linen uniforms is reported in the minutes of 1869 as the old bone of contention (*Zankapfel*).

As early as 1850 the need was felt for a closer union of all *Turner* societies in order to furnish a basis of mutual cooperation as well as for the sake of self-protection. At the instigation of the *Sozialistischer Turnverein* of New York a meeting was held in Philadelphia in October, 1850.

Many differences of opinion came to light at this first meeting, particularly on political questions, for one party wished to make the promotion of Socialism one of the main functions of the organization, while the other faction advocated that the *Turnverein* should confine itself solely to physical training. On one point, however, all were agreed, that the *Turnerbund* should manifest a tendency toward freethought in the broadest sense.

At the first national gymnastic festival held in Philadelphia in 1851 it was decided, after heated debate, to name the association *Sozialistischer Turnerbund*. It is of interest here to give the definition of socialism as understood by the *Turner:*

Socialism of to-day, in which we Turners believe, aims to remove the pernicious antagonism between labor and capital. It endeavors to effect a reconciliation between these two, and to establish a peace by which the rights of the former are fully protected against the encroachments of the latter.

In short, socialism wishes to set up business honesty. There is no doubt that the next European revolution will primarily exhibit a social character, and it is difficult to foresee the outcome. However, since self-preservation is the inherent impulse of the human race, the ultimate solution of this vital problem will be in the final victory of the oppressed classes. They, in their turn, must not violate justice in their demands. They must not endeavor to build up some sort of a new aristocracy of the working class upon the ruins of the old aristocratic class, with its manifold privileges and numerous monopolies and its unwarrantable advantages—an heritage bestowed by the blind accident of birth.

We wish all men to be working men, sustaining themselves by the product of their labor, but by no means do we favor the creation of new class distinctions upon the overthrow of the present ruling class.

Also quite characteristic for the *Turner* throughout the years is a statement from the report of their executive committee in 1872:

The Turners of America have nothing in common with the Turners of the old fatherland, except the system of physical training. Of our endeavors for reform in political, religious, and social fields, of the struggle against corruption and slavery in all forms, the Turners in Germany know nothing, although this has been the object and the inspiration of our *Turnerbund*.

The Philadelphia meeting in 1851, after settling the question of the name of the organization, adopted the following resolution regarding its political attitude: "The *Sozialistischer Turnerbund* in general subscribes to the principles underlying the radical Free-soil Party and urges all members to support that party in every way possible." Perhaps even more important than the question of the name was the establishment of a newspaper which was to be the official organ. This newspaper was to be kept free of all personal polemics and of any tendency toward partisanship. Every society subscribed for as many copies of the newspaper as it had members. At the end of 1851, twenty-two societies were in existence, of which twenty had joined the *Turnerbund*. The total membership amounted to 1,672. In 1853 the organization, due to its growth, was divided into five districts, according to locality.

As we have seen, the first years of the *Turnerbund* were chiefly devoted to the advocacy of a type of socialism for the realization of which the *Turner* had fought in Germany. The great problems which disturbed the internal situation in America, such as slavery, prohibition, or nativism, could not be disregarded by the *Turner*. The *Turnzeitung*, under the able guidance of Wilhelm Rapp, and Gottfried Becker in Philadelphia, took a very strong stand for the "full independence of the individual." It is there-

fore not at all surprising that the uncompromising attitude of the
Turner and their publications attracted the attention of their opponents and led to many violent arguments in the daily press
and to many attacks by the nativistic rowdies.

The changes forced upon the *Turner* as the result of happen-
ings in the fifties are reflected in the proceedings of the National
Convention held from September 24 to 27, 1855, in Buffalo,
New York. This meeting marks a turning-point in the history of
the *Turnerbund*. By taking a position on the most burning problems of the time, particularly by their stand against slavery, the
Turner entered practical politics. At the same time, this new era
is marked by internal strife and dissension which soon destroyed
the unity of the national organization.

The platform adopted, after violent debate, by the representatives of the forty-seven societies, begins by pointing out the necessity for "social, political and religious reforms" which can be
accomplished by elimination of certain abuses, and then continues:

The *Turnerbund* states that slavery, nativism and prohibition are the
worst abuses of the time and in full realization of this fact sets up the
following principles:

   1) The *Turner* will vote for no man who is a member of the Know-
   Nothing party, or who is identified with any nativistic organization or party, or who does not declare himself openly as opposed
   to any organization of this nature.
   2) The *Turner* are opposed to slavery; particularly they are against
   extension of slavery to the free territories, and regard this institution as definitely unworthy of a republic and contrary to all
   concepts of freedom.
   3) The *Turner* are opposed to all prohibition laws as undemocratic
   and unjust in theory and not feasible in practice.

The die had been cast, and as a consequence these gymnastic
societies whose *Turnfeste* appeared so queer and ridiculous to
native Americans, found themselves under the leadership of
Forty-eighters, in the midst of the most violent conflict of the
century:

The attitude and the spirited agitation of the Turners induced many of
the early German immigrants who had become identified with the

Democratic party to change their minds, and to fall in line with the Unionists. The Turners not only manifested the courage of their convictions in debate, in the press and in public discussions, but they braved personal danger for the anti-slavery cause whenever the opportunity presented itself. Such was the case in Boston and Cincinnati, when Wendell Phillips, the celebrated Abolitionist orator, was defended by the Turners against the furious attacks of hostile mobs; again, in New York, when the Turners responded to a call to act as guards at a Fremont demonstration.

The great sectional issues divided also the *Turner*. A number of the Southern societies—the *Turner* organizations in Charleston, Savannah, Mobile, and Augusta—seceded from the *Bund* because of the newly adopted antislavery paragraph in the platform. The Charleston group attempted to unite all the *Turnvereine* in the South. However, the proposal was rejected by the *Turner* of St. Louis, Wheeling, Baltimore, Louisville, Covington, and Newport, who remained faithful to the Union. An attempt to win back the Southern groups was made at the annual convention of 1858, held in Bloomingdale, New York. It was decided to substitute for the explicit platform of 1855 a very general statement that could be accepted possibly even by partisans of slavery, namely, the principle of a "struggle against all existing abuses." But those were not days when people accepted mental reservations for the sake of peace and harmony, and no reconciliation between North and South was effected. The *Turner* were ready: at the inauguration of President Lincoln, March 4, 1861, two *Turner* companies from Washington and Baltimore formed part of his bodyguard.

Events moved fast. On April 12, 1861, came the attack on Fort Sumter and on April 15 President Lincoln called for seventy-five thousand volunteers. That the *Turner* were willing to back their resolutions by deeds was soon demonstrated by their members everywhere. Under the date of April 19, 1861, there appeared in the Baltimore *Wecker* a call for enlistment signed by a former fighter in the Revolution, Alexander Schimmelpfennig, and also the following news item:

Turner depart for Washington. Yesterday afternoon sixteen *Turner* and sixteen other Germans left for Washington for voluntary enlistment.

They received an enthusiastic send-off from the large patriotic crowd which had gathered at the station. The people, mostly native Americans, broke out in loud cheers whenever the Union was mentioned.

On April 19 there occurred violent riots on the streets of Baltimore when a Massachusetts regiment passed through the city en route to Washington. On the same day a mob appeared before the *Turnhalle* demanding that the *Turner* lower the Stars and Stripes and hoist the Maryland flag; the *Turner* replied that they would rather blow up their hall than pull down their country's flag. Meanwhile many more *Turner* departed for Washington, thus arousing fierce resentment among the numerous Southern sympathizers, and on April 20 a mob stormed the hall, smashing everything to bits. From there they proceeded to the office of the Baltimore *Wecker*, the only Republican paper in Maryland, founded in 1851 by the Forty-eighter Carl Heinrich Schnauffer; the *Turnzeitung* was at this time issued from the same printing establishment. What happened there is graphically described in a letter to his father in Germany written by Wilhelm Rapp, Forty-eighter and *Turner;* Rapp tells of his support of Lincoln in 1860, and then continues:

Supported by gallant German and American friends, I arranged public meetings in the interest of the Republican presidential candidate. Two of these meetings were broken up by the raging mob of the Democratic party; in the course of the one held in the open air in the Richmond marketplace, the howling mob bombarded us with bricks, rotten eggs, and other Democratic missiles, and fired their pistols at me and several other Germans and Americans who were standing with me on the speaker's platform. There were no serious injuries, but I returned to my editorial office dripping egg yolk from my neck and chest (I must have looked like a canary bird) and sat down to give my thanks to the Democratic party for the orders which they had conferred on me at the Richmond Market. On another occasion a band consisting of several thousand ruffians surrounded our meeting hall (the Front Street Theater) and hurled bricks and bottles of vitriol at us, and on my way home threatened me with hanging—which however was prevented by a squad of policemen who protected me with their revolvers against the surging mob.

Better times arrived for me when on the sixth of November last year Abraham Lincoln emerged victorious in the election, and it appeared that he had received in Maryland, in spite of the terrorism of the slave-holders, and their helpers, a stately number of votes far exceeding all expectations. As one of the earliest defenders of the victorious party, I was now flattered by those who had previously persecuted me. After February, 1861, however, matters became very much worse, for also in Baltimore the horrible Southern conspiracy began gaining ground, and its chief, to whom I had been particularly obnoxious, placed me high on his proscription list. During the course of March, they con-tented themselves with various threats with which they tried to drive me out of the city; but when, after the bombardment of Fort Sumter, the Southerners became more and more bold, my life was no longer safe in Baltimore. In broad daylight I was insulted on the street and overwhelmed with murderous threats. The Friends of the Union lost their courage more and more, and one after the other my most de-pendable adherents fled for safety. Every attempt to unite the patriots in armed resistance against the conspirators was in vain.

The Government of the Union at that time had as yet no troops at its command. The police, who had always been unfavorable toward the Republicans, now inclined entirely toward the side of the traitors. Various friends gave me the advice to go into hiding or leave the city entirely. However, I would not quit my post, but fought every day firmly but calmly against the conspiracy; then came the bloody seces-sionist rising of the 19th and 20th of April; it was noon on the 20th of April when several men called on me in my home and asked me in-sistently to retreat into some hiding place, since the drunken mob which was roaming around the streets was shouting my name in preparation for a march to the office of the *Wecker* where I was to be lynched. I ate my dinner and then went calmly to the office of the *Wecker* in order possibly to organize armed resistance against the mob; however, aside from Mrs. Schnauffer, the wife of the publisher, all had lost their courage. No one except Mrs. Schnauffer and myself, and a refugee from the mob who came in all out of breath to hide in the *Wecker* office, remained there. Suddenly the entire street was filled with drunken rowdies, some of them armed, who advanced toward the doors shouting "We want Rapp." I was on the ground floor, separated only by a door from the raging mob.

The crowd shouted again and again that they wanted only me and had no intention of harming Mrs. Schnauffer in any way—(respect for womanhood is instinctive with even the lowest and commonest Ameri-cans). Stones flew against the house and the beasts outside got ready to storm the building and fetch me out, when finally a platoon of police appeared and hung a Secessionist flag out of one of the windows. At the same time they told the mob that I had escaped, and gradually the crowd scattered. On the street corners in the vicinity, however, some of the most dangerous rioters remained, in order to keep an eye out for me. With the coming of dusk, I left the house and fled past one of the corners occupied by these murderous fellows, down the street to the Berlin *Weissbier* brewery of Mr. Pringsheim. His building, like all other business houses in Baltimore, had been shut up for fear of these monsters in human form, but when I called, I was admitted without being noticed by the fellows at the corner, and placed in a safe hiding spot. From this point of vantage I heard two hours later a new and bigger mob coming down the street, howling, firing pistols, shouting "Where is Rapp? Hang him! Hang him!" They marched to the *Wecker* office, and smashed the entrance door, but departed again when the terrified neighbors assured them that I had long ago fled.

The next morning at eight o'clock I left my hiding place and went to the office, which was absolutely deserted. Several drunken Irishmen were staggering about and told me with great cordiality that they would find "that damned black Republican journalist and hang him." It was my good luck that none of them knew me personally. Urged by the neighbors, I returned to my hiding place, and since during the rest of the day the mob continued its orgies in various streets, I was unable to leave it for the time being. In the evening I sent for a barber who was my friend and got him to shave off my beard. At three o'clock on the following morning I left my hiding place, dressed entirely in black, clean shaven, and walked with measured tread to the railway station in order to escape to Washington on the early morning train. But this train was not running; the railway traffic was interrupted. I could not very well go back, because by daylight in the streets of the city, which by now was entirely in the hands of the Secessionist bands, drunk with victory, I would have been recognized in spite of my changed appearance. I decided, therefore, to make my escape on foot and marched ahead on the railroad tracks. Since all along the way everyone seemed to take me for a peaceful clergyman, I experienced no further inconveniences and arrived in Washington the same day, thanks to a kind soul who gave me a lift. That is the story of my flight from Baltimore.

Since the presses of the *Wecker* had been damaged by the mob, the paper could not be printed for some weeks, and it is only in the issue of May 20, 1861, that we read further news about the *Turner*. After an apology for the delay, the editor states that these brave men who gathered in time of crisis about the banner of freedom would receive recognition when the history of these tragic days was written. The article continues:

When the troops sent by Pennsylvania and Massachusetts for the protection of Washington were prevented from passing through Baltimore, it appeared as if the Capitol had been completely isolated from the North. The two German *Turner* companies in Washington were about the only reliable troops there, and it is not at all surprising that the most important tasks were assigned to them. Washington, in those days, had a garrison of not more than a thousand soldiers, whose officers proved to be generally indifferent if not men of Secessionist sympathies. Thus, prior to the arrival at the steps of the Capitol of the Eighth Massachusetts Regiment and the Seventh New York Regiment, the German *Turner* placed themselves unconditionally at the disposal of the Government. Confident of their loyalty, General Scott is reported to have said that he could entrust to them the most dangerous and important tasks. And that is exactly what he did. When it was a question of guarding and securing the railroad line between Washington and Annapolis Junction and of protecting the rear and left flank of the Massachusetts and New York regiments, advancing from Annapolis toward the Junction in order to restore the interrupted train service, the two German *Turner* companies were the only trustworthy troops the Government could use for this highly dangerous and important work. These two companies marched to Annapolis Junction, cleared the environment of traitors, subdued the farmers of that region who inclined toward secession, and protected the railroad line until the Massachusetts and New York troops arrived. In addition, they found time to supply the Capitol with fresh meat, of which there was great scarcity, by requisitioning cattle from the hostile farmers who were no longer willing to bring their products to Washington.

In the preceding chapter mention was made of the great influence exerted by Forty-eighters as journalists in Missouri in imbuing the German population of that state with a strong anti-slavery and pro-Union spirit. As a result, when the crisis came, the *Turner* were ready.

The critical importance of Missouri in the struggle between North and South has been succinctly stated by General Grant:

There was some splendid work done in Missouri, and especially in St. Louis, in the earliest days of the war, which people have now almost forgotten. If St. Louis would have been captured by the rebels it would have made a vast difference in our war. It would have been a terrible task to have recaptured St. Louis—one of the most difficult that could be given to any military man. Instead of a campaign before Vicksburg, it would have been a campaign before St. Louis.

Since Missouri was a slave state, the greater and by far the most influential part of the population sympathized with the Secessionists. Governor Claiborne F. Jackson replied to Lincoln's call for volunteers by rejecting the demand for troops as illegal and unconstitutional and asserting that Missouri would not place so much as a single man in the field for the unholy cause. At the same time, Governor Jackson advanced by all means in his power the formation and equipment of "Minute Men," as the armed groups of Southern sympathizers were called. For this purpose, as well as for the entire war that was just beginning, the control of the arsenal in St. Louis with equipment for approximately thirty thousand soldiers was most important.

The arsenal was protected by only two hundred soldiers under the command of Captain Nathaniel Lyon, who, however, was firmly determined to hold it for the Union. In this he was supported by a distinguished St. Louis citizen, Francis P. Blair, editor of the Republican newspaper, the St. Louis *Democrat*. After the fall of Fort Sumter, the Secessionists established a camp in St. Louis, called Camp Jackson in honor of the Governor, where they gathered together a fighting group that reached the number of two thousand men. Although it was obvious that the purpose of these troops was to seize the arsenal, Captain Lyon was not in a position to act against them because his superior officer, General Harney, forbade any move in that direction.

The *Turner*, as early as December, 1860, had begun their preparations. Every night they practiced military drill in the *Turnhalle* and companies of *Turner* were organized as well as some other German militia groups who called themselves *Schwarze Jaeger* (ambiguously termed Black Guards by the Southern sympathizers). Toward the end of April, five regiments of Union men had been formed, consisting largely of Germans. The first regiment, composed mostly of *Turner*, elected Francis Blair as their colonel; the second chose Heinrich Boernstein, editor of the *Anzeiger des Westens;* the third chose Franz Sigel, the fourth, the "Black Guards," Nicholas Schuettner; and the fifth C. E. Salomon. All but Blair were Forty-eighters.

But these troops were only scantily armed, while the Seces-

sionists received more and more weapons, particularly after they
had, on April 20, seized a smaller arsenal located at Liberty,
Missouri. General Harney made no move to restrain them. But
Francis Blair turned directly to President Lincoln, whereupon,
on April 22, an order came from Washington deposing General
Harney and placing Captain Lyon in command of the United
States troops in Missouri. On that very morning three companies of *Turner* under the command of Colonel Blair, after
having camped in the *Turnhalle* during the night, moved to the
arsenal where they were equipped and mustered in by Captain
Lyon. In the course of the day the other regiments followed
suit and all were enrolled in the Union Army.

There were thus in St. Louis two hostile camps and the situation was extremely tense. Some of the local color is caught in
bits of dialogue in Winston Churchill's *The Crisis:*

"Let me go, Anne!" he cried. "Do you think I can stay here while
my people are shot down by a lot of damned Dutchmen"!

"John," said Mr. Brinsmade sternly, "I cannot let you join a mob.
I cannot let you shoot at men who carry the Union flag."

"You cannot prevent me, sir," shouted the young man in a frenzy.
"When foreigners take our flag for their own, it is time for us to shoot
them down."

．　　．　　．

". . . Away, away,
Away down South in Dixie."

The song ceased amid peals of girlish laughter. Stephen was rooted
to the spot.

"Jinny! Jinny Carvel, how dare you!," came through the shutters.
"We shall have a whole regiment of Hessians in here."

Old Uncle Ben, the Catherwoods' coachman, came out of the stable
yard. The whites of his eyes were rolling, half in amusement, half in
terror. Seeing Stephen standing there, he exclaimed:—

"Mistah Brice, if de Dutch take Camp Jackson, is we niggers gwinter
be free?"

Stephen did not answer, for the piano had started again.

"If ever I consent to be married,—
And who could refuse a good mate?—
The man whom I give my hand to
Must believe in the rights of the State."

On the day of these fictitious conversations, May 10, 1861,

Lyon, now Brigadier General, by a skillful maneuver surprised
the troops in Fort Jackson and demanded surrender within half
an hour. Before the time was up, the Secessionists surrendered,
delivered up their arms, and were paroled. The most important
city in the West had been saved for the Union. There had been
no fighting and no flashy deeds of valor in the course of this action, but the *Turner* had proved true to their ideals and ready to
die for them. To them it was "The Second Fight for Freedom,"
as a Forty-eighter, Fritz Annecke, called his book of memoirs.

Just as had been the case in St. Louis, so in Boston, New York,
Philadelphia, Cincinnati, Indianapolis, Chicago, Milwaukee,
and other cities, the *Turner* came forward as volunteers. An
enumeration has been made by an historian of the movement,
of the more important regiments composed wholly or in part of
Turner, under the leadership of Forty-eighters where the names
appear in italics: First Missouri, Colonel Francis P. Blair; Third
Missouri, *Colonel Franz Sigel;* Twelfth Missouri, *Colonel Peter
Joseph Osterhaus;* Seventeenth Missouri, Colonel Franz Hassen-
deubel; Ninth Wisconsin, *Colonel Friedrich Salomon;* Twenty-sixth
Wisconsin, *Colonel Hans Boebel;* Ninth Ohio, Colonel Robert
McCook; Twenty-eighth Ohio, Colonel August Moor; Thirty-
seventh Ohio, *Colonel Eduard Siber;* One Hundred Sixth Ohio,
Colonel Gustaf Tafel; One Hundred Eighth Ohio, Colonel George
T. Limberg; Ninth Illinois, *Colonel Mersey;* Forty-third Illinois,
Colonel Adolf Engelmann; Twenty-fourth and Eighty-second Illi-
nois, both in turn organized by *Colonel Friedrich Hecker;* Thirty-
second Indiana, *Colonel August Willich;* Twentieth New York,
Colonel Max Weber; Second Minnesota Cavalry, *Colonel Wilhelm
Pfaender;* Hofmann's Battery, *Colonel Louis Hofmann;* Colonel
Robert McCook, one of the "Fighting McCooks" of Ohio, was
made colonel of the *Turner* regiment at the suggestion of Judge
Johann Bernhardt Stallo; though an Irishman, the Colonel spoke
German and commanded his regiment in that language.

After the conclusion of the Civil War, the *Turnerbund* flourished
more than ever. Members could turn from the army life or the
relief work that had occupied them for the duration of the con-

flict, to the practice of gymnastics and cultural activities. The annual national competitions were resumed and the quality of the theatrical productions in *Turner* clubs reached a high level in the seventies. The socialistic trend gradually disappeared, but the resolutions at the annual meetings remained distinctly liberal, in some cases anticipating reforms adopted by the nation decades later; for instance, a manifest of 1871 favors woman suffrage. In the preceding chapter mention was made of the training school for teachers of gymnastics, the graduates of which became instructors in schools throughout the country. As an estimate of the wide interest in physical training generated by the *Turner*, to which President Truman alludes in the letter cited at the beginning of this chapter, a quotation from Dr. Edward M. Hartwell's report to the United States Commissioner of Education of the year 1898, may serve:

Neither the colleges nor the athletic organizations of the country have earned the right to speak with authority on the question of what constitutes a well-ordered and practical system of physical training for elementary and secondary schools. Therefore, the more or less successful introduction of school gymnastics, since 1884, by the cities of Chicago, Kansas City, Cleveland, Denver, Indianapolis, St. Louis, Milwaukee, Cincinnati, St. Paul, San Francisco and Boston, through the action of their respective school boards, has been chiefly due to the zeal and insistence of the advocates of the German and Swedish systems of gymnastics, who were prepared to speak with knowledge and to act with intelligence. In every city named above, excepting Boston, German free and light gymnastics have been adopted, and the directors of physical education are graduates of the Seminary or Normal School of the North American Turnerbund. In Boston, Worcester, Cambridge and a considerable number of other cities in Massachusetts and New England, Swedish gymnastics have been introduced more or less completely into the public schools. Mixed systems of an eclectic character are in vogue in the schools of Brooklyn, Washington, New York, and Providence. The promotion of gymnastic teaching in the public schools has ever been one of the cherished aims of the *Turnerbund*.

The centenary of the *Turner* celebrated in St. Louis (where a Jahn memorial stands in Forest Park) exemplifies the give and take in the acculturation of groups in the American melting pot. The program lists competitions in the traditional gymnastic exercises on horizontal and parallel bars that formed part of the earliest *Turnfeste* held in this country, and along with them track and field events, basketball, volleyball, and similar innovations that would cause a Forty-eighter immense amazement if his ghost could return after a hundred years. Balancing the physical competitions there are always "mental gymnastics," much in the old manner—song writing and poetry, essay writing, singing and choral contests. The old Forty-eighter would be surprised and pleased to note that women have an equal share in the physical and mental competitions. The program contains an essay on "Mental Training in the Turners" by Mr. George Seibel, an old *Turner* and director of the Allegheny Carnegie Library of Pittsburgh, in which he tells how the old tradition is being continued:

Today also the Turners have a far-reaching educational program, like the Y.M.C.A., which adapted the Turner idea to its own province. In our Turner societies, which appeal to every member of the family, there are classes and study groups in many mental and cultural activities, from basketry and weaving, ceramics and sculpture, to the study of history and economics. Photography and other "hobbies" have been organized. There are libraries and chess clubs, hikers seek nature's haunts to learn her secrets, all the interests of the Boy Scouts and the Campfire Girls.

Mr. Seibel concludes by quoting some lines of poetry expressing what he has been describing as the *Turner* philosophy. The verse is not by Schiller or any other German poet dear to the Forty-eighters, nor by one of the several score of *Turner* poets in this country, but by James Russell Lowell, who is called by Curtis Hidden Page "our noblest patriot-poet and our most complete and well-rounded man":

> We speak the truth, and what care we
> For hissing and for scorn,
> While some faint gleamings we can see
> Of freedom's coming morn.
> Let liars fear, let cowards shrink,
> Let traitors turn away;
> Whatever we have dared to think,
> That dare we also say.

Chapter Five

THE FORTY- EIGHTERS
IN POLITICS

*By Lawrence S. Thompson
and Frank X. Braun*

THE PERIOD before the arrival of that dynamic group known as the Forty-eighters could well be called the *Biedermeier* (that is, early Victorian) period of the German element in the United States. The Germans who arrived at these shores in the various waves of immigration before the middle of the nineteenth century were on the whole honest and hard-working artisans, farmers (some "Latin," mostly otherwise), and laborers, with a thin sprinkling of intellectuals. Most of the latter were refugees from the political disturbances in Germany in 1830. Among them were men like Gustave Koerner, who in 1845 was appointed justice of the Illinois Supreme Court and who later was to be elected lieutenant-governor of that state and to become a close friend of Lincoln; Philipp Dorchheimer, the postmaster of Buffalo and later state treasurer of New York; Karl Follen, professor at Harvard University and an ardent abolitionist at an early date; Friedrich Muench, state senator of Missouri; Karl Gustav Memminger, secretary of treasury, CSA; Albert Lange, state auditor of Indiana; Christian Roselius, state prosecutor of Louisiana; Franz Huebschmann, in 1852 an unsuccessful candidate for the Democratic nomination for governor of Wisconsin; Franz Hoffmann, elected lieutenant-governor of Illinois in 1860; and General John A. Wagener, CSA. However, those individuals who made a name for themselves in politics represented, numerically speaking, an infinitesimal portion of the mass of German immigrants, who were politically inexperienced and uninterested and who became, at most, passive voters.

Julius Froebel (nephew of "Kindergarten" Friedrich Froebel), one of the earliest Forty-eighters to reach the United States, declared bluntly and with a somewhat superior air that Germans of previous migrations had fully earned the epithet *Stimmvieh* ("voting cattle," dull followers of an oxlike leader), by their limited political interest which never extended beyond such obvious side issues as temperance and Sabbath laws. The new note characteristic of the Forty-eighters is clearly evident in Froebel when he expresses his impatience with the German Americans because of their insistence on making a sacred cow of their beer; he says the thought has occurred to him that it is perhaps not fortuitous that in various countries the emphasis on and devotion to beer, wine, dance music, and *Gemuetlichkeit* stands in inverse ratio to political maturity and political freedom. In sharp contrast to the Forty-eighters, the mass of the former immigrants accepted slavery as simply another strange phenomenon in a strange country. Only a small minority, men of the type of Karl Follen and Francis Lieber, was antagonistic, although not yet belligerently, to this peculiar institution of the South.

The older German immigrants were mostly Jacksonian Democrats, supporting and believing in the principles laid down by the Declaration of Independence—freedom and equality of all men, especially white men. Applied to their specific case, this meant, of course, the equality of native-born and naturalized Americans. According to Friedrich Kapp, around 1850, it was considered the proper thing for a German immigrant to be a Democrat and practically heretical for him to be a Whig. To the newcomer, unacquainted with American party alignments, the mere word "Democrat" was a sort of shibboleth, for he imbued it with his own preconceived and idealized conceptual content which was not necessarily congruent with reality.

The Democratic party in the middle of the last century was commonly and traditionally considered the party "friendly" to the immigrant, and the Irish as well as the Germans flocked to it. The Whigs, on the other hand, had the reputation of being money-bound aristocrats. "Don't trust the Whigs," counseled a

Wisconsin German newspaper in 1846; "they have always opposed the rights of the foreign-born."

The average German immigrant was, in general, content to
be left alone to work out his own destiny, to settle in sections of
the country that topographically and climatically bore the greatest resemblance to his native region, to dwell, if possible, among
his fellow countrymen, and to retain some of his cherished old-
country patterns of living. These Germans, who enjoyed a good
reputation as skilled workers, tenacious settlers, and thrifty and
enterprising tradesmen, as a matter of good political form gave
their votes to the "friendly party" and expected little more in
return than the right to enjoy the fruits of their labor in their
own way. The general impression is one of a political passivity
which might be attributed to a number of reasons: the language
barrier, the lack of political experience, and the paucity of leaders who could turn the passive voter into an active and politically
conscious citizen.

This is the accepted picture of the pre-1848 German immigrant. However, it should be noted that most of the brushwork
in this composite portrait of the *Biedermeier* in America was
daubed in by the more articulate, aggressive, and politically
hypersensitive Forty-eighters, the young and self-appointed
teachers of the old immigrants. It is a picture of the "Grays"
painted by the "Greens," and it reflects some of the impatience
felt by highly active teachers toward their stolid, conservative,
and none too easily moved pupils.

The first indications that this rather uneventful period of political *Biedermeiertum* of the German immigrant might be terminated became manifest with the appearance of nativistic societies. These antiforeign protest movements recruited from the
native Protestant population were primarily directed against the
Catholic Irish immigrants who were arriving in droves in the
forties and fifties of the last century. German Catholics, however, were also included by them as being a part of this irritating
and clannish foreign element. Rioting and bloodshed ensued
in Baltimore, Philadelphia, and New York.

Related to this aggressive movement or directly descending from it were those secret societies which from about 1850 on comprised the Know-Nothing movement. This movement, which came out in the open as the American Party, gained rapidly in strength and at the height of its power could control 63 per cent of the Massachusetts vote. Nativism was, of course, by no means attributable only to apprehension over the increasing immigration of Catholic foreigners. Economic reasons were perhaps equally important, at least in some sections of the country, and gave the movement a general nonsectarian and anti-foreign stamp.

Many of the poorer and less enterprising immigrants remained in the East and began to clog the labor market. This was quickly resented by native-born American workers. In the slaveholding South cheap immigrant labor, however, was equally undesired. When a German farmer, by hiring fellow immigrants, could enter into successful competition with the planter operating with less efficient slave labor, the latter quite correctly interpreted such a condition as a serious threat to a whole economic structure built on slave labor. The incursion of immigrants, of "free" labor, even though it might be neutral or indifferent to the social institution of slavery as such, was diagnosed by Southern political leaders as tending to weaken the social and economic bases of their society. Southern plans to extend slavery into the new territories, the leaders feared, might come to naught because of the infiltration of Northern and immigrant labor. Know-Nothingism, then, with all its appendant bigotry, violence, and intolerance was in reality a defensive reaction by both the Eastern proletariat and the Southern planters.

This antiforeign, nativistic feeling was further fed by cultural friction, especially in the Eastern sections of the country with their old traditions and Puritan background. Carl Wittke depicts this condition vividly: "Blaring bands, Sunday picnics, dances, parades and noisy German beerhalls deeply offended many Americans and challenged the long-established customs of many a community."

The Know-Nothing movement grew in strength and violence

in the early fifties as a direct result of heavy Irish and German immigration in those years. Large-scale election frauds in the metropolitan areas of the country came to light, in which very recent immigrants were "made" citizens on election day. Conservative American property holders felt that near-pauper immigrants, who often had to be supported at public expense, were responsible for higher taxes, and American labor accused the employers of deliberately importing pauper labor in order to lower wages. Whether it is to be considered an historical coincidence or a direct casual relationship, it would appear that the period when nativism reached its height coincided with the very moment when the Forty-eighters started to assume political and intellectual leadership of the German masses. And it would seem that the Forty-eighters added fuel to the flames.

In politics and social relations a sizable number of the latter could be counted among the most radical groups of the day. From a religious point of view most of them were freethinkers; they also believed in universal suffrage, abolition of the Sunday laws, taxation of church property, establishment of the eight-hour day, government ownership of railroads, and a number of other equally pernicious heresies. These "socialists and rationalits, atheists and desecrators of the Sabbath" caused great dismay in the ranks of the descendants of the old colonial families. The *North American Review* in 1856 commented: "Among the Forty-eighters there are too many of those turbulent, restless spirits who are always evoked from obscurity by civil commotions . . . they stamp kingcraft and priestcraft with a common brand of infamy. The great majority of the wealthy and educated are atheists or radicals." Radicalism carried some of the left-wingers to such bitter opposition to organized religion that they objected to the mention of God in the records of the 1864 Frémont Convention in Cleveland. It is significant that of all the outstanding Forty-eighters only Friedrich Schuenemann-Pott and Eduard Schroeter were ministers, and they very radical ones at that. In other fields of human endeavor the Forty-eighters were later to distinguish themselves in the country that had adopted them, but none of these intellectual disciples of Feuerbach is anywhere recorded as a leader in the religious field, that is, among the conventional denominations.

German radicalism increased that militant fury of the Know-Nothings which had heretofore been directed against Irish popery, and the German immigrants found themselves in a defensive position. As early as 1837 there is on record a convention of Germans which, as one of its expressed objectives, sought "to counteract the efforts of nativistic American societies." Similar mass protests were voiced by the Germans of Milwaukee in 1843 and those of Chicago in 1844. Local piecemeal defense against a movement of national dimensions was of no avail, and the need for broad organized self-defense became more and more evident and pressing. Intellectual and political leadership was badly needed, for there had been an abundance of bloody troubles, such as the nativistic riot in Cincinnati in 1855. In the front ranks of the politically inexperienced German immigrants there were posts aplenty for political leaders. Into this political vacuum the Forty-eighters plunged with an abundant enthusiasm. Their first manifestations, coming from the radicals among their number, were less practical than utopian; therefore, the Wheeling Congress and the Louisville Platform find their place in the next chapter.

The term "radical" did not fit the majority of the Forty-eighters, for they represented all the political shadings of the German revolutionary movement. There was among them the German nationalist, who, in place of thirty-six small fatherlands, aspired to one united Germany with a vigorous and popular emperor at its head; in the eyes of the German authorities such a sentiment, of course, was subversive. There was the German political humanist, who under a monarch or within the framework of a republic wanted above all political and personal liberty and freedom for individual development. In these two categories, without drawing rigid lines, might be included most of the liberals among the Forty-eighters. A typical individual was Friedrich Kapp, who participated in the revolutionary uprising in 1849 and fled to Switzerland. There, in his association with German and Italian revolutionists, he became convinced of the stupidity and futility of their plottings. In New York he became a member of the law firm Zitz, Kapp, and Froebel, and later, editor of the New York *Abendzeitung*. "His political notions were idealistic," writes Frank Monaghan, "and he entertained an optimistic belief in the capacity of the people for leadership."

Carl Schurz, a young man of nineteen at the outbreak of the Revolution, was in Veit Valentin's rather sharply expressed opinion not a typical revolutionary: "He had no opinion of big, solemn speeches, and so he never developed into a sly conspirator or a greasy roaring tavern orator." Schurz arrived with convictions, but his political personality was formed by the practical and realistic American environment. His views as politician and journalist alike bore the stamp of moderation.

Carl Heinrich Schnauffer fought a number of engagements under the Revolutionary leader Hecker, was taken prisoner and escaped. He was a literary man and the author of a number of lyrics and a drama. In contrast to his fellow refugees, he was relatively conservative, though definitely antislavery.

Friedrich K. F. Hecker, doctor of laws of the University of Munich, has been described as the romantic embodiment and the hero of the German Revolution. Politically he was a democrat, but above all he was a man who lived for action, no matter whether we see him as "half a hero and half a highwayman," or as the "scholar and gentleman who exemplified all the social graces of his native Baden." In Belleville, Illinois, where he joined a colony of "Latin farmers," he became a successful cattle raiser and viticulturist. Hecker was among the early German supporters of the Republican Party.

Nor could Franz Sigel, graduate of the military academy at Karlsruhe, Hecker's associate in the Baden insurrection and leader of an army of revolutionists, be called a political radical. He merely fought for what he considered right on both sides of the ocean.

Among the moderate revolutionaries was Oswald Ottendorfer, later the well-known editor and owner of the New York *Staatszeitung*. In Austria he fought Metternich's troops and participated in the Saxon rebellion. Another moderate was Hermann

Raster, former secretary of the Landtag in Dessau who was arrested and freed on condition that he emigrate to the United States. In 1851 Raster became the editor of the Buffalo *Demokrat* and later of the New York *Abendzeitung*, and finally of the *Illinois Staatszeitung*. From Mannheim came attorney Lorenz Brentano, the one-time chairman of the five-man executive commission in charge of the Grand Duchy of Baden. After burying himself for nine years on a farm near Kalamazoo, Michigan, he moved to Chicago and became in 1859 editor of the *Illinois Staatszeitung*, helping to make it one of the most influential German dailies in the country. Georg Hillgaertner was an attorney until the outbreak of the Revolution. Seeking safety first in Switzerland, he then went to London and there met Gottfried Kinkel. As Kinkel's secretary he came to the United States, where Kinkel had decided to campaign in order to raise money for a second revolution. For one year Hillgaertner was editor of the *Illinois Staatszeitung*. Gottlieb Theodor Kellner, editor of the Philadelphia *Demokrat*, once taught at the University of Goettingen, and at the outbreak of the Revolution founded a social-democratic *Verein*. He was captured near Paderborn and escaped from jail the same day he was to be sentenced.

It might be said that the great majority of the leading Forty-eighters, in spite of their religious radicalism, ranged politically from somewhat right to somewhat left of center. Definitely left were, of course, Karl Heinzen and Friedrich Hassaurek in his earlier years in America. It was in that period that Karl Heinzen, in his usual savage manner, dubbed him the "beerhall Demosthenes" because Hassaurek traveled about in the Middle West delivering radical lectures before groups of workingmen.

It is clear that the Forty-eighters were by no means a homogeneous group. They represented all the variations of the Revolutionary movement at home and transplanted into new soil their old opinions with all their concommitant factional and ideological strife. It was only later that most of them learned to subordinate their personal wishes and individual aims to a common cause, when, because of a combination of impelling circumstances, a metamorphosis was effected from utopian visionary or impatient reformer to realistic American politician.

The initial stimulus in the early fifties which caused the Forty-eighters to begin to participate actively in American politics was probably self-protection. Nativism, fanned by injudiciously bold reform proposals of "impudent foreign elements," reached the peak of its power in these years, and the Forty-eighters, now America-conscious and America-wise, took up the cudgels and returned pressure with pressure. They answered with all the time-honored devices of practical politics, with political agitation and organization, with party maneuvers, platforms and demonstrations, promises and threats. They discovered that the German voting power, if organized, had a bargaining value. To organize and to fuse the potential strength of the German immigrant vote was their first problem, which they tackled with enthusiasm and vigor.

The first manifestations of this defensive organizational activity were a number of state conventions of the *Bund freier Maenner* in 1853 and 1854 to "coordinate the political thought and activity of the German-Americans." It was their declared intention not to form a German political party, but rather to protect their rights as stated in the Declaration of Independence and as guaranteed by the Constitution. Bernhard Domschke, once co-editor of Heinzen's *Pionier* and co-author of the radical "Louisville Platform," gave typical expression to this sentiment. With his characteristic slant he wrote to Roeser's *Wisconsin Demokrat* at Manitowoc on August 17, 1854:

The idea of forming a union of foreigners against nativism is wholly wrong, and destroys the possibility of any influence on our part; it would drive us into a union with Irishmen, those American Croats. In our struggle we are not concerned with nationality, but with principles; we are for liberty and against union with Irishmen. . . . The Irish are our natural enemies, not because they are Irishmen, but because they are the truest guards of Popery.

The more docile and passive Germans of the previous wave of immigration, though restive under nativist pressure, were none too eager to follow the call of the up-start politicians, and bitter newspaper campaigns were fought between the "Grays" and the "Greens." The dislike and distrust of the former by the latter can easily be understood. It was not only radicalism which made the "Greens" suspect, but, as Wittke points out, many Forty-eighters

took keen delight in flaunting their Continental tastes in the face of Americans whom they regarded as little better than barbarians—men without art, music, culture, or refinement, who were suppressed and crushed by the bigotry of Puritanism. The conflict between the champions of two diametrically opposed philosophies of life was especially acute in the Middle West, and neither party to the struggle distinguished itself for tact or tolerance.

A better understanding and even a partial fusion between the "Grays" and the "Greens" came about when both found a common cause in the newly born Republican party. A combination of powerful ideological and practical motives first drove the Forty-eighters to the party which mustered its initial strength from antislavery Whigs, anti-Nebraska Democrats, and Free-Soilers. That this "spontaneous overflow of powerful feelings," a phrase aptly borrowed by Dr. Shuster from the poet to describe the rise of the Republican Party, should engulf the politically sensitive Forty-eighters was to be expected. This party, the outward expression of the greatest protest movement of the century, counts among its founders and early organizers many of the German nonconformists who saw in the struggle against slavery, injustice, and class rule an historical parallel to their own lost cause in the fatherland. They made the Republican party and its ideals their new cause.

An emotionally charged attitude toward slavery initiated the Republican landslide in the ranks of the Forty-eighters and united extreme radicals like Heinzen, Hassaurek, and Struve with moderates like Kapp and Schurz. From the very beginning of their stay in America, and even before they had come to a complete comprehension of the complexities of the peculiar institution of the South, many of the Forty-eighters had become militant abolitionists. Not content to raise their voices in editorial protest from a safe distance, some of them moved South and their antislavery printing establishments became storm centers in the slave states. Heinzen edited the Louisville, Kentucky, *Herold des Westens* for three months in 1853 and won five hundred new subscribers with his uncompromising antislavery views boldly distributed in the metropolis of a slave state until the offices and presses were burned on December 3, 1853. Schnauffer's Baltimore *Wecker*, founded in 1851, was for many years the only antislavery organ, in German or English, in Maryland; and after his death Mrs. Schnauffer continued to run the office and the paper with Wilhelm Rapp as editor. A previous chapter cites Rapp's account of the attack of a mob on the *Wecker* office. There is a version of this story which relates an event that Rapp did not report, namely that Mrs. Schnauffer made a dramatic appeal to the mob, holding a small child in her arms, and thus saved the establishment from complete destruction. In San Antonio, Texas, Douai founded a small antislavery paper which he printed, published, and distributed himself until he was compelled to leave town two jumps ahead of a mob. In St. Louis, Missouri, it was Georg Schneider, later the editor of the influential *Illinois Staatszeitung*, who became notorious for his opposition to the extension of slavery. The presses and premises of his organ, the *Neue Zeit*, were destroyed by fire.

In the South and the North, the editorial drums of the Forty-eighters beat out the insistent and continuous line that slavery, not temperance nor Sabbath observance, was the really important issue, the crux of American politics. They scrutinized the problem from all angles. Friedrich Kapp, a leading abolitionist in New York viewed slavery from the ethical and political side. In his discussion of the slavery question in the United States he writes:

"The problem of slavery is not the problem of the Negro. It is the eternal conflict between a small privileged class and the great mass of the non-privileged, the eternal struggle between aristocracy and democracy."

Struve and Heinzen attacked slavery on a humanitarian basis. Struve's abhorence of slavery reached its climax after he had spent a year and a half in slave states. In *Diesseits und Jenseits des*

Ozeans, he castigates the moral depravity of slaveholders, the animal-like status of the Negro, and the degenerating effect of the institution of slavery on both slave and master. "The dirt that clings to this institution is so nauseous and repulsive that it is impossible to describe it in a book that is intended for a mixed audience," he wrote.

Karl Heinzen, notorious for his complete lack of a sense of compromise, and equally deficient of insight in most matters pertaining to economics, stoutly refused to consider any but the purely human approach to the slavery problem, namely that it is wrong for one man to hold another in bondage. For Heinzen the term Republican was equivalent to abolitionist, and when years later Seward, as candidate for the Republican nomination for the Presidency, moderated his "irrepressible conflict" sentiment, Heinzen commented bluntly: "Seward stopped being a Republican when he saw the White House." When Carl Schurz campaigned for the great moderator Lincoln, the disappointed radical, Heinzen, called his countryman a "mere American politician."

In the late fifties, when the slavery issue had come to a head, it was Carl Schurz in his Republican campaign speeches who crystallized the antislavery sentiment more eloquently than any other Forty-eighter. In his English and German speeches, he not only discussed slavery from a Constitutional and philanthropic point of view, but went on to show the injury it wrought upon the country at large, and above all, upon the slave states themselves. His philosophical approach blended eloquence, logic, and historical and economic insight to an admirable degree and was, according to the testimony of contemporaries such as Andrew D. White, something entirely new which greatly enhanced the young politician's stature in the eyes of both Germans and native-born.

Slavery, although the great issue of the day, was not the only one that loomed large on the political horizon. Nativism, for the bulk of the German immigrants, was quite as important and of much more immediate concern. It was recognized by the Forty-eighters and the leaders of the new Republican party that, if the great masses of the German immigrants were to be drawn into the new party, a clear statement as to the status of the foreign-born was essential. Here again the Forty-eighter acted as the political catalyst. As early as 1854, in the period of Republican organizational activity on a state-wide basis, we find Georg Schneider, then editor of the powerful *Illinois Staatszeitung*, in collaboration with Abraham Lincoln. Schneider, the crusading Forty-eighter, had faith in the tenets of the nascent party, but "he was unwilling that it fall in the hands of those former Whigs who had Know-Nothing tendencies." The earliest results of the collaboration of Lincoln and Schneider was a plank in the Illinois state platform of the Republican party recognizing the rights of the foreign-born citizen, an example which was followed by other Republican state conventions and by the national convention in 1856.

Not only in Illinois but also in Wisconsin, Michigan, and other states, the Forty-eighters were on hand when the new party was formed. Representing the Germans at the organizational convention in Madison were Carl Roeser, editor of the Manitowoc *Demokrat* and Christian Esselen, editor of *Atlantis*. In Michigan it was Dr. Hermann Kiefer, chairman of the Freiburg mass meeting in 1848 and participant in the encounters of Phillipsburg and Ubstadt in 1849. Five years later he was again a chairman, but this time of the German Republican executive committee in Michigan. He was twenty-nine years old at the time. In later years he became Presidential elector of Michigan, United States consul to Stettin, and regent and professor emeritus of the University of Michigan.

Within a short period, the leading Forty-eighters assembled under the banner of the Republican party. With scores of editors in their ranks as an increasingly powerful propaganda factor, they were courted by both parties but threw themselves whole-heartedly into the fight for their new cause, antislavery. Bringing the mass of the German immigrant vote within the fold of Republicanism was their immediate aim, and to this end they turned into veritable Republican flying squadrons. With pen and speech they labored untiringly; they shepherded, cajoled, and whipped their cautious and still suspicious countrymen into breaking old allegiances and joining them in the ranks of freedom.

The example of Gustave Koerner, a refugee of 1830, who turned Republican at the expiration of his term as Democratic lieutenant-governor of Illinois, made a profound impression on the older generation of Germans. His eloquent speeches in the campaign of 1856 contributed greatly in winning over his countrymen to the Republican cause. Koerner was joined by his friend Friedrich Hecker, who stumped the East and West against slavery and for the Republican party.

Carl Schurz, "known locally as a tenacious holder of minority views in politics and to a few of the native-born as an educated young German who was opposed to slavery," was drafted by the Wisconsin Republican leaders to help turn the tide in their state. In following his friend Hecker, he redeemed an old pledge, namely that they would join forces in the battle against slavery when the time was ripe. They met again later, in the uniform of the North. So Schurz did for Wisconsin what Koerner and Hecker had previously done for Illinois, and what Hoffmann, a spiritual relative of the Forty-eighters, was doing in Chicago. Hassaurek, the former extremist and now editor of the Cincinnati *Hochwaechter*, organized with Judge Johann Bernhard Stallo the Republican party in Cincinnati, a Democratic stronghold, while Charles Ruemelin and Stallo were equally active in outstate Ohio.

Friedrich Kapp, editor of the New York *Abendzeitung* and originally, for cultural reasons, one of the very few Whigs among the Forty-eighters, had become a highly successful lawyer and publicist. Perhaps the most influential personality among the Germans of New York, he was among the first to join the new party and was soon recognized by Germans and Anglo-Americans alike as a leader and a powerful polemicist. Gustav Struve, the socialist who in the middle fifties was engaged in writing his nine-volume *Weltgeschichte*, came out in support of Republicanism. Reinhold Solger, who fled Germany with a price on his head and subsequently was twice chosen as lecturer at Boston's Lowell Institute, became an enthusiastic member of the party.

Limitations of space prohibit an enumeration of the Forty-eighters among the early Republican pioneers, but it can safely be said that by 1856 all of the prominent men among them were active in the ranks of the new party, with the exception of Oswald Ottendorfer, editor of the New York *Staatszeitung*, who remained a Northern anti-Breckenridge Democrat, Otto Dresel of Ohio, and Emil Rothe, a Wisconsin editor.

The virtually unanimous support of the Republicans by the Forty-eighters was by no means equivalent to a general exodus from the Democratic party on the part of the bulk of the German voters. The older generation was exceedingly reluctant to break the bonds of allegiance that tied them traditionally to the "friendly party." However, there were growing indications that German faith in the Southern-dominated Democratic party was being shaken. This process of estrangement was initiated by antiforeign Democratic legislation and was deliberately accelerated by the Republican party and its crusading Forty-eighters. Consistent blocking of the homestead bill by Southern Democrats had long been a source of irritation to immigrants of all nationalities, but the real turning point came in 1854. This year saw the passage of the Kansas-Nebraska Act and the repeal of the Missouri Compromise, thereby bringing to a head simultaneously two issues in which the Germans were deeply interested and involved, slavery and nativism. The law which created the new territories of Kansas and Nebraska, with the stipulation that the agreement of the Missouri Compromise of 1820 be inoperative, opened up these territories to slavery. Appended to the bill was Senator John M. Clayton's (Delaware) nativistic amendment which, although couched in polite terms, stated quite unequivocally that slaveholders and their human chattel would be more welcome in the new territories than free immigrants from Europe. The reaction to the Kansas-Nebraska Bill with "the Devil's cloven hoof sticking out without covering" (Clayton's Amendment) was immediate and direct, and the first link of a chain reaction within the mass of the German voters. It was, according to Herriott,

a major cause in disturbing their political alignments, shaking and
almost shattering their loyalty to the Democratic party, with which
three-fourths of the Germans were then affiliated, inducing secessions
in large numbers in 1856, and it set in motion among them forces in
opposition to slavery that made the Germans a determining factor in
the overthrow of the Democratic party in 1860 and in the election of
Abraham Lincoln.

The immediate results of the passage of the bill were a number
of protest meetings of German immigrants, most of them inspired
by the vigorous idealism of Forty-eighters. In Chicago, Georg
Schneider convoked a public meeting to draft resolutions against
the bill, and at a later mass meeting he branded Douglas, the
author of the bill, as "an ambitious and dangerous demagogue"
—at the conclusion of this meeting an effigy of Douglas was
publicly burned. The nativistic counterblow to this "indignity
to Senator Douglas by a German mob" was delivered at once
by Senator Adams of Mississippi, who introduced a naturalization bill which proposed to increase the period of probation to
twenty-one years. An open split in Congressional Democratic
ranks greatly reinforced the anti-Southern sentiment and gave
it, in a sense, official approval.

Senators Chase from Ohio and Sumner from Massachusetts
with a number of Eastern representatives, all of them independent Democrats and later Republicans, signed an "Appeal of the
Independent Democrats in Congress to the people of the United
States." It denounced the Kansas-Nebraska Bill as a "gross
violation of a sacred pledge," "part and parcel of an atrocious
plot" to exclude immigrants and free laborers from the unoccu-
pied territories and convert them into "a dreary region of despotism, inhabited by masters and slaves." Added to it was a
statement addressed directly to the Forty-eighters. "We earnestly
request the enlightened conductors of newspapers in the German
and other foreign languages to direct the attention of their readers to this important matter." Needless to say, the Forty-eighters
responded to this appeal, both as antislavery men and as Germans. In Douglas they saw "a traitor to the cause of human
freedom" and they were always ready to strike a blow at the

Southern Democrats to whom Douglas, a man with Presidential aspirations, had in their opinion sold himself.

There was no love lost between the Forty-eighters and the Southern Democrats, for it was the latter who had most violently opposed the intervention of the United States in favor of revolutionary foreign governments. Southern Democrats repeatedly blocked the passage of the Homestead Act, terming it a Northern election bribe to win the Irish and the "Dutch." The final stinging insult to Iowa Germans in particular came from Senator Butler of South Carolina. During the debate on the Kansas-Nebraska Act, he attacked foreign immigrants (specifically excluding his Irish constituents) and declared: "The intelligent and judicious master, having his slaves around him in Missouri or Nebraska, would be as acceptable a neighbor to me and, as I thought would be to Iowa, as one of these new immigrants." The Germans in Iowa, with their strong contingent of Forty-eighters, seethed with resentment. Newspapers announced that Judge Butler preferred Negroes in Nebraska to "emigrants from the land of the Kraut," and James W. Grimes, Whig candidate for governor of Iowa, exploited the incident to the fullest. Butler's "playful" remark, it is alleged, gave Iowa its first and last Whig governor. Grimes won the state by such a narrow margin that a shift of the German vote might easily account for his victory.

The events of the year 1854 pointed to a gradual estrangement between the German voters and the Democratic party. The Iowa election took on national significance, for Grimes, in soliciting German support, had judiciously concealed his original nativistic tendencies and had practically ignored the "dry" plank in the Whig platform. The fact that this successful strategy was emulated by the young Republican party is in itself sufficient evidence of the increasing importance accorded to the bulk of the German vote in localities where it had been organized.

In the Republican national convention and the Presidential campaign of 1856 it became evident that the organizational activity of the Forty-eighters and their friends was recognized and that it was to bear fruit. Hecker, Muench, and Froebel appeared on a platform, and Hecker was a candidate with Abraham Lincoln on the Republican electoral ticket in Illinois. Charles Ruemelin's speech at the national convention in Philadelphia, arraigning Know-Nothingism as a "scheme of bigotry and a mischievous side-issue," was enthusiastically applauded and a plank against Know-Nothingism was inserted. The Republican party, to all appearances, had decided that it was worth while to please the Germans rather than the nativists and proceeded to purge itself of some initial nativistic and temperance tendencies, unmitigated iniquities in the eyes of the Germans.

Frémont, the Republican Presidential candidate, had his platform, together with the Constitution of the United States, printed in the German language. The returns of the election showed that Frémont carried the German sections of the Middle West; but it also revealed that there was no evidence yet of a stampede of the mass of the German voters to the Republican side and that the Democratic party still possessed a strong appeal for the Germans, especially in the North and in the South. To quote Andreas Dorpalen: "Probably no voter was harder to move than the German farmer."

Nevertheless, by 1856 the solid phalanx of Republican Forty-eighters looked upon the fruits of their labor with a great deal of satisfaction. They had contributed to the destruction of the German Democratic front and in doing so had dealt a telling blow to slavery. They could point out to their constituents that it was the "Black Republicans," not the "friendly Democrats," who championed foreign born citizens. Although they had channeled only a fraction of the "Grays" into the Republican current, this initial success and its recognition was a powerful stimulus to the Forty-eighter who had become politically Americanized by now. It was also salve to the injured ego of the German immigrants in general.

Political leaders of both parties began to reckon with the potentialities of the German vote. If the numerical strength of the German constituents seemed to justify the sacrifice, the issues of nativism and temperance were soft-pedaled on state platforms, and citizens of German descent were included on the state tick-

ets. In 1855, in Wisconsin for instance, a German was the
nominee for state treasurer on both tickets; and Karl Roeser, a
Forty-eighter, was defeated by his Democratic countryman
Charles Kuehn. Carl Schurz, still a few weeks short of naturalization, won the Republican nomination for lieutenant-governor in
1857, another effort to strengthen the party ticket and win the
German vote, according to A. M. Thompson. Senator Sam
Houston of Texas had Seward's anti-Nebraska speech translated
and distributed in western Texas, but his German supporters
abandoned him a year later on the basis of alleged nativistic
sympathies.

The contemporary press felt that the Germans were the back-
bone of the Republican party. To quote the Detroit *Free Press* of
April 17, 1859: "Nothing has been more evident for a long time
than the fact that the main dependence of the Black Republicans
in all the states where they have an existence is on the German
vote." The numerical strength of the Forty-eighter press with
Republican sympathies in itself was imposing. Some of the most
prominent editors were Brentano, Becker, Daenzer, Douai,
Guelich, Hassaurek, Heinzen, Hielscher, Hillgaertner, Kapp,
Kellner, Olshausen, Preetorius, Rapp, Raster, Roeser, Schneider, Stibolt, Vortriede, Weber, and Weydemeyer. In Chicago
alone more than thirty German periodicals were published between 1848 and 1871, and in 1873 nearly three hundred German
daily or weekly publications were scattered in twenty-eight states.

By 1859 it would appear that a feeling was prevalent among
the German voters that, due partly to their determined show of
strength, nativism was retreating. They enjoyed a feeling of
security and political equality in their powerful ally, the Republican party. However, Know-Nothingism still held considerable
power in a number of Eastern states, sometimes as a sort of
"loyal" opposition within the Republican party. As late as
April, 1859, Senator Henry Wilson of Massachusetts requested
Carl Schurz to aid him in his fight against the Know-Nothing
movement, at which occasion Schurz delivered one of his most
famous speeches, "True Americanism."

The German feeling of security among the Republicans was

to experience a severe shock within the same year. In the state of Massachusetts, Republican leaders proposed and the voters ratified the "Two-Year Amendment" to the state constitution, adding a two-year period of probation to the five years required for original naturalization, during which a naturalized citizen could not vote nor hold office. This nativistic amendment was, in the opinion of contemporary political observers, a preelection Democratic maneuver to discredit the Republicans. Herriott quotes Clark Dunham in the Burlington, Iowa, *Hawkeye* of May 17, 1859:

The truth is that three-fourths of the Democrats stayed at home for the express purpose of letting it pass and a large majority of those who did go to the polls voted for it in order to throw the odium of the measure upon the Republicans.

If it was a political maneuver it came close to being a successful one. The more radical German Republicans reacted violently. According to Gustav Koerner's *Memoirs*, a number of German societies in Cincinnati under the leadership of August Willich, military commander in the Baden Revolution, editor of the Cincinnati *Republican* and later a general in the Union Army, passed a resolution "requesting some so-called prominent Germans [Stallo, Schurz, Hecker, Douai, Nicholas J. Rusch, Fritz Anneke, Kapp and Koerner] to issue a manifesto declaring the principles of the German Republicans, and protesting particularly against discrimination between native and naturalized citizens." It was Willich's idea to appeal to Republicans as well as Democrats to desert their parties and to form a new party on the basis of "general humanity, social reform and political morality," in short, secession from the Republican party. The level-headed "prominent Germans" were, however, rather cool toward the proposal, and it never materialized.

Heinzen's *Pionier* in Boston came forth with a similar remedy for "Republican Know-Nothingism." In response to protests coming from German organizations in a score of cities, Heinzen called a meeting in the Boston *Turnhalle* and was elected president of the assembly. Ignoring the advice of an Irish Democratic speaker to shift their allegiance to the Democrats, the assembled

Germans adopted Douai's resolutions which called for repudiation of the Republican party and the formation of an independent organization which "does not measure civil rights by place of birth, or human rights by color of skin." Heinzen was all in favor of calling a national convention to launch a new party under German leadership. This plan, according to Wittke, found some support among German newspapers, but the great majority of them were opposed to it, as well as Hecker, Koerner, Willich, Stallo and others. It was Schurz, the youngest of them all, who tamed the old firebrand. Wittke writes:

Schurz, with whom he had discussed the problem in Boston, wrote from Milwaukee, on May 18, 1859, fixing the entire blame for the amendment on Governor Banks. He urged the Germans to take revenge on him but argued strongly against any scheme to organize his fellow-countrymen into a separate party group. . . . Strangely enough it had its intended effect. Heinzen agreed to await developments.

German sentiment began to go against the Republican party in Iowa, a state which it had controlled since 1854, although by a narrow margin. Karl Rotteck, editor of the Muscatine, Iowa, *Zeitung*, declared that his faith in the party had been shattered and that he and his paper would be Democratic henceforth. A group of forty German leaders in Iowa addressed a circular letter to the Congressional delegation of their state requesting definite statements of 1) their views on existing naturalization laws, 2) their interpretation of the basic Republican attitude towards adopted citizens, and 3) their approval or disapproval "of the late action of the Republicans in the Massachusetts legislature." Senator Grimes of Iowa as well as Governor Chase of Ohio replied to the letter expressing themselves unequivocally in favor of equal rights for naturalized citizens.

Nicolas J. Rusch, who became lieutenant-governor of Iowa the next year, wrote in a letter to Samuel J. Kirkwood, who was elected governor on the same ticket:

I have said before that my own confidence in our party in this respect, especially in the Northwestern States, stands firm, it is deeply to be regretted that the question is earnestly agitated in the entire Republican press in the Union, whether it might be a safe policy for us to help the

Republican party to success and to the possession of the power to trample us down. . . . The Germans are anxious to bury the tomahawk, which you may judge from the fact that more than eight-hundred of them in Scott County voted for W. Vandever, notwithstanding that it was generally known and strongly used by the other side to irritate their prejudice, that he formerly did belong to the Know-Nothing Party.

Judge W. W. Hamilton, of Dubuque, Iowa, wrote to Kirkwood on May 19, 1859:

To naturalize a man and disrate him for two years, for *two* years afterwards, won't do in the free West, in the Great West. The emigrant here does not stand in the same footing with one in Massachusetts. Here, all God's earth lies unappropriated before him, just as it did in New England before the Pilgrim Fathers, who were equally emigrants. More than one half of our population, in this country, are foreign born. . . . To keep these with us is a point of utmost nicety, and even a slight mistake on this point will give the north to the Democrats this fall, and probably the State.

Of the many declarations and open letters published in the Republican press by Republican leaders condemning the Massachusetts incident, Abraham Lincoln's letter of May 17, 1859, to Dr. Theodor Canisius, editor of the Springfield *Illinois Staatsanzeiger*, did more than anything else to ease the tension among Germans. It was reprinted far and wide in both the English and the German press:

Dear Sir:
   Your note asking, in behalf of yourself and other German citizens, whether I am for or against the constitutional provision in regard to naturalized citizens, lately adopted by Massachusetts, and whether I am for or against a fusion of the Republicans and other opposition elements, for the canvass of 1860, is received.
   Massachusetts is a sovereign and independent state; and it is no privilege of mine to scold her for what she does. Still, if from what she has done an inference is sought to be drawn as to what I would do, I may without impropriety speak out. I say, then, that as I understood the Massachusetts provision, I am against its adoption in Illinois, or in any other place, where I have a right to oppose it. Understanding the spirit of our institutions to aim at the *elevation* of men, I am opposed to whatever tends to *degrade* them. I have some little notoriety for commiserating the oppressed condition of the Negro; and I should be

strangely inconsistent if I should favor any project for curtailing the existing rights of *white men*, even though born in different lands and speaking different languages from myself. . . .

I have written this hastily, but I believe it answers your questions substantially.

Yours truly,

A. Lincoln

Herriott says of this letter: "Its clarity, its force, its courteous consideration for all concerned, its adroitness and tact, its insight and foresight in contrast with sundry other letters written and proclaimed by his confreres in politics in Illinois at the time compel the admiration of the most critical."

The Republican party in most of the Midwestern states with a heavy German population countered the effects of the Democratic maneuver by special declarations against the amendment and by the nomination of German-born candidates on their state tickets. Hawgood's *Tragedy of German-America* lists the reasons why the German Republicans did not secede from the party and summarizes succinctly the views held by such farsighted and cool leaders as Koerner and Schurz.

First of all, they knew that some Republicans, like Lincoln and Seward, disapproved of the amendment and had never possessed any nativist leanings; next, they had acquired enough influence in the Republican party to feel themselves equal to crushing out this heresy from within —a political confidence that was new to the Germans in America— and finally, there was no possible alternative to the Republican party, for they had burned their Democratic boats, and they were not prepared and too wise to attempt to form a national party solely of Germans and other immigrants.

The large-scale desertion from the Republican party had been averted by the cooler heads among the German leaders. Schurz and most of the more experienced German Republicans were fully aware of the fact that whatever gains the citizens of German descent had made in terms of political equality and recognition, had been made as party members, as Republicans, and not as independents or as Germans. It was for this reason that Schurz and Koerner viewed with rather mixed feeling the so-called "Meeting at the *Deutsches Haus*" in Chicago. This meeting was called by the German Republican Central Committee of New York for May 14–15, 1860, a few days before the Republican national convention in Chicago. The purpose of the preconvention caucus was to formulate resolutions to be presented to the national convention. All states with an organized German Republican party were to be represented by three delegates, and Herriott's enumeration of those who answered the call reads like a "Who's Who" of the Forty-eighters and of prominent German Republicans in general.

Schurz and Koerner, both present at the meeting, completely ignore the German preconvention caucus at the *Deutsches Haus* in their memoirs. Both of them were fully aware that such an open show of German solidarity and political strength might not only be viewed with disapproval by the country at large, but might become the signal for a renewed outburst of nativism on the convention floor. But the wisdom and restraint exhibited by this group of German Republicans made such fears superfluous.

The delegates at the *Deutsches Haus*, after violent debates, agreed to submit to the national convention five resolutions as representative of the "sentiment of the majority of German Republican voters."

1. Adherence to the principles of the Republican Philadelphia platform of 1856, "applied in a sense most hostile to slavery";

2. Full and effective protection at home and abroad of the rights of all citizens, adherence to the old naturalization laws, and condemnation of the so-called "Massachusetts Amendment";

3. Immediate passage by Congress of a liberal homestead law, by which the public lands of the Union may be secured for homesteads of the people and from the greed of speculators;

4. Admission of the Territory of Kansas as a sovereign state and without slavery.

5. The pledge to "support any aspirant for the presidency and vice-presidency who stands on this platform and has never opposed the Republican platform of 1856, nor has ever been identified with the spirit of the Massachusetts Amendment."

The "pledge," based strictly on principle alone without endorsing any particular candidate, following the policy initiated by the Davenport Republican Club in their March 7 resolution, gave proof of the good political sense and wisdom of these men. Specific endorsement of a candidate in the form of a German ultimatum would undoubtedly have been promptly rejected by the convention and was, in fact, impossible, because there was no unanimity in this respect among the German delegates. Most of them favored Seward, and the German preconvention meeting was even regarded in some quarters as a pro-Seward gesture. Herriott writes in summing up the importance of the meeting:

the shrewdest of counsels controlled the leaders in refraining from saying anything about this or that candidate and especially in refraining from endorsing any one or disapproving of this one or that—save as they might be affected by the discriminating terms of the resolutions. The friends of all candidates would perforce be constrained to regard the resolutions with favor and to vote for them—just to secure what votes the Germans might command for their candidate, so far as such action might attract their favor. It put a stop to the Seward talk that the Conference would declare for him. This restraint enhanced the political potency of the resolutions many fold.

A few days later the Republican national convention, where Koerner, Schurz, Hassaurek, and Arnold Krekel functioned as state delegates, treated the German resolutions with considerable respect, for as noted by Herriott, the Germans in 1860 held the balance of power in the states of Missouri, Iowa, Minnesota, Illinois, Wisconsin, Indiana, Ohio, Michigan, Maryland, Pennsylvania, New York, New Jersey, and Connecticut. Broad as this statement may appear, there seems to be some truth in it, for the Democratic *Free Press* of Detroit stated on May 9, 1860: "Since they hold the controlling power in the Black Republican Party they consider it no more than right that the party should yield to their preferences."

Carl Schurz, as member of the platform committee, secured the embodiment of the second and third resolutions, commonly known as "Dutch planks," in the Republican platform of 1860. There was, however, an attempt in the nativistic camp to counter this move by German Republicans. Andrew G. Curtin, candidate for governor of Pennsylvania, and Henry S. Lane, candidate for both the governorship and Senatorship of Indiana,

appeared at the convention and let it be known to many delega-
tions that an enemy of the Know-Nothings could not carry
either one of these states.

In the grand strategy of the Republican party it would seem
that two facts were weighed against each other—the importance
of the German vote against the equal importance of the nativistic
vote. The adoption of the antinativistic "Dutch plank" left no
doubt as to which side, in the opinion of the party leaders, carried the most weight. That Abraham Lincoln, in 1859, had
already clearly discerned these facts and with extraordinary
foresight and political prudence had reached a definite conclusion is apparent not only in his stand against nativism as outlined
in the letter to Canisius, but also in a second, less well-known
political transaction. This was Lincoln's secret purchase on May
30, 1859, of the Canisius printing establishment, the *Illinois
Staatsanzeiger* in Springfield. To quote Carl Sandburg:

Lincoln was past fifty years of age, a seasoned and hardened player
in the great American game of politics, the national sport of watching
candidates and betting on who would win or arguing as to which was
right or wrong. Without the cunning of a fox, without a wilderness
sagacity, without natural instincts such as those guiding wild geese on
thousand-mile flights he would have gone down and under in stalking
a presidential election.

Outside himself or Theodore Canisius, hardly anyone in Springfield
or Illinois knew that Lincoln was the owner of the German language
newspaper, the *Illinois Staatsanzeiger*. Canisius, the editor, had run into
debt, and his landlord, John Burckhardt, took over the newspaper
property and sold it to Lincoln through Canisius for $400.

Lincoln drew up a contract which he and Canisius signed. The type,
the press, and other equipment were declared the property of Lincoln,
the contract read, and Canisius was free to use the property to publish
a Republican newspaper in the German language with occasional
articles in English.

Any time the paper should fail to operate as a faithful Republican
mouthpiece and organ, Lincoln could take over his property and
Canisius would move out; thus the contract written on legal cap paper
dated May 30, 1859.

So it happened that while the leading German newspaper of Illinois,
the *Chicago Staats-Zeitung*, was for Seward for president, Lincoln was
the owner of a German newspaper downstate and could walk into its

office, ask for favors and get consideration. Furthermore, he had kept
a live political asset from falling into Democratic hands and served his
party to that extent in the close fighting for control of the Northwest.

In taking possession of a printing plant and newspaper he had been
"honest Abe" with a still tongue. Not even Herndon was told, nor
Swett, nor Whitney, nor Bunn the banker. Canisius, the editor, looked
like the proprietor of the *Illinois Staats-Anzeiger* and walked the streets
of Springfield as such. Lincoln had plenty else to do.

The resolutions stemming from the *Deutsches Haus* and, especially, the pledge to support any candidate who had never been
identified with nativism was again to play a role in the actual
nomination of the Republican Presidential candidate. To quote
Hawgood:

The German preference actually boiled down to support of Lincoln's
nomination, for though they would have accepted such a candidate as
Seward or Chase, neither of these had enough following in the convention (or they both had too many enemies) to secure election. Lincoln's
strongest opponents were Banks and Bates, the latter being particularly strong. But, it has been argued [by Herriott], "The last resolution
or pledge, effectually ruined the chances" of both. In the face of that
pronouncement from the "Deutsches Haus," neither had a ghost of a
chance. The nomination of either would have driven the Germans into
a third party, or into their old Democratic circles again, or they would
have stayed away from the polls and the Democratic party would have
had a more than fighting chance for re-entering the White House.

It has been hotly argued, and equally hotly denied, that Lincoln owed his nomination in 1860 to consideration given by
Republican leaders to the German vote. If the premise that the
Germans held the balance of power in a number of key states is
acceptable, if preconvention resolutions were evaluated on this
basis, and if, as Herriott propounds, "the question of the status
of the foreign-born naturalized citizen and not slavery was the
major cause of dissention in the National Republican Convention," then it may be said that German preferences, by a process
of elimination, helped to lay the groundwork for Lincoln's
nomination.

Not long after the sensational campaign of 1860 during which
the Germans revealed their potency as a national political force,
the legend began to grow that Lincoln would not have been

elected if he had not had the wholehearted support of the leaders among the Forty-eighters. It has been inferred that the Forty-eighters herded the German vote into the Republican fold, that it would otherwise have gone to other factions who presented candidates in the 1860 election, and that this vote was the decisive factor. Although Schurz denied categorically the allegation that he was responsible for Lincoln's election, the legend has been repeated time and again. German audiences were informed by such books as Julius Goebel's *Das Deutschthum in den Vereinigten Staaten von Nord-Amerika* (1904) that "It is no exaggeration to say that Abraham Lincoln would not have been elected president without the support of the Forty-eighters and that slavery would not have been abolished at that time." The late William E. Dodd's frequently cited essay on "The Fight for the Northwest, 1860" states flatly that Indiana, Illinois, and Iowa "would have given their electoral votes to Douglas but for the loyal support of the Germans and other foreign citizens led by Carl Schurz, Gustave Koerner, and the editors of the *Staatszeitung* of Chicago."

Certainly the Forty-eighters had fought and bled for their political ideas during the Buchanan administration, and they had much at stake in the election of 1860. "Dutch planks" for a homestead law and for equal rights for foreign-born citizens had been firmly nailed into the Republican party's platform; and nominee Abraham Lincoln was squarely opposed to slavery and legislation of the Massachusetts Amendment variety. There was no special loyalty to the man Lincoln, for prior to Chicago the Germans had been for Seward (although even more *against* Bates), and in 1864 they would flee from the regular Republican camp in droves. Neither was there any party loyalty (never a Forty-eighter virtue—or vice, whatever it may be), for a few months of Grant would send them packing off to the Liberal Republicans and even to the Democrats.

Just how much effect the Forty-eighters had on the German vote and, in turn, how much effect the German vote had on the election is a moot point. Certainly the Forty-eighters never commanded the whole German vote. The Catholics would hardly have been willing to vote Republican merely at the insistence of such an "anti-Christ" as Schurz, and the "Grays" were never thoroughly reconciled to the leadership of the Forty-eighters. There is no objective measuring stick to determine exactly how many Germans turned Republican and how many of those who actually did were motivated specifically by the leadership of men such as Schurz, Kapp, Solger, Koerner, and other leaders or rather by the mere presence of the "Dutch planks" (the work of the Forty-eighters, whether the multitude admitted it or not). For this reason an attempt has been made to evaluate the exact weight of the German vote in selected localities.

The first study along this line was an essay by the late Joseph Schafer entitled "Who Elected Lincoln?" and published in the *American Historical Review* in 1941. By the analysis of a presumably reliable sample of the Wisconsin vote, Schafer found that most Germans (probably predominantly Catholic) and the Irish stuck by Douglas and the Democrats, the party that had always been kindly disposed to the immigrant. Although some Germans (undoubtedly Forty-eighters and possibly some liberal Lutherans) supported the Republicans, just as they had done in 1856, that portion of the vote was rather negligible. Revolutionary *émigrés* apparently were unable to impress the conservative and Catholic Germans. Schafer concludes that the tight little nucleus of Forty-eighters helped save enough Wisconsin German votes for Lincoln to give him a clear majority, but that "Lincoln would have won in Wisconsin if all German votes had been given to Douglas, as doubtless five-sixths of them were."

In 1942 J. Monaghan published a similar study, "Did Abraham Lincoln Receive the Illinois German Vote?" in the *Journal of the Illinois State Historical Society*. He points out that it was easy enough for historians to have been misled by the boundless enthusiasm of German liberals for Lincoln and the Republican cause and that Democratic vituperation of the "lop-eared Dutch" had no small part in strengthening the assumption that German sympathies were with the Republicans. But Lincoln considered the German vote sufficiently important to invest in a newspaper which might sway them; and any doubts cast upon the importance of the German vote in 1860 would also involve a reevaluation of Lincoln's political acumen. Furthermore, the Illinois Germans were largely urban, organized into unions, *Turnvereine*, and so on, in contrast with the rural and unorganized Wisconsin Germans outside of Milwaukee. Monaghan concludes, "There is no warrant for a serious revision of the accepted interpretation of the importance of the Illinois German vote in the election of 1860."

In 1947 the Minnesota situation was reviewed by Hildegard Binder Johnson in *Minnesota History* with an essay entitled "The Election of 1860 and the Germans in Minnesota." Minnesota, by the way, had the most liberal laws of any state in the Union for the enfranchisement of immigrants: the newcomers could vote within four months after applying for citizenship. Since every seventh potential voter in Minnesota was a German, the English-language press and the politicians of both parties tried to secure the German vote for their candidates. Both parties had Germans on their state tickets, and the best German orators from Wisconsin (Carl Schurz, Republican, and Emil Rothe, Democrat, also a Forty-eighter) were sent to attempt to persuade the Germans of Minnesota to follow their political leadership. Mrs. Johnson concluded that it is questionable whether the Germans in Minnesota contributed a very significant absolute number of votes for Lincoln but that they did contribute their share to the Republican victory of 1860 as indicated by a sample from a region in which Germans constituted more than half the population.

On the other hand, in the Southwest neither Lincoln nor Douglas were acceptable, if the situation in New Braunfels, Texas, may be considered as typical. Rudolph L. Biesele found that in this community of 3,000 Germans and less than twenty Anglo-Americans, neither Douglas nor Lincoln received a single vote. Andreas Dorpalen's review of "The German Element and the Issues of the Civil War" published in the *Mississippi Valley Historical Review* in 1942 concludes that the Germans did no more to assure the victory of Lincoln than did their Anglo-American neighbors, either in any particular section or in the nation as a whole. He does suspect that the influence of the Forty-eighters in the election has been rather frequently overestimated, pointing out the snobbish attitude of many Forty-eighters and their refusal to fraternize even with the politicians of their own nationality. No study has been made of the Ohio situation; and while Hassaurek helped bully the Wigwam delegates into accepting the "Dutch planks" with the threat of taking 20,000 Ohio German votes to the enemy camp, no one really knows whether his influence was actually that strong. Certainly he had many enemies among the "Grays," who could hardly forget the anti-clericalism and socialism of the *Hochwaechter*.

Lincoln certainly appreciated the services of the Forty-eighters and saw to it that they were appropriately rewarded. On June 18. 1860. he wrote Schurz that "to the extent of our limited acquaintance, no man stands nearer my heart than yourself," and shortly afterward appointed him as minister to Spain. There were those who were alarmed by Lincoln's appointment of an ex-revolutionary to conservative Spain. However, Lincoln did not hesitate to send back the rebels to the very countries that represented the reaction against which they had rebelled in 1848. To be sure, Gustav Struve was not accepted as consul to the Thuringian States because of his record in 1848, but no other difficulties seem to have arisen on this score. Canisius was appointed consul to Vienna and in 1862 embarrassed the government by indiscreet actions in the negotiations of the State Department with Garibaldi, which had for their purpose the appointment of the Italian hero as commander of a Northern Army; later Canisius held consular posts at Bristol, England, and the Samoan Islands.

On the whole, Lincoln's appointments of Forty-eighters to diplomatic and consular posts seem to have been wisely conceived, and his policy was imitated by subsequent administrations. Georg Schneider did yeoman service in spreading Northern propaganda in Scandinavia while he was consul in Elsinore, but he was recalled by the administration before the war was over in the vain hope that he could bring the pro-Frémont *Staatszeitung* back into line. Koerner left a creditable, if less colorful record as Schurz's successor in Madrid. His assignments to head off European recognition of the Confederacy and to cultivate the traditionally friendly relations with Spain were well performed. The record speaks for the former, and the sympathetic interpretation of Spain in his *Aus Spanien* is evidence enough of the latter. Friedrich Hassaurek occupied the "highest" post any government can grant, at Quito, as minister to Ecuador. Although he left this job to come home to campaign for Lincoln's reelection and to secure exchange of a half brother who was held by the Confederates in Libby Prison, he did accomplish valuable services in settling indemnity claims of Ecuador against the Northern government. Like Koerner, he did his best to understand the people to whom he was assigned, and he recorded his experiences in the book, *Four Years among Spanish Americans*. Heinrich Boernstein and Carl Bernays were appointed consuls in Bremen and Zurich respectively.

Other Forty-eighters also received their rewards in executive departments. John Albion Andrew, war governor of Massachusetts, said of Reinhold Solger that he had done as much to secure the support of Eastern Germans for Lincoln as Schurz had done in the West; but this may possibly be discounted somewhat inasmuch as it was in a letter urging the appointment of Julius Solger, age fourteen, to a pageship in the United States Senate. At all events, Lincoln appreciated Solger's services to the extent of having the special office of assistant register of the Treasury created for Solger to occupy until the position of register fell vacant. Carl Roeser, editor of the *Demokrat* of Manitowoc, Wisconsin, and a bulwark of Republicanism since the middle fifties, also received a Treasury post.

It must be something of a tribute to the value of the Forty-eighters as diplomatic and consular agents under Lincoln that subsequent administrations saw fit to reward them in the same manner. Jakob Mueller, elected lieutenant-governor of Ohio as a Republican in 1860, later turned Democrat and was sent to Frankfurt as consul. Grover Cleveland appointed Edmund Juessen, not a Forty-eighter proper but a liberal sympathizer and a brother-in-law of Carl Schurz, as consul in Vienna. Dr. Her-

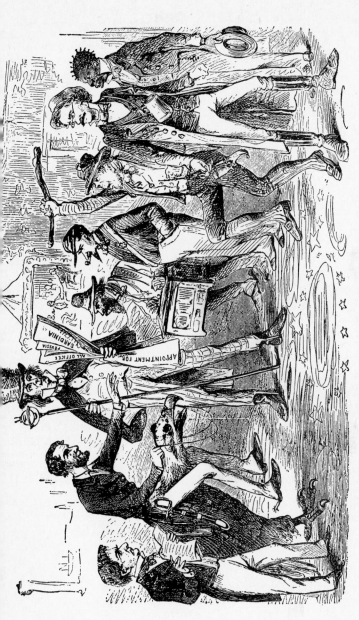

LINCOLN'S POLITICAL INDEBTEDNESS TO CARL SCHURZ

From the *Budget of Fun*, New York, as reproduced in Albert Shaw,
Abraham Lincoln, The Review of Reviews Corporation, 1929

At the left is Senator Seward. At Lincoln's left are Uncle Sam and a group of "adopted fellow-citizens." Carl Schurz, with stein and pipe, is second from the right. Lincoln is saying: "My dear friends, I cannot express to you in words how deeply I am obliged to you for your generous votes. They have made me what I am. Without you I should have remained what I was—nothing. My emotions overpower me, as you can easily perceive. Be assured that I will do for you whatever *lies in my power!*"

mann Kiefer served as President Arthur's consul in Stettin. General Peter Joseph Osterhaus was appointed consul in Lyons in 1866 and in Mannheim in 1898.

Numerous Forty-eighters and other Germans allied with them were rewarded after 1860 with state offices. It is safe to speculate that they would literally have swarmed through Washington and the state capitols had they not answered the Northern call to arms when the War between the States broke out. Their records as officers and enlisted men are treated elsewhere in this book. Suffice it to say of their value as public servants, in not one instance was a Forty-eighter ever known to be guilty of corruption or malfeasance in office, something that can be said of few comparable groups of Anglo-Americans who held office, civil or military, state or federal, in the same period.

The Forty-eighters supported the Northern side almost to a man during the War. Fifty-six-year-old Gustav Struve, aging Friedrich Hecker, and Peter Joseph Osterhaus enlisted in the ranks and left with commissions. In the spring of 1862 Carl Schurz resigned his diplomatic post in Madrid to enter the army. He was impatient to come home in order to persuade Lincoln that the fight against slavery should be made a clear-cut issue. On this side, a large proportion of Germans, radicals as well as moderates, were unhappy about Lincoln's delaying tactics in the progress to emancipation. Impetuous and even insubordinate officers such as Frémont issued emancipation proclamations without governmental authority and embarrassed the administration but received the applause of Heinzen and the rest of the extremists. Schurz, diplomat, master of the "art of the possible," and, above all, statesman, actually accomplished far more than the firebrands in the smoke-filled rooms of freethinking clubs ever could have done. He helped convince Congress of the incompatibility of slavery and democracy, headed off the progress of Confederate agents in Europe, and helped Lincoln through a difficult situation. But Heinzen, always finding the world out of step with himself, remarked that Carl Schurz knew as much about military affairs as Lincoln knew about Hegelianism.

Few of the Forty-eighters were nearly so mindful of the enormous political problems in the way of emancipation, and many
of the radicals criticized Lincoln severely. One of the most outspoken critics of the President was Caspar Butz of Chicago, and
his attacks on the administration are symptomatic of what must
have been going on in the minds of others who were later to
support Frémont for the Presidency. Encouraged by Frémont's
unauthorized emancipation of the slaves of Confederate planters
in Missouri on August 31, 1861, Butz appeared on November
10, 1861, before a German mass meeting in North Market Hall,
Chicago, viciously attacked Lincoln, and proposed Frémont as
a Presidential candidate in 1864. For the next three years, Butz
laid the groundwork for his subsequent campaign, and in 1864
he began to publish the *Deutsch-Amerikanische Monatshefte fuer
Politik, Wissenschaft und Literatur*, a journal somewhat of the type
of the *Atlantic Monthly*. It boasted of such outstanding contributors as Karl Blind of London, Douai, Muench, Olshausen,
Preetorius, Solger, and Bayard Taylor. The very first issue revealed clearly that the basic purpose of the journal was to engineer the nomination of Frémont instead of Lincoln. The *Monatshefte* was circulated to over three thousand subscribers and reflects very clearly the rise and fall of the Frémont campaign. It
survived the elections of 1864, but in 1867 it went the way of all
political ephemera.

Meanwhile Heinzen, assiduously promoting *teutscher Radikal-
ismus* as usual, had not been idle. In the fall of 1863 he managed
to bring together in Cleveland the representatives of a number
of radical, freethinking German clubs whose political sentiments
were anti-Lincoln and pro-Frémont. Many of the best elements
refused to participate, and the rolls of the convention were conspicuous for the absence of such names as Schurz, Koerner,
Stallo, Hassaurek, and Solger. Similarly, the press of both languages gave little, if any, attention to the meeting. The program
reflected Heinzen's own notions on remodeling the entire Constitutional structure of the federal government.

In the spring of 1864 the activities of men like Butz in the
West and Heinzen in the East on behalf of Frémont began to

coincide. Both began to intensify editorial and forensic activity, both began to organize Frémont clubs in their respective areas, and both began to beat the drums for the Frémont convention scheduled for Cleveland at the end of May.

Frémont, aptly described by President Shuster as "a fearfully hard fanatic," stood on weak grounds. The anti-Lincoln elements were composed of all shades of political discontent, including everyone from Horace Greeley and Governor Andrew of Massachusetts, as secret supporters, to vituperative German radicals. One of the greatest political weaknesses of Frémont was that such a relatively large proportion of his supporters were Germans. In addition, it has been observed that after Salmon P. Chase withdrew his candidacy for the Presidency, he devoted himself to the promotion of a convention of radicals, Germans, and war Democrats at Cleveland and that he intended to use Frémont as a cat's paw much as Calhoun had used John Tyler in a side convention in 1844 to force the Democrats to scuttle Van Buren. Many of the Germans were rather overconfident in the belief that they could have "the decisive word at the next election," as Butz stated in the *Monatshefte* for January, 1864.

A gathering of German radicals was called in advance of the Cleveland convention. On May 29, Germans representing ten states and the District of Columbia and twenty-two clubs assembled and adopted resolutions that called for a new party, repudiated all compromise with Lincoln Republicans, and reaffirmed action taken in the meeting of the previous autumn. The document was printed in English with the endorsement of Frémont himself and distributed to all delegates at the convention. Heinzen's reward was election to membership on the executive committee and (together with five other Germans) on the platform committee of fourteen.

The 400-odd delegates at the convention proper were mainly from the Midwest, with a good representation from Pennsylvania. Although Germans held many key committee appointments, officers were Anglo-Americans. The platform demanded, of course, prohibition of slavery through the Constitution, popular election of the President (and for a single term only), Con-

gressional reconstruction, reaffirmation of civil rights and the
Monroe Doctrine, and confiscation of the property of adherents
of the Confederacy with redistribution to Northern soldiers regardless of race. Frémont, of course, was nominated for President.
Just as they had preceded the convention with a private
caucus of their own, the German delegates met in rump session
and approved the acts of the convention proper.

Despite the weakness of the Frémont movement, there were
some doubts in the air as to Lincoln's ability to win the election.
Greeley's New York *Tribune* published a statement to this effect
on August 5, 1864, by Senators Wade and Davis (Republicans),
but the country waited for the results of the Democratic convention scheduled for Chicago on September 1. In the hope that
the Democrats would make Frémont their choice, Butz wrote
an article entitled "The Wade-Davis Protest, a Last Appeal to
the Democratic Party," which was subsequently translated into
English and distributed widely in pamphlet form—even personally to the delegates at the Democratic Convention! Lincoln's accomplishments and ability were deprecated, and it was
stated that Frémont alone could bring 400,000 German votes to
the Democratic Party. But the Democrats nominated General
McClellan. On September 22, Frémont withdrew his candidacy
rather awkwardly as the result of a deal whereby Lincoln immediately dismissed the ultraconservative Montgomery Blair
from his Cabinet. German Frémont clubs became Lincoln clubs
overnight. Butz reluctantly announced in October that he would
support Lincoln under protest. Chase and Wade joined Schurz
and Koerner to campaign for Lincoln, and Republican victory
was assured. It has been stated that many Germans stayed away
from the polls, but, in the absence of definite evidence, it may
be surmised that the majority probably voted against the Democrats rather than for the Republicans.

The assassination of Lincoln opened a new chapter in the political history of the Forty-eighters. President Johnson's many
weaknesses and his unexpected conciliatory attitude toward the
South displeased the Forty-eighters as much as the radical Re-

publicans in Congress. The views on the South in Carl Schurz's famous report (Senate Document 2, 39th Congress, 1st Session) are typical of other opinions expressed in the German-language press during the period immediately after Appomattox. But the Forty-eighters, liberals to the core, shifted to a more conciliatory position toward the South at the end of the decade when the passions of the War had died and they saw that the South was neither prospering nor improving on acts of reprisal by the North. At the Republican convention of 1868, of which Schurz was the keynoter, a resolution was inserted in the party platform calling for the removal of disqualifications imposed on the "proud traitors." By 1870 Schurz had reversed himself to the extent of making a speech in the Senate on January 14 of that year urging the restoration of civil rights to former Confederates. Before Bernhard Domschcke died in 1869, he had advocated a pardon for President Jefferson Davis in the columns of the Milwaukee *Herold* of which he was then the editor. Hassaurek, radical of radicals in earlier days, now softened and cried out against the injustice of the Republican program for reconstruction. Only a *teutscher* radical such as Heinzen could continue to kick the prostrate South in the seventies. But the South never buried the hatchet.

In 1868 there was general satisfaction among the Germans with the nomination of Grant, for they knew not what manner of man he would turn out to be after he assumed office. But there was hardly even a honeymoon for U. S. Grant in the White House and Carl Schurz on Capitol Hill. The story of Schurz's alliance with Charles Sumner to fight the corruption of the Grant administration is now a classic: the condemnation of the move to annex the Dominican Republic, the battle for civil service reform and the ending of the spoils system, the consistent advocacy of sound monetary policy to protect the forgotten man of the sixties and seventies (and later), the condemnation of the War Department's sale of arms to France in 1871. Schurz was only the leader of the anti-Grant forces, for other Germans, led by the Forty-eighters in their last grand political gesture as a group, rallied to the fight against the party they had once helped to power.

The new movement, soon to become known as Liberal Republicanism, attracted the best elements among the German Americans. Unlike the Frémont movement in 1864, the anti-Grant forces included conservatives and radicals, natives and foreign-born in proportional quantities. Only Heinzen refused to participate, and he again plugged for "abolition of the monarchial office," although it has been observed that he actually hoped for Grant's reelection so that the Presidency could be discredited once and for all! As early as 1870 Preetorius and the *Westliche Post* had supported the Liberal Republicans in Missouri, and in 1872 this paper came out for a national Liberal Republican drive to defeat Grant. In Chicago, Caspar Butz joined in the chorus of opposition to Grant and found himself for the first time in a dozen years on the same side of the political fence with such moderates as Koerner. In the southern Illinois-Missouri area Hecker saw the chance for one more battle. In Cincinnati, Hassaurek, now editor and part owner of the *Taegliche Cincinnatier Volksblatt*, vigorously opposed all aspects of paternalism and held that the one function of government was the protection of private rights, views that led him into direct conflict with the pro-Grant groups. Cincinnati was indeed the focal point of Liberal Republicanism as far as the Germans were concerned, and the most interesting smoke-filled rooms at the convention were in the residence of Judge Stallo.

Schurz, organizer and acknowledged leader of the movement, was elected permanent president of the 1872 Liberal Republican convention in Cincinnati where the new party was formally organized. Schurz's personal choice as well as that of most of the other Forty-eighters was Charles Francis Adams, a man who even in defeat could have established the prestige of the new party and enabled it to do some lasting good. "Under the influence of some manipulation and a wave of curious enthusiasm" (James Ford Rhodes), Horace Greeley was nominated. The Germans were shocked. Butz and Hecker stalked out of the convention hall without taking formal leave; and the latter even spoke

UNITED STATES SENATE THEATRE; CARL SCHURZ AS IAGO

From *Harper's Weekly*, March 30, 1872

Harper's Weekly favored Grant; its cartoonist, Thomas Nast, here portrayed Schurz as the leader of the opposition to Grant's renomination in 1872. The others are from left to right, Charles Sumner, Francis Blair, Thomas W. Tipton, Lyman Trumbull, Reuben E. Fenton, and Horace Greeley

against Greeley in the ensuing campaign, although he did support the Illinois state Liberal Republican ticket headed by Koerner for governor and Rummell for secretary of state. Koerner reluctantly lent his support to the national ticket. Greeley was endorsed halfheartedly by the Democrats in Philadelphia in July, although many members of that party subsequently bolted. The low tariff element represented by the *Nation* was alienated; and old Forty-eighters such as Preetorius, who realized that protectionism was a major issue, could display little enthusiasm for Greeley, although the *Westliche Post* supported him after a fashion. Oswald Ottendorfer, although a successful candidate for alderman on the New York City Liberal Republican ticket in 1872, would have nothing to do with Greeley as a candidate for the Presidency.

Schurz was in a quandary, and, after some soul-searching and a rather strange correspondence with the candidate his new party had selected, decided to support Greeley. Greeley's uncertainty as to the true nature of the Germans' dislike for him is reflected in a letter to Schurz dated May 8, 1872: "Of course, the most of the Germans dislike me, not so much that I am a Protectionist as that I am a Total Abstinence man. They will not vote for me so generally as they would have voted for Adams or Trumbull." Perhaps many a head of "voting cattle" would go against Greeley as a prohibitionist, but Greeley would have done well to have reread Forty-eighter editorials from the antebellum period. For example, he might have pulled from his shelf a back file of Christian Esselen's *Atlantis* (I,194) and checked on the true attitude of the Forty-eighter, no less firm in his opposition to protectionism than he was to slavery:

We agree perfectly with the *New York Abendzeitung* and the *Illinois Staats-Zeitung* in this, that where no other way can be found we ought to lay principal stress on the slavery question in state and congressional, but on the temperance question in municipal elections. To those who would fain draw us into the ranks of the pro-slavery party by showing us a beer mug, we will reply that we would rather submit to annoying measures than to betray the grand principles of liberty.

Now, since the Forty-eighters would not lead their compatriots to the polls to vote for Greeley on account of his notions on the tariff, Hermann Raster, editor of the *Staatszeitung* and partner of Boss Anton Caspar Hesing of Chicago, saw a golden opportunity to force temperance as a national issue upon the Republican Party. In 1872 Illinois had antagonized her German citizens by passing a "Personal Liability Law" (temperance legislation). Raster had little difficulty persuading the state Republican convention in Springfield in 1872 to insert the famous "Raster plank" in its platform, denouncing categorically "all unconstitutional legislation for the cure of any of the disorders of society, whether irreligion, intemperance, or any other evil."Encouraged by his success in Springfield, Raster leveled his sights at the national convention; and, by threatening to lead the Germans over to Schurz and Greeley unless resolutions were adopted to confirm "the right to drink what one pleases" and "the right to look upon the day on which Christians hold their prayer meetings as on any other day," he committed the regular Republicans to the same planks he had put into the Springfield platform. As a result of the well-known "Raster Resolution of 1872" the Republican party was for years suspected by the Anti-Saloon League and the Women's Christian Temperance Union as being an enemy of the cause. Heinzen, by the way, would not recognize temperance as a legitimate political issue, and he condemned *Vereinsleben* and *Bierbaenkelei* as the lowest forms of Philistinism. Temperance for him was a matter for the Sunday Schools and the "snooper" press.

Whatever may have been the cause, there is little doubt but that the Germans contributed their share to the defeat of Greeley, although their vote would not have been enough to save him from his humiliating defeat had it gone to him 100 per cent. What is significant is that 1872 was the last date when the Forty-eighters saw a cause in which they could fight as a unit; and that cause ended in a fiasco of discord, leaving the "voting cattle" with no leadership other than the variety offered by a Forty-eighter who had gone against the very principles which Esselen and others had so ably propounded before the War. On one point the Forty-eighters were absolutely and almost unanimously loyal to their traditions in 1872: total disregard of party allegiance as a final determinative factor in deciding whom they should support politically.

Relatively few Forty-eighters returned to Europe, although hardly any had considered himself as a permanent resident upon first arriving, viewing America as a temporary haven until the next revolutionary outbreak. Prussia declared a general amnesty in 1862, and Struve took almost immediate advantage of it. Johannes Gambs, a leading *Turner* and a New York delegate to the *Deutsches Haus* conference, returned to Germany in 1862 to preserve his pension rights, but he always continued his battle against oppression and in behalf of liberty. Similarly, Carl Daenzer, once the associate editor of the *Anzeiger des Westens* and subsequently the founder of the *Westliche Post* (1857), retired from active politics soon after the outbreak of the War because of ill health and returned soon after amnesty was announced. Theodor Olshausen, militant editor of the Davenport *Demokrat* and subsequently associated editorially with the *Westliche Post*, left for Europe shortly after Appomattox. Friedrich Kapp was the so-called *Weltbuerger* among the Forty-eighters, winning a prominent place both in American and German politics; he served as a deputy in the *Reichstag* after naturalization as a Prussian in 1872. Kapp once wrote to his father that he had become involved in the slavery controversy "not because this question [slavery or freedom] is American, but because its answer has a great ethical significance for the entire civilized world." To the end he remained a fighter for freedom and against oppression which is shown, for example, by his publication after his return to Germany of a book on the sale of soldiers by the German princes during the eighteenth century—very unflattering to their contemporary descendants!

One of the Forty-eighters even turned reactionary. It is amazing that an old reformer like Raster should lead the mob crying for the blood of the anarchists after the Haymarket riots and oppose trade unions and the struggle for the eight-hour day. In all fairness to him, however, he must be given credit for fighting

for school reform before the Cook County Board of Education—
so successfully in fact that a schoolhouse was subsequently named
for him. But Raster's reactionary position is probably unique
among Forty-eighters, unless one would describe an approval of
the empire established by Bismarck in 1871 as reactionary. The
developments in the old fatherland placed former revolutionaries in a dilemma, for they had fought for freedom *and* unity.
When, therefore, the many principalities were replaced by a
united Germany, it meant that one of their aims had been realized. However, the means by which this had been accomplished
were roundly condemned by a number of Forty-eighters—
strikingly so by Friedrich Hecker in an eloquent speech at a
meeting in St. Louis called to celebrate the end of the Franco-
Prussian War in 1871. Heinzen of course never relented in his
feelings toward William I or Bismarck; he expressed his disgust
when he learned that Carl Schurz had in 1868 sat down with
the latter to a Havana and a bottle of Mosel. Schurz set the
pattern for the attitude toward Bismarck by expressing admiration for his frankness but maintaining certain reservations about
his other views. As early as 1866 Schurz had written, "Bismarck
can now be more useful to Germany than any other man if he
can only be forced into the right track." Reactions of other
moderate to conservative leaders such as Koerner and Claussen
were similar.

Schurz's attitude toward the sound money problem deserves
more extensive comment. Perhaps it harked back to the 1859
panic in Wisconsin when Schurz complained bitterly against the
wildcat banks of Wisconsin which were issuing worthless paper
notes by the ton. From the end of War on he fought the various
proposals to issue greenbacks as a remedy for recurring financial
crises. When greenbackism was proposed as a panacea for the
nation's economic ills in 1873, Schurz opposed further issues of
paper money. In 1875 the issue came to a head once more in the
Ohio gubernatorial campaign between Rutherford B. Hayes,
Republican, and William Allen, put forward by the Democrats,
together with the idea that "the volume of currency be made
and kept equal to the wants of trade." Schurz and John Sher-

man, later to serve as Secretary of the Treasury under Hayes from 1877 to 1881, stumped for Hayes and sound money in a campaign which even attracted Senator Oliver P. Morton. Hayes's victory in Ohio was his key to the Republican nomination the following year and ultimately to a Presidential term during which he and his two friends from the Ohio campaign of 1875 struck many a good blow for sound money and against the uncontrolled coinage of silver.

Schurz continued the fight for sound money long after he retired from public office in 1881. In 1896 he opposed William Jennings Bryan bitterly on the free silver issue (although he supported him just as strongly four years later as an anti-imperialist). In 1896 he spoke on the monetary issue before the American Honest Money League and the *Deutsch-Amerikanische Gutgeld-Liga* (of which he and Oswald Ottendorfer were honorary presidents). Schurz was so effective in the 1896 campaign that the Republican National Committee reprinted his principal speech and distributed 1,500,000 copies throughout the country.

Another Forty-eighter who adopted an aggressive attitude in favor of sound money was Raster. As editor of the *Staatszeitung* he served on the platform committees at the National Republican conventions in 1868 and 1872, and on the former occasion he was able to throw his weight against threatened resumption of greenbackism by forcing into the platform the plank denouncing "all forms of repudiation as a national crime."

In the issue of woman suffrage, the Forty-eighters performed yeoman service, even though their ideas did not come to fruition until the nineties and thereafter. The most vigorous of the Forty-eighters in this cause was Mathilde Franziska Anneke, wife of Captain Fritz Anneke (later colonel, United States Army). Even before her arrival in 1849 she had waged a good battle in Germany; and although Anglo-American feminist leaders had been active, she found a *tabula rasa* in this field as far as pre-1848 *Hausfrauen* in America were concerned. When she moved to Milwaukee in the early fifties, she began editing and publishing the militant *Deutsche Frauen-Zeitung* and soon won adherents for the emancipation of women in cultured circles of Milwaukee and

to political issues was equaled only by their tenacious devotion to the ideals of liberalism.

In recent years the statement has frequently been made that the Germans lack political ability, and this criticism can be supported by a great deal of evidence from German history, for example that of the Republic of 1919 to 1933. However, this charge cannot be made against the Forty-eighters. We have seen that they eagerly and astutely espoused the causes of liberty and of progress and that they placed principle above mere party loyalty. Particularly in the course of perhaps the most crucial Presidential nomination and election, that of Lincoln in 1860, they showed a political wisdom that made the weight of their influence count to the last ounce. Abraham Lincoln appreciated the qualities of these men and expressed himself to that effect. Throughout this chapter an effort has been made not to claim too much for the Forty-eighters, but it can certainly be stated that they caused to burn brighter the flame of freedom that had beckoned them to these shores.

Chapter Six

THE RADICALS

By Eitel W. Dobert

EVERY political movement has its dreamers, its radicals, its "lunatic fringe." They are a constant source of embarrassment to the leaders of their own party because of their uncompromising attitude and their extravagant political demands. Ridicule has always been a weapon that can be used against them. It is very difficult to draw the line between an uncompromising "man of principle" and an intolerant "visionary." As one radical once said about himself: "I am trying to do two things, daring to be a radical and *not* a fool, which, if I may judge by the exhibitions around me, is a matter of no small difficulty."

But to judge radical ideas fairly one must disregard contemporary prejudice, because the fools of yesteryear are frequently called prophets today. Often hindsight shows that political disaster could have been prevented if their counsel had been followed. But their contemporaries have never acknowledged this fact; they have not even given them credit for the courage to differ from the masses and to risk all because of an ideal. Emerson once said of the American radicals that their spirit was destructive and aimless, not loving and without ulterior ends. It is doubtful whether he would say the same today of the thousands of American utopians including the radical wing of the Forty-eighters whose political and social demands in many instances have been accepted as a matter of course today.

Admittedly, the radical Forty-eighters were not always comfortable company. They were obsessed by an idea, the demand for freedom, social progress, and true democracy. They were intolerant. They thought in terms of black and white. They began

with a program and in the heat of the battle the program became a cult. They were impractical, impatient, and at times
tactless. And they were, like all utopians, irritatingly optimistic
and firm in the belief in the possibility of realizing the good. As
typical children of the Frankfurt *Parlament* they were great believers in the power and primacy of the word. Veit Valentin in
his *1848: Chapters in German History* writes:

Beautiful, genuine, great, true words were for these people deliverance
and solution of all problems. They fought with words, won victories
with them and were astonished that there could still be powers that
refused to bow to words, despising and abusing them.

No wonder, then, that a great majority of the leading spirits
turned to journalism in this country. President George N.
Shuster of Hunter College stated in a recent commemorative
address at the Library of Congress:

They yearned for newsprint. It cannot be said that all of them wore the
editorial mantle with easy grace. Sometimes they went about, figura-
tively speaking, with several fingers on the triggers of verbal derringers,
to be fired at a moment's notice.

It is a strange experience to leaf through the fragile yellowed
pages of magazines and dailies published a hundred years ago
and to discover with what holy zeal these radicals pleaded their
cause, how they spent hours in their meetings to find the right
wording for a resolution, as if the fate of the future depended on
an "also" or a "but." Their language is surprisingly clear, simple
and direct, very different from the bathos that made the effusions
of the Nazis so offensive and ludicrous to unbelievers. The one
among their number who later became effective in national politics, Friedrich Hassaurek, said of his early period of *Sturm und
Drang* that some of his radical companions had gone to ruin and
some had gone stale, but that all had been in their time a kind
of spiritual leaven.

What distinguishes the radicals among the Forty-eighters from
the moderate elements is not obvious. Radicalism is a question
of temperament. Radicals are born, not made. An unwillingness
to follow the well-trodden path, a very sensitive social conscience,
the feeling of a personal responsibility for the world about, an

urge to reform—all these go into the making of a radical. His natural antagonists are the passive masses which regard all change with distrust, and marshaled with them are the privileged classes fiercely defending their vested interests. The struggle against these forces generates that impatience and exaggeration which characterizes the radical through the ages.

After the feverish tension of European conspiracy, the Forty-eighters found themselves suddenly in the tepid atmosphere of a democratic country where comparative complacency seemed to prevail. An idealist who has worked for a great idea can never forget the feeling of intoxication in which he has lived, and the revolutionaries who readily slip back into normal life are few indeed. Many Forty-eighters had naturally idealized American democracy. In their simplicity they had believed that freedom inevitably ennobles the character of a people and perfects its institutions. Instead they found a federal government in the hands of slaveholders, election frauds in many of the states, and a growing xenophobia in a country where, after all, everyone was a newcomer. The intolerance of puritanism, its "holier than thou" attitude seemed to them worse than a Prussianism maintained "by the grace of God." To their horror they saw at every fifth street corner a church, and that an ugly one. Thus America seemed a caricature of freedom.

America was growing. Its natural resources were being unlocked; everywhere there was planning and building and creating, the laying of the foundation of a world power. For this in turn, the Forty-eighters had no understanding. It was sheer materialism! It may have been *Zivilisation*, but certainly not *Kultur*. They consoled themselves with the thought that their sojourn in America was only temporary and awaited the storm signals of revolution that would call them back. In the meantime they earned their livelihood at menial labor and, when the daily work was done, they met to discuss and forge the future of the Republic of Germany. Some lines of contemporary doggerel expressed their ironic situation—it was written by a revolutionary refugee with the perhaps symbolic name of Wilhelm Sauerwein:

Woll'n die Fürsten wissen	If the princes ask you,
Wie's dem Flüchtling geht,	"How's the fugitive?"
Sagt, er ist zerrissen	Say that he's in misery
Wo er geht und steht.	Wherever he may live.
Hängt nicht an einem Baume,	He does not hang on any tree,
Hängt nicht an einem Strick,	Nor at the end of a rope,
Sondern an einem Traume	To a republic for Germany
Der deutschen Republik.	He hangs with wistful hope.

Some of the revolutionaries who had remained in London began to realize that idealism and patience unaided would never produce a new revolution in Germany. Money was needed, and the example of the Hungarian patriot, Louis Kossuth, showed that it could be found in America. Therefore the moderate faction of the London "Revolutionary Committee" sent to the United States the German professor, poet, and agitator, Gottfried Kinkel, whose name was widely known because of his liberation from prison by Carl Schurz. He was received with enthusiasm everywhere, and fairs and dances were held for the benefit of German freedom.

But in spite of some initial success, Kinkel's mission failed of its goal. Quarrels broke out over what should be done with the relatively small sum of $8,000 which he had collected. A report exaggerating Kinkel's achievement caused the more radical faction in London to send their own man. They chose Amand Goegg, at one time a member of the provisional government in Baden. After his arrival in Philadelphia, he founded the "German Revolutionary League," and in one of its first meetings a wonderful plan was hatched which looked very promising, at least on paper. If each of the three million Germans in the United States contributed weekly but one cent for the cause of the Revolution, this would mean the sum of $1,560,000 a year. Kinkel had proposed that the money be spent for the immediate fomenting of revolution in Germany. But Goegg was in favor of spending the money in longer range planning for the organization of revolutionary committees in foreign countries in order to train leaders for the masses. Many well-known revolutionaries, Karl Heinzen, Gustav Struve, Arnold Ruge, August Becker,

Karl Blind, and Franz Sigel, fell in with this idea. The plan failed utterly because Goegg's radicalism repelled most of the older German settlers, and likewise the more practical among the Forty-eighters.

However, Goegg's agitation was not without its effect since it brought about a new intellectual attitude on the part of these radical Forty-eighters. Hitherto they had regarded American democracy as an experiment which had miscarried. Now, suddenly they assigned the United States the major role in the plan for world revolution. They adopted a resolution which read:

That in the opinion of the present congress, every people upon throwing off the yoke of its tyrants, ought to demand admission into the league of free states, that is, into the American Union, so that these states may become the nucleus of the political organization of the human family and the launching of the World Republic.

The idea of a steadily expanding American Republic was of course widely held at the time, and by no means only by radical Forty-eighters. There was general talk of "the manifest destiny" of the United States. No limits seemed to exist for the growth of the Republic, and each newly acquired territory was firmly believed to mean at the same time the liberation of enslaved populations. The Republic reached now from ocean to ocean and in the south to the Rio Grande. The census of 1840 showed a population of seventeen million and by 1850 it recorded twenty-three million. At the same time the number of immigrants increased astonishingly from year to year. The young giant was flexing his muscles and glorying in his strength. The New England poet, Jonathan M. Sewall had written:

> No pent up Utica can hold our powers.
> The whole, the boundless continent is ours.

It is characteristic of the radical Forty-eighters that they conceived of this expansion as global and at the same time tried to convert it into a force in the realm of ideas. America was after all not a nation in the usual sense of the word; it was a new beginning. Diverse races and religions had established themselves here and were living peacefully side by side; the mere example of such a community of free people was bound to make tyrants uneasy and the oppressed hopeful. In comparison with a possible remedy of all of humanity's ills even the liberation of Germany became of secondary importance.

To study this program in all its details, a meeting was called in Wheeling in September, 1852. The fact that only sixteen delegates appeared out of a possible eleven hundred and twelve, and that those who came were predominantly from the East, could not dampen the prevailing enthusiasm. The leading role in the discussions was assumed by Charles Goepp, who was not a Forty-eighter—his father had emigrated in the thirties from Herrenhut in Silesia to Bethlehem, Pennsylvania—but one who made their cause his own. He had thought much about America's mission in the world and had written a pamphlet entitled "E pluribus unum." He found a kindred spirit in Theodor Poesche, a former German student of philosophy, fighter on the barricades, and refugee from the reaction, who surprisingly enough, had developed similar thoughts in far away Germany and had set them down in a manuscript, called "The New Rome," which unfortunately had fallen into the hands of the Prussian police. Goepp and Poesche then collaborated on a book *The New Rome*, with the subtitle *The United States of the World*, published by Putnam in New York in 1852. The resolutions adopted by the Wheeling Congress are largely those contained in this volume.

First of all, Poesche and Goepp compared America's geographical position with that of ancient Italy which was "moored like a great battleship in the midst of the Mediterranean."

The American Continent divides the Ocean as Italy the Mediterranean, and just as ancient Rome overlooked the circle of lands which skirted this island-sea, so the United States shall overlook the whole of the world. The Universal Empire of the Future belongs to them.

In a few lines they then retraced the early history of Rome, listing parallels with the foundation of the British colonies and they conclude:

And exactly as the first step to acquire a World Empire was for the Romans the conquest and colonisation of the whole of Italy, as important it is for us Americans to unfurl our flag over the whole, wide American continent.

According to the authors, the first step the United States should take in the Western Hemisphere would be the annexation of Cuba and the Dominican Republic, to be followed by that of Canada, where they thought they perceived a growing sentiment for union. Simple too, seemed to them the annexation of Mexico: "down to the Isthmus of Panama, the gardens of the world are dying for want of annexation."

Seven-eights of the population are composed of Indians and Mestizoes who are either highwaymen and thieves, vagrants or peons. They constitute the working class, and as they do not labor, no work is done. The Creoles form an apology for a middle class, and furnish the small businessman, but because there is no labor there is little business. And there are the more ambitious individuals who seek a sphere in church or army, whence they try to derive incalculable revenues extorted from a desperately hopeless people. God and Liberty mean the Bishop and the General. They love the excitement of pronunciamentos, presidencies of four weeks duration and as many little revolutions as possible with very little danger of the over-use of ammunition.

In fact, the prospects of an early annexation of Mexico must have appeared favorable at the time. William Walker was filibustering in Latin America, and Commodore Vanderbilt had considerable financial footholds there—but of course their motives were not those of the Wheeling idealists. The authors berate General Winfield Scott for having refused, after the conclusion of the American-Mexican War in 1848, the governorship of Mexico. It seemed to some that during his stay in that country at the head of the military occupation forces the Mexicans for the first time since the outbreak of the revolution had enjoyed security of person and property.

The first European country which should be infederated was of course England. Two facts, the very serious decrease in population and the bad financial condition of that country seemed to point to its diminishing power. Australia, India, and Africa also should be included. America's influence in Australia, they state, is already greater than that of England.

The next in line would be Germany. The Forty-eighters had
previously favored intervention, but for the authors this did not
suffice. They demanded annexation! Prophetically they wrote:

Germany is the hearthstone of Europe, physically and morally. All the
burdens of Europe are poured into its lap and it is constantly atoning
by its suffering not only for its own sins, but for the sins of all other
nations. Can we hope for a revolution in this unhappy Germany?

And their answer is a flat "No."

The liberal leaders are all in exile and those who remain behind have
lapsed into their former state of contented servitude. It remains therefore the task of the liberal Germans in America to propogate the
American World State in Germany itself.

Thus they took up country after country, tried to solve the
Jewish question and even dealt with Palestine:

The idea, for some time entertained, of purchasing Palestine and making Rothschild a Jewish king was one of those phantastic confusions!
Every Jew will hasten to claim the protection of the American flag,
and Rothschild will not shut his eyes to the only prospect of enabling
the European states to liquidate the debts they owe him.

But now, what about Russia?

This goal to liberate the world will not be realized before a great
World War which is forever seen to hang, like the sword of Damocles,
over the passing joys and troubles of the hour. This great World War
will break out between the forming Union and the Russian Empire.
The real fountain of power in Europe is Russia. No political step can
be taken on this unhappy continent without taking into account the
Russian rulers and their tricky bureaucracy, incapable of any combination out of their usual routine of espionage. . . .

It were idle to belittle the power of such an organization opposed to
the distracted condition of the Occidental states of Europe with their
collapsed aristocracy and smothered democracy. Russia must either
deal or drink destruction. Europe will be first Cossack, but then
Yankee. . . .

European democracy cannot withstand her, for it is disorganized,
unsteady, theoretical and unstatesmanlike. There will be therefore no
concerted rising to repel the slowly advancing repression. Isolated districts may rebel, not in hope, but in despair, their certain defeat serving only to hasten and perfect the utter subjugation of the whole. The
reign of Russian absolutism is an inevitable phase of Europe.

At this last stage of future world development Poesche and Goepp see the lines clearly drawn, the choirs marshaled on each wing of the world stage, Russia leading the one, the United States the other. But as the world will have become too small for both, the contest must end in the downfall of the one and the victory of the other.

Political freedom and national wealth go hand in hand according to the authors. Where there is power in the few the many cannot but suffer. Where there is free economic intercourse between individuals within the state or between different nations, political emancipation follows. They continue:

Freedom of trade between nations requires free government. Free world trade is impossible as long as the world is half free and half slave. If our goods could flow freely all over the world without being impeded by egotistical barriers of some cliques or some rulers, freedom all over the world would gain; the living conditions could be improved, and improved living conditions lead to greater social interdependence among nations and that is what is needed to build the World State.

Then followed a series of remarkable prophecies, many of which have by now been fulfilled. The authors predicted that only the iron, screw-propelled steamship had a future, a device that was just being tested in England at the time of their writing. They spoke enthusiastically of the transformation of the globe into "one head"; although Congress had only a few years earlier voted the tiny sum of $30,000 for telegraphic experiments.

One day, every principal part of the earth's surface will be so connected as to form, for all purposes of intelligence, a single town. The fire that glides upon these wires will scorch away the differences of race and nations, and the fetters of custom and tradition, and their light will illume man with a wisdom he has never known. And why should our modern steamers not have wings and a motive power to impel them forward? What else has the proud condor that surges around the American Alps?. . . A little alteration of adjustment and these iron ships will leave their native element and ride in mid-air.

They produced this remarkable prophecy twenty years before the Wright brothers were born:

We are on the eve of aerial navigation. The experiments of steaming and towing in the atmosphere by means of a screw-propeller raised and supported by a balloon, will one day be tried out; the balloon, which is a toy, must be discarded and then we shall have the practical navigation of the air. The airplane is fitted for universal navigation, its shores are everywhere, and why should not man fly over the poles? Aerial navigation alone will give us the victory over Russian Continentalism.

And they explained how this would enable America to destroy the Russian garrisons in their own territory. Once victory was achieved and unity won,

Even language will be no hindrance. It may be true, that nations are based on a unity of speech. The American will replace it by a union based on unity of thought. It is the office of America to vindicate individualism against nationality. When the dominion of nationality is crushed everywhere and everyhow in the world and the sovereignty of the individuals attained, the mission of the American revolution will be accomplished.

This thesis was propounded in Wheeling. Amidst general applause, Goepp declared:

We demand the extension of American freedom! A war to extend our institutions is not a war of conquest, for in as much as the spirit of our government is the principle of self-government, its expansion does not necessitate the introduction of violence, but rather abolition of the latter. It is the purpose of our government to restore the sovereignty of the individual by striking off the shackles against which he has striven in vain. An Empire, not of conquest and of subjugation, not of inheritance, not of international frictions and hatreds, but of fraternity, of equality and of freedom. We implore it to fulfill its destiny and out of *many* worlds create *one*.

The delegates of the Revolutionary League were electrified. They were impressed by the "grandiose simplicity" with which the interests of the Old and New World were to be reconciled. America had a mission in the world! It was the nucleus of the future World State. It was the point at which to apply the lever to lift the world. Suddenly, to be an American seemed to make sense. At once it was decided to change the Revolutionary League into a "People's League for the Old and New World." The goal was to found an American party which would proclaim this annexation of Europe in its platform. A resolution to this effect was drawn up, signed by the president, Dr. Conradin Homburg, and the secretary, Edward Schlaeger.

Fired with enthusiasm for the new idea, the delegates parted. *The New Rome* captured the interest of a certain public for a while. The scholarly background of its authors was readily acknowledged. But enthusiasm soon subsided. The "People's League for the Old and New World" died a peaceful death, and for years there was many a laugh over the cranks of Wheeling who, in their zeal to better the world, had asked for nothing less than the annexation of the universe by the United States!

Even some participants of the congress who had cheered the speaker tried later on to excuse their enthusiasm as youthful folly and political immaturity. But we can now see no reason for their embarrassment. Forty-eighter idealism and yearning after a new world order, free and united—all that was noble and good in the spiritual world of these revolutionaries was expressed by the Congress of Wheeling. People smiled at the small number of participants. There had been no more than sixteen and they all found room around one table. But these men were not the first to dream of an empire "not of inheritance, not of international frictions and hatreds but of fraternity, of freedom" and the hope for "One World" still lives in the hearts of millions.

The Congress of Wheeling marks a turning point in the spiritual development of the radicals among the Forty-eighters. They had occupied themselves with America, and had even deemed it worthy of a mission in spite of its many shortcomings; now since the possibility of a revolution in German lands seemed more remote than ever, they began to criticize the institutions of the Republic in detail and to make proposals for reform.

In fact that was very simple. They had only to open desk drawers and pull out the old plans with which in the late forties they had planned to build the German Republic. Of course, the social and economic conditions in America differed basically from those in Germany. Hardly one among the planners had studied American history. What did they know about the compromises made by the authors of the Constitution and the history of slavery, which after all was a heritage from colonial times? In their inexperience these radicals did not stop to think that social institutions must grow organically and are related to certain needs of time and place.

Parochial as these immigrant radicals were, they launched their attacks chiefly at the older German groups in the United States, the "Greys" whom they taunted for their laxity in the fight against Puritanism and slavery. This accusation infuriated the "Greys." They could prove they had drawn up antislavery platforms as early as 1844 and 1848. Had not the first antislavery society been brought to life already in 1829 by Karl Follen in Boston with the result that he had not only lost his professorship at Harvard but had even been exiled from the city of Boston? Francis Lieber, Friedrich Muench, and others had attacked the institution of slavery long before the "Greens" had ever seen a Negro. The very impatience of these newcomers who felt that all reforms had to be realized at once showed plainly how "green" they were. Evidently these radicals, along with hundreds of other utopians in the New World, felt that the millennium could be attained if only Old World institutions were abolished. Thus a certain Dr. Hobelmann advocated the total abolition of money; without this he believed any social reform impossible. Fritz Hassaurek snd some others considered the Catholic Church the great danger to America. Some preached the abolition of the office of the President, the emancipation of women, the nationalization of the railroads, or the abolition of all class distinctions. But Dr. Friedrich Sorge from Hoboken outdid them all, when he arose in a meeting and solemnly declared: "Gentlemen, I am against everything that exists!" The violence of these proposals led an American observer, Frederick Law Olmsted, to comment:

free thinking and a devotion to reason carried . . . to the verge of bigotry, and expanded to a certain rude license of manners and habits. . ., an insane mutual jealousy and petty personal bickering that prevents all prolonged and effective cooperation—an old German ail which the Atlantic has not sufficed to cleanse.

The markedly anticlerical attitude of many radicals and their attempt to replace the Bible with Feuerbach's philosophy encountered general criticism. Their atheism was not based solely on philosophic materialism, but on the firm conviction that all churches, Catholic as well as Protestant, were in league with reaction and narrow nationalism and consequently were barriers to progress. They had observed this phenomenon in Germany and the attitude of American clergymen strengthened their belief. Naturally enough, churchmen did not approve of the radicals, as a report of a missionary priest in Milwaukee to the Archbishop of Vienna of the year 1853 shows:

It must not be forgotten that such rotten elements have stolen into this country in large numbers since 1848 with the crowd of troublesome fugitives, and caused annoyance to church and state, for to certain people even Washington is a despot. So how can the Catholic Church, with its Pope, find favor in their eyes? Followers of Hecker and Kossuth are most annoying and disgusting to Catholics.

"To certain people even Washington is a despot" is a remark that applies especially to Karl Heinzen, the radical most remarkable for sharpness of invective and biting scorn. Had Heinzen been an American by birth and had he written in English, he would certainly have his niche in the history of American journalism. Horace Greeley said of him:

Of all the exiles whom the European revolution brought to our shores none wields so trenchant, merciless and independent a pen as Mr. Charles Heinzen . . . he necessarily often shocks the feelings of his readers and makes foes where he might make friends, but he also often tells the truth.

It is difficult to do justice to this upright man who combined an absolute devotion to freedom with an equal lack of the practical. Symbolic of the man is the following paradox reported by his recent biographer: "Heinzen favored punishing violations of the freedom of the press by death, though he believed capital punishment should be abolished for all other crimes." He appreciated American democracy with superlatives: "The true greatness of America consists in its freedom for intellectual combat, and this is a virtue which outweighs many an evil and places this country, in spite of its many failings, above that of any other nation on earth." In spite of all the warmth of his heart, Heinzen never hesitated, whenever it was a question of the purity of radical principles, to scourge with cutting scorn and ridicule even his best friends. Feared, hated, and loved, he belonged to the few radicals who remained faithful to their youthful convictions to the death. The Frenchman's well-known saying, "Whoever has not been a radical in his youth has something wrong with his heart; whoever remains one in his old age, has something wrong with his head" has a definite application in his case. Unlike some other Forty-eighters, he never made peace with the German Reich under the *Kartaetschen Prinz*, ("the shrapnel prince," afterward William I, who had shot down many Forty-eighters).

Older than most Forty-eighters, Karl Heinzen was born near Duesseldorf in 1809. His youthful years were filled with revolt. He lost his mother at the age of four and with her disappeared probably the only being that could have had a moderating influence upon the impetuous boy. The irritating insistence of his foster parent on his becoming a Catholic priest aroused his antagonism and sowed the seed of his pronounced anticlericalism. From his father, who resented Prussia's absorption of the Rhineland, young Heinzen imbided as a child his hatred of the Prussian spirit that was never to leave him.

Heinzen graduated neither from a German *Gymnasium* nor from the Bonn University. Both institutions complained of his lack of discipline and of interest in his studies. The authorities even expelled him from the University in 1829, when Heinzen accused his teachers of narrow-mindedness and condemned the lack of academic freedom. A short sojourn in Batavia in the service of the Dutch colonial military forces undertaken in a spirit partly of adventure, partly of despair, only strengthened his dislike of all kinds of coercion, and one year in the Prussian army filled him with a hatred of militarism.

He fell in love with a young widow and for several years supported her and her four children by taking a job as a tax official, and when she died in 1835 he undertook the care of her four children. His service was a continuous battle with his superiors, who, he felt, treated him unjustly, or with whose administrative methods he disagreed. He must have been the most un-Prussian of Prussian officials, and one can only marvel at the forbearance of the Prussian authorities toward Heinzen during eight long years. Whoever heard of a Prussian tax official who wrote lyrical ballads and comedies in his spare time, that is, when he was not writing letters of complaints to his superiors, not omitting the King of Prussia!

In 1839 he married the oldest daughter of the late widow, a marriage which he never regretted, although it laid him open to the slander by his enemies that he had married his own daughter. Heinzen paid fulsome tribute to his wife as his devoted companion throughout a long life of great poverty and the one person who made the publication of the *Pionier* possible by her aid in setting the type.

With his resignation from officialdom began his political career. Instead of the usual letters of complaint he wrote a pamphlet in which he attacked the system of espionage practiced within the Government bureaus. It appeared in 1844 and was entitled *Die preussische Buerokratie*. Not only the content but the virulence of its language earned its suppression by the government and Heinzen was summoned before a court. His flight across the border was followed by a warrant, which he answered with flaming articles making a return to his homeland impossible. Now began his wanderings, a time of even greater trial for the exile: fights with foreign authorities who for reasons of diplomacy would not permit political conspirators in their countries, difficulties of earning a livelihood and the maddening wait for the revolution in Germany.

He met the poet Freiligrath with whom he formed a lasting friendship, and Karl Marx, for whom he later conceived the most bitter hatred. In Switzerland he held discussions with the philosopher Feuerbach, the freethinker Arnold Ruge, and many others for whom the German homeland had become too narrow. He tried to publish a magazine entitled *Die Opposition*, which he envisioned as a weapon against Prussian reaction.

At first he opposed a bloody upheaval in Germany, because he deemed a systematic enlightenment of the people sufficient to bring about peaceful reforms. Moreover, he was of the opinion that such reforms must be undertaken in unison with all European nations. But slowly he changed his mind. In his publication *Die teutsche Revolution* (one of his many crotchets was the use of the pseudo-learned form "teutsch"), Heinzen advocated tyrannicide and recommended open revolt and mutiny in the army, and referred to 449 princely drones and their bureaucracies who could be hurled from their position of power only by revolution. By this time Geneva was the one Swiss Canton willing to give him and his family a permit of sojourn.

Thanks to various German editors, his name began to be known in America. On the advice of Freiligrath and with the help of friends he came to America late in 1847. After three months he returned to Europe with borrowed money, for the March Revolution had broken out!

But this intransigent fellow did not find his place even among corevolutionaries. He failed in his attempt to be selected as a representative of Hamburg in the Frankfurt *Parlament*. During the abortive revolt of 1849 he quarreled with Hecker over the political goals of the revolution. The moderate element now branded him "Bloody Heinzen" because in his fanatical fury against the Prussian tyrants he called for a military intervention by France. Obviously he was a ready target for mild satire.

In 1850 he returned to America and became editor of the *Schnellpost*, and after its failure a year later, editor of the New York *Deutsche Zeitung*. This paper also, because of pecuniary difficulties, had to suspend publication only three months later, and the *Janus* which he edited afterward suffered the same fate within twelve months.

In spite of these troubles, which would have exhausted a person of ordinary vitality, Heinzen continued his fight for truth and justice with undiminished fire and eagerness. Difference of opinion was ground for him to part company with people who would have been financially helpful in the realization of his plans. Uncompromising and stubborn, always true to himself, he went his way. He received an offer of the editorship of the *Herold des Westens* in Louisville and, in a stronghold of slavery, Kentucky, he raised the banner of human freedom. But this undertaking, too, was of short duration, for a fire (of accidental origin, according to his biographer) destroyed the printing shop. Finally, Heinzen founded, with the help of friends, *Der Pionier* which remained until his death the organ of the radicals. It was first published in Cincinnati, then in New York, and from 1859 to 1879 in Boston, his favorite city, the "Athens of America."

It was in Louisville that Heinzen, together with other radical Germans, forged in 1854 the Louisville Platform which they hoped to make the foundation of a new reform party. Though it is signed by Burgeler, Stein, L. Wittig, B. Domschke and Ch. Heinzen, one can detect Heinzen's thought and language in each of its twelve points. It was addressed to "All True Republicans of the Union," and began:

Liberty, prosperity and education . . . have become the privilege of classes and races who control the legislature and the administration of the country. . . . Peoples are overruled by parties, parties governed by cliques, persons taking the place of principles and names are substituted for rights. . . . This thing must be stopped.

An alliance is proposed between the liberal German element and the progressive Americans "for the purpose of carrying into full effect those grand principles of the Declaration of Independence." All those who adhere to these principles are asked to support only such men and parties as uphold the same ideas.

The first point takes up the thorniest question of the day: "Slavery should at least be excluded from all new territories." Secondly: "Religion is a private matter, hence it is despotism to compel citizens by political means to religious manifestations contrary to their private persuasion." The entire platform constitutes a catalogue of the shortcomings of American democracy according to Heinzen: "No one should remain over five years in the United States without rendering an oath to uphold the constitution," and "the public land belongs to actual settlers and not to speculators." It demands "the creation of an office for the protection of the immigrants who are now helplessly exposed to so many sufferings, wrongs and abuses, from the place of embarkation to the place of their settlement in America.

North America is neglecting herself when neglecting immigration, for immigration is the mother of this Republic."

It advocated furthermore "the protection of the laboring classes from the capitalists" and asked "that the State should mediate as the arbitrator of all contending interests, fixing minimum wages and maximum working hours." It also demanded that justice should be administered without fees, and as a means for facilitating popular instruction "the gratuitous forwarding of newspapers and pamphlets."

As to political procedure, Heinzen asked that "all elections should issue directly from the people" and "any representative and officer should at any time be recalled by the constituents and replaced." He favored "free trade, where reciprocity is accorded," that "public works that are of national interest . . . be carried out by national means," and that "the policy of neutrality must cease to be an article of national creed and ought to be abandoned as soon as contrary to the interests of North America."

Heinzen championed the rights of women. "All men are born equal . . . and we are of the opinion that women too are among 'all men.' " He pleaded in his platform for "the right of the free negroes," for "penal reforms," "abolition of the penalty of death," "the revision of military laws," and finally for the abolition of temperance laws because "they encroached upon individual liberty."

These twelve points, Karl Heinzen's credo and his program for America resemble the plan he had elaborated for a German republic. For him these were the requisites for any democratic order and none could be sacrificed.

The supporters in Louisville decided to send a copy to each member of Congress, the Cabinet members, even the President. Eagerly they folded copies of the finely printed document and put them into envelopes. Then somehow, as the story goes, the envelopes disappeared, and only many weeks later were discovered under the sofa in the office of the editor of the *Louisville Anzeiger!*

Heinzen also had some proposals for the revision of the American Constitution. He felt that too much power had been given to the President, an executive not elected directly by the people, but by the electors who are not bound by the will of the people. The President, Heinzen argued, is commander-in-chief of the army, navy, and of all the militia. He has no right to declare war, but, if he desires it, he can easily bring on war with a foreign power through his Secretary of State. Though he is dependent on the Senate for the ratification of treaties, he can maneuver that body in such a way that it must submit to his will or else seriously compromise the government. He nominates the Justices of the Supreme Court and thereby may make his creatures members of that Court whose office it is to decide upon violations of the Constitution. Heinzen also attacked the President's power of veto by which two-thirds of the legislative body of several hundred members are required to counteract the will of a single man. He harshly criticized the immense patronage power which each President employed as a means to secure his position for the next term, or to maintain his party in possession of the booty. For Heinzen, the President, as provided by the Constitution, is nothing but "a king in morning coat" and the American Constitution merely a document based on English tradition. "And it is well known that it only depended on Washington's will to be made king of North America. Had this man, like the brand of European princes, possessed so little self-respect as to consider it compatible with his dignity as a man and a human being to be degraded to an oppressor of his fellow citizens by having a crown put on his head, this country would now have His Majesty Washington X."

To Heinzen, Switzerland seemed the perfect example of a democracy in which the will of the people can be expressed in the most direct manner. He called attention to the advantage of the frequent plebiscites demanding, as they do, the constant participation of the people in all matters pertaining to the general welfare. In this exemplary republic the power of the president is more restricted. The executive power rests in a confederate council which is elected by the confederate assembly from all eligible citizens of the country. It is this council which elects the president for the duration of one year only. In this way party politics are made almost impossible and the evil of political patronage is largely avoided.

For the American Constitution, Heinzen demanded even more. He wanted the abolition of the Presidency and of the Senate, and proposed the institution of an executive council under the supervision of a Congressional committee to safeguard the interests of the people and to combat the evils of party politics and lobbies.

Many radicals, among them Edward Schlaeger (who had attended the Wheeling Congress), Hassaurek, and Kapp finally made their peace with the German Empire and pretended that it fulfilled their old dreams. Heinzen never repented. These "cheap conversions" only confirmed his old suspicion that the others never had been sincere radicals and that his fierce attacks on these men in the fifties and sixties had been justified. Prussia, according to him, had simply annexed Germany, and soon Prussian bureaucracy would be in full command, and Prussian militarism penetrate the whole *Reich*. The nationalistic intoxication which had seized not only the *Reich*, but many Germans in America disgusted him and led him to warn the immigration authorities against monarchistic Germans who could endanger Republican ideas in this country. Heinzen preferred an immigration based on political conviction rather than on empty stomachs, and he would require as a condition of naturalization a thorough knowledge of the language, history, and government of America, thus anticipating the present practice.

Such were the ideas of this man "from whom," as Wendell Phillips said in his memorial address, "many prominent men gained without acknowledging their obligation." And we in our day have seen the fulfillment of many of his prophecies, for example those concerning Prussian Germany.

One can differ from Heinzen's views but one cannot characterize his criticism as negative and destructive. He believed firmly that the American Constitution was for the people a living thing which had to grow and adapt itself to changing conditions from generation to generation. Marxistic thinking was foreign to his nature, and though he admitted the existence of classes he loathed the doctrine of class warfare as an approach to social problems. The Communists called him therefore the "bourgeois democrat" and the "doubtful friend of the poor." Heinzen lashed back with "Communist hell-hounds" and declared that a Marxist was to him as repugnant as the Emperor of Russia, being equally inimical to liberty and culture and just as barbaric in his method. He was farsighted enough to see that "the struggle for the victory of a particular class would only lead to another form of tyranny." He would reconcile class differences by an unceasing social education of all citizens. This program would consequently lead to economic justice and despite all shortcomings, the American democracy seemed to him quite capable of attaining his ideal.

The Communists and Marxists who were so bitterly attacked by Heinzen also had their representatives among the radicals of the Forty-eighters. Their history deserves closer examination.

The inhuman factory conditions and the abysmally low wages in the young German industry of the first half of the past century were the chief reasons for the great stream of emigrants to America. The German countryside seemed to be overpopulated, and thousands of the surplus rural workers had gone to the cities and centers of industry. The sudden change from country to city meant a sharp break in the life of each individual. For generations the peasant had known but two authorities: the great landowner and the curate. Work had been hard, but daily existence had been secure. Spiritual stimulus had come only from the church, and reading and writing were taught from the catechism. Furthermore, there was military service, but there, too, the system made certain that nobody forgot where he belonged. The sons of the landowners were the officers and they received the same obedience as on their estates.

But the vast slums of the growing industrial cities with their new stimuli, the more painful contrast between poverty and wealth, the many opportunities for discussion with one's equals, helped to reveal to the German worker the true wretchedness of his position. Those who in the forties and fifties went to America were not "class conscious" in the Marxian sense, but they carried with them the bitterness born of injustice and the firm decision to resist similar evils in the new country.

Much of what they found in America they disliked. Together with the Irish, those Germans who gravitated to the cities lived again in slums and only a few achieved economic security within a short time. The Anglo-Saxons regarded immigrants as inferiors. This feeling of inferiority, together with the memory of unhappy experiences in the Fatherland, prepared them for the message of socialism. They were therefore ripe for the intellectual leadership which the Communist element of the radical Forty-eighters offered.

Perhaps the foremost figure in the German labor movement of the fifties in the United States was Wilhelm Weitling. He appears to have been the only one among the German Communists who earned the admiration of Karl Heinzen. Weitling's European past was just as tempestuous as Heinzen's, but while the editor of the *Pionier* had enjoyed many cultural and educational advantages, Weitling owed his success entirely to his own efforts. For him, Communism was an ethical system in full harmony with Christianity. He put his ideas into several books: *The World As It Is and As It Should Be* which had been printed secretly in Prussia in 1838, *The Guarantees of Harmony and Freedom* and *The Gospel of a Poor Sinner*.

Weitling recognized the almost unbridgeable differences between classes, but he, too, shrank from preaching class warfare. The ideas he brought to America were the result of practical experiences. For years he had wandered through Europe as a tailor's apprentice, had instructed workmen in Germany and associated with leading intellectuals in France, Switzerland and England, among whom were the educator Friedrich Froebel, the anarchist Michael Bakunin, the communists Marx and Engels, and the poet Heine. He had organized cooperative restaurants for workingmen in France and Switzerland and had secured a faithful following. Naturally enough, he had managed to arouse the special fury of His Prussian Majesty's police.

In 1846 *Die Volkstribuene* called him to New York, but shortly before his arrival the paper died. On the outbreak of the Revolution of 1848, the *Befreiungsbund* which Weitling had founded, sent him back to Germany, but like Heinzen, he soon returned to the United States. The next years he devoted to the German-American labor movement. He was successful in coordinating the various groups and in creating a central organ for the movement, *Die Republik der Arbeiter*, which from 1850 on appeared almost every month for five years. A Central Committee of United Trades was formed in New York which engaged in intense propaganda. Slowly the movement gathered momentum; groups of other nationalities joined. Weitling succeeded in stirring up even the farmers in New Jersey and the Negroes in New York.

In the fall of 1850 the "General Workmen's Convention" was called in Philadelphia. Delegates came from St. Louis, Louisville, Baltimore, Pittsburgh, Philadelphia, New York—in fact from all the cities which had large German populations. Compared with the millions of members of today's trade unions, the 4,400 members which were represented in Philadelphia by 44 delegates were pitifully few, but for Weitling and his time it represented a considerable organizational triumph. Topics discussed with great seriousness were the means of propaganda, education, and Weitling's pet idea, the founding of a Labor Exchange Bank which was supposed to promote bartering among producers. The twelve political demands made by the Philadelphia Convention were the same as those of the Free-Soil movement and were based on the democratic slogan "equal rights and equal duties." Furthermore, the congress resolved to publish *Die Republik* in a monthly edition of 4,800 copies and created central committees for the different cities which were to protect the interests of the movement at state and national elections. Finally a new name was adopted: *Allgemeiner Arbeiterbund* (The General Workingmen's League).

Naturally the state of the future, as envisioned by Weitling, would have no place for capitalists because his state served the "ethos of work." Government offices were open only to workers and teachers, who, Weitling believed, would have purer motives to strive for the general good. The ultimate goal should be a

World Republic. The first step toward this World Republic was the purchase by the League of a thousand-acre farm in Iowa. Conditions for admission were easy: ten dollars, good health and good behavior. "Communia" sheltered forty persons in 1852. All work was done in common and at the same time care was taken, that the different types of labor were rotated.

Weitling's Workingmen's League enjoyed but a short life. His newspaper failed because it was never adapted to a laborer's intellect. Torn by quarrels "Communia" ran into debts and was finally auctioned off in 1853. Weitling retired from public life, became a clerk in the Bureau of Immigration and devoted his last years to astronomy!

Whatever remained of his Workingmen's League came under the influence of Joseph Weydemeyer, a former Prussian officer, then a fighter in the Revolution, personal friend of Marx and Engels, and later a colonel in the Union Army. For the first time, the teaching of Marx was heard in America. In 1858, the League published a new weekly *Die Soziale Republik*. It was first edited by Gustav Struve, who filled its columns with romantic phrases, assumed the mannerisms of the typical revolutionary, and admitted only such persons into the League as had sworn "on life and death to break the chains that tie labor to capital." *Die Soziale Republik* and the General Workingmen's League disintegrated in the general turmoil of the Civil War.

A Communist Club founded in New York in 1857 was composed mostly of well-educated radicals. The abolition of private property was one of their tenets. The club had been founded by Friedrich A. Sorge, a refugee of the Baden revolution, an enthusiastic partisan of Marx and Engels. It was eventually merged in 1867 with the "German General Labor Union," which in turn, was the direct ancestor of the first modern socialist party on the American political scene, "The Socialist Party of New York and Vicinity."

The names of the Forty-eighter radicals are today generally unknown to the American public. Whoever heard of Kinkel's and Goegg's attempts to finance a German revolution with

American dollars, or who knows of the Congress of Wheeling? Karl Heinzen even in his lifetime had a very small following, but today more than ever, we need men who fearlessly proclaim the truth, who do not flatter the masses but inspire men to realize their dignity. Granted that Weitling was a dreamer and his attempt to solve the evils of the world were doomed to failure, yet what he and all the radical Forty-eighters strove for in fiery debates and in innumerable resolutions, in the founding of unions and leagues and clubs, was justice and freedom in the world. Democracy needs its radicals.

Chapter Seven

THE FORTY-EIGHTERS
IN THE CIVIL WAR

By Ella Lonn

IT HAS BEEN pointed out repeatedly that Germany suffered a great loss in the migration after the revolutionary failure of 1848 of several thousands of cultivated, educated persons, a loss difficult to sustain without spiritual impoverishment. Spain had earlier sustained a greater loss in the migration of the Moors, and France an even greater loss in the Huguenot emigration. Such mass migration always means gain to the country welcoming the migrants. This chapter endeavors to show the gain to the United States in the Civil War from the addition of several thousand Forty-eighters whose crusading spirit was dedicated to the expansion of human freedom. Men who had been held, as they declared, in servitude by the barons would naturally embrace a cause denying expansion of slave territory toward that Northwest in which so many of them were vitally interested.

The importance of these new adherents to the doctrine of extension of freedom to the slaves—for in the last analysis that is what the formation of the new Republican party meant—appeared most effectively in the second campaign of that party in 1860. The antislavery movement entered its important political stage at the time when the Forty-eighters had definitely given up hope of another revolution in Germany and had gained some experience in American politics. Before these firebrands a field of new activity opened and by hundreds they went into the election as agitators to lead the German Democrats into the new Republican Party. They were inspired by the inner conviction that the cause they were espousing was righteous, even holy.

Their speeches were straight abolitionist speeches, filled with clear, sound argument, free from the demogogic hyperbole so often found in the mouths of the native Americans speaking for the same party but following the party line.

Compromise, evasion of the fundamental issues, seemed to these Germans despicable. Ignorant of American history, unaware of the compromises out of which the Union was born, unaware of the existence of widely differing cultures in the Northern and Southern sections of the country, despising the Southern aristocrats for social conditions which they had inherited without seeing how they could be eradicated, utterly impervious to considerations of practical politics at which American politicians were adept, these foreign-born felt that the vaunted freedom in the "land of the free" rang false and hollow. Americans discussed the states rights issue, belabored the Constitutional aspects, carefully insisted on the immunity of slavery within the territory where it already existed—or, as the somewhat bored and repelled German listeners charged, "sneaked around" the main issue. The humble people, foreigners as well as natives, had with sound instinct sensed the really vital question and wished an end of sophistry. The leaders among the Forty-eighters spoke out to the German settlers who came in hordes, even in the backwood districts of Wisconsin and Iowa, to listen to the *Schnurbarts*, as they termed the mustachioed Forty-eighters. In a tone similar to that which they had struck in Germany, these idealists attacked, not crowned tyrants this time, but the slaveholders.

Here was a tangible field which could absorb a part of their zeal for that thorough reform of America which seemed to them so greatly needed. The Negro, as a human being, was endowed according to the United States Constitution with inalienable rights with which the German crusaders were burning to invest him. Leaders and followers, old and new settlers could all understand slavery as a moral issue; hence they almost solidly arrayed themselves against it. The presence of slavery in the United States they regarded as a serious reflection on the republic; as zealots for the cause of civilization and free government, they were necessarily sturdy opponents of the institution. Many Forty-eighters espoused the antislavery cause with all the ardor and enthusiasm they had given to the principles of the Revolution of 1848. As to the other aspect of the issue which was rendering America into two sections, the right of secession, it seemed evident to them that the Union must be preserved. The one outstanding republic in the world, whatever its faults—and they found plenty of them—must not be allowed to disintegrate. They had had in their homeland glaring proof of the dangers of disunion—particularism, as they termed it—and recognized an obligation to prevent that calamity in their adopted country. To translate into American terms, the Germans were opposed to "states rights." It was the Forty-eighters who educated the German farmers, often apathetic and uninterested in abolition and constitutional niceties, to a realization of what the war meant.

Motives for enlisting in the war were of course seldom unmixed; ambition to capitalize on military training for military rank, a sense of obligation to repay America for the opportunities they enjoyed, a desire not to allow the Germans to be outdone by the Irish or other nationality groups, the temptation of the huge bounties—all entered into the complex, but the humanitarian impulse was almost always a strong factor.

The idealism which inspired most of the Forty-eighters is beautifully summed up in a letter by Carl Schurz to his friend, Theodor Petrasch, written October 3, 1863, from a camp in Alabama:

What a tremendous problem and what a mighty cause! I am happy to live in this country at this time. In comparison with the splendid goal, what are our little sufferings and our individual sacrifices? Slavery is being driven out of its last citadel; the insulted dignity of human nature has been avenged. The people of the new world are taking an immeasurable step forward in its cleansing and ennobling.

Elsewhere in this volume a discussion of the numbers swept to our shores as a result of the revolutionary wave of 1848 are estimated as between three and four thousand. It is impossible to hazard any conclusion as to the proportion which entered the army, since army records naturally did not enter data on this subject. This group, often too little regarded by us Americans of non-German ancestry, was of the greatest importance, as leaders among the Forty-eighters organized or directed thousands of their fellow countrymen enlisted in German regiments and performed through them great military feats. It is fortunately possible, however, to give some account of those military leaders, selected from various ranks and various fields of activity in the army, and through them to indicate what the Forty-eighters contributed to the Union cause. This method is somewhat like trying to understand the work of an orchestra by observing the performance of the director, though here there are many directors to study. Nevertheless, whatever may be true as to numbers and however later generations of German Americans may idealize the entire group of Forty-eighters, students of German Americans of the Civil War period are agreed that they had a great leadership. In the group of Forty-eighters, as a whole, there were a few well-read merchants and craftsmen but many were quite ordinary men soon lost in the American population, while the leaders were intellectuals, physicians, journalists, reformers, and philosophers, all men of rigid and uncompromising ideals.

Since the highest rank in the entire army, that of lieutenant general, was accorded only to Grant, we are concerned here first with the major generalships. The entire number was relatively few, and of the six allotted to men of foreign birth, the Germans carried off more than half. There can be no question that the government in some instances used this distinction as a means of rewarding nationality groups for their response to the call to arms. First with a claim for consideration as a nationality group stood the Germans, for the government was fully aware of what it owed to the Germans. However, the according of one of the newly created major generalships to Franz Sigel was not a spontaneous act of gratitude, for the German element clamored loud and long for the appointment of someone of German nationality to this high rank. There can be little doubt that the selection of Sigel for this great honor was in direct response to a readily understandable enthusiasm of his countrymen for this leader of the Badensian Revolutionary army. In the case of Carl Schurz political and personal considerations weighed heavily; Lincoln owed him a considerable debt for his part in capturing so large a share of the Teutonic vote for the Republican candidate. Schurz was on close, not to say intimate, terms with the President. The nomination of Osterhaus to the highest rank, in the absence of any influence to further his cause, must be ascribed to merit and demonstrated military ability. General Adolf von Steinwehr cannot enter this story as he was not a Forty-eighter: he arrived in 1847 and served also in the Mexican War.

Franz Sigel, first in the hearts of his countrymen, makes on the whole a poor showing for military talent and skill, even after all due allowances are made for unquestionable misfortunes. Since this chapter is not intended to be a mere series of biographies, biographical data will be reduced to a minimum, except as they bear upon a given career in the Union Army. Sigel was born at Sinsheim, Baden, in 1824, and hence was a South German. He received his military training at the Karlsruhe Academy, where he graduated in 1840. Entering the army of the Duke of Baden, he won rapid promotion so that by 1847 he held the post of chief adjutant and was accounted one of the best artillerists in Germany. Resigning from the ducal army because his liberal views did not comport with those of the regime and also because in a duel he had killed his opponent, he preferred to go to Heidelberg to study law. He took an active part with Friedrich Hecker in the Baden Revolution and soon found himself appointed as a trained military man to the chief command of one of the revolutionary armies and, even in 1849, when the insurrectionary government was established, appointed to the post of minister of war. He distinguished himself in the unsuccessful campaign of that year against the intervening Prussian army. American Germans never forgot the report that on the retreat into Switzerland he opposed eighty thousand with thirty thousand—a fact not substantiated by Sigel himself, who claims the escape into Switzerland of only eight thousand. It is notable that he effected this retreat with almost no loss of men or artillery. Forced by the Swiss government to leave in 1851, he sought refuge first in England and then in the United States. The generalship displayed in these brief Baden campaigns won for him among German Americans a prestige which amounted to idolatry. "I fights mit Sigel" was a passport to the good will of German civilians everywhere in the West.

In the new homeland he earned his living during the interval before the Civil War by teaching first in New York and after 1857 in St. Louis at the German American Institute. That put him in the crucial state of Missouri when the President issued the call to arms in April, 1861. Sigel's instant response was to organize one of the first regiments in Missouri, the Third Missouri Volunteers, and, what an artillerist could hardly neglect, a battery of artillery.

After helping to save St. Louis with its important arsenal, he shared in the defeat at Wilson's Creek and lost most of his men on the retreat to Springfield; then he partially retrieved this record by his bravery and skill as commander of a division in Frémont's army at Pea Ridge in a decisive Union victory which definitely held Missouri within the Union. Transferred to the East in March, 1862, with promotion to a major generalship, Sigel failed to escape having to serve again under General Henry W. Halleck (his evil genius, who thoroughly disliked him), for the latter was soon called to Washington as Chief of Staff. Even though Sigel commanded the Eleventh Corps and under Pope a Grand Division including two corps, he did little to increase his reputation. Only at the second battle of Bull Run did he reveal ability, for here he fought with distinction on the second day and ably covered the retreat. An unfortunate temporary withdrawal from the army on the eve of the battle of Chancellorsville because of his health deprived him of a great opportunity, for he would probably not have committed the tactical blunders of Howard. Return to the service in the Department of West Virginia in 1864 brought only a humiliating defeat at New Market by a force partly composed of mere cadets from Virginia Military Institute and half the size of his own army. It is seldom remembered to his credit that when the Confederate General

Jubal Early threatened Washington in July, 1864, Sigel detained him near Harpers Ferry with a greatly inferior force for four days, thus affording time for supporting forces to come to the defense of the capital. Certainly there is nothing phenomenal in this entire record; as Wilhelm Kaufmann points out, Sigel was engaged in only six actions, a single great battle, the second battle of Bull Run; one battle of secondary importance, Pea Ridge, where he was second in command and appears as the real victor; and two greater skirmishes, Wilson's Creek and New Market, in both of which Sigel with independent command met utter defeat; and two rear-guard skirmishes at Bentonville and Carthage. The defeat at New Market brought about his removal and thereafter he held no commands of importance.

German admirers blame everyone and everything for Sigel's bad luck, and *Pechvogel* is certainly a term that can properly be applied to him. Granted that he was unfortunate in his entire relationship with Halleck, granted that the West Point officers in the army viewed him as an interloper usurping one of the few highest ranking positions from their number and frankly showed their resentment and prejudice against a foreigner, granted that there were extenuating difficulties at New Market, even then it is evident that a large part of the difficulty goes back to Sigel. His personality, cold and reserved, was little adapted to winning over his resentful colleagues, especially when combined with lack of marked military ability. "A love for free government," to quote the *Dictionary of American Biography*, "had been the ruling motive of Sigel's life. His military successes were not of the greatest, but his prompt and ardent espousal of the Union cause was a great factor in uniting the large German population of the North, with which he was extremely popular, solidly behind the Union." The evaluation of Sigel may be summed up in the terse comment of Kaufmann that he could not prove himself capable of commanding a corps. He is by far the least impressive of the four German major generals. Part of that unimpressiveness may be attributed to his physical appearance, for "on horseback the small, thin man with the fixed death-like expression gave no impression of the heroic. . . . One needed to be a German really to know and appreciate him."

This chapter deals only with that portion of the career of Carl Schurz which has to do with his activity in the army during the Civil War. His slight experience in the South German revolt and his assiduous study of military science while serving as ambassador to Spain constitute the military background for his duties as a major general. That his desire from the beginning was for military service is evidenced by his activity at the outbreak of war in forming the first cavalry regiment, command of which he renounced reluctantly. He craved field service so greatly that during a leave from ministerial duties early in 1862 he succeeded in securing from Lincoln a commission as brigadier, an appointment which can only be designated as political. The scorn of some Forty-eighters for the "Zivilist Schurz," their refusal to admit his military ability can be explained only by a fear that he was usurping first place from the professional soldier, their favorite Sigel. Schurz's war record affords no justification for this attitude, while the fact that Schurz, according to a published letter of his wife, was instrumental with the President in the appointment of Sigel to succeed Frémont should disprove charges that he tried to steal any of Sigel's glory.

The pronouncement of his superiors, as of the officers and men under him like Schimmelfennig and others, was that Schurz was an able commander. This was demonstrated at the second battle of Bull Run, where his division, constituting Sigel's right wing, sustained a bitter fight in the woods before the railroad embankment for eight hours, and then managed to cover the retreat; at Chancellorsville, where his repeated protests to the corps commander, General Howard, against the ill-advised placing of the Eleventh Corps proved his understanding of tactics; at Gettysburg, where, again forced to take the brunt of the Confederate attack as temporary commander of the Eleventh Corps, he was still able to withdraw his somewhat disordered corps to Cemetery Ridge. Transfer with the entire corps to the western field of action brought him to the Chattanooga area in time for the battle of Missionary Ridge, but he had to stand in reserve during the main portion of that conflict.

When Schurz was put in charge of a training station for recruits at Nashville, he was apparently shelved by the War Department, but the truth is that he had become involved in a bitter quarrel with General Joseph Hooker when the latter reported failure by Colonel Hecker to execute an order. Schurz instantly assumed responsibility for the officer acting under his instructions and recognized the criticism as really directed at himself; he demanded an inquiry in which he fully vindicated himself, but attacked Hooker so sharply that his continuance under the latter became impossible. When the Eleventh Corps was joined to the Twelfth as the Twentieth Corps under Hooker, he voluntarily decided to take over the training corps. Soon it became clear that he could render better service in the reelection campaign of Lincoln than in the field. Some months after the election Schurz reported to Sherman for a command and was serving as Chief of Staff to that general when the surrender came.

Schurz's yearning for active military service is shown in the following letter of September 24, 1863, again to Petrasch: "I belonged to the party that had brought on the crisis; I could not avoid the chances of the struggle. . . . Then I will return to my old activities with the satisfaction not only of having labored definitely for the future of the country, but also of having loyally shared its fate."

Schurz seems to have been obscured after the autumn of 1863 but it is beyond question that he had the respect of superiors and inferiors for courage and ability. He was often complimented in dispatches and at a review of the Army of the Cumberland his division impressed the Presidential party as the best drilled of all the troops. Schurz seems to have been particularly gratified by a tribute from Colonel Leopold von Gilsa who came one day to headquarters to say to Schurz, "General, I owe you an apology. When you were appointed brigadier, I regarded you as a mere civilian, and indulged in some hard language. I want to say in the opinion of everybody you have fully earned your rank, and I have come to pay you my profound respects." In the command of a division, and of a corps at Gettysburg, he rendered his adopted country on the field of battle service no less valuable than that he later gave as a statesman.

The third in the trio of Forty-eighters in the highest possible rank rose from private to major general. Peter Joseph Osterhaus had had a limited Prussian training in a military academy in Berlin and had served in an infantry regiment in the Schleswig-Holstein War. Participation in the Baden Revolution of 1848–49 led to his flight to the United States. The Civil War found him in St. Louis and he instantly enlisted in the Second Missouri Regiment. His previous military experience impressed his superiors so that he was promptly made major of a battalion in that regiment, sharing as such in the battles of Dug Springs and Wilson's Creek during the three months' campaign. In December he was commissioned colonel of the Twelfth Missouri and shared in the campaign to rid the southwestern part of the state of bushwhackers. At the battle of Pea Ridge, March 6–8, 1862, he headed one of Sigel's two divisions; it was Osterhaus who discovered the position from which Sigel's decisive attack was made. After the artillery had caused the Confederates to waver, Osterhaus stormed the enemy's main position at Eldhorn Pass, a feat which may have furthered his promotion to a brigadiership the following June. For most of the first two years of the war he had only difficult, ungrateful jobs to perform, disassociated from opportunity for distinction, such as cleaning the bushwhackers out of Missouri and northern Arkansas, or the task of preventing supplies from reaching the Confederates during the siege of Vicksburg. They involved, however, constant fighting. Even the attempt to storm Vicksburg on May 22, 1863, during which his division penetrated the outer works, brought him little glory. In the campaign down the river south of Vicksburg, he found a new foe in malaria and yellow fever but no opportunity for distinction.

Not until the Chattanooga campaign did the chances of war favor him, but then he figured as the hero of the Battle of Lookout Mountain. Osterhaus sought and secured from Hooker the task of attacking the mountain, which necessitated crossing the swollen Tennessee River by a pontoon bridge thrown over it during the night. In a double attack by General John W. Geary from the South and Osterhaus from a point nearer the city both were successful, as the Confederates lacked the strength to defend the widely separated points and were forced to flee down the other side of the mountain into Chattanooga. At Grant's headquarters toward evening the Union flag was noted fluttering on the peak of Lookout Mountain. As it was unfurled, one of Grant's staff said, "That's the work of 'Fighting Joe,' " meaning Hooker. Quietly with a shake of his head, Grant replied, "I don't think it is 'Fighting Joe,' I think it's 'Peter Joe,' " a designation among the soldiers for Osterhaus. This remark is not only a tribute to Osterhaus' daring but also a revelation of Grant's familiarity with the men in his command.

After the capture of Lookout Mountain, Osterhaus led the vanguard to the south side of Missionary Ridge, fought there also with distinction and directed the pursuit of the defeated Confederates. At Ringgold, where he encountered the fugitives, he directed independently the bloody battle with virtual destruction of the Confederate army there. He received the well-earned promotion to major general before he participated in the Atlanta campaign and the march to Savannah with Sherman. He rendered significant service in the many battles of that campaign: at Resaca, Dallas, Pumpkin Vine Creek, and the frightfully hard battle of Kenesaw Mountain, where he broke through the Confederate line and made untenable General J. E. Johnston's defensive position on that mountain. He was present at the decisive battles of Peachtree Creek, and before Atlanta. By September, 1864, he held command of the Fifteenth Corps and shared in the taking of the key fortress which delivered Savannah into Union hands as Sherman's Christmas present to Lincoln. He concluded his war career as Chief of Staff for General Canby in the Mobile sector and on the lower Mississippi.

An important factor in his promotion was his adaptability to American ways and methods of warfare. When the end of war came he had been in no less than thirty-four battles, and whenever he led independently had never met defeat. The Confederates called him the "American Bayard." Probably his finest tribute came from Sherman, who said concerning the three-day battle around Chattanooga, "I left one of my best divisions, that of Osterhaus, to act with Hooker, and I know it has served the country well and reflected honor to the Army of the Tennessee."

Less niggardly with the title of brigadier general, and repeatedly conferring it as a brevet title, the government bestowed this rank on no less than nine Teutons, of whom only the Forty-eighters engage our attention.

We need give only brief consideration to Louis Blenker, who is generally spoken of as a soldier of fortune. He had been one of the Bavarian Legion, raised in 1833 to accompany the Wittelsbacher recently elected King of Greece; in six years of service he attained the rank of lieutenant. Not unnaturally for an adventurous spirit he was swept into the Revolution of 1848, occurring almost a decade after his return from Greece to Baden, and became a member of the insurrectionary government. He followed the usual course of the defeated Badensians—flight into Switzerland and, after he was ordered out, to America. He could not resist the call to war in 1861, promptly became colonel of the Eighth New York Regiment which he had raised, and at the first important battle of the war commanded the brigade into which the regiment was incorporated. His reward for covering the retreat of the demoralized Union army at the first battle of Bull Run was a brigadier's commission.

Carl Schurz sees much that is amusing in Blenker's pomp and ostentation, but he gives a favorable view of the man's character:

When in the course of events he had been, deservedly, promoted to a brigadier-generalship, his headquarters in the field were the wonder and envy of the whole army of the Potomac. His tent was unique in the elaborateness and taste of its appointments. Not only officers of the army but civilians from afar came to see it, and he was lavish in his hospitality. Great things were told of the reception he gave to General McClellan when that commander visited him. Our war had attracted many German officers who sought service in our army, among them noblemen of high rank. Some of these were attached to General Blenker's staff as "additional aides-de-camp." He was thus enabled to form a sort of court around him which abounded in high titles. A story was passing from mouth to mouth that General Blenker was often heard to give orders in this wise: "Prince A., you will instruct Count B. to inspect the pickets to-night, and to take Baron S. with him."

But Blenker proved that a man can be a perfect stage-general and at the same time a very efficient soldier. He was a thoroughly brave man, an excellent organizer, and an efficient commander. The regiment he had formed was a model regiment, and the brigade commanded by him on the ill-fated day of the first battle of Bull Run stood firm as a rock, in perfect order, when the rout of our panic-stricken army seemed to sweep everything else with it. While he amused his friends by his theatrical oddities as a type, he still enjoyed their sincere respect.

Whenever General McClellan had on his hands a foreign officer whom he found it difficult to place, he sent him to Blenker, with the result that the latter soon had a staff of eighty. These men, not on salary until assigned to a regiment, felt they deserved distinguished treatment and Blenker was not niggardly with hospitality in keeping with the "champagne taste" of these noblemen. McClellan enjoyed the hospitality of Blenker's camp, of which he received a full share. In November, 1861, Blenker organized a torchlight procession in Washington in honor of McClellan, with two thousand soldiers carrying torches. Blenker, followed by fifty-six staff officers, rode at the head of the parade; all had splendid chargers and gaudy uniforms. Twelve bands were in the line of march and fireworks crowned the event. It was a sensation in Washington and Lincoln also reviewed the "circus." However, all of this cost a lot of money and Blenker was obliged to retire from the army for mismanagement of regimental funds, though he was not thought personally corrupt.

Friedrich Salomon, the most important of the four famous brothers, brought with him, when he was forced into exile because of participation in the Prussian Revolution of 1848, the military training acquired as a one-year volunteer in artillery and as a lieutenant in the reserve. He also brought with him, what is more than some Forty-eighters possessed, a means of earning a livelihood, for he was trained in surveying. He was located in St. Louis when the war came; there he entered as captain the Fifth Missouri Regiment (the regiment of his brother,

Carl Eberhard Salomon) and was present at Sigel's defeat at Wilson's Creek. Early in the war he received at the hands of another brother, Governor Edward Salomon of Wisconsin, the command of a German regiment which the governor had been zealous in raising, the Ninth Wisconsin. By June, 1862, Colonel Friedrich Salomon was promoted to a brigadiership and sustained a defeat in trying to capture Newtonia. His most important and even brilliant service was the victory at Helena, Arkansas, where he led independently and hurled the foe back with heavy loss. Although his superior, General Prentiss, who observed the battle from a cannon boat on the Mississippi, later claimed the victory, the entire group of officers who had participated in the encounter signed a statement that Salomon had independently conducted the defense. It was charged that Grant, because of an old grudge against Carl Eberhard Salomon, who had defeated him for a minor office in St. Louis, did not allow this paper to reach Lincoln. Although General Salomon fought in many battles, they were almost always in remote theatres of war in the West and Southwest so that he never played a role in any decisive conflict. It must, however, be acknowledged that the award of a major generalship by brevet late in the war was an acknowledgment of particular service to the Union and recognition of two victories won with independent command, Helena and Jenkins Ferry.

In Alexander von Schimmelfennig appears one of the ablest of the German leaders in actual combat. Born in 1824 in Prussia, he fought as an officer while still in his twenties in the Schleswig-Holstein disorders and moved on into the Revolution in Baden where, though an experienced officer, he was subordinated to amateurs in the game of war. An educated, trained, military man, largely free from the crusading spirit of the Forty-eighters, he emigrated and settled in Philadelphia. He entered the Civil War as colonel of the Seventy-fourth Pennsylvania, raised among the Germans of Pittsburg and regarded as one of the élite units of the Potomac army. It was not unnatural that his regiment should be assigned to Blenker's division, and so came under fire at the battle of Cross Keys, where Schimmelfennig fought with distinction. He next shared in Pope's Virginia campaign of 1862 under Sigel, where he was especially noted for his fighting at the second battle of Bull Run, since his brigade pressed forward over the railroad jetty and drove Stonewall Jackson's troops back beyond Cushing Farm. It was probably as a reward for this work that he was named brigadier general. He next appeared at Chancellorsville in Schurz's division of the Eleventh Corps; he made several reconnaisances which disclosed the approach of the Confederates and duly warned his superior officers of the impending flank attack. He made as strong a stand as possible with his brigade under Schurz at Hawkins Farm and in the earthworks defended by Colonel Adolf Buschbeck, another German, but not a Forty-eighter.

No one felt more keenly than he the injustice of making the Germans the scapegoats for the failures of Generals Joseph Hooker and Oliver O. Howard; he personally had occasion to know the stupidity of the latter in refusing to heed danger signals. At Gettysburg, the promotion of Howard to general direction of the field and of Schurz to command of the Eleventh Corps for the first day's fighting brought Schimmelfennig to the command of Schurz's division. As noted elsewhere, the poor placement of the Eleventh Corps, just as at Chancellorsville, invited disaster at the hands of a vastly superior foe and so two divisions of the corps were driven back into the streets of the town of Gettysburg in confusion. Struck down by the butt of a gun, Schimmelfennig had wit enough when he recovered consciousness to seek refuge in a neighboring cellar, or pigsty, according to some accounts, where he hid two days, thus escaping capture by the Confederates. After this battle, no longer wishing to be associated with the corps, he had himself sent to the Carolinas, but here he had to fight another enemy, malaria, in the swampy regions about Charleston. However, he had the satisfaction of being the first at the head of his troops to enter the cradle of secession after the surrender of Charleston. The skill of this Prussian-trained officer contributed much to the cause he had espoused. He was an intimate friend of Carl Schurz; in the fighting in Baden he had been Schurz's superior, but in the American

Civil War their roles were reversed; Carl Schurz generously acknowledged that Schimmelfennig had taught him much.

Now we come to two of the most picturesque members of the group, Max von Weber and August von Willich. The colorful United Turner Rifles, the Twentieth New York, called for a colorful commander, which it certainly had in its organizer, Max von Weber. He had fought with the rank of colonel under Generals Ludwig Mieroslawski and Sigel in the Baden revolt, and in addition to that war experience he had had the training of the Karlsruhe Military Academy and of a lieutenant in the ducal army.

It was a great day for New York Germans when von Weber led through the streets of New York for its departure for the front the Twentieth New York Regiment, darling of the Teutons, especially of the *Turner*, fitted out with many necessities by the "*Turner* Sisters." The various German societies gathered to bid the regiment farewell. It would be simpler to name the societies absent than those present, so generous was the list. At two in the afternoon, June 14, 1861, a delegation from the various *Turner* societies of the city escorted this *Turner* regiment from its camp in Turtle Bay to Union Square where a tremendous gathering of societies awaited the arrival of the departing soldiers. As the procession moved down Broadway to City Hall through the packed streets, onlookers waved greetings from all the doors and windows and threw flowers. At City Hall the usual presentations of beautiful American and German flags were made, along with appropriate speeches. Finally, the regiment was escorted to its ship by the *Turner* societies.

When this regiment was assigned to Blenker's brigade at the beginning of the war, Weber refused to serve under that officer and was therefore sent with his regiment to the Peninsula. After he was separated from the *Turner* regiment by promotion to brigadier general in April, 1862, he was on duty at Fortress Monroe where troops were landed for the Peninsular campaign. He won distinction by his performance in the battles at Norfolk, but it was at Antietam that he attracted attention in significant fashion. As leader of a brigade in General E. V. Sumner's corps,

he was stationed at Rulett's House where he held firm even after
General John Sedgwick's left had crumbled. He held out against
a deadly cannonading until a brigade was sent to his assistance.
He was able repeatedly to hurl the enemy back and retreated
only after four additional batteries were put into action against
him. It must have gratified him that his old regiment, now under
the Swedish Baron Ernst von Wegesack, rendered distinguished
service at Antietam. At this battle Weber received such a severe
wound in the shoulder that he was confined for months to the
hospital. It was only in May, 1864, that he appeared again on
the battlefield and then he shared in Sigel's Shenandoah Campaign by helping to defend Harper's Ferry against General Early
in late June, but with only eight hundred men he did not again
win special attention. However, the government gave proof of
appreciation for Antietam by bestowing on him in 1865 the
accolade of the title of major general by brevet.

Probably the most picturesque personality among all the
Forty-eighters was August von Willich, who along with Osterhaus traversed the distance from private to general. Despite the
oft-repeated rumor that he was of Hohenzollern descent the bald
facts seem to point merely to an old noble family. With an inherited interest in things military, for his father had served as
Rittmeister in a regiment of Hussars in the Napoleonic wars, he
was sent at the age of twelve to the cadet house at Potsdam, and
afterwards to the Berlin military academy. By the time he was
thirty years old he had advanced to captaincy of artillery, but
then came an abrupt break, for he had adopted the communistic
ideas seething through young Germany. As the result of a conflict between a part of his brigade and the government he offered
his resignation, and when the government attempted to remove
him to Further Pomerania away from "seditious" influences, he
refused to go. Oddly enough, the court-martial which followed,
instead of condemning him, favored acceptance of his resignation. He became an outcast with his relatives when he turned
carpenter and flouted his old associates by marching over the
parade ground with his ax on his shoulder and girt with the
conventional leather apron.

At the outbreak of the Revolution in Baden it was entirely in character for him to hasten there to cooperate with Hecker, Schimmelfennig, and Blenker. He made a reputation as leader of volunteers. Collapse of the movement meant for him, as for others able to escape, exile, first to Switzerland and then to England where he joined the reddest of the radical clubs. Though Willich was a zealous disciple of communism, Karl Marx ridiculed him as the "knight of the noble conviction" and as a "spiritual communist."

More fortunate than most Forty-eighters, he had in his carpenter's trade a means of livelihood when he landed in New York in 1853; soon his mathematical training opened a post in the Coast Survey which position he forsook for the editorship of the workingman's paper, the *Deutsche Republikaner*, in Cincinnati.

Like an old warhorse he responded to the President's call, entering the Ninth Ohio and becoming at once adjutant and as such drillmaster. When the regiment entered active service, he became its major and took part in the West Virginia campaign. About this time, August, 1861, Governor Morton of Indiana was looking for someone to organize a German regiment which later became the Thirty-second Indiana, and offered the colonelcy to Willich. In both these German units, Willich had fine material, but it was he who fashioned them into brilliant fighting units. In battle the Indiana men of this regiment maneuvered in Prussian fashion by trumpet signals and to the astonishment of American officers conducted themselves in their first battles like veterans, after only one month's training. A report on Willich's conduct in the Battle of Shiloh is given by General Lew Wallace in his *Autobiography*. The general describes how the troops supporting his position found themselves in grievous straits and then returned to the woods from which they had recently emerged, "reminding me of blackbirds in their migratory fall flight." Next he saw the enemy setting out in pursuit with triumphant yells. Wallace says that this caused him to tremble for his division. Shortly afterward he saw a body of troops emerging from the forest. He did not know whether they were friend or foe, until through his field glasses he noticed their flag, the stars and stripes. He forgot everything else, intently watching the actions of these troops.

They were but a regiment; yet at sight of them the enemy halted, about-faced, and returned to his position in the woods. There he struck out with a fire so lively that the new-comers halted and showed signs of distress. Then an officer rode swiftly around their left flank and stopped when in front of them, his back to the enemy. What he said I could not hear, but from the motions of the men he was putting them through the manual of arms—this notwithstanding some of them were dropping in the ranks. Taken all in all, *that* I think was the most audacious thing that came under my observation during the war. The effect was magical. The colonel returned to his post in the rear, and the regiment steadied as if on parade, advancing in the face of the fire pouring upon them and actually entered the wood.

On my part, then, no time was lost pressing the division forward; and while the order was in delivery I dispatched an orderly to the colonel of the unknown regiment with my compliments and asked his name. "August Willich of the Thirty-second Indiana Volunteers," was the reply brought me.

This daring procedure, which occurred also at Perryville and Chickamauga never failed to steady his men and never failed to draw an audience of American officers.

The soldiers were inclined at first to be amused at the old man who spoke bookish English with a strong East Prussian accent; but after a first battle there was only respect, for he was always where the bullets fell thickest. He served uninterruptedly from April, 1861, to February, 1864, when he was incapacitated by a severe wound in the shoulder; he was in more than thirty battles, among them the great battles of Shiloh, Perryville, Murfreesboro, Chickamauga, and Missionary Ridge. He was rewarded by a brigadier's commission for brilliant service at Shiloh where he caused the first break in the Confederate lines by a bayonet charge and thus played a decisive role.

At Murfreesboro he was guilty of his only recorded lapse from proper military procedure; after posting pickets and giving directions in case of attack, he himself rode back to brigade headquarters, instead of sending an aide, to report the left wing hanging in the air. When the attack came, he was still at headquarters and while galloping back to his men he was captured. He was exchanged within four months' time to lead his brigade in September at Chickamauga. There he stood with Thomas at the Rock of Chickamauga, executed several brilliant coups, and with the Russian Colonel Turchin covered Thomas' retreat. Willich was especially proud of his victories at Hoover and Liberty Gaps for there, in his only independent command, he forced the foe entirely out of position and made possible the advance of Rosecrans' army on Chattanooga.

His most spectacular performance was at Missionary Ridge; after having carried the breastworks at the foot of the mountain he found himself exposed to violent Confederate fire. He is said to have reasoned with himself as follows: "I cannot, because of the enemy's bullets, remain where I am and I will not turn back. I am going forward, even if I am court-martialed for it." Therefore, without waiting for orders, he allowed his nine regiments to scale the summit. Their enthusiasm swept neighboring troops with them and thus they gained the heights before General Grant had intended them to be scaled. In the battle of Resaca, May, 1864, at the beginning of Sherman's march through Georgia, a bullet put an end to his active service. Even so he was made commander of the Cincinnati district and went in March, 1865, to Texas with his corps until its muster-out the next October. Only then was he accorded his final recognition, brevet rank of a major general.

Willich belongs among the most eccentric but also the most remarkable figures of the war. His best friends pronounced him a *naerrischer Kerl*, but his extraordinary courage, his coolness and caution in danger, and what may be termed without exaggeration, nobility of spirit, lifted him above the ordinary man. He combined the contradictory qualities which typify in some respects the Forty-eighters. Though a stern disciplinarian—he once expected after a twenty-mile march to hold the usual regimental drill—he would share with his men his last morsel. This radical extremist would assemble his soldiers in camp, address them as "Citizens of Indiana," and then harangue them on communism. Probably the greatest tribute to him was the fact that his warmest admirers were the American officers who served under him.

The Germans, and among them some Forty-eighters, were especially conspicuous among the colonels. Here were to be found some of the best fighters in the army, for it is the colonels who determine the execution of the general's strategy by the way in which they handle their regiments.

Dr. Friedrich Hecker may well head the list, not only for his services in the War but also for his prominence in the entire German-American population. Through his mother he was descended from the nobility, a background still further accented by his rearing at court. As a student of jurisprudence he was naturally exposed at the university to the new liberalism in Germany, and, being an impractical idealist by nature, he was certain to embrace it with ardor. A leader in the movement for parliamentary government, he logically became one of the chief leaders in the uprising in Baden. After the first defeat of the revolutionaries at Kandern, Hecker went to America to raise funds among German Americans there, but in 1849 when the movement manifested fresh strength, he set out to return to Germany. Before his arrival in the homeland, the Revolution had completely collapsed and there was nothing for Hecker to do but return to the farm he had purchased not far from Belleville, Illinois.

Hecker, like Osterhaus, was willing to enter the Union service as a private and presented himself with his son in St. Louis to enter in this humble position Sigel's Third Missouri Regiment. Almost immediately the command of the Twenty-fourth Illinois, a German-Hungarian unit, was tendered him but, when friction developed between him and the other officers, he withdrew from the command. Straightway a second Hecker regiment was organized by his admirers, the Eighty-second Illinois. Laying down conditions to prevent the dissension which had arisen in the earlier regiment, he accepted the command of what became one of the best regiments in the West. At Chancellorsville, his most significant battle, his regiment in Schurz's division of the Eleventh Corps was stationed on the Hawkins Farm, in the path of Jackson's onslaught. Almost immediately after the opening of the battle, Hecker was shot from his saddle while trying to

rally his men, but by a fortuitous circumstance the bullet re-
bounded from a large silver snuffbox which he always carried in
his pocket so that he suffered only a flesh wound and in a few
months was again capable of service. He shared in the Chattanooga campaign, in the night battle at Wauhatchie, and in the
great victory at Missionary Ridge. He was directly involved, as
has been related, in the controversy between Schurz and Hooker.
Hecker resigned at the beginning of 1864, partly from pique, it
might be said, but it is not strange that he felt neglected at being
passed over in all promotions during nearly three years of service.
Hecker lives in American history for his devotion to the antislavery cause, his gripping oratory, and his charming personality
rather than for any great contribution on the battlefield.

Colonel George von Amsberg presents one of those rare cases
where a German qualifies as a Forty-eighter by virtue of participation in the Hungarian revolt. Though born in the Hanoverian
city of Hildesheim, he had enlisted in the Austrian army and in
1848 was serving as an officer in one of the Hungarian Hussar
regiments. Here he had so completely mastered the Hungarian
tongue that he preferred it to his native German. After the outbreak of war for Hungarian independence, he accompanied his
regiment into the revolutionary army. An adjutant to General
Henry Dembinski with the rank of colonel, he distinguished himself in several battles. After suppression of the revolt, he was
sentenced to sixteen years' imprisonment, actually served nine
years, and was then pardoned on condition of leaving the country. At the commencement of the Civil War he was supporting
himself at Hoboken as a riding master. He became colonel of the
Forty-fifth New York Regiment composed mostly of old soldiers.
His previous combat experience undoubtedly explains his early
selection for regimental office and promotion to command of a
brigade under Sigel and later under Schurz.

Adolf Dengler, colonel of the Forty-third Illinois Regiment,
was a distinguished exile of the Baden Revolution who had defended Freiburg against the ducal forces. As a "Latin farmer"
in the Belleville settlement he organized, after Lincoln's call, a
company of second generation Germans from Belleville and led

them to St. Louis into the regiment of his intimate friend Sigel. He survived the battles of Carthage, Wilson's Creek, and Pea Ridge only to be killed at the grand assault on Vicksburg on May 22, 1863.

Colonel Joseph Gerhardt, a native of the Rhenish city of Bonn, rose to the command of a battalion in the uprising in Baden by virtue of the confidence his courage and caution inspired. He suffered imprisonment in the famous fortress at Rastatt but succeeded in effecting an escape and fled via Switzerland to America to settle ultimately in the national capital. Here he made his living at first by playing the violin at theaters, and then as a restaurateur; after a time he progressed to the ownership of the Germania Hotel. At the outbreak of the war he organized a *Turner* company in Washington, leadership of which gave him rank as captain. Later he was called to be major of the Fifty-sixth New York Regiment and soon rose to be its colonel. Distinguished service in several battles brought him by the end of the war to a brigadier's title by brevet.

Carl Eberhard Salomon, brother of the general of that name, cannot be omitted, for he too had a war record in Germany. He went from the *Gymnasium* to Magdeburg as a one-year volunteer in the pioneer section of the army; after one year he proved able to pass the examination for officer in his branch of the service. The collapse of the Revolution threatened him with dire consequences for he was condemned in 1849 to two years in prison but he was already on the ocean bound for the United States. After a brief residence in Wisconsin he settled permanently in St. Louis in 1860. Within a month after the country was plunged into war, he had organized a regiment, officially the Fifth Missouri Volunteers; as its colonel he fought in the battle of Dry Forks near Carthage.

In Wilhelm Heine and Konrad Krez were found picturesque characters who combined with artistic talent the qualities that make able military men. Krez was regarded by his contemporaries as the finest poet among German Americans. *An mein Vaterland*, certainly among the most inspired songs written by a Forty-eighter, was said to have deeply affected the suppressor of the South German revolution, Emperor William I, even though it was the outpouring of a revolutionary fugitive. Krez rendered service at the siege of Vicksburg, in the campaign in Arkansas, and against Mobile, as commander of the Twenty-seventh Wisconsin, and for his activities at Mobile emerged from the war as brigadier general by brevet. Heine, who attained exactly the same rank, had pursued a painter's and writer's career at Leipzig; he found his continued residence there impossible after his participation in street fighting in the revolt of 1848. The story of his life in America from his arrival in 1851 to the war reads like a romance, compared with that of many Forty-eighters who existed by violin-playing in cheap beerhalls or by acting as porter in low-class inns. He took service with the American fleet and became an able seaman and engineer. When the war came, he entered the Potomac army as an engineer; when he took command of the One Hundred and Third New York in 1863, he reached the rank of colonel and in the last year of the war that of titular brigadier.

Another outstanding engineer, who had brought his trained skill to the United States because of participation in the revolt of 1848 as a captain of a company of army engineers, was Henry Flad. Here he rose during the Civil War to be colonel of Josiah Bissell's Missouri Regiment of Engineers and became one of the outstanding engineers of the Union army, rendering his finest service in building bridges.

Another colonel of the individualistic type among the Forty-eighters was Fritz Anneke. He had been a Prussian artillery officer but because he could not refrain from criticism of his superiors, he had been dismissed from the army. He later joined the Revolutionary army in Baden, in which he had as his adjutant the nineteen-year-old Carl Schurz, and there manifested some skill in strategy. Flight was the only alternative to execution offered an ex-Prussian officer, and so he came to America. After serving briefly as a colonel of artillery on General J. B. McClernand's staff he was, probably because of his European experience, commissioned by Governor Salomon colonel of the Thirty-fourth Wisconsin Infantry. His old lack of self-control was

another opportunity for a military career. In response to the first call for troops he raised a company which as captain he led into the Fifty-second New York, a regiment to be noted for its hard fighting and frightful casualties. In little more than six months he was serving as major; a year later he had advanced to lieutenant colonel, and commanded a regiment at Chancellorsville. He was twice wounded, so desperately at Gettysburg that he had to resign, though he still served in the veteran reserve corps where by April, 1864, he again ranked as lieutenant colonel. Toward the close of the war the government recognized his gallantry by the rank of colonel by brevet.

An Austrian revolutionary of the Hungarian revolt was Ernest F. M. Faehtz, who fought in Austria in 1848 and then in Baden in 1849; when the movement collapsed, he turned his back on Europe for the new world where he found a teaching career possible. The Civil War brought him back to the field in the Fifth Maryland, and ultimately he became lieutenant colonel of the Eighth Maryland.

The second in command of the Forty-sixth New York was Germain von Metternich, a former dragoon officer in the Austrian army who had fought under Sigel in the Baden revolt; in America he met his unfortunate end on the island of Tybee off Savannah when an infantryman accidentally bayoneted him.

Hermann Ulffers, as a trained civil engineer after his flight to America following the failure of the Revolution, readily found work on the railroads. He entered the army in 1861 as an engineer officer and saw much action in the West before Sherman called him to his staff. One of the fortunates who escaped from Andersonville, he finally reached the Union lines, wrapped in rags, reduced to a skeleton, unrecognizable but alive, and able after a time to return to service. Also in this group should be mentioned Hans Boebel of the Twenty-sixth Wisconsin; Edward C. Wratislaw of the Forty-fifth New York; and Adam Senges, whose long imprisonment with Otto von Corwin at Freiburg had not quenched his ardor for combat as is testified to by the fact that he went out as colonel of the Fifteenth New York Artillery in the Potomac Army.

Eliciting special interest are several Forty-eighters who served in the army as artillerists with the rank of lieutenant colonel. Andrew Brickel (spelled in official records Brickell) commanded the First New York Battalion of Light Artillery, more generally referred to as Brickel's Artillery, consisting of four batteries. This revolutionary of the Baden uprising, enjoyed one of the most widely known reputations in the Potomac army, and that is saying a great deal, for there emerged during the war a large number of distinguished artillerists. Brickel fought during the entire war with the greatest brilliancy. Albert Arndt, mentioned here to avoid repetition though his rank was only that of major, was in charge of Battery A and had, like his chief, joined the insurgents in Baden. He fell at Antietam.

Outstanding among the officers of the next grade, that of major, was Franz Backhoff, holding this rank in Sigel's artillery during his Missouri campaign. Backhoff had already achieved a reputation in Baden by his participation in the disaffection of the national army at Rastatt in 1848. As early as 1842 he entered the artillery, was advanced after seven months over many old soldiers to head cannoneer, became in a year a corporal, and then sergeant major. In 1847 he passed the examination for riding warden of the border, but was unable to accept the post as he still had two more years to serve in the army. When the Revolution broke out in Baden the next year, he was posted with a battery, along with other portions of the national army—infantry and cavalry—in the courtyard at Rastatt and was commanded to order the guns fired on the insurgents. Instead he had the guns turned around. A superior officer who tried to force the soldiers to fire was badly wounded and obliged to retire. One of the leaders of the revolutionaries in a brief speech to the military pleaded with them to make common cause with the people; the cannons were trained on the infantry and cavalry and in a few minutes the fortress was in the hands of the insurgents. Backhoff was made captain of artillery by the insurrectionary Executive Committee and ordered to accompany a battalion of infantry to Karlsruhe with a battery. Before his arrival the duke, disguised as a cannoneer, had fled the city, together with his ministry and his battery of cannon. Charged with the duty of pursuing the duke, Backhoff captured the minister of war, some six hundred men, and the cannon. He was made chief of artillery on Sigel's staff and helped Sigel develop the plan of operations; he won distinction in the battles on the border and in defense of the fortress at Rastatt. After the capitulation, he was thrown into the casements. Instead of death he drew ten years' imprisonment, two of which he had served when the duke pardoned him on condition of his leaving Europe. He settled in St. Louis as building contractor in 1861 and was at hand when Sigel was seeking officers for his artillery. The European experience of this officer illustrates well how the Forty-eighters were advanced in their American fortunes by that experience and how, in turn, the European training and relationships made it possible to bring able men at once to the front. Backhoff's career with Sigel in Missouri was distinguished, almost brilliant. A capable man at the guns certainly helped win the victory at Pea Ridge and fix Missouri in the Union.

Representing another specialized field was Ernst F. Hoffman, an engineer officer originally in the Prussian army, who might readily be classified as a soldier of fortune. After the brief interlude of the Baden revolt, he fought in Schleswig-Holstein, then went over into the English service and fought in the Crimean War. Next he was enrolled as staff officer with Garibaldi. Oddly enough, he was then honored with a post carrying the rank of major in the engineer corps of the regular Italian army. As soon as the war broke out in the United States he appeared here, where his services were highly significant. He established the topographical bureau for the Eleventh Corps and later in 1864 for Thomas's army in Tennessee. He restored the bridge over the Hiwassee River in Tennessee, which had suffered destruction at the hands of the enemy. To the astonishment of one of the most important engineers of the army, General James H. Wilson, he erected the bridge during a single dark night and thus enabled Sherman's troops to cross the next morning to come to the relief of General Ambrose E. Burnside at Knoxville. This deed

Wilson could scarcely praise enough and said of Hoffman, "Sober, serious, and untiring, as brave as any paladin, and as punctilious as any knight errant, he was always ready and always practical. It was his high proudest boast that he was indeed a Dutch Yankee. Modest and gentle as a woman, industrious and patient as a navvy, an accomplished musician, and an interesting conversationalist, he was one of the most useful and most lovable men I ever came in contact with."

Undoubtedly the most distinguished of the Forty-eighters who bore the designation of captain in the Union army was Gustav von Struve, referred to occasionally as "the leader of the Revolution in Baden." It is unnecessary here to stress his radical views, his activities as a political agitator, or his work in New York between his exile and the outbreak of the American war. It is quite in character that in 1861 he was instantly ready to fight in behalf of another cause; hence he enlisted as a private in Blenker's Eighth New York Regiment though he was promptly raised to captain in that unit—another evidence of the results of the European associations. He made himself rather ridiculous after Prince Felix zu Salm-Salm became colonel of this regiment by declaring, "I cannot be a servant of princes." Since the prince was the simple colonel of a regiment, Struve's indignation was ridiculed in the army more than the old revolutionary enjoyed. During his brief war career here he was the loyal supporter and defender of Blenker, his old Baden comrade. In the midst of the war he returned to Germany, an embittered man to judge by the sharp strictures in his writings.

Several other captains could boast of military experience in the struggle of 1848. Adam Schumacher's story is interesting enough to narrate and may be typical of others who, like Backhoff, went over to the people's army. He had been called for military service in the spring of 1848 and was stationed at Freiburg. Five days after being mustered in, his regiment was ordered to march to Kandern against Hecker, but this unit was not used in the campaign of that year, possibly because of distrust of raw recruits. In 1849 when the army deserted to the side of the insurrectionaries, he went over with his comrades. Although hardly more than a recruit, he was promptly advanced by the insurrectionary provisional government to a noncommissioned post to drill new recruits. He served under Sigel as sergeant until that officer led his army into Switzerland. By the next November, Schumacher was in Cincinnati. He went to the field in the summer of 1861 with the first German Ohio regiment, the Ninth, saw active service in almost all its battles, and had by February, 1864, advanced from private to captain. A second illustration of a Forty-eighter of this rank is Captain Sixtus Ludwig Kapff, who served at the head of Company G in the Seventh New York under his brother, Colonel Edward Kapff.

Since chiefs of batteries rank as captains, we must add also the following: Christian Essig, who had been Sigel's adjutant in Baden and commanded a battery under Backhoff during the three months' campaign in Missouri; William Hexamer, who commanded Battery A of the First New Jersey Light Artillery, and at Antietam frustrated an attack on General Winfield S. Hancock's left wing, entirely exhausting his munition in the process and losing heavily in men; Louis Hofmann, another testimony to Sigel's partiality to old comrades in arms, who fought with such distinction at Vicksburg that a memorial to his Fourth Ohio Independent Battery stands on the battle grounds. Peculiar interest attaches to Captain John Albert Neustaedter, a former Prussian artillerist, because with Schurz he made his escape from the fortress at Rastatt as the latter reveals in his *Reminiscences*. In America, by 1851 he was continuing his association with his old comrades in arms by working with Boernstein on the *Anzeiger des Westens*. A battery which he organized came into action in the first battles in Missouri. He not only proved himself one of the most capable artillerists in the Western army, often distinguishing himself in the battles of the Army of the Cumberland, but also an important engineer, building Fort Anderson. Late in the war he served on Sherman's staff.

Probably many more Forty-eighters than we know or could find space for here found their way into the lower commissioned and noncommissioned offices, for the lower the rank the less the

information forthcoming. Lieutenant Hermann Ignatz Dettweiler of Company C, Sixth Kentucky Infantry, is an example.
Research has revealed a few Forty-eighters as privates who did
not rise from the ranks; one such is Fidel Schlund, whose talents
apparently lay in the political rather than the military field.
He sat in the Bavarian legislative chamber from 1845–49 and
in the famous Frankfurt Assembly of 1848. For his part in the
uprising he languished long in the public jail at Kempten. The
sincerity of his crusading spirit is manifest through his action
after coming to America in entering the Union service with his
four sons, one of whom was killed and a second severely wounded.

In the field of special services the physicians and chaplains
prove of special interest. The number of doctors in the Union
army who had participated in the revolutionary movement of
1848 is truly astonishing. The superiority of medical training in
Europe at the time insured that the services of German-trained
medical men would be welcome to the Northern authorities.
Among them were some of the outstanding surgeons in the
United States, and even some with an international reputation.
It is certainly interesting to find in the list the name of Dr. Adam
Hammer, who stood at the very top of his profession. Although
his father came to America before the Revolution, the son stayed
on in Germany to complete his training at Heidelberg. He became involved in the insurgent movement in Baden through his
friend Hecker and with him fled to this country. He established
a practice in St. Louis, where, after his return from a period of
study in Europe, he founded the first German medical college in
America, the Humboldt Institute. It is not too much to say that
Dr. Hammer was one of the most zealous among the Germans
in promoting the patriotic uprising in St. Louis. As early as
March preceding the outbreak of war, he organized and armed
his students as a military unit; they hid at night in a near-by
brewery, ready to fall on the rebels in case of an attack on the
arsenal. Upon the outbreak of war, he closed the Institute and
entered the Fourth Missouri Infantry as lieutenant colonel. At
the end of three months' service he assumed for the greater part

good revolver; hence, they might expect to see him, when they were involved in battle, not on his knees but in the front with the fighters. He is quoted as closing with the words: "Make way for freedom—Death to the traitors!" This type of sermon, very typical of the Forty-eighter spirit, seemed to please his Ohio Germans. To this group should probably be added Joseph A. Fuchshuber whose "sermons" were freethinking lectures. However, the soldiers were content with their chaplain, for he was a true humanitarian—giving sound advice, writing letters for the soldiers, and serving the sick in the hospital.

That every army regulation can be circumvented is illustrated by the case of Albert Kraus, who served in Osterhaus's Twelfth Missouri Regiment under the technical title of chaplain though he was decidedly a freethinker. By this time a law had been passed by a scandalized Congress requiring that only regularly ordained clergymen should be appointed to the post of chaplain, but Kraus's friends neatly met the letter of the law by founding a *freie Gemeinde* to enable him to prefix the title of "Reverend" to his name. The choice was a wise one, for this particular chaplain went constantly under fire to give aid to the wounded.

But in Blenker's division the so-called "chaplains" were often largely a farce. Every regiment had its official who, to the scandal of the devout, was referred to as *Seelsorger*. The soldiers in Blenker's division felt little craving for spiritual comfort, for their chaplains, often compared to Schiller's humorous parson in *Wallensteins Lager*, prided themselves on being "liberal" in religion, a liberalism which usually translated itself into atheism. "I don't believe in any such nonsense," was a phrase often on the lips of the Forty-eighters. However, since under the law Blenker was entitled to one chaplain for each regiment, he saw to it that all appointments were duly made. It was rumored that his first requirement was that any chaplain must be a devout disciple of Bachus. In the main they were journalists, who could work for their papers without interference and repay Blenker by sending in eulogistic articles about the commander of this division.

There were of course also serious journalists associated with the army, and Otto von Corwin, probably the most distinguished in the group, deserves recognition at this point. One of the outstanding leaders of the uprising in Baden and commander for a time of the fortress at Rastatt, he was naturally condemned to death at the collapse of the revolt and languished for many years in prison. As correspondent of the *Augsburger Allgemeine Zeitung* and of the London *Times* during a part of the Civil War, he became one of the best known of the war reporters. His most distinctive activity in the war, however, was the effort in 1863 to bring over to the service of the Union 20,000 trained German soldiers. Lincoln at first reacted favorably to the idea but soon dropped it in the face of the opposition of Secretary of War Edwin M. Stanton. It was probably doomed from the moment that it became apparent that Corwin hoped to make the venture financially profitable to himself.

Another very important journalist, a bit too young to be classed exactly as a Forty-eighter but imbued with quite the same spirit was Henry Villard. As a boy in school he had rebelled against joining in a prayer for the King and otherwise found the reactionary regime of his native land so oppressive that at the age of eighteen he fled to the United States, arriving in 1853 without either funds or a knowledge of the English language. But with great gusto and application he made his way as correspondent first of German language papers as reporter of the Lincoln-Douglas debates and during the Civil War as correspondent for the New York *Herald* and the New York *Tribune*. He was present at the battles of Bull Run, Shiloh, Perryville, Fredericksburg, and Chattanooga. Later in life he became a great railway magnate and made of the New York *Evening Post* a liberal paper with Carl Schurz as one of the editors. His valuable memoirs report many of his experiences at the front.

The value of the presence of the Forty-eighters in the Union army was threefold: first, their help in winning the war; second, the reaction on the Forty-eighters themselves; third, the advantage to the United States in appreciable assimilation of a hitherto critical group. It would be impossible to write or read this chapter without realizing how much these German-born leaders contributed by their trained skill, their knowledge of military science, and their combat experience toward winning the victory. First of all, a raw, undisciplined citizenry had to be made into a fighting machine. The North had far too few trained officers for the colossal task. Officers must be able to stand up without flinching under fire and the North in the veterans of the Mexican War had only a handful of men who had ever experienced fire. The Union desperately needed officers with skill in handling brigades and divisions and men who could handle the thousand men of one regiment; it also needed men with the judgment on occasion to lead independently. To call a roll of those noted in this chapter is to show men who could do just that—Osterhaus, Willich, von Weber, Salomon, Schurz, Schimmelfennig—to name the chief among the Forty-eighters. Then the cause must have fighters, men of lower rank, the kind of men who could stand up against the hardest odds—men like Gerhardt, Backhoff, Brickel, Freudenberg, Dengler, Mahler, von Metternich, and Mersey. Men of specialized skills were also necessary—engineers like Flad, Hoffman, and Ulffers; and men high in the medical profession who could organize the care of the wounded on a huge scale, like Drs. Hammer, Weber, and Schmidt. The many other Germans who had come before or independently of the movement of 1848 and the excellent leaders from other nationality groups must not be forgotten, such as the Hungarians, Poles, Norwegians, Swedes, and French. Certainly, however, the number of top leaders from the group of the Forty-eighters in proportion to the three or four thousand who came over is striking.

The aspect which most German Americans, as well as native Americans, tend to overlook is what the war and the preliminary debate of the preceding decade did for the Forty-eighters and hence for their countrymen who followed the leaders. As a result of the war they abandoned completely the lingering hope of a renewed revolution in Germany, in which they were to have a leading role. In truth, they now definitely became a part of America, accepting this as the future home for themselves and their children. By rubbing shoulders with Americans in every type of military relationship, as superiors, equals, and inferiors, they came to understand their native fellow citizens better and, by the same token, to appreciate them better. The things in American life which the Forty-eighters had criticized so harshly assumed a new aspect when they saw the essential fairness and generosity of the average soldiers, the devotion to an ideal which made Americans pour out their blood and treasure to a degree that no Forty-eighters could surpass. Crudeness which had so grated on the cultivated strangers seemed under the common hardships of camp and field, where all niceties drop away, less annoying than it had in time of peace. Face to face with stark realities the dream of an ideal state seemed less alluring. Furthermore, when men faced day after day the eternal verities of life and death, the importance of proving the follies of religion, the inconsistencies of church or creed, loomed less and less, so that the zeal for anti-ecclesiastical warfare tended to disappear.

Many had thrown themselves into the war with whole-souled ardor—the same ardor with which they had fought for the freedom of Germany a decade earlier. During the election campaigns of 1860 and 1864 they had an active share in the political field and that meant dealing practically with a problem. Hence, most of the Forty-eighters cast aside some of their radicalism and adapted their views to actual conditions. Compromise no longer seemed merely moral cowardice. They were losing some of their extreme liberalism or, to put it metaphorically, the war had rubbed down some of their sharp corners. Some of the younger revolutionaries, fifteen years older by the close of the war, had toned down to moderate progressives, worthy of leadership among their own people, and some, like Schurz, ready for leadership in the country as a whole. They cast off the impractical extravagances which had characterized a majority of the refugees in 1850 and some few began to see that they were partly to blame for the nativists' attitude which they had so cordially loathed. In 1848 they had been theoretical and idealistic politicians, treating statecraft as a philosophy; in America they learned that it was a practical matter to be dealt with on the basis of the possible. They saw that what they had condemned without reservation as American corruption was human nature, much the same everywhere. The common hatred of slavery had thrown radical Puritan abolitionist and radical Forty-eighter into the same melting pot. The war had served to broaden the rigid mind of the fanatical idealist.

Probably the greatest good of all came to the United States, for nothing is more unwholesome than unassimilated groups in the body politic, especially a group which could generate so much intellectual ferment as these independent-thinking Germans. Much as the common intellectual struggle against slavery, in the debate over which leaders among the Forty-eighters had taken a real part, had done to promote amalgamation, the war did far more. There is an old truism that to love something one must fight for it. The Forty-eighters had thrown themselves into the war to end slavery and to preserve the Union. They knew that they had helped to win the great triumphant victory. As we have seen in a previous chapter, the claim that the Germans were the determining factor in Lincoln's first election can probably not be substantiated; the German uprising in Missouri, however, cannot be challenged but must stand as the greatest single contribution by the Germans, and especially by the leading Forty-eighters, to the Union cause. The consciousness among Germans and Forty-eighters of their great contribution to the ultimate victory of the Union cause consolidated them in the Union.

Chapter Eight

CARL SCHURZ

By Bayard Quincy Morgan

THERE can scarcely be any doubt that if a single person were chosen to represent, in the minds of the American public, the peculiar essence of the German immigration of '48, its idealism and its ideals, its vigor and independence, its youthful buoyancy and optimism, the name of Carl Schurz would head any list of nominees for that position. No other member of the group combined within himself so many of the characteristics which set the entire body apart from any other company of immigrants to this country, either before or since. Few if any others played such a part in building up in the eyes of our people the portrait of the German-American. To this day, the name of Carl Schurz commands a respect which transcends his person; it has become a symbol behind which the man himself tends to disappear. Desirable as that development is in many respects— for Schurz has long been dead, but that for which he stood has not died and should not die—it is more than appropriate that in the present volume the man himself should once more be recalled, to take his proper place at the head of the distinguished company of men and women with whom his memory is indissolubly linked.

Karl Schurz (he changed the spelling to Carl soon after beginning his political career in this country) was born on March 2, 1829, as the oldest child of Christian and Marianne (Juessen) Schurz in the village of Liblar, a few miles from Bonn on the Rhine. The immediate family was engaged in farming, and the boy grew up in a rural environment and in an atmosphere on which he congratulated himself in later years. He was compelled to learn thrift, yet without suffering actual want or the sacrifice of any essential form of training; his relatives, though not highly educated themselves, had a high respect for education; and the healthful physical, mental, and moral conditions of his youthful years doubtless laid the soundest foundations for his future well-being. Moreover, as the village contained only the ordinary *Volksschule*, Karl had to go to Brühl, eight miles away, at the age of nine, and to Cologne at the age of ten, and was therefore never a home-boy, strictly speaking. This must have promoted an early maturity in him, encouraging the development of that strength of character, self-reliance, and initiative which were to be of supreme importance in his future political career.

A thirst for knowledge and for intellectual conquest was fundamental in him, and not long after he had learned to read and write he began the mastery of Latin. In view of recent disagreements as to the place of the classical languages in a modern curriculum, it is interesting to read the reasoned opinion of this successful man of affairs on that point. "Were I once more given a choice," he writes in his *Reminiscences*,

between classical studies and the so-called utilitarian ones, I should unquestionably choose for myself essentially the same course of study that I pursued. I should do so with the less hesitation that in later life I should probably never have been able to take up the classics, had I not begun them in the *Gymnasium*, and that my knowledge of the ancient languages was of inestimable value to me later on in the acquisition of the modern languages.

His training included rather thorough schooling in music and in the appreciation of art. Wide acquaintance with the masterpieces of German literature helped to form his sense of style and at the same time encouraged him to try his hand at all sorts of literary creation: lyric poetry, fiction, drama. However slight their intrinsic merit, these youthful productions may well have contributed to that mastery of the word which, once gained in one language, is then more easily attained in others. Only on some such assumption can we understand the remarkable eloquence which Schurz developed in English after a relatively short residence in this country. The oratorical ability which he had displayed as a youth in Germany seems to have been somehow transferred to his use of the English language in the United States.

More important to him than literary accomplishment was political achievement, which came closer to him through his study of history. Beginning with personal narratives of the Napoleonic period supplied by his father and grandfather, he was soon led into three separate provinces of historic interest, two of them destined to be decisive in his own life.

First of all, he became an ardently patriotic German, with a strong desire to see a united Germany; this had of course a direct bearing on his conduct during the year 1848.

Second, and in the end perhaps more significantly, even as a boy Schurz came to take a keen interest in America. This interest had its inception in the fact that neighboring families emigrated to that land of incredible dimensions and seemingly inexhaustible resources. In the course of the interminable conversations regarding this migration, the mind of the boy took in, never to lose them again, vivid pictures of the vast forests and the mighty rivers and lakes of America. Once aroused, his interest was fed by the letters of the emigrants, and by all sorts of printed matter. Schurz never forgot his first sight, in the *Pfennigmagazin*, of the face of George Washington, whom his father had already described to him as the noblest of men. It seems likely that Washington was his first "hero," and helped to arouse in him the admiration of human greatness which was to be one of the motivating forces in his character.

For it was not only the marvels of nature and the material promise of undeveloped territory that made America seem like the place of a new Golden Age. To the political enthusiasts of Europe, America was the bulwark and the home of freedom, and it was no accident that thousands of those who had striven in vain to achieve their political ideals on European soil turned their faces and their feet westward. Many who did not convert such a dream into reality did cherish it as a hope, and the Schurz family was among these. Certainly the idea of migration to America became familiar to Karl Schurz from his earliest youth.

Ultimately most of the Schurz family actually did migrate to America, hoping to find liberty there.

At the *Gymnasium* in Cologne, Karl not only broadened his knowledge but also, as he writes in his *Reminiscences*, "learned how to learn." To master and digest a set of facts, to put in order a mass of unrelated details, to subdue with celerity and ease a rebellious or resistant spiritual territory—this is the mark of the trained mind; and when family misfortune compelled Schurz to quit the *Gymnasium* before his course was ended, he had so thoroughly grasped the fundamentals of learning that he put himself through the remaining subjects while attending university classes at Bonn. Though the rigid final examinations of the *Gymnasium* were then made especially severe for those who prepared for them outside of school, Karl passed them brilliantly, astonishing his examiners by translating the assigned passage from the *Iliad* without looking at the Greek, as he knew the text by heart.

Even in his youth Schurz was to taste public triumph, and though the occasions were not of great importance, the results may have been lasting. For one of the "rewards" of the public figure must be acclaim and applause, cheers and admiration. It was in 1848, when Schurz was nineteen, that he delivered his first extemporaneous speech in public. He writes: "I have never been able to recall exactly what I said. I only know that I was in a state of excitement which was wholly new to me, that my entire body was trembling, that ideas and words came to me in unbroken flow, that I spoke with impetuous rapidity, and that the ensuing applause had the effect of waking me from a dream." If there is such a thing as a born orator, must not this be a good description of his characteristic essence?

While this is not the place for a full account of the memorable year of 1848, we must at least outline those events which led, in the end, to the exile of Karl Schurz and his eventual removal to this country.

Among the early ideals and hopes cherished by Schurz was the unification of the German people, involving at the same time

a democratization of government which had indeed been promised the Prussian people by their King, when he summoned
them to arms to overthrow the tyranny of Napoleon. Actually,
however, King Friedrich Wilhelm III, who ruled from 1797 to
1840, became one of the most absolute autocrats of the day, and
when his son Friedrich Wilhelm IV proved to be even more
autocratic than his father, the restiveness of the German people
reached a new peak. The "United Diet" of 1847, which the
king was forced to convene, did nothing to lessen the rising tide
of discontent, and open resistance to tyranny began to find
expression.

Like a bombshell in a powder magazine fell the news that the
French had deposed Louis Philippe and proclaimed a new republic. Schurz, who like many other students at Bonn had been
following the course of public events with keen interest and increasing zeal, was now so powerfully stirred that we may call
this the turning point of his entire life.

Galvanized into action by the example of France, the German
people staged public demonstrations of more or less violent
character in all the provinces. News of exciting character from
all over the land kept the Bonn students on the alert. The bloody
clash in Berlin, from which many deaths resulted, and which
wrested from the King the promise of a new and more liberal
constitution, had an electrifying effect.

Schurz and other enthusiasts felt that their high hopes were
about to be realized. Schurz went about the countryside preaching the new gospel, and spent a great deal of time helping to
edit and publish the *Bonner Zeitung*, founded by Gottfried Kinkel
in 1848 as a democratic organ. This experience must have been of
the utmost importance for the shaping of Schurz's political ideals
and convictions, and a definite preparation for his life in America, where he was to see in action, and help to guide, the forces
now struggling for their very existence in Germany.

It is interesting and perhaps significant that Schurz first came
into contact with Kinkel by taking his course in public speaking
—an indication that Schurz was not indifferent to the appeal of
oratory. Then about thirty-two, Kinkel was well qualified to

win Schurz's admiration: talented as a teacher and speaker, with a genuine gift for poetry, and a man of great personal charm, Kinkel only had to offer affection in order to lay the grounds for a real friendship.

It was natural that Kinkel's unshrinking espousal of the revolutionary cause should be emulated by his younger friend; and it followed naturally that Schurz became involved in the military actions which carried Kinkel into prison. What happened after that was merely the logical concatenation of character and circumstance.

The story of Kinkel's rescue has been told in exemplary fashion by Schurz himself, and the interested reader may be referred to his *Reminiscences* for the fascinating details, which do as much credit to Schurz's head as to his heart. It will suffice here to provide the merest outline of a great and complicated action.

Condemned to life imprisonment, Kinkel was incarcerated in the fortress at Spandau, where he was treated with inhuman contempt, including the denial of all intellectual occupation. This meant not so much a restriction of liberty as a living death. His wife Johanna, a woman of high intelligence and great tenacity, never for a moment abandoned the hope that he might be liberated. First assembling funds sufficient for an attempt at rescue, she wrote to Schurz, who had fled to Switzerland, that she was in search of a man who would, even at the risk of his own life, undertake to manage Kinkel's escape.

Schurz responded promptly to the unstated but clearly implied appeal, and laid his plans with such extraordinary foresight and imagination that in November, 1850, some nine months after the receipt of Johanna Kinkel's letter, Kinkel and Schurz were on board the brig "Anna" bound from Rostock to Leith—and freedom.

Schurz's subsequent indecision, which lasted a full year, was finally terminated by the *coup d'état* of Louis Napoleon in December, 1851. Now he realized, apparently for the first time, that he must rebuild his life plans from the bottom up. Return to Germany was impossible; liberty, or at least democratic liberty, was at an end in France. Where then could one find democracy? His eyes turned to America. There was "a new world, a free world, a world of great ideas and purposes." Thinking such thoughts, Schurz tells us, on a chilly December day in Hyde Park, he became aware of a small man sitting on the same bench, whom he presently recognized as Louis Blanc, leader of the French socialists, now an exile like himself. As Schurz rose to go, without having said a word, Blanc fastened sleepless eyes on him and said simply, "Ah, c'est vous, mon jeune ami! C'est fini, n'est-ce pas? C'est fini!" It was as if the way-worn Frenchman, seemingly at the very end of his road (he was to remain in exile till the fall of the Second Empire in 1870), were handing over to the impetuous young German the torch of liberty, that its flame should not die in the world.

On the 6th of July, 1852, Karl Schurz was married to Margarethe Meyer of Hamburg in Marylebone Church in London, and in August of that year the young couple set sail from Portsmouth for their new home.

The rise of Karl Schurz, an unknown immigrant of twenty-three years, who upon his landing in New York knew virtually no English at all, to the rank of United States Senator Carl Schurz, in the comparatively short space of sixteen years, is a development that may be fairly called sensational. Without doubt this result was in part due to the peculiar configuration of things in the United States, and to the fact that Schurz's native gifts happened to meet the needs of the situation, while his personal philosophy responded with natural eagerness to the challenges that his new home presented to him. When we consider, however, that of the thousands of German Forty-eighters who sought a home in the American republic no other achieved anything like such eminence as Schurz, we are justified in attributing a major portion of his success to those outstanding qualities of mind and character that his friends and admirers stressed during his lifetime.

We are fortunate in having from Schurz's own pen a summary account of the first ten of these sixteen years, written down for his former fellow student Theodor Petrasch of Bonn. We can

hardly do better than to quote a portion of that letter, which is
dated September 24, 1863, at Catlett Station, Virginia:

In the year 52 I put an end to my refugee life in London, because
I was painfully conscious of its untenableness and was longing for some
real activity. Here in America I lived for several years quietly and un-
obtrusively in an ideally happy family circle. . . . I studied, observed,
and learned assiduously, until at last in the year 56, when the movement against slavery developed magnificently, I found myself drawn
into public life. I knew that I should accomplish something. America
is the country for ambitious capability, and the foreigner who studies
its conditions thoroughly, and with full appreciation, can procure for
himself an even greater field of activity than the native. My success
surprised even myself; I found my boldest expectations outdone. I suddenly realized that I had become a celebrity in America. I flung myself with all my heart into the Antislavery Movement and thus showed
the Americans something new. The broad world-view of the German,
which opened up wider horizons for them; the peculiar speech of the
foreigner which, although formed after the best models in English
literature, presented a multitude of unfamiliar phrases; the power of
true conviction, which is not found too often in its purity—all this had
an uncommon appeal for the Americans, and so I gained, perhaps
more rapidly than anybody in the land, a nation-wide reputation, a
reputation which went far beyond my deserts. My activities covered a
wide territory and had a great and direct influence on the political
development of the country. It is said that I made Lincoln President.
That is certainly not true; but the fact that people say it indicates that
I did contribute something toward raising the wind which bore Lincoln into the presidential chair and thus shook the slave-system to its
very foundations. I had put my full strength into it, and the Herculean
labor had tired me greatly.

As one does in moments of exhaustion, I sought rest, and so I went
as ambassador to Spain. But I soon found that in such a time as the
present one "rest" was for me the most exhausting effort of all. The
gigantic struggle which is to decide the future of this country suddenly
took on enormous proportions. . . . The stillness about me grew un-
canny to me; the forced apathy of an insipid diplomatic existence became a crushing burden upon my temperament and my conscience. . . .
I was one of those who had accelerated the crisis; I must share in the
vicissitudes of the conflict. . . . I shall probably remain in the service
till the end of the war. Then I shall return to my former activities with
the satisfaction of not only having had a part in determining the future
of this country, but also of loyally sharing its fate. In the political re-

construction which this revolution is bound to produce, I shall probably play an important role, and my voice will be heard.

It will be of interest to follow Schurz a little more in detail in the rather extraordinary career thus succinctly outlined.

Upon reaching this country, his first objective was to learn English as soon as possible. The method he adopted was wholly his own and might be called a "reading method," since it involved to begin with the daily reading of a newspaper, soon to be supplemented by the works of Goldsmith, Scott, Dickens, Thackeray, Macaulay, the commentaries of Blackstone (as he was looking forward to a legal career), and last of all, because of their enormous vocabulary, the plays of Shakespeare. Soon he added active exercises to these passive ones, taking the "Letters of Junius," translating them first into German and then back into English, and then comparing his English version with the original. Though this was a very slow and laborious process, it gave him, as he says, "a sense of the logic and also of the music of the language." When the time came for Schurz to talk on his feet, as we say, these basic studies in the forms of English expression were of inestimable benefit to him, providing him with an almost infallible linguistic guide and mentor.

With the eagerness of youth he surveyed all that he could see of the new land; with the eye of the born politician and statesman he took in its folkways and its public ways, and with the optimism of the true idealist he resolved to look for all that was good and sound in American life. The year 1852 was one of a Presidential election, and although Schurz knew nothing of American politics and parties, his attention was naturally directed to that feature of American life. Very soon, with that philosophic reflectiveness which was natural to him, he began to make his observations contribute to a philosophy of democracy, of which we have some traces in one of his letters:

Here in America you can see every day how little a people needs to be governed. There are governments, but no masters; there are governors, but they are only commissioners, agents. The great institutions of learning, the churches, the great commercial institutions, the lines of communication, etc., almost always owe their existence not to official

A third factor was one of a more practical character, involving the part which German-Americans, particularly the Forty-eighters, were to play in American politics. These recent immigrants were in general of a high class: intelligent, hard-working, and largely idealistic. Few of them knew any English before they came to America, and many of them never learned English really well, living as they did on so-called "language islands" populated by their compatriots, while the general stream of American life flowed past them without immersing or even wetting them. It came to be one of the principal assets of the antislavery party that it had in Carl Schurz a speaker who could address these Germans, who had settled very thickly in the Middle West, in their own language.

Schurz had taken up residence in Watertown, Wisconsin, where relatives had already settled, and the campaign of 1856 launched him as a political speaker. Although he spoke only in German, he was beginning to get the "feel" of an audience, to learn how to handle a crowd, how to take a heckling; in short, he underwent an invaluable schooling in his own language before he attempted to use a foreign one. Moreover, he had tasted once more the peculiar thrill of public oratory, this time on American soil; it was not likely that he would long resist the lure of enlarging his audience by making the language of the land his medium of utterance.

First, however, he was to undergo another decisive—one might almost call it fateful—experience, destined to establish in him still more firmly the consciousness of his allegiance in the conflict which was already foreshadowing the Civil War. This was his attendance at one of those great debates between Lincoln and Douglas which went far to change the course of American history, and which introduced Schurz to Lincoln. In the debate at Quincy, Illinois, Schurz's abhorrence of Douglas was deepened, while the foundations were laid for that affectionate admiration of Lincoln that does both men so much credit. From now on Schurz was a Lincoln man through and through.

With the preparation he had enjoyed, and the convictions he had formed, Schurz was ready for a special mission in which his peculiar position as a recent immigrant made him the man of the hour. The address, "True Americanism," which he delivered before a great audience in Faneuil Hall, Boston, on April 18, 1859 (shortly after Massachusetts had adopted the Two-Year Amendment), not only made his name nationally known; it also gave him the prestige which he employed with good effect in the campaign of 1860. Hereafter he was "Carl Schurz of Wisconsin," and no important measures could be taken by the Republican party without his being consulted.

This then was the ardent young idealist who plunged with heart and soul into the campaign for Lincoln. The spirit which animated him and which found ever new expression in his campaign speeches is still appealingly audible in this sentence from the *Reminiscences:* "I think it can be said without exaggeration that there has never been in the history of this Republic a political movement in which the purely moral motive was so strong —indeed, so dominant and decisive." There can be no doubt that this was Schurz's profound belief, and the conviction that he himself was battling for Right against Wrong, for Liberty against Servitude, for Humanity against Greed, lent him an assurance of success that nothing could shake. He spoke

day after day, often more than once, [from June] until the day of election in November. . . . A large part of my work, my specialty, consisted in addressing meetings of German-born voters in their and my native language. . . . As a public speaker I gathered . . . a very valuable experience . . . that with such audiences . . . the desire to be informed and instructed is greater than the desire to be amusingly entertained. . . . He who aims at making a lasting impression upon the minds and hearts of his hearers . . . should take care not to underestimate their intelligence, their normal sense, and their self-respect.

No less a judge of good oratory than Lincoln attested to the effectiveness of Schurz as a speaker. After listening to him once, Lincoln said, "You are an awful fellow. I understand your power, now."

His most telling if not his ablest campaign speech, and the one which attracted the most notice, was one in which he devoted his sole attention to Senator Douglas, delivered in New York on

September 13, the day after Douglas had spoken there himself. Schurz prepared for this speech with a care unusual to him in this campaign, analyzing with great acumen a number of Douglas's public utterances, and memorizing much of what he meant to say. When Schurz told the chairman of the meeting that his address would take two and a half hours to deliver, the response was consternation: "Good heavens!" he cried. "No New York audience will stand a speech as long as that!" But Schurz had a sounder instinct. The immense crowd that filled the great hall of Cooper Institute was ready to hear Douglas denounced, and their applause and laughter took up so much time that the speech lasted more than three hours. Schurz himself tells with glee of a certain old gentleman in the front row who pounded the floor with his umbrella until it broke, after which, unable to make any further noise with it, he would wave it in the air like a banner. "I have to confess," says Schurz, "that of my printed speeches this has remained one of my favorites." No wonder: it was his third and most serious onslaught upon the man who more than any other stood for the foe he hated with a righteous wrath, and he put into it such a combination of clear thinking, noble idealism, and forceful speech, together with a brilliant display of savage irony and sarcastic wit, as only a young man on the crest of an enthusiasm could have produced. Schurz says modestly he "was told that it cost Mr. Douglas many votes."

Impelled by the necessity of improving his finances, which had suffered from his campaigning, Schurz decided to go out lecturing. In so doing, he became aware of the rapidly growing unrest throughout the country, the increasing danger of secession on the part of the slave states, and the seriousness of the entire situation. At the same time he made up his mind to the no-compromise policy which was characteristic of his political integrity and which history has justified in fact as well as in theory.

Hardly had Schurz been appointed minister to Spain when the attack on Fort Sumter signalized the beginning of the Civil War. Schurz at once offered to resign from the Spanish post and take an active part in the military preparations called for by the

situation. But Lincoln and Seward urged him to proceed to
Spain, where they felt his services to be needed just then even
more than at home. This proved to be true in a sense different
from that which they had had in mind.

At such a distance from the scene of action, Schurz sensed two
things quite clearly, first, that the danger of having the Confederacy formally recognized as an independent government by
the powers of Europe was greater than Washington realized,
and second, that the most effective means for forestalling such
action was the public statement that the principal objective of
the Civil War was the abolition of slavery. Unable to convince
Secretary Seward of the soundness of his policy, and suspecting
that Seward had not even transmitted his urgent message to
Lincoln, Schurz returned to Washington to see the President in
person. To him he then communicated the substance of his
despatch, obtaining Lincoln's consent to sound out public opinion and report back to him. For some weeks Schurz pursued
these inquiries, becoming convinced that the time was ripe for
the beginning of an open movement in favor of emancipation.
Returning to Washington, Schurz told Lincoln that a public
meeting of this character was to be held on March 6, 1862, in
the great hall of Cooper Institute. "Good!" said he. "And at
that meeting you are going to make a speech?" "Yes." "Well,
now go home and sketch that speech. Do it as quickly as you
can. Then come and show me your arguments and we will talk
it over."

Schurz realized that he could not base his arguments on the
need for preventing foreign intervention. Instead, he took his
stand, with statesmanlike vision, upon the broad ground of the
incompatibility of slavery with truly democratic institutions, to
which this republic is dedicated. If the Union were to be maintained, then slavery, which put loyalty to the Union in second
place, must be abolished. Schurz read the speech to Lincoln,
who merely said, "You go and deliver that speech at your meeting on the 6th of March. And maybe you will hear something
from me on the same day." The "something" was a despatch
which announced that on that day President Lincoln had re-

quested of the Congress, in a special message, a joint resolution looking to the gradual abolition of slavery in the United States.

Schurz had read the signs correctly. The open adoption of a policy which distinctly stamped the war for the Union as a war against slavery so strengthened the hands of the antislavery groups in England that the movement for foreign interference was effectively nullified. Perhaps no act of Schurz's entire career had a more far-reaching effect; none was more striking as a demonstration of his ability as a statesman. And he was only thirty-three years old.

It was almost a foregone conclusion that Schurz would not return to Spain, and that he would take part in the military operations which were enlisting the full energies of the States in a life-and-death struggle. His military services to the nation are discussed elsewhere in this volume and need not be taken up here.

It was likewise a foregone conclusion that Schurz would inevitably be drawn into the Presidential campaign of 1864. His relation to Lincoln had grown to be so close that the President could and did talk to him with singular frankness. The simple honesty of Lincoln's words is still vibrant in Schurz's record of the conversation.

They urge me with almost violent language to withdraw from the contest . . . in order to make room for a better man. I wish I could. . . . Perhaps some other man might do this business better than I. . . . But I am here, and that better man is not here. . . . God knows, I have at least tried very hard to do my duty—to do right to everybody and wrong to nobody. And now to have it said . . . that I have been seduced by what they call the lust of power, and that I have been doing this and that unscrupulous thing hurtful to the common cause, only to keep myself in office! Have they thought of that common cause when trying to break me down? I hope they have.

This was a man for whom Schurz could campaign with all his heart, and again he girded his loins and sallied forth to do battle with the Enemy. "I made many speeches . . . but that they contributed much to Lincoln's success, I candidly do not believe," he writes with engaging modesty. But it is likely that this campaigning did something for Carl Schurz, in whom we have already discerned—not as weakness but strength of character—a tendency to hero worship. First there was Washington, then there was Kinkel, and now came Lincoln. It was on October 12, 1864, that Schurz wrote to his old friend Petrasch words about Abraham Lincoln which testify eloquently to his intellectual acumen and his statesmanlike vision. "I will make a prophecy," he wrote, after a critical analysis of Lincoln's character and record, "that may now sound peculiar. In fifty years, perhaps much sooner, Lincoln's name will be inscribed close to Washington's on this American Republic's roll of honor. And there it will remain for all time. The children of those who persecute him now will bless him."

The thoughtful student of Schurz's record may very well feel that not the least of the tragic aspects of Lincoln's assassination was the loss of Carl Schurz to Washington. There can be no doubt that upon the termination of the Civil War Schurz would have been made a member of Lincoln's Cabinet; there can be as little doubt that, seeing eye to eye with Lincoln as he did, and enjoying his confidence and even affection to a remarkable degree, he would have delighted in helping Lincoln carry out a very different plan of reconstruction from that which American history records.

Schurz's relation to Andrew Johnson could never have been as cordial as that which bound him to Lincoln: at first sight he had rather disliked him, and when Johnson was made the Republican candidate for the Vice-Presidency, Schurz was "one of those who received the news with a certain uneasiness of feeling." Once more we get an impression of Schurz's sound instinct and shrewd judgment of human character, and the record of Johnson's administration proves that Schurz was only too well advised in feeling uneasy.

At first, however, Johnson inherited, so to speak, something of Schurz's loyalty to Lincoln, and this led to an important mission. Johnson was doubtful, even anxious, about the Gulf States, with their very large black population, and he asked Schurz to visit those states and gather information for him. In hundreds of conversations during some three months Schurz was told substantially the same things over and over: "The negro will not work without physical compulsion. He is lazy. He is improvident. He is inconstant. We want steady, continuous work, work that can be depended upon." His own personal observation led him to surmise "that the success of negro free labor would depend not only on the aptitudes of the laborer, but also on those of the employer." All in all, Schurz carried away with him a picture of the South which probably could not have been duplicated then or subsequently, and which gave him a sense both of assurance and of power in the troubled times that were to follow. The great general report which Johnson, who had in the meantime changed front, tried to suppress because it conflicted with the policy he had begun to follow, was finally furnished to the Senate and ultimately became widely known throughout the country. Schurz says of it, "I do think that this report is the best paper I have ever written on a public matter." And he records with satisfaction "that none of those statements of fact has ever been effectually controverted."

Schurz had lost one great avenue to the service of the nation by the death of Lincoln; the journalistic one still remained open to him. After serving under Horace Greeley on the *Tribune* and then editing the Detroit *Post*, he took charge in 1867 of the German daily newspaper of St. Louis, *Die Westliche Post*. The move was destined to be a significant milestone in his career.

Schurz soon found himself in the midst of Missouri politics, which presented a special brand of Republicanism. To make a long story short, Schurz came to be proposed as a nominee for the Senate, opposing a certain General Ben Loan who had been put forward by the other Senator from Missouri, Charles D. Drake. Schurz's name proved so attractive to the voters that Drake hurried home from Washington to bring about the election of his candidate. Schurz promptly followed Drake to Jefferson City, then the capital of Missouri, to do some campaigning in his own behalf.

Guided by his astute manager, Schurz met the extravagant accusations of his opponent with moderation and strict truthfulness, shunned any personal attack on Loan, and conducted himself with such sobriety and modesty that Drake grew overconfident.

As a result, Drake was induced to meet Schurz in public debate just prior to the Republican caucus. It was arranged that two meetings should be held on consecutive evenings. First Schurz would deliver a speech of specified length. On the second evening Loan and Drake were to answer that speech, and then Schurz would have the final rebuttal. The announcement went out all over the state and drew crowds of people to the capital.

It was ten years since Schurz had listened to the Lincoln-Douglas debate at Quincy, Illinois, but he had not forgotten the tactics employed at that time by Lincoln, and he resolved to lure Drake into the same trap into which Douglas had fallen. "I kept my opening speech in calm, somewhat tame, defensive tone, reserving my best ammunition for my closing argument and putting forth in a somewhat challenging manner only a few sharp points which I wished Drake to take up the next evening." Drake was completely fooled and boasted publicly, "Gentlemen, tomorrow night about this hour General Carl Schurz will be as dead as Julius Caesar!"

Drake's speech—that of Loan was wholly negligible—was quite as arrogant and as incautious as Schurz had hoped. The body of it consisted of "a violent attack on the Germans of Missouri, for whose political character and conduct he made me responsible. He denounced them as an ignorant crowd, who did not understand English, read only their German newspapers, and were led by corrupt and designing rings . . . and whose presence in the Republican party hurt that party more than it helped it."

This speech was not well received, for the Germans were a large and powerful element in Missouri, and many members of the Legislature were fully aware of the fact. This gave Schurz a fearful weapon with which to belabor the unfortunate Drake. Who, he asked, had saved Missouri to the Union and been foremost on its bloody fields? "The Germans," shouted the audience. Where was Mr. Drake in those days? Sitting in his law office,

Schurz answered his own question. Stung by this thrust, Drake attempted to defend himself and claimed to be a friend of the Germans. Then, retorted Schurz, they must take what he had said of them that evening as a specimen of Mr. Drake's characteristic friendship.

And now Schurz advanced to the final attack, his remarks punctuated by increasing applause as he pictured Drake in the guise of a leader who would lead out of the party every man and every newspaper that would not take his word as law. Thus, said Schurz, he would finally stand "lonesome and forlorn, surrounded by an immensity of solitude, in desolate self-appreciation." When the laughter and cheering had died down, Schurz shrewdly changed his tone and offered the olive branch, assuring the listeners that they need not apprehend the possibility of enmity between him and Drake in the Senate. "I was sure, if we ever differed, Senator Drake would respect my freedom of opinion, and I certainly would respectfully recognize his." Drake left the meeting before it adjourned, hurried to the railroad station, and took the night train for the East.

On the 4th of March, 1869, Carl Schurz of Missouri took the oath of office in the Senate of the United States. It was two days after his fortieth birthday.

"For forty years or more," says Claude M. Fuess in his excellent book, *Carl Schurz, Reformer,* "he was the self-constituted, but exceedingly useful, incarnation of our national conscience." Moreover, he goes on to say, "historians have been forced to admit that he was right on most issues; and even when he was wrong, he was sincere." And then, it seems to me somewhat grudgingly, "Naturally he did not make himself popular, but he did, without being at all sanctimonious, become a mighty spiritual force."

It is characteristic of Schurz that his spectacular elevation to high office, so far from turning his head, as it might well have done, seemed to him a solemn call to duty. No ordinary officeseeker wrote down the reflections, as recorded in his *Reminiscences,* which his first day in the Senate inspired in him:

I remember vividly the feelings which almost oppressed me. . . . Now
I had actually reached the most exalted public position. . . . Little
more than sixteen years had elapsed since I had landed on these shores,
a homeless waif. . . . And here I was now, a member of the highest
law-making body of the greatest of republics. Should I ever be able . . .
to justify the honors that had been heaped upon me? To accomplish
this, my conception of duty could not be pitched too high. I recorded
a vow in my own heart that I would at least honestly endeavor to fulfill that duty; that I would conscientiously adhere to the principle
salus populi suprema lex; that I would never be a sycophant of power
nor a flatterer of the multitude; that, if need be, I would stand up
alone for my conviction of truth and right.

Over against this manly statement of principle I like to set
the words of righteous indignation with which Schurz, in reply
to the charge that he had abandoned the regular Republican
party, set forth in almost epigrammatic clarity the policy of political independence which alone could satisfy his high moral
sense. Senator Morton of Indiana, with whom he was then crossing swords, had boasted, "I have never betrayed my principles;
I have never betrayed my friends; I have never betrayed those
who elevated me to power, and sought to use that power for
their destruction." Schurz was to become the outstanding leader
of the "Independents" in course of time, and Senator Morton's
charge, intended as a crushing rebuke, merely gave him a chance
to affirm his political faith: "I want him to point out in my
record," he cried, "a single principle that I ever betrayed. I
want him to show, in platforms of policy I have favored, a single
contradiction. He will not find one. He has never left his party;
I have never betrayed my principles. That is the difference between him and me."

In their Prefatory Note to the "Sketch of Karl Schurz's Political Career," Frederick Bancroft and William A. Dunning say,
"During the last three decades of the nineteenth century Mr.
Schurz's political influence was unique." And even in the 140
large pages at their disposal they have not felt that they could
do more than "describe the salient features of his activity in
public affairs." A complete record, indeed, would have occupied
as much space as the three volumes of Schurz's own *Reminiscences.*

There is hardly an important political issue in that entire period
in which Schurz did not take an active interest; only one Presidential campaign (he was in Europe in 1888) in which his voice
was not raised in the advocacy of the policies he favored and in
attack upon those he rejected; hardly a cause involving public
morals in which he could not be found engaged in his favorite
pursuit, that of slaying the dragon.

For as the knight of old went forth to rescue the oppressed, to
defend virtue, and to assail the powers of evil, regardless of his
material fortunes, scorning all personal advantage, so Schurz
felt irresistibly drawn into every conflict in which he sensed a
moral issue, a struggle between right and wrong, and infallibly
championed the right, as he saw it. It is a tribute to his ability
as well as his moral integrity that his efforts were so often
crowned by success.

What was the source of that spiritual power which Fuess
ascribes to him? I find three main sources. That influence which
we commonly call "political" was not one of them. Schurz was
Senator for six years, and a Cabinet officer for four, but in
neither case did he have to redeem campaign promises or dis-
pense patronage. Schurz won thoughtful men and women to his
way of thinking solely by the power of the word, by persuasive
reasoning, by invincible logic, by that masterly ordering of the
facts which we have already pointed out as the attribute of
the trained mind.

The second factor in Schurz's consistently successful and influential public career was that, with characteristic German
thoroughness and the instinct of the true historian, he never
addressed himself to any important issue without getting up the
facts of the matter as thoroughly as the available information
permitted. This was strikingly illustrated in the celebrated debate with Roscoe Conkling in 1872, after Sumner had charged
the War Department with a violation of the rules of neutrality
in selling munitions to France during the Franco-Prussian War.
Schurz replied to Conkling's defense of the administration, says
Fuess, "with an array of facts which dazzled his auditors." Now
Conkling, whose vanity was aroused, took the floor again, after

careful preparation, and delivered so brilliant a speech for the administration that Schurz's own wife advised him against attempting to answer it. But Schurz, who also felt that the test was a decisive one, sat up half the night to study the documents once more and arrange his ideas for the reply which he had already announced he would make. The Senate galleries were filled, and on motion the floor of the chamber was opened to the eager visitors, who filled every square foot in it. "This audience was indeed inspiring, and he never in his life spoke with so much nervous energy, fire, and immediate effect." Mrs. Schurz, who was not well, had declined to accompany him to the Capitol, but her uneasiness finally drove her to the Senate, where she saw the crowd pouring out. Senator Sumner rushed to shake her hand and cried, "Oh madam, I congratulate you. Your husband has just made the greatest speech that has been heard in the Senate for twenty years."

The third source of Schurz's power was his own moral integrity. In vain his enemies—and he had plenty of them as time went on—sought to pierce the shining armor of this modern Bayard *sans peur et sans reproche.* In vain they set secret investigators at work to unearth some indiscretion or private vice, some hidden intrigue, some evidence that he had been or could be swayed by bribery or flattery. Again and again these hired agents found that his private life was spotless, that he was an aspirant for fame but not willing to pay for it by betrayal of principle, and that neither the lure of power nor the natural desire for a comfortable living could induce him to deviate in the least from the course that his own sense of right dictated.

Thus prepared and equipped, Schurz attacked problem after problem in much the same manner: he would gather together men of common interests for convention or conference, he would persuade them by argument and carefully assembled facts—never by cajolery, bribery, or any force but that of truth and reason—to adopt resolutions and publish them; and he would himself write letters, both public and private, in which the same patient marshaling of facts, the same relentless logic, were made vibrant by the moral fervor of the writer. Says Fuess, "He was aggressive, tireless, irrepressible . . . [his critics] could not help respecting the rare combination of patience and audacity with which Schurz impressed his ideas upon the more intelligent voters."

It goes without saying that in dealing with Schurz's public career, which was bound up with the entire political history of the United States for over forty years, an account like the present one must bear in mind the exigencies of space and the patience of the general public. It must suffice us here to focus attention briefly upon some outstanding features of his final phase, trusting that the interested reader will turn to the fuller discussions of these matters already available in print. It will be found that virtually all of Schurz's public acts grew out of a few fundamental political principles, applied, like so many burning torches, to the fuses which touched off the energizing forces of his dynamic nature.

The principal issues of a moral character which enlisted Schurz's interest and which stirred him to action were ten in number: the abolition of slavery, the establishment of a merit system in the civil service, the insistence on honesty in public affairs, the subordination of partisanship to principle, the maintenance of sound money, the rehabilitation of the Indians, the conservation of natural resources, the continuance of free trade, the promotion of international peace, and the battle against American imperialism. Every one of these issues involved him in conflict with persons and groups whose interests would be adversely affected by the measures he proposed or supported; in every case his stand was based not upon expediency but upon principle, upon a review of the facts rather than an appeal to sentiment, and upon what he stoutly believed to be the best good of his country. He could be defeated but not cowed; he never reversed himself on any fundamental question; and in many cases he saw his predictions verified by the outcome and his opponents, though they might command the force to outvote him, eventually subdued by the indisputable verdict of the event.

Let me pass in brief review two of the great issues just listed, in the light of Schurz's relation to them.

Civil Service Reform. Next to the slavery question, no public reform attracted Schurz's advocacy as early, and stirred him as deeply as this one; none held his attention as persistently. On the occasion of his first visit to Washington he had been enlightened as to the "spoils system" and had been deeply horrified by the revelation. So soon as slavery was done for, and Schurz was in the Senate, he fixed his eyes upon this horrid monster and resolved to scotch it. His first speech in the Senate was delivered on this subject, and from that time on he never relaxed in his vigilant attention. The reform bill which he offered in the same year doubtless paved the way for the bill which established the Civil Service Commission in 1871. His next opportunity to advance the cause was afforded by his appointment as Secretary of the Interior by President Hayes. He at once instituted competitive examinations for admission to the service, and based promotion on similar tests coupled with efficiency records. Intelligent advocates of civil service reform commended Schurz on his quiet but effective promotion of the cause. In the year 1881, when his term as Secretary came to an end, he supported the founding of the National Civil Service Reform League. The efforts of the League, seconded by liberal opinion in various parts of the country, resulted in the passage of a bill embodying the principles that Schurz had long advocated. By 1884 over fourteen thousand government employees had been classified and placed under civil service rules. For this important and indeed decisive forward step Carl Schurz is almost universally given the chief credit. He became president of the League in 1892, and his active interest in the subject never flagged. In his summary of Schurz's achievements, Fuess says,

Schurz's most definite contribution to his adopted country was doubtless through his promotion of civil service reform . . . the rapid adoption of the merit system by successive Presidents was probably due more to him than to any other one man. In achieving his aims, he employed every legitimate device; he threatened, he bargained, he persuaded, he pleaded, he argued. . . . No matter what else was going on, Schurz had always a watchful eye for government appointments and seldom let a poor one slip by without protesting to the person responsible for it.

It is a frequent if discouraging observation that the man caught in wrongdoing, instead of mending his own ways, turns upon the one who catches or exposes him in it, and there is no phase of Carl Schurz's career in which this aspect of human conduct affected him more painfully than with respect to "snivel service reform," as one enemy sneeringly put it. As he was tireless in uncovering the unsavory tricks of the spoilsmen, so they were equally persistent in trying to make his life miserable. Unable to fight him in the open, they tried to choke him off in other ways, notably by ridicule. "Something about his irregular features," says Fuess, "lent itself readily to caricature, and his whiskers became as well known as Roosevelt's square teeth or Mark Twain's shaggy moustache." Carl Schurz the man still labors under much of that "unpopularity" which Carl Schurz the civil service reformer drew upon himself, but which was certainly anything but a discredit to him.

Schurz the Indians' Friend. Among the varied and wholly disparate problems which Schurz found lying on the threshold when he entered his office as Secretary of the Interior in 1877, there was none which was more trying or more desperately urgent than that of the American Indians and their relation to the United States government and people. Nor is there a chapter in American history of which this country has less reason to be proud. Without going into these matters in any detail, we may say that the disastrous fight between Chief Sitting Bull and General Custer on the Little Big Horn in 1876 had been a logical outcome of the bad policies of the past: exploitation of the Indians, misuse of their own faults, ignorance of their character and their needs, and their abandonment to the spoilsmen, the profiteers, and the Western desperadoes.

It is not unlikely that Schurz's consciousness of his own alien birth rendered him especially receptive to the Indians' complaints; but in the light of his general record we should expect him to come to the rescue of any person or group whom he found unfairly treated and incapable of effective self-defense. His immediate response to the challenge of the situation was to issue a call for the facts, and the commission he appointed brought in

a report in 1878 which was a startling revelation, accusing the
Indian Bureau of "cupidity, inefficiency, and the most barefaced
dishonesty," and asserting that the management of Indian affairs had been "a reproach to the whole nation."

Schurz acted promptly, discharged the inefficient and corrupt,
and began a complete reorganization of the whole department.
Almost as promptly, he announced a positive program which
has been conceded to outline "every feature of the policy which
was destined to achieve such signal success in the break-up of
tribal life during the ensuing quarter century." His main object
was "to absorb the Indians by legal means into the citizenry of
the United States, and, when this had been accomplished, to
treat them in all respects like other inhabitants of the country."

Schurz was both resourceful and energetic. With convincing
logic he opposed the proposal to transfer the control of the Indians to the War Department, which, as he rightly said, was not
well fitted to carry out the protracted scheme of education that
the proper treatment of the Indians involved. In August, 1879,
he himself made a tour of inspection, lasting six weeks, among
the various Indian agencies. In the previous year he had tried
out one of his pet ideas, namely that the Indians should be educated and brought into touch with modern life. Satisfied that
young Indians were entirely capable of assimilating the customs
of our civilization, Schurz opened up the famous industrial
school which later came to be known as the Carlisle Institute.
This experiment was followed by others, and although there has
been dispute as to the type of training which is most beneficial
to the Indians, Fuess says that "adult Indians regarded these
experiments with favor and encouraged the continuance of the
policy through later schools at Chilocco, Haskell, and elsewhere."

It goes almost without saying that the advocate of fair treatment of the Indians would not be any better loved by those
whom he deprived of their illegal perquisites than the political
spoilsmen whom he despoiled; but it is ironic that the relatively
insignificant case of the Poncas—for which he was not even responsible, but which he did his best to settle in a practical fashion—should have laid him open to the abuse of the very idealists

of whom he himself was one. Taking advantage of this split in the liberal ranks, his enemies sought to spike the guns that were so effectively trained upon them. One of these attacks brought from his pen a retort that may well be quoted here as an example of his savage irony when aroused. In the winter of 1881 Senator Henry L. Dawes had criticized some of Schurz's summary measures, saying,

It has been a relief to me, in examining our treatment of these weak and defenseless people, to find that these methods are not American in their origin, but bear too striking a resemblance to the modes of an imperial government carried on by espionage and arbitrary power. They are methods which I believe to be unique and which I trust will not be naturalized.

Schurz replied in kind, but gave back better than he got:

You have succeeded in making yourself understood. From the Pequot War to our days there never was an Indian unjustly killed in this country until a German-born American citizen became Secretary of the Interior. All has been peace, love and fraternity. The red man has for three centuries reposed upon the gentle bosom of his white brother, and no man to make him afraid, until this dangerous foreigner in an evil hour for the Republic was clothed with authority to disturb that harmonious accord and to disgrace the American name with espionage in Indian camps and the blood of slaughtered victims; and all this he did in an effort to naturalize on American soil the dark and cruel methods of imperial governments, of which this foreigner is, and has always been, a faithful worshiper and champion. And "it is a relief" to your patriotic soul that there is hope this wicked naturalization scheme will never succeed. It is pleasant to reflect that there is one man at least among us who even under such threatening circumstances will not despair of the Republic.

It seems unnecessary to take up in detail the other public issues which occupied Schurz's attention and enlisted his support at one time or another in his life. From what has already been said the interested reader will correctly infer both his attitude toward any given problem and his general method of dealing with it. As Secretary of the Interior he was one of the first to point to the necessity of forestry reform—a field in which Germany has long led the world—as one important phase of the conservation of our national resources. A consistent advocate of free trade, he opposed to the last the "protective tariff" as to which, in the opinion of the present writer, the last word has not yet been said. He promoted to the utmost of his ability the conditions on which a sound policy of international peace could be based. He fought bitterly every manifestation of that American imperialism which began in the Presidency of Grant and is only dying out in our day. His stout and unflinching advocacy of public honesty and a sound monetary system is in line with the best political thinking of all ages.

Finally, a word is in order as to his relation to Germany and the German people. Carl Schurz stands before us as an ideal representative of the "hyphenated American." Without ever losing love and sympathy for his native land, he never flagged in his active devotion to his adoptive country, into whose service he flung every advantage of his birth and training, and whose political progress he viewed from the historic perspective of the European student of human affairs. Without advocating the wholesale transfer of German institutions to American soil, he never ceased to apply to American conditions the lessons which he had learned in the study of German history. In other words, Schurz was a true German-American, with a double loyalty but not a divided one, a citizen whose foreign birth was not a detriment to his Americanism but an asset to it.

On the occasion of the death of Carl Schurz, the erstwhile Mississippi Pilot, Mark Twain, wrote the following tribute to the statesman in terms of the calling from which his own *nom de plume* was derived ("Carl Schurz, Pilot," *Harper's Weekly*, May 26, 1906):

We all realize that the release of Carl Schurz is a heavy loss to the country; some of us realize that it is a heavy loss to us individually and personally. As a rule I have had a sufficiency of confidence—perhaps over-confidence—in my ability to hunt out the right and sure political channel for myself, and follow it to the deep water beyond the reef without getting aground; but there have been times, in the past thirty years, when I lacked that confidence—then I dropped into Carl Schurz's wake, saying to myself, "he is as safe as Ben Thornburgh." When I was a young pilot on the Mississippi nearly half a century ago, the fellowship numbered among its masters three incomparables: Horace Bixby, Beck Jolly, and Ben Thornburgh. Where they were not afraid to venture with a steamboat, the rest of the guild were not afraid to follow. Yet there was a difference: of the three, they preferred to follow Thornburgh; for sometimes the other two depended on native genius and almost inspirational water-reading to pick out the lowest place on the reef, but that was not Ben Thornburgh's way; if there were serious doubts he would stop the steamer and man the sounding-barge and go down and sound the several crossings and lay buoys upon them. Nobody needed to search for the best water after Ben Thornburgh. If he could not find it, no one could. I felt that way about him; and so, more than once I waited for him to find the way, then dropped into his steamer's wake and ran over the wrecks of his buoys on half steam until the leadsman's welcome cry of "mark twain" informed me that I was over the bar all right, and could draw a full breath again.

I had this same confidence in Carl Schurz as a political channel-finder. I had the highest opinion of his inborn qualifications for the office: his blemishless honor, his unassailable patriotism, his high intelligence, his penetration; I also had the highest opinion of his acquired qualifications as a channel-finder. I believed he could read the political surfaces as accurately as Bixby could read the faint and fleeting signs upon the Mississippi's face—the pretty dimple that hid a deadly rock, the ostentatious wind-reef that had nothing under it, the sleek and inviting dead stretch that promised quarter-less-twain and couldn't furnish six feet. And—more that all—he was my Ben Thornburgh in this: whenever he struck out a new course over a confused Helena Reach or a perplexed Plum Point Bend I was confident that he had not contented himself with reading the water, but had hoisted out his sounding-barge and buoyed that maze from one end to the other. Then I dropped into his wake and followed. Followed with perfect confidence. Followed, and never regretted it.

I have held him in the sincerest affection, esteem, and admiration for more than a generation. I have not always sailed with him politically, but whenever I have doubted my own competency to choose the right course, I have struck my two-taps-and-one ("get out the port and starboard leads"), and followed him through without doubt or hesitancy. By and by I shall wish to talk of Carl Schurz the man and friend, but not now; at this time I desire only to offer this brief word of homage and reverence to him, as from grateful pupil in citizenship to the master who is no more.

APPENDIX

ABBREVIATIONS

The abbreviations listed here serve for the Bibliographical Notes as well as for the Biographical. No page references are given when the work referred to is well indexed. The DAB contains good bibliographies and, therefore, when reference is made to this work in the biographical sketches, no further sources are cited, except in a few cases where later valuable works have appeared.

AGR: *American-German Review*, Philadelphia, Carl Schurz Memorial Foundation.

Appleton: *Appleton's Cyclopaedia of American Biography*, ed. by James G. Wilson and John Fiske (10 vols., New York, Appleton and Co., 1887–1924).

Bess: F. B. Bess, *Eine populaere Geschichte der Stadt Peoria* (Peoria, Ill., 1906).

Boernstein: Heinrich Boernstein, *Fuenfundsiebzig Jahre in der alten und neuen Welt* (2 vols., Leipzig, 1884).

Carman: Harry J. Carman and Reinhard H. Luthin, *Lincoln and the Patronage* (New York, Columbia University Press, 1943).

Chicago: *Chicago und sein Deutschthum* (Cleveland, German-American Biographical Publishing Co., 1901).

Commons: John R. Commons, *History of Labor in the United States* (4 vols., New York, 1918).

Cunz: Dieter Cunz, *The Maryland Germans* (Princeton, N. J., Princeton University Press, 1948).

DAB: *Dictionary of American Biography*, ed. by Allen Johnson and Dumas Malone (21 vols., New York, Charles Scribner's Sons, 1928–1944).

DAG: *Deutsch Amerikanische Geschichtsblaetter*, after 1912 under editorship of Julius Goebel, *Jahrbuch der deutsch-amerikanischen historischen Gesellschaft von Illinois*.

DPV: *Mitteilungen des deutschen Pionier-Vereins von Philadelphia*, ed. by C. F. Huch (26 numbers issued from 1906 to 1912, Philadelphia).

Eiboeck: Joseph Eiboeck, *Die Deutschen von Iowa und deren Errungenschaften* (Des Moines, 1900).

Elson: L. C. Elson, *The History of American Music* (New York, Macmillan, 1924).

Froebel: Julius Froebel, *Aus Amerika. Erfahrungen, Reisen und Studien* (2 vols., Leipzig, 1858).

Fuess: Claude Fuess, *Carl Schurz, Reformer (1829–1906)* (New York, Dodd Mead, 1932).

Gert Goebel: Gert Goebel, *Laenger als ein Menschenleben in Missouri* (St. Louis, 1877).

Julius Goebel: Julius Goebel, *Das Deutschthum in den Vereinigten Staaten von Nord-Amerika* (Munich, J. F. Lehmanns Verlag, 1904).

Hansen: Marcus Hansen, *The Atlantic Migration 1607–1860* (Cambridge, Mass., Harvard University Press, 1940).

Hawgood: John Hawgood, *The Tragedy of German-America* (New York and London, 1940).

Heinrici: Max Heinrici (ed.), *Das Buch der Deutschen in Amerika* (Philadelphia, Deutsch-Amerikanischer Nationalbund, 1909).

Heitman: Francis B. Heitman, *Historical Register and Dictionary of the United States Army from its Organization, September 29, 1789 to March 2, 1903* (2 vols., Washington, Government Printing Office, 1903).

Hense-Jensen: Wilhelm Hense-Jensen, *Wisconsins Deutsch-Amerikaner* (2 vols., Milwaukee, Die deutsche Gesellschaft, 1909).

Herriot: F. I. Herriot, "The Conference of the German-Republicans in the Deutsches Haus, May 14–15, 1860," *Transactions of the Illinois State Historical Society*, 1928.

Hillquit: Morris Hillquit, *History of Socialism in the United States* (New York, Funk and Wagnals Co., 1903).

Huhn: Heinrich Huhn, "Gedenkblatt" (two articles consisting of biographical sketches of *Turner*), *Amerikanischer Turner-Kalender*, 1886 and 1887.

Hyde and Conart: William Hyde and Howard L. Conart, *Encyclopaedia of the History of St. Louis* (St. Louis, 1899).

IJHP: *Iowa Journal of History and Politics*.

JDAT: Heinrich Metzner, *Jahrbuecher der deutsch-amerikanischen Turnerei* (New York, 1890–1894).

Kalender: Carl Doerflinger, *Amerikanischer Turner-Kalender* (Milwaukee, 1879–1893).

Kapp: Friedrich Kapp, *Aus und ueber Amerika* (Berlin, Julius Springer, 1876).

Kaufmann: Wilhelm Kaufmann, *Die Deutschen im amerikanischen Buergerkriege* (Munich, Verlag Oldenburg, 1911).

Kiefer: Warren Washburn Florer (ed.), *Liberty Writings of Dr. Hermann Kiefer* (New York, G. E. Stechert, 1917).

Koerner: *Memoirs of Gustave Koerner, 1809–1896, Life-sketches Written at the Suggestion of His Children*, ed. by Thomas J. McCormack (2 vols., Cedar Rapids, Iowa, Torch Press, 1909).

Koss: Rudolf A. Koss, *Milwaukee* (Milwaukee, 1871).

Kottinger: H. M. Kottinger, *Leitfaden fuer den Unterricht in den Sonntagsschulen freier Gemeinden* (Milwaukee, 1871).

Krez: Konrad Krez, *Aus Wisconsin* (New York, 1875).

Lacher: J. H. A. Lacher, *The German Element in Wisconsin* (Milwaukee, 1925).

Lamb: *Lamb's Biographical Dictionary of the United States*, ed. by John Howard Brown (Boston, James H. Lamb Co., 1900–1903).

Legge: James G. Legge, *Rhyme and Revolution in Germany* (London, 1918).

Lemke: Theodore Lemke, *Geschichte des Deutschtums von New York von 1848 bis 1892* (New York, 1891–1892).

Lenel: Edith Lenel, *Friedrich Kapp, 1824–1884* (Leipzig, T. C. Hinrichs, 1935).

Magazin: H. A. Ratterman (ed.), *Deutsch-Amerikanisches Magazin* (Cincinnati, 1887).

Metzner: Henry Metzner, *A Brief History of the American Turnerbund* (Pittsburgh, 1924).

MH: *Minnesota History.*

Mo: *Monatshefte,* formerly "fuer den deutschen Unterricht" (Madison, Wisconsin).

Muench: Friedrich Muench, *Gesammelte Schriften* (St. Louis, 1902).

NCAB: *National Cyclopaedia of American Biography* (39 vols., New York, James T. White Co., 1893–1946).

OWR: *The War of the Rebellion; a Compilation of the Official Records of the Union and Confederate Armies* (Washington, Government Printing Office, 1880–1904).

P: *Der deutsche Pionier* (Cincinnati, Deutscher Pionier-Verein, 1869–1886).

Phisterer: Frederick Phisterer, *New York in the War of the Rebellion* (Albany, Weld, Parsons, and Co., 1890).

PSHSW: *Proceedings of the State Historical Society of Wisconsin* (Madison).

Richter: August P. Richter, *Geschichte der Stadt Davenport* (Davenport, Iowa, 1917).

Rombauer: Robert J. Rombauer, *The Union Cause in St. Louis in 1861* (St. Louis, 1909).

Rosengarten: Joseph Rosengarten, *The German Soldier in the Wars of the United States* (Philadelphia, J. B. Lippincott, 1886).

Russell: John A. Russell, *The Germanic Influence in the Making of Michigan* (Detroit, 1927).

Ruetenik: Hermann Julius Ruetenik, *Beruehmte deutsche Vorkaempfer* (Cleveland, 1888).

St. Paul: *Das Deutschtum St. Pauls* (St. Paul, 1924).

Schem: Alexander J. Schem (ed.), *Deutsch-amerikanisches Conversations-Lexicon* (New York, 1869–1874).

Schlegel: C. W. Schlegel, *German-American Families* (New York, American Historical Society, 1917).

Schurz: Carl Schurz, *Reminiscences* (3 vols., New York, McClure, 1907–1908).

Schurz Intimate Letters: *Intimate Letters of Carl Schurz*, tr. and ed. by Joseph Schafer (Madison State Historical Society of Wisconsin, 1928).

Schurz Papers: *Speeches, Correspondence and Political Papers of Carl Schurz*, ed. by F. Bancroft (New York, Putnam, 1913).

SHGM: *Society for the History of the Germans in Maryland, Reports* (Baltimore, 1887).

Shuster: George N. Shuster, *The Forty-eighters in America*, an address delivered in the Coolidge Auditorium of the Library of Congress, 12 May, 1948 (Washington, Library of Congress, 1948; processed).

Stevens: Walter Barlow Stevens, *St. Louis, the Fourth City, 1764–1911* (St. Louis and Chicago, S. J. Clarke Publishing Co., 1911).

Struve: Gustav von Struve, *Diesseits und Jenseits des Ozeans* (4 vols., Coburg, Streit Verlag, 1863–1864).

UJE: *Universal Jewish Encyclopaedia* (New York, 1939–1943).

Valentin: Veit Valentin, *Geschichte der deutschen Revolution* (2 vols., Berlin, 1930).

Valentin 1848: Veit Valentin, *1848: Chapters on German History* (London, George Allen and Unwin, 1940).

Wittke, A. C.: Carl Wittke, *Against the Current* (Chicago, University of Chicago Press, 1944).

Wittke, Marx and Weitling: Carl Wittke, "Marx and Weitling," *Essays in Political Theory* (Festschrift in honor of George H. Sabine; Ithaca, N. Y., Cornell University Press, 1948).

WMH: *Wisconsin Magazine of History*.

Zimmermann: G. A. Zimmermann, *Deutsch in Amerika* (Chicago, 1892).

BIBLIOGRAPHICAL NOTES

Since the first two chapters are of very general nature, their content is here not documented by notes; however, these brief selective, by no means exhaustive, bibliographies may be of interest.

CHAPTER I

Thomas S. Baker, *Lenau and Young Germany in America*, 1897; Wilhelm Busch, *Die Maerztage von 1848;* Friedrich Engels and Carl Marx, *The Communist Manifesto*, 1848, and *Class Struggles in France*, 1851 (especially the Preface of the 1895 edition); Friedrich Meinecke, *Radowitz und die deutsche Revolution*, 1913; Friedrich Meinecke, *Weltbuergertum und Nationalstaat*, 1922; Hermann Oncken, "Die deutsche Auswanderung. . ." in *Historisch-politische Aufsaetze und Reden*, I, 37ff.; Hermann Oncken, "Zur Genesis der preussischen Revolution von 1848," in *ibid.*, II, pp. 1ff.; Vernon L. Parrington, *Main Currents in American Thought*, 1927–1930; Heinrich von Sybel, *The Founding of the German Empire*, 1890–1898; Valentin, 1848; H. von Treitschke, *Deutsche Geschichte im Neunzehnten Jahrhundert*, Vol. V, 1894; Franz Schnabel, *Der Zusammenschluss des politischen Katholizismus 1848*, 1910; Franz Schnabel, *Deutsche Geschichte im neunzehnten Jahrhundert* 4 vols., 1929–37; John A. Walz, *German Influence in American Education and Culture*, 1936.

CHAPTER II

Carl Russell Fish, *Rise of the Common Man*, and Arthur C. Cole, *Irrepressible Conflict 1850–1865* (Vols. VI and VII of the *History of American Life*, New York, 1927, 1934); E. C. Kirkland, *History of American Economic Life*, New York, 1932, and *Men, Cities, and Transportation*, Cambridge, Mass., 1948; Oscar Handlin, *Boston's Immigrants, a Study of Acculturation*, Cambridge, Mass., 1941; Hansen; Commons; Merle Curti, *Growth of American Thought*, New York, 1943, Part IV; A. F. Tyler, *Freedom's Ferment; Phases of American Social History to 1860*, Minneapolis, 1944; A. B. Hart, *Slavery and Abolition*, New York, 1906; Allan Nevins, *Ordeal of the Union*, New York, 1947.

CHAPTER III

Page 43. Appearance and dress, etc.: Froebel, pp. 14–15; Joseph Rudolph, "Kurzer Lebensabriss eines achtundvierziger politischen Fluechtlings," DAG, VIII (1908), 21–30. Example of a diary: Dr. Otto Heller, "Aus dem Tagebuch eines Achtundvierzigers (Dr. Enno Sanders)," DAG, XIII (1913), 309–340. Titles of poems: Caspar Butz, *Gedichte eines Deutsch-Amerikaners*, Chicago, 1879, p. 1; Krez, p. 55.

Page 45. Number of Forty-eighters: Valentin, I, 493. Number of emigrants: II, 552; Hansen, p. 274.

Page 47. Kapp: Kapp, II, 290–306.

Page 48. Hecker's letter: *Deutsch-Amerikanischer Hecker Denkmal Verein*, Cincinnati, 1881, pp. 22–23. Hecker's farmstead: Koerner, I, 529. Hecker's granddaughter, Mrs. Harris A. Reynolds of Belmont, Massachusetts, agreed in a letter to the author that Hecker was not a typical pioneer farmer.

Page 49. German language papers—opportunity: Gert Goebel, pp. 154–155. A good story of the schoolman who turned to journalism is found in "G. A. Roesler," DAG, II, ii (1902), 39–41.

Rusch's campaign in 1859: F. I. Herriot, "The Germans in the Gubernatorial Campaign of Iowa in 1859," DAG, XIV (1914), 504, 522–526. Rothe's encounter with Schurz: Hildegard Binder Johnson, "The Election of 1860 and the Germans in Minnesota," MH, XXVIII (March, 1947), 29. Claussen: Hildegard Binder Johnson, "Hans Reimer Claussen," AGR, X (June, 1944), 30.

Page 50. Romantic elements: Muench, pp. 349–356.

Page 51. For amusing incidents: Gert Goebel, p. 151; Hildegard Binder Johnson, "German Forty-eighters in Davenport," IJHP, XLIV (January, 1946), 6; Hense-Jensen, I, 143–146.

Page 52. German settlements in Iowa: Eiboeck, pp. 314–526; C(arl) K(oehne), "Eine Turn- und Wasserfahrt aus der guten alten Zeit," *Kalender*, I (1880), 33–39.

Guttenberg: Eiboeck, pp. 528–532.

Page 53. German immigration to Wisconsin: Kate Asaphine Everest Levi, "How Wisconsin Came by Its Large German Element," *State Historical Society of Wisconsin Collections*, Vol. XII (1892). Milwaukee: Koss, p. 264, for "Three-Cents Society."

Page 54. Political situation in Milwaukee and Wisconsin: Hense-Jensen, I, 164–182; Lacher, pp. 30, 37–40; Ernest Bruncken, "German Political Refugees in the United States during the Period from 1815–1860," DAG, IV (1904), 54–55.

Page 55. Quotations about German political influence: Hense-Jensen, pp. 276–279; for Bruncken's more reserved description: Ernest

Bruncken, "The Political Activity of Wisconsin Germans," PSHSW, 1901, 190–211.

Turner societies: Koss, pp. 313, 318, 320; Hense-Jensen, I, 156–157. Freethinkers' societies: Koss, pp. 336, 341, 366, 391–394, 404–406; Preface in Kottinger. Advertisement of the textbook by Friedrich Schuenemann-Pott, *Blaetter fuer Freies Religioeses Leben*, January, 1872, p. 137.

Page 56. Thiensville and picture of the Hall of the *Freie Gemeinde* in Sauk City: Fred L. Holmes, *Old World Wisconsin*, Eau Claire, Wisconsin: E. M. Hale and Co., 1944, pp. 60–61. The *Freie Gemeinde* of Milwaukee celebrated its 85th anniversary in 1947 and maintains Jefferson Hall, 2617 West Fond Du Lac Avenue, Milwaukee.

Page 57. Data about Engelmann's school: *Festschrift zur Einweihungsfeier der neuen Heimstaette deutsch-amerikanischer Erziehung in Milwaukee*, 1891.

Page 58. Data for German free schools: Lacher, pp. 29–30; Hense-Jensen, I, 137, 162. Knapp: Cunz, pp. 230ff.; Henry L. Mencken, *Happy Days*, Knopf, 1940, pp. 20–24.

Page 59. Music: Hense-Jensen, I, 152–155.

Page 60. The new theater: Hense-Jensen, I, 149, 151, 225; Heinrici, pp. 454–458.

German population of Chicago: Andrew Jacke Townsend, "The Germans of Chicago," DAG, XXXII (1932), 1–153. Canal Bill: Koerner, I, 482.

Page 61. Protest against Nebraska Bill: F. I. Herriott, "The Germans of Chicago and Stephen A. Douglas in 1854," DAG, XII (1912), Hoffmann's address on pp. 394–395.

Page 63. Dr. Ernst Schmidt: Andrew Jacke Townsend, "The Germans of Chicago," DAG, XXXII (1932), 22–23; Otto C. Schneider, "Abraham Lincoln und das Deutschthum," DAG, VII (1907), 69.

Page 64. Dr. Otto Schmidt: Max Baum, "Otto Leopold Schmidt," DAG, XXXIII (1937), 10.

Data on Germans in St. Louis and Missouri before 1848: Friedrich Schnake, "Geschichte der deutschen Bevoelkerung und der deutschen Presse von St. Louis und Umgegend," P, III, 232, 304, 335; IV, 85 ("Message to German People"); V, 100 (banquet of January, 1849).

Page 65. Kossuth's triumph: Koerner, I, 580–581.

Page 66. Political situation in St. Louis: Rombauer, p. 127. Goebel's testimony: Gert Goebel, p. 149. Danger to rural Germans: Muench, pp. 123–124. James's address: DAG, VI, 67–68.

Page 68. Davenport: Hildegard Binder Johnson, "The Forty-eighters in Davenport," IJHP, XLIV (1946), 3–60. Claussen's political maneuver, *ibid.*, p. 48.

Page 70. Prohibition: Eiboeck, p. 150. Mathias Frahm: pp. 436–439.

Page 71. New Ulm: Hildegard Binder Johnson, "The Founding of New Ulm," AGR, XII (June, 1946), 8–12. Details from clippings and manuscript material in the New Ulm Historical Society.

Pfaender: *Kalender*, 1886, pp. 60–68.

Page 72. Settlement Society: *Ansiedlungsverein des sozialistischen Turner-bundes von Nordamerika.*

Page 73. Sioux War in New Ulm: "Die Deutsche Ansiedlung New-Ulm Minnesota," P, III, 13–17; Rev. Alexander Berghold, "Ge-schichte von New Ulm, Minnesota," P, IV, 122–128, 162–170. Church destroyed: Robert P. A. Nix, "New Ulm in Truemmern —Huelfe fuer New Ulm," *Kalender*, 1882, 63–69.

Page 76. Many became cigar makers: Kaufmann, p. 107.

Page 77. Arrested development: Hawgood, p. 253.

CHAPTER IV

Page 79. Jahn: Augustus J. Prahl, "The Ideological Background of the American *Turner*," *Comparative Literature News-Letter*, November, 1944.

Page 80. Nimbus of poetry: Translations are from Legge; Schnauffer's poem by Lois Miles Zucker.

Page 89. Laube: Heinrich Laube, *Das erste deutsche Parlament*, I, 22; quoted in Legge, p. 352.

Page 91. James's speech: DAG, VI (1906), 71.

Page 92. First Turner society: R. (H. A. Rattermann), "Die Pionier-Turngemeinde Amerikas," P, VII, 178–187; Heinrich Huhn, "Die Gruendung des nordamerikanischen Turnerbundes," *Kalen-der*, 1889, p. 32. One record says New York was the first.

Page 93. Arthur C. Cole: Arthur C. Cole, *The Era of the Civil War*, McClung, 1922, p. 215.

Page 96. Baltimore City Election: J. Thomas Scharf, *History of Mary-land*, Baltimore, 1897, III, 250. Know-Nothing oath: *ibid.*, III, 249. *Turner* picnic: JDAT, p. 88.

Page 98. Straw Hat: Augustus J. Prahl, "History of the German Gym-nastic Movement in Baltimore," SHGM, XXVI (1945), 22.

Union of Turner societies: Metzner, pp. 8ff. Definition of Socialism: *ibid.*, p. 26. The attitude: *ibid.*, p. 14.

Page 101. Two *Turner* companies: Kaufmann, p. 127.

Page 102. Rapp letter: Unpublished letter printed by permission of Mr. William R. Kemper, Chicago, grandson of Wilhelm Rapp.

Page 105. General Grant: John Russell Young, *Around the World with General Grant*, New York: American News Company, 1879, II,

465; cf. also DAB, Francis Blair, Nathaniel Lyon, and Franz Sigel.

Page 107. Winston Churchill: Winston Churchill, *The Crisis*, New York, 1901, Chapter XVIII.

Page 108. Historian of the movement: Heinrich Huhn, *Kalender*, 1890, p. 33.

Colonel McCook: Kaufmann, p. 535.

Page 109. Hartwell's report: WMH, IX, 134.

Page 110. Program: George Seibel, "Mental Training in the Turners," *Souvenir Program of the American Turners Thirty-seventh National Festival, June 30–July 4, 1948*, St. Louis, Missouri, p. 62.

CHAPTER V

Page 112. "Voting cattle": Froebel, I, 500. Rattermann states (*Magazin*, I, 238) that Judge Hume, a Republican member of the Ohio legislature, invented this expression and applied "voting cattle" to the Germans in 1856.

Jacksonian Democrats: Kapp, I, 316ff. Contrasting earlier immigrants with the Forty-eighters.

Page 114. Blaring bands: Quotations on American reaction to "continental" habits in Wittke, A.C., pp. 282ff.

Page 117. Frank Monoghan: Article on Kapp in DAB.

Carl Schurz: Valentin 1848, p. 416.

Page 119. Domschke to Roeser: Ernest Bruncken, "The Political Activity of the Wisconsin Germans, 1854–1860," PSHSW, 1901, 196ff.

Page 121. Mrs. Schnauffer: L. P. Hennighausen, "Reminiscences," SHGM, Seventh Annual Report.

Friedrich Kapp: Lenel, p. 96.

Gustav Struve: Struve, I, 35.

Page 123. Hermann Kiefer: Kiefer.

Page 126. A major cause: F. I. Herriott, "The Germans of Chicago and Stephen A. Douglas," DAG, XII (1912), 381.

Page 130. The truth is: F. I. Herriott, "The Germans of Iowa and the 'Two-Year Amendment,'" DAG, XIII (1913), 250.

Page 131. Schurz: Wittke, A.C., 290–291.

Circular letter of Iowans: F. I. Herriott, "The Premises and Significance of Abraham Lincoln's Letter to Theodore Canisius," DAG, XV (1915), 181–254. This is a major contribution to the history of the Forty-eighters in politics. Circular letter, *ibid*., p. 189.

Rush letter: F. I. Herriott, "The Germans of Iowa and the 'Two-Year Amendment,'" DAG, XIII (1913), 281–284. Hamilton letter: p. 286.

Page 132. Lincoln letter: F. I. Herriott, "The Premises and Significance of Abraham Lincoln's Letter to Theodore Canisius," DAG, XV (1915), 219.

Page 133. First of all: Hawgood, p. 249.

Conference in the *Deutsches Haus:* Herriott. The resolutions are on p. 189; this is the most important single study of the Forty-eighters' political activity prior to the War. It contains a wealth of biographical material.

Page 136. Sandburg: Carl Sandburg, *Abraham Lincoln, The Prairie Years,* Harcourt Brace, 1926, p. 421.

Page 137. The German preference: Hawgood, 251.

Page 138. Schurz denied: Schurz, *Intimate Letters,* p. 283.

It is no exaggeration: Julius Goebel, p. 59.

Fight for the Northwest: William E. Dodd, *American Historical Review,* XVI (1911), 786.

Page 140. New Braunfels: Rudolph Leopold Biesele, *The History of the German Settlements in Texas, 1831–1861,* Austin, Texas: Press of Von Boeckmann-Jones Co., 1930.

Page 141. Lincoln to Schurz: Schurz letters, Library of Congress, June 18, 1860.

Canisius: H. Nelson Gay, "Lincoln's Offer of a Command to Garibaldi," *Century Magazine,* November, 1907, pp. 63–74.

Page 142. Andrew letter: quoted in Milton Allan Dickey, "Reinhold Solger," University of Pittsburgh, unpublished Ph.D. thesis, 1930, p. 25.

Edmund Juessen: Information regarding relationship of Carl Schurz to Juessen from Dr. Arthur Hogue of Department of History of the University of Illinois, who has examined the library of Carl Schurz, now in possession of Mrs. Edith Steinbrecher of Chicago. This collection contains a large number of unpublished letters of Carl Schurz and many others which were published only after bowdlerization by Agathe Schurz.

Page 144. Caspar Butz: Hildegard Binder Johnson, "Caspar Butz of Chicago—Politician and Poet," AGR, XII (August, 1946), 4–7.

Frémont: Shuster, p. 6; *Deutsch-amerikanische Monatshefte fuer Politik, Wissenschaft und Literatur,* ed. by Caspar Butz, January, 1864 to December, 1865. A copy of the English pamphlet distributed by Butz at the Democratic Convention of 1864 can be found at the library of the University of Michigan under the title, *Campaign Literature, 1864,* "The Wade-Davis Manifesto, a Last Appeal to Democracy," 1864. German radical Republicanism is treated in Ruhl Jacob Bartlett, *John C. Frémont and the Republican Party,* Ohio State University, Columbus, Ohio, 1930, pp. 74–83, but here the role of the Germans in Chicago is greatly underestimated. The present evaluation is based chiefly on data from the *Illinois Staats-*

zeitung, Monatshefte, New York Times, Missouri Republican, and *Chicago Times.*

Page 146. Chase and Wade: Burton J. Hendrick, *Lincoln's War Cabinet,* Boston: Little Brown, 1946, p. 435.

Page 147. Schurz and the South: Fuess, p. 167.

Domschke: J. J. Schlicher, "Bernhard Domschke, I: A Life of Hardship," "II: The Editor and the Man," WMH, XXIX (1945–46), 319–332, 435–456.

Page 148. James Ford Rhodes: *Carl Schurz (1829–   ),* in Charles Dudley Warner, ed., *Library of the World's Best Literature, Ancient and Modern,* XXII, 12974–12978.

Page 149. Greeley to Schurz: Schurz, III, 350.

Page 151. *Westliche Post:* Thomas S. Barclay, "Emil Preetorius," DAB.

Raster: Peter H. Olden and Harvey Wish, "The Influence of the Illinois Staatszeitung upon American Politics," AGR, VI (February, 1940), 30–32, 39.

Kapp's letter: Lenel, p. 103.

Page 153. Woman Suffrage: Lillian Krueger, "Mathilde Franziska Anneke, an Early Wisconsin Journalist," WMH, XXI, 160–167.

Page 154. Willkie: Wendell L. Willkie, "There Were Giants in Those Days," AGR, IX (December, 1942), 4–5.

CHAPTER VI

Page 158. Primacy of the Word: Valentin 1848, p. 177.

Shuster: Shuster, p. 4.

Sturm und Drang: Friedrich Hassaurek, "Rede zum 7. Stiftungsfest," P, VII, 112–125.

Page 159. The intolerance of puritanism: Kaufmann, pp. 101–117. A good characterization of the Forty-eighters.

Page 160. *Woll'n die Fuersten:* quoted in P, VII, 116. Translated by Lois Miles Zucker.

Kinkel: P, VII, 116–118; C. F. Huch, "Revolutionsvereine und Anleihen," DPV, No. 18, 1–19; No. 22, 28–29.

Page 162. Wheeling: Edward Schlaeger, "Der Wheelinger Congress im Sept. 1852," P, VIII, 90–97; Julius Goebel, Jr., "A Political Prophecy of the Forty-eighters," DAG, XII (1912), 462–498; Charles Goepp and Theodor Poesche, *The New Rome,* New York: Putnam, 1852, pp. 10, 16, 71, 81, 95, 104, 105, 107, 109, 141, 144, 147, 155, 156.

Page 166. The People's League for the Old and New World: Friedrich Hassaurek, "Eine Antwort an Schlaeger," P, VIII, 155–159.

Page 168. Grays and Greens: Heinrich A. Rattermann, "Das deutsche Element in den Vereinigten Staaten, 1800–1850," *Gesammelte Werke,* Vol. XVI, Selbstverlag, 1912.

Dr. Hobelmann and Sorge: Jakob Mueller, *Aus den Erinnerungen eines Achtundvierzigers*, Cleveland, Ohio, 1896, p. 206.

Frederic Law Olmsted: *A Journey through Texas; or, A Saddle-Trip on the Southwestern Frontier*, New York, 1859, p. 430.

Page 169. Catholic circles: *"Letters of the Reverend Anthony Urbanek,"* WMH, "Documents," X (1926–27), 91.

Karl Heinzen: Julius Goebel, "German-American Political Thought," DAG, XXV (1925), 143–222; Paul Otto Schinnerer, "Karl Heinzen, Reformer, Poet, and Literary Critic," DAG, XV (1915), 84–144.

Greeley letter: Wittke, A.C., p. 90.

Capital punishment—American democracy: Wittke, A.C., pp. 201, 303.

Page 173. The Louisville Platform: quoted in excerpts in P, XIII, 162f.; the original document (English version) available in the Labadie Collection of the University of Michigan Library and the University of Kentucky Library.

Page 174. The supporters in Louisville: "Aus Louisvilles Vergangenheit," P, I, 109.

Page 175. His Majesty Washington X: Julius Goebel, "German-American Political Thought," DAG, XXV (1925), 158.

Page 176. Wendell Phillips: Julius Goebel, "German-American Political Thought," DAG, XXV (1925), 155.

Page 177. Heinzen and the Communists: Wittke, A.C., pp. 240ff.

Page 178. Weitling: William F. Kamman, *Socialism in German-American Literature*, Philadelphia: Americana Germania Press, 1917; Carl Wittke, "Wilhelm Weitling's Literary Efforts," Mo., XL (1948), pp. 63–68; Wittke, Marx and Weitling, pp. 179–193.

Page 180. The Socialist Party: Hillquit.

CHAPTER VII

The material in this chapter is treated more fully in a forthcoming book by Dr. Lonn to be published by Louisiana State University Press.

Page 184. Carl Schurz letter: Schurz Intimate Letters, pp. 287–288.

Page 185. Franz Sigel: DAB; Kaufmann, pp. 448–466.

Page 186. Numbers in Sigel's army: T.E.C., *Battlefields of the South*, London: Smith, Elder and Co., 1863, Preface xxviii–xxix; Franz Sigel, *Denkwuerdigkeiten des General Franz Sigel aus den Jahren 1848–49*, Mannheim: Wilhelm Blos Co., 1902, p. 123.

Page 188. Comment on Sigel: Kaufmann, p. 460.

Page 189. Carl Schurz: DAB; Kaufmann, 468–470; Schurz.

Page 190. Schurz letter: Schurz Intimate Letters, p. 282.

Page 191. Osterhaus: Friedrich Schnake, "Der Ausbruch des Buergerkrieges in Missouri," P, XII, 57n; Emil Mannhard, "General Peter Joseph Osterhaus," DAG, IV, 354-363; Kaufmann, 445-449; DAB.

Page 193. Blenker: William J. Tenny, *The Military and Naval History of the Rebellion in the United States*, New York: Appleton and Co., 1866, p. 769; Kaufmann, 483-484; Schurz, II, 233ff.

Quotation on Blenker: Schurz, II, 235-236.

Page 194. Friedrich Salomon: Kaufmann, 389 and note, 545; recorded in Heitman.

Page 195. Schimmelfennig: Kaufmann, 549-550; Lamb, VI, 435.

Page 196. Episode at Gettysburg: Frank Moore, *Rebellion Record*, 12 vols., New York: G. P. Putnam, 1861-1868, Vol. VII, Part 3, p. 52; Schurz, III, 36.

Page 197. Max von Weber: NCAB, XII, 264; Kaufmann, 561-562; Lamb, VII, 527-528.

Page 198. August von Willich: "General August Willich," P, IX, 439-445, 488-495, X, 68-71, 114-117, 144-147; Appleton, VI, 538-539.

Page 200. They were but a regiment: Lew Wallace, *An Autobiography*, 2 vols., New York and Boston: Harper and Brothers, 1906, Vol. II, pp. 560-562.

Page 202. Friedrich Hecker: DAB; Koerner, I, 518-520, 528-530, II, 150-152, 193-194.

Page 203. George von Amsberg: Edmund Vasvary, *Lincoln's Hungarian Heroes*, Washington, D. C.: Hungarian Reformed Federation of America, 1939, p. 47; Kaufmann, 478.

Adolf Dengler: Kaufmann, 491.

Page 204. Joseph Gerhardt: "General Joseph Gerhardt," P, XIII, 282; Kaufmann, 502.

Carl Eberhard Salomon: Kaufmann, 545; number of his Missouri Regiment corrected by Heitman, I, 867; P, XII, 450-451.

Konrad Krez: DAB; H. O. Brown and M. A. W. Brown (eds.) *Soldiers' and Citizens' Album of Biographical Record*, Chicago: Grand Army Publication Co., 1890, pp. 597-599.

Page 205. Wilhelm Heine: Rosengarten, 174-175; Kaufmann, 510.

Henry Flad: DAB; Rombauer, p. xii.

Fritz Anneke: Hense-Jensen, I, 202-205; Kaufmann, 478-479.

Page 206. Franz Mahler: Schurz, I, 209, II, 233, III, 12; Kaufmann, 529-530.

Heinrich Boernstein: Koerner, II, 147-148; Richard Edwards and M. Hopewell, *Edwards' Great West and her Metropolis, Embracing a General View of the West and a Complete History of St. Louis*, St. Louis, 1860.

Page 207. Adolf von Hartung: Kaufmann, p. 508; Address of von

Hartung, *Dedication of Monument of 74th Pennsylvania Regiment at Gettysburg*, Harrisburg, Pennsylvania: E. K. Meyers, 2 vols., 1893, Vol. I, pp. 400–402.

Edward Kapff: P, VIII, 515.

Augustus Mersey: Koerner, II, 120–123, 151–152; Kaufmann, 531.

Friedrich Poschner: Whitelaw Reid, *Ohio in the War*, 2 vols. Columbus, Ohio: Eclectic Publishing Co., 1893, Vol. II, pp. 290–291; Kaufmann, 519.

Franz Wutschel: Kaufmann, 307, 565.

Rudolf von Rosa: Phisterer, p. 408; Kaufmann, 543–544.

Franz Wilhelmi: Kaufmann, 563.

Heinrich von Trebra: Kaufmann, 263–264, 556–557.

Nickolaus Schuettner: Rombauer, pp. 198, 394; Kaufmann, p. 551.

Albert Sigel: Kaufmann, p. 553. Interesting facts appear in an obituary of his father, Moritz Sigel in the New York Democrat, August, 1863 (gathered from a clipping in the possession of his daughter, Miss Lena Sigel).

Carl Gottfried Freudenberg: Rosengarten, 118–119; Kaufmann, 500.

Page 208. Ernest F. M. Faehtz: P, XIV, 115; Kaufmann, 497.

Germain von Metternich: Kaufmann, 532.

Hermann Ulffers: "Hermann Ulffers," P, XI, 395–396; Kaufmann, 558.

Edward C. Wratislaw: Phisterer, 407–408; Kaufmann, 565.

Page 209. Andrew Brickel: Phisterer, 350; Kaufmann, 486.

Albert Arndt: Kaufmann, 479; for details as to the composition of the Brickel First New York Light Artillery, see General Richard C. Drum, *List of Synonyms of Organizations in the Volunteer Service of the United States during the Years 1861, '62, '63, '64, and '65*, Washington: Government Printing Office, 1885, pp. 98, 100.

Franz Backhoff: "Major Franz Backhoff," P, XII, 216–217; Kaufmann, 480.

Page 210. Ernst F. Hoffman: Kaufmann, 513–514; General J. H. Wilson, *Under the Old Flag*, New York: Appleton, 1912, pp. 309–312. Quotations on p. 311.

Page 211. Gustave von Struve: DAB; see also Struve for evidence of his bitterness.

Adam Schumacher: P, X, 451–452.

Page 212. Sixtus Kapff: P, VIII, 515.

Christian Essig: Kaufmann, 496; OWR, Series I, Vol. III, p. 17.

William Hexamer: Kaufman, 512.

Louis Hofmann: Kaufmann, 514.

John Albert Neustaedter: Friedrich Schnake, "Der Ausbruch des Buergerkrieges," P, XI, 359*n*; Schurz, I, 215–231, 236–238; OWR, Series I, Vol. VII, p. 449.

Page 213. Hermann Ignatz Dettweiler: P, X, 272.

Fidel Schlund: Kaufmann, 550.

Dr. Adam Hammer: "Dr. Adam Hammer," P, X, 242–244; DAB.

Page 214. Dr. Gustav C. E. Weber: Kaufmann, 562; DAB.

Dr. Rudolf Neuhaus: Kaufmann, 535–536.

Dr. Emil Haas: Kaufmann, 506.

Dr. Julius von Hausen: Kaufmann, 509.

Dr. Adolf Zipperlen: Kaufmann, 565–566.

Dr. Johann Zitzer: Kaufmann, 566.

Page 215. Edmund Maerklin: Kaufmann, 531; checked by the Descriptive Rolls in the National Archives and the State Rolls in the office of the Adjutant General in Madison, Wisconsin.

Dr. Philipp Trau: P, XV, 333–334.

Dr. Karl Hartmann: Kaufmann, 508.

John A. Foersch: *Illinois Staatszeitung*, July 20, 1861. The fact of his service is established by the Descriptive Rolls both in Washington and in Albany.

August Becker: *Illinois Staatszeitung*, July 20, 1861; P, III, 61, 290–294.

Wilhelm Stengel: Huhn, I, 33.

Page 216. Joseph Fuchshuber: Kaufmann, 501; *Official Roster of the Soldiers of the State of Ohio in the War of the Rebellion*, 1861–66, II, 265.

Albert Kraus: Kaufmann, 521.

Otto von Corwin: Kaufmann, 489–490.

Page 217. Henry Villard: DAB; *Memoirs of Henry Villard*, New York, 1904.

Page 218. Effect of the War on the Forty-eighter: Ernest Bruncken, "German Political Refugees in the United States from the Period 1815–1860," DAG, III, 33–46, IV, 31–59.

CHAPTER VIII

The chief works relating to Carl Schurz, in addition to those quoted below, are: C. V. Easum, *The Americanization of Carl Schurz*, University of Chicago Press, 1929; Fuess; Joseph Schafer, *Carl Schurz, Militant Liberal*.

The memory of Carl Schurz has not been and will not be allowed to die. Of monuments in the narrower sense we may mention the bronze statue by Karl Bitter which stands on Morningside Heights at 116th Street in New York City, a few hundred feet from Low Library at Columbia University. In Oshkosh, Wisconsin, in a small park overlooking Lake Winnebago there is a statue of Schurz larger than life size. It bears the inscription: "Our Greatest American, Carl Schurz. Presented to the City of Oshkosh by John Hicks, 1914." Another impressive memorial is the stone seat erected by his friends at Bolton Landing on the western shore of Lake George, where Schurz spent

many happy months in the summers of 1892–1905. A tablet marks—
or marked—the room where Karl Schurz was born, in the castle near
Liblar.

Still more lasting commemoration is promised by the endowments
founded in his name. The first of these was the Carl Schurz Memorial
Professorship, established by means of funds donated largely by public-
spirited German Americans, and devoted to the memory of Schurz as
one-time Regent of the University of Wisconsin. The income of this
endowment has been used to bring a number of prominent German
professors to the University from time to time, to deliver lectures in
their special fields.

The second of these endowments is the Carl Schurz Memorial
Foundation, with offices in Philadelphia, which is dedicated to the
task of promoting cultural relations between the people of Germany
and of the United States. The Foundation publishes an illustrated
magazine, *The American-German Review*, promotes cultural exchanges
of every sort between the two peoples, and carries out in its policies
that enlightened German-Americanism—if one may call it so—which
Carl Schurz exemplified so signally in his own life.

Page 227. Blanc: Schurz, I, 400.

Page 228. To Petrasch, September 24, 1863: Schurz Intimate Letters,
   p. 282.

Page 229. Here in America: Schurz Papers, I, 8.

Page 231. Douglas: Schurz, II, 32.

Page 236. They urge me: Schurz, III, 103.

Page 237. To Petrasch, October 12, 1864: Schurz Papers, I, 251.
   Report on the South: Schurz, III, 204.

Page 239. I kept my opening speech: Schurz, III, 297.

Page 240. Schurz becomes Senator: Friedrich Schnake, a pre-'48 immigrant, states (P, V, 333) that the first German immigrant to be
   elected Senator was Henry Geyer of Missouri who assumed his
   seat about twenty years before Carl Schurz. Geyer had come to
   this country as a child of three and later graduated from West
   Point. Rattermann, editor of the *Pionier*, who as a "Gray" had no
   love for the Forty-eighters, underlines in a footnote that thus
   Carl Schurz was not the first German-born Senator!

Page 241. I remember vividly: Schurz, III, 302.
   I want him to point out: Schurz, III, 358.

Page 248. You have succeeded: Schurz, III, 392.

BIOGRAPHICAL DICTIONARY OF THE FORTY-EIGHTERS

By A. E. Zucker

AN MEIN VATERLAND
Kein Baum gehoerte mir von deinen Waeldern,
Mein war kein Halm auf deinen Roggenfeldern,
Und schutzlos hast du mich hinausgetrieben,
Weil ich in meiner Jugend nicht verstand
Dich weniger und mehr mich selbst zu lieben,
Und dennoch lieb ich dich, mein Vaterland!

TO MY FATHERLAND
In all thy forests was no tree mine own;
No blade of rye in all thy fields was mine;
Thou cast me out defenseless and alone,
So young and simple I could not divine
That I should love thee less, myself the more.
Still, Fatherland, I love thee as before!

THE poem of which the first stanza heads these biographical
sketches of slightly more than three hundred Forty-eighters has
been widely acclaimed as the best poem by a Forty-eighter. This
judgment indicates that the sentiment found a wide echo among
thousands of readers on both sides of the Atlantic. It is placed here to
call attention to the fact that each of these sketches deals with an uprooted life, with all the hardships and handicaps that such a career
entails. While the Forty-eighters enjoyed and appreciated the freedom
and the asylum the United States offered them, they naturally enough
found the strange land a cold world and remembered many pleasant
aspects of the Fatherland. Nor was it possible for them to hate an entire
nation for the injury the men in power had done them.

The reader must bear in mind that several hundred immigrants out
of the perhaps 4,000 Forty-eighters who came to America (a conservative estimate, I believe) are not an average group. I cannot claim to
have searched all records; of those men who disappeared from sight as

laborers, bartenders, janitors, and all manner of menial workers, no account is extant. Of the soldiers in the Civil War only officers are counted here. Consequently, statistics based on my figures are not to be taken too seriously as typical; even of those listed some data, such as place or date of birth, are not available.

Still, a few counts may serve to support some generalizations that have been made. It has been said that the Forty-eighters were young men; of 242 with birth dates listed 148 (over 60 per cent) were born in 1820 or later, with the year 1827 giving the largest number, namely 20, and no year before 1820 furnishing more than 9. Thus most of them were in their early twenties when they risked their lives for freedom.

Furthermore, it is commonly said that the greatest number of Forty-eighters came from southwestern Germany. Of those whose birth places are ascertainable the list runs as follows: Baden 40, Hesse 29, Wuerttemberg 20, Palatinate 19, Rhineland 17—total 125. Among the much larger states, Prussia has only 25, Saxony 16, Bavaria 16, and Austria 15. It is surprising that there are as many as 15 from Silesia and 12 from Schleswig-Holstein.

I have also tried to list the professions. Regarding this count it must be borne in mind that one man frequently must appear more than once, Carl Schurz, for example, was diplomat, politician, soldier, Senator, Secretary of the Interior, and author.

Journalist	74	Musician	11
Soldier	67	Engineer	9
Physician	37	Pastor	9
Teacher	25	Poet	8
Turner	25	Innkeeper	7
Lawyer	22	Legislator	7
Businessman	21	Goldsmith or Jeweler	6
Author	16	Banker	5
Farmer	12	Pharmacist	5
Diplomat	11	Speaker of *freie Gemeinden*	5

A number of categories have fewer than five representatives: apothecary, actor, architect, astronomer, baker, bookkeeper, botanist, brewer, butcher, caricaturist, carpenter, chaplain, cigar maker, Congressman, cooper, customs official, dentist, engraver, ethnologist, geologist, governor, immigration commissioner, inventor, labor leader, laborer, lieutenant governor, lithographer, mayor, notary, policeman, printer, professor, rabbi, sculptor, soapmaker, Secretary of Interior, Senator, statistician, stone mason, surveyor, tanner, tailor, viticulturist.

There is listed also one suffragist, the only woman among the Forty-eighters, Mrs. Mathilde Giesler-Anneke.

No one who has read this book is surprised that journalists lead the field. The number 67 listed as "soldiers" fails to include not only the privates or noncommissioned officers, but also the regimental surgeons, quartermasters, chaplains, and so on. This means that practically one-third of the recorded Forty-eighters took part in the Civil War. The number of authors would be much larger if works of scientists or all books of verse had been included; the number of Forty-eighters who published verse would have to include at least 50 per cent, I should guess, but the exact figure would be very difficult to determine. One surprise is the fact that there are nine pastors of conventional churches among the Forty-eighters; if all who at one time or another served as "speakers" of *freie Gemeinden* were included, the number would be much greater than five. Strange too, it seems that only five (Kiefer, Jacobi, Weber, Stoeckel, and Peters) attained the position of university professors; in the much less numerous immigration of the twenties, Beck, Follen, and Lieber received such appointments, and among later immigrants there are many such instances.

The term "politician" applied to 18 men is by no means intended as derogatory, but simply to mean that they did their duty as citizens and took an interest in public affairs, usually by running for office. This designation has been applied somewhat arbitrarily and the number so described could well be much larger. *Turner* is used to designate gymnastics teachers or others who were practically professionally connected with the organization.

It is rather interesting to note the large number who escaped from prison. This probably indicates that the Forty-eighters were resourceful, daring men, and also that the general populace, including some prison guards, sympathized with the revolutionaries. From all accounts it seems too that the police in the numerous German states of a hundred years ago were not nearly so efficient as was Hitler's *Gestapo*. There are many instances of prison sentences that were reduced, showing that the fierceness of the persecution of the revolutionaries relaxed somewhat after a few years.

Generalizations aside, the list of biographies contains many exciting lives. As usual, probably Carl Schurz heads the group when it comes to a colorful career, but there are many others far from drab. Very remarkable, to mention just a few, are: Baumbach, Behrendt, Bernays, Brentano, Degener, Otto Dresel, Eickmeyer, Gerhardt, von Gilsa, Hartmann, Hassaurek, Heine, Kapp, Theodor Kaufmann, Loehr, Peters, Reichmann, Peissner, Pfaender, and Mrs. Giesler-Anneke.

Quite a number have been included whose lives, except for the one gallant moment of the fight for freedom, can be summed up in "the short and simple annals of the poor"; they are listed here to show that not all Forty-eighters were intellectuals. Some who have not been listed for lack of data nevertheless stir one's curiosity; for example, there is mentioned as present in Cincinnati in 1848 "Schoeninger who had shot

Gagern," referring to the commander of the regular Baden troops in the Battle of Kandern. (The brother of this general was Heinrich von Gagern, president of the Frankfurt *Parlament*.) And there is reported another man who, very shortly after he had enlisted in the Union army, died perhaps the most futile death—shot by a jealous lover who mistook him for someone else!

I am indebted to Rabbi Bertram W. Korn of American Jewish Archives, Cincinnati, for the names of a number of distinguished Jewish Forty-eighters.

AMSBERG, GEORGE von (1817–?), soldier, riding master, b. Hildesheim. Served as officer in the Austrian army in command of a Hungarian Hussar regiment. On the outbreak of the Hungarian Revolution he joined this movement with his troops. After the revolt had been crushed, he was condemned to a long term in prison and came to the U.S. in the late fifties, when he became a riding master in Hoboken. He served with distinction as a colonel in the Civil War. (Kaufmann, 478.)

ANNEKE, EMIL P. (1823–?), journalist, auditor, lawyer, b. Dortmund. Studied at University of Berlin. As result of revolutionary activity, he fled to U.S. in 1848. Until 1854 he was reporter for the New York *Staatszeitung* and in 1855 he joined the staff of August Marxhausen's *Volksblatt* in Detroit. Elected auditor general of Michigan in 1862 and established himself in law practice in Grand Rapids in 1866. (Russell, 94, 277, 296.)

ANNEKE, FRITZ (Jan. 31, 1818–?, 1870), army officer, journalist, b. Dortmund. After graduation from a *Gymnasium*, he joined the Prussian army. Despite the fact that he was an officer, he held democratic convictions and lived up to them by organizing democratic clubs among soldiers and workers. Like Willich he was dishonorably discharged from the army and joined the revolutionary forces in South Germany. He distinguished himself as commander in the battle of Ubstadt, but was forced to take refuge in Switzerland. He arrived in U.S. in 1849 with his wife, Mathilde Giesler-Anneke. Before and after the Civil War he followed a journalistic career in St. Louis and Chicago and served also as correspondent for the *Augsburg Allgemeine Zeitung*. He was a colonel of the 35th Wisconsin Regiment, but because of his criticism of his superiors his army career was terminated. (Schem; Valentin; Hense-Jensen; Huhn, I, 37; Kaufmann, 478f.)

ANNEKE, MATHILDE FRANZISKA GIESLER- (April 17, 1817–Nov. 25, 1884), suffragist, author, educator, b. Westphalia. Educated in Catholic schools. At an early age she wrote verse in a devout strain. Her unhappy marriage at nineteen and her divorce a year later accompanied by a long struggle to secure custody of her child turned her into an advocate of women's rights. In 1848 she edited a *Frauenzeitung* in Cologne, which was suppressed by the authorities. In 1847 she married Fritz Anneke and, when he in 1848 became one of the commanders of the Revolutionary armies in Baden, she accompanied him as his mounted orderly. Carl Schurz, then Anneke's aide-de-camp, describes her as "a young woman of noble character, beauty, vivacity, and fiery patriotism." Upon the failure of the Revolution, the Annekes went first to Switzerland and then in 1849 came to the U.S., settling in Milwaukee. Mrs. Anneke continued writing and lecturing for the cause of woman suffrage and was highly esteemed by Susan B. Anthony as well as other leaders of the movement. From 1852 to 1858 the Annekes lived in Newark, N. J., where she edited the *Frauenzeitung*. When her husband entered the Union army, she went to Switzerland, supporting herself as a newspaper correspondent. In 1865 she returned to Milwaukee and founded a girls' school which she conducted for the rest of her life. Her husband died in 1870 and many other misfortunes overtook her, but she bore them all in a brave spirit, retaining her youthful idealism and interest in humanitarian causes. She published, aside from her social writings, a number of novels, dramas, memoirs of the Revolution, and some charming verse. As the one woman among our Forty-eighters, Mathilde Giesler-Anneke may well be considered an embodiment of the noblest traits of this group. (DAB; Hense-Jensen)

ANSCHUETZ, CARL (Feb., 1813–Dec. 30, 1870), musician, b. Koblenz. Trained in music by his father and a number of noted musicians and became director of a school of music in his native town. In 1848 his sympathy with the Revolution cost him his position. After some wanderings to Amsterdam and London, Anschuetz arrived in New York where he remained for the rest of his life. He became the conductor of Ullmann's Opera Company and later of the German Opera Company. Anschuetz is one of the important pioneers of opera in the U.S. (*Magazin*, I, 515 ff.)

ARNDT, ALBERT (d. 1862). Fought in the Baden Revolution, though a former South German officer. In the Civil War he commanded a battalion of artillery. Major Arndt fell at Antietam. (Kaufmann, 479.)

AULENBACH, KARL (Aug. 6, 1813–Sept. 25, 1881), pastor, b. Homburg. Student of theology at Erlangen. Was dismissed in 1835 because of participation in liberal movements. Continued studies in Goettingen and became pastor in Schmieheim, Baden. He showed his liberal attitude through the publication of numerous poems in democratic vein and in 1848 became involved in the Revolution. He was forced to flee to Switzerland and later immigrated to the U.S. in 1849. Unlike most Forty-eighters, he was orthodox in religious matters and occupied various pulpits in Ohio, chiefly that of the Evangelical Church in Zanesville. He continued to publish verse, chiefly of religious and didactic character. (P, XIII, 331–339.)

BACKHOFF, FRANZ (Nov. 28, 1821–?), contractor and soldier, b. Weschbach, Baden. Trained for building trade. Took valiant part in fighting in Baden where he was taken prisoner at the surrender of Rastatt. He was sentenced to ten years imprisonment, but pardoned after two years on condition that he leave Europe. He arrived in the U.S. in 1851, settling in St. Louis where he established himself as contractor. He was repeatedly elected member of the city council. He served as major of artillery under General Sigel in Missouri. (P, XII, 216 f.; Kaufmann, 480.)

BALATKA, HANS (March 5, 1826–April 17, 1899), musician, b. Hoffnungsthal, Austria. Studied music at University of Vienna. In 1848 he joined the Vienna Academic Legion, but upon the suppression of the Austrian Revolution he was forced to flee and arrived in U.S. in 1849. Imbued with the romantic notion of idyllic country life, he bought a farm in Wisconsin but after a short time abandoned this occupation. He then settled in Milwaukee and, under considerable difficulties, began a musical career that was to continue for fifty years with great success. In 1860 he accepted the post of director of the Chicago Philharmonic Society. The great fire in 1871 destroyed his home and musical library and left him impoverished; but after two years of concert tours he returned to Chicago. Balatka, in addition to being a musical director, sang various operatic roles, wrote some original compositions, and published some humorous poems. Among the pioneers to introduce good music in America, Balatka ranks very high. (Chicago, 119–123; P, XIII, 119.)

BALBACH, ———. Fought in the Baden Revolution as a member of the general staff. After his arrival in the U.S. he was employed on the U.S. Coast Survey. In the Civil War he served as a major and fell in one of the first battles. (Kaufmann, 480.)

BARUS, KARL (Oct. 12, 1823–?), musician, b. Brieg, Silesia. Trained in music in Breslau. Took part in the Revolution and arrived in the U.S. in 1849. He tried farming in Michigan and then went to Cincinnati to engage in a musical career. At first he conducted the orchestra of the German theater and in 1856 was chosen as director of the Philharmonic Society. Barus introduced symphonic music in Cincinnati. (P, XII, 274f.)

BAUER, CARL FRIEDRICH (1824–1889), journalist, b. Baden. Studied chemistry. Took part in the Revolution and arrived in the U.S. in 1849, settling in Pittsburgh. At first he worked as apothecary and later established the *Volksblatt*, which he conducted successfully as a liberal, independent paper from 1853 to 1885. In 1885 he was called to Milwaukee to become the editor-in-chief of the *Herold*. He was an enthusiastic *Turner*, one of the founder members of the Pittsburgh *Turnverein*, as well as a national officer. It was under his presidency in 1855 that the *Turner* passed their antislavery resolution branding it an institution unworthy of a republic and contrary to the principles of liberty. (Huhn, I, 34; WMH, IX, 130.)

BAUMBACH, LUDWIG VON (April 22, 1799–Jan. 26, 1883), politician, gentleman farmer, consul, b. Hesse. Trained for the army, he resigned a captaincy to devote himself to the cultivation of his family estates. Of extremely liberal political views, he was elected to the Hessian diet where he presided very ably in 1848 when numerous reforms were voted. He was also a member of the Frankfurt *Parlament*. Dissatisfied with conditions under the reaction, he sold his estates in 1857 and brought his family to the U.S. to permit his children to grow up in a free atmosphere. He first went to Ohio where, as a "Latin farmer" he took great interest in politics and wrote articles for German papers. In 1857 he went to Milwaukee, serving as consul for Bavaria. At the same time he founded a real estate firm with his two sons. His writings attracted numerous immigrants as well as German capital to the young state of Wisconsin. Ludwig von Baumbach as a man of nobility and of wealth exemplifies unselfish idealism in his devotion to freedom. One of his daughters married Rudolf von Kaltenborn, the father of H. V. Kaltenborn. (P, XV, 355f.; Valentin.)

BAYRHOFFER, KARL THEODOR (Oct. 14, 1812–?), professor of philosophy, farmer, lecturer, b. Marburg. Studied philosophy at Heidelberg and was made full professor at Marburg. Because of his radical political lectures delivered to the general public, he was suspended in 1846 and accused of "blasphemy and incitement against the government." In 1848 he wrote for revolutionary papers and was elected to the Hessian diet. Upon the suppression of the Revolution he fled to Switzerland and was sentenced *in absentia* to fourteen years' imprisonment. He arrived in the U.S. in 1852, and for 17 years lived as a farmer near Monroe, Wisconsin. He was an ardent member of the Republican party and his son volunteered for service at the outbreak of the Civil War.

In 1869 he accepted the position of speaker of a *freie Gemeinde* in La Salle, Ill. He published articles and books setting forth his democratic and humanitarian ideals. (Schem; DPV, XI, 21.)

BECKER, AUGUST (1813–March 26, 1872), journalist, chaplain, b. Biedenkopf, Hesse. Studied theology in Giessen. Before 1848 he was involved in revolutionary activity, was imprisoned for three years, and then lived in exile in Switzerland. In 1848 he returned to Germany and was elected member of the Hessian diet. Forced into exile again by the reaction, he went to Switzerland and in 1853 arrived in Baltimore where for some years he was editor of the *Wecker*. As such he was a staunch adherent of the Republican party and an antislavery man. Then he went to Cincinnati, continuing his journalistic career in turn on the *Hochwaechter* and *Courier*. He had the distinction of serving as member of the Ohio delegation to the Republican convention in Chicago in 1860. On the outbreak of the Civil War he joined the New York Steuben Regiment as chaplain, serving for three years. Afterward he returned to journalistic activity. He was an unbending man of firm conviction, sometimes called *der rote Becker* because of his radical tendencies. He wrote some striking verse glorifying the fight for freedom. In his regiment he was known as "the word of God on horseback." (Herriot, 71; Ruetenik, 343f.; Cunz; Huhn, I, 32; Zimmermann; Kaufmann, 481; Schem; P, III, 61, 290–294.)

BECKER, GOTTFRIED (1827–1867), *Turner*, soldier, b. Frankenthal, Palatinate. After participating in the Revolution, he fled to Switzerland and arrived in U.S. in 1850. For several years he was editor of the *Turnzeitung*. At the outbreak of the Civil War he entered the 28th Ohio Regiment and served as colonel from 1863 to 1865. In the Battle of Antietam his was the first regiment to cross the Antietam and attack the strong position of the Confederates. (Huhn, I, 32; Kaufmann, 481.)

BEHLENDORF, FREDERICK (July 4, 1829–?, 1889), soldier and customs official, b. Dresden. Studied law in Dresden, where, when the Revolution broke out, he joined the student corps fighting on the barricades. He escaped and arrived in the U.S. in 1849. He followed various occupations in a number of states. The year 1860 found him in New Orleans where he was mobbed as a Union sympathizer. He went to St. Louis and enlisted in the regular army as a private and rose to the position of major in 1864. After the war he was appointed Deputy Collector of Customs in Chicago as a reward for his courageous efforts in bringing about the exposure and conviction of a number of corrupt customs officials. Behlendorf left fascinating reminiscences of the Dresden street fighting and his early days in the Union army. (DAG, XV, 310–351.)

BEHR, ALFRED VON (d. Jan. 1, 1863), physician, b. Koethen, Prussia. Studied medicine in Paris. Elected member of Prussian constituant assembly, 1848. Forced to flee when the Revolution was suppressed, he arrived in the U.S. in 1849 where he practiced medicine, at first in Texas and then in St. Louis. He is described as a most generous and self-sacrificing doctor, somewhat eccentric and devoted to the bottle. It is related that on one occasion after a loss of much sleep he was called to attend a woman patient and listened to her heart action; a little later a colleague entered, to find him sleeping gently, his head on the lady's bosom. (DAG, XIII, 316f.)

BEHR, HANS HERMANN (1818-?), physician and scientist, b. Koethen, Prussia. Studied medicine in Halle and Berlin. Traveled widely in Australia, Asia, and Africa. On his return to Germany, he took part in the Revolution. Forced to flee, he arrived in the U.S. in 1850, establishing himself as a physician in San Francisco where he also served as professor at the Pharmaceutical College. Later on he abandoned the practice of medicine to assume the post of custodian of the Academy of Sciences. He published verse in praise of the beauties of nature. (Zimmermann.)

BEHRENDT, KARL HERMANN (Nov. 12, 1817–May 12, 1878), physician, ethnologist, b. Danzig. Studied at various universities, receiving his M.D. at Berlin in 1842. He established himself as lecturer at the University of Breslau. In 1848 he was a member of the Frankfurt *Parlament* and lost his post at the University because of his democratic opinions. He came in 1851 to the U.S., settling first in New York. He then went to Central America and later to Mexico where he became interested in archeological and ethnological studies. His publications attracted the attention of the Smithsonian Institution in whose interest he set out in 1866 for Guatemala to explore some hitherto unknown district. This was followed by a number of other expeditions for the Peabody and the Berlin Museums. His chief interest was the Mayan civilization. After his death the Smithsonian Institution acquired his voluminous manuscripts, which included a grammar and a dictionary of the Mayan languages. (P, XII, 251–256.)

BERGER, HEINRICH (June 9, 1816–?), sculptor, b. Breslau. Studied painting and sculpture in Breslau and Vienna. Because of revolutionary activity in Vienna, he fled to the U.S. in 1848 and, after many hardships established himself as a sculptor in New York. In 1877 he published a book of verse, including a vivid eulogy of General George A. Custer. (Zimmermann.)

BERGMANN, CARL (April 11, 1821–Aug. 10, 1876), musician, b. Ebersbach, Saxony. Studied music in Breslau and was conductor in various European capitals. Involved in the Revolution, he was forced to flee and arrived in New York in 1849. He joined the Germania Orchestra as violoncellist, but soon became conductor. In 1858 he became conductor of the New York Philharmonic Society. In the period from 1865 to his death he introduced many works by Wagner, Liszt, Rubinstein, Berlioz, and Brahms to this country. He also gave the first complete performances in this country of Beethoven's *Fidelio* and Wagner's *Tannhaeuser*. At the height of his career he was "the most respected and admired musical leader in the country." (DAB.)

BERNAYS, CARL L. (1815–June 22, 1879), journalist, consul, b. Mainz. Studied law in Munich, Goettingen, and Heidelberg. Engaged in liberal journalism and had to leave Germany in 1842 when he joined Boernstein in Paris who was editing the revolutionary *Vorwaerts*. In 1848 he went to Vienna and because of his involvement in the Revolution he was forced to flee to the U.S. With Boernstein he edited the St. Louis *Anzeiger des Westens* and is accounted one of the best journalists among the Forty-eighters. He had the distinction of being a member of the Missouri delegation to the Republican convention in Chicago in 1860. He was a close friend of Lincoln's and spent the election night with him watching the telegraphic returns. When on the outbreak of the Civil War the situation in St. Louis between Union and Confederate sympathizers became critical, Bernays went to Washington to inform Lincoln of the willingness of the *Turner* to act and secured from Lincoln permission for the arming of the German regiments. In 1861 Lincoln appointed him consul in Zurich. In 1862 Lincoln appointed Bernays to a paymastership in the army, a sinecure, to enable him to return to the *Anzeiger* for the sake of holding the German Republicans as supporters of the administration instead of following Preetorius into the radical camp. (Herriot, 70; Kaufmann, 483; Boernstein, II, 297; P, XI, 458ff.; Carman, 199.)

BEST, ADAM (Aug. 7, 1827–Dec. 26, 1880), cooper, b. Osthofen, Hesse. Took part in the Revolution and was forced to flee, arriving in the U.S. in 1848. He settled in Cincinnati and continued successfully at his trade as cooper. Best also was a devoted member of the *Pionierverein*, an historical society of the Germans in Cincinnati. (P, XIII, 34.)

BEST, MICHAEL (Feb. 25, 1829–?), merchant, soldier, b. Schifferstadt, Bavaria. Served four months in the Revolutionary Army and came to St. Louis in 1852. He engaged in steamboating. In 1861 he enlisted as a private in the First Regiment Missouri Volunteers and advanced to the rank of captain by the time his regiment was mustered out after one year's service. In 1864 he again enlisted as a private and after 15 days was promoted for gallantry to first lieutenant and served as such to the end of the war. After the war he started a successful flour business. (Hyde and Conart.)

BETZ, PHILIPP, *Turner*, soldier. Took part in Revolution in Baden and suffered three years imprisonment, after which he was released on condition that he emigrate. He came to America where he settled in Davenport, Iowa, was an enthusiastic *Turner*, and served in the Union army. (*Kalender:* 1887, 91–101; 1888, 83–88.)

BEYSCHLAG, CARL (Feb. 4, 1816–?) editor, chaplain, b. Noerdlingen, Bavaria. For his revolutionary activity as editor of *Donauzeitung* in Ulm he was condemned to six months' imprisonment and then released on condition that he emigrate. He arrived in the U.S. in 1851 and served as editor of a number of papers in Indianapolis. During the Civil War he served as chaplain of the 28th Ohio Regiment. In 1863 he published a humorous work, *Eisele und Beisele im Westvirginischen Feldzuge.* After 1866 he edited the *Mississippi Schulbote* in St. Louis. (Schem.)

BIEN, JULIUS (Sept. 27, 1826–Dec. 1, 1909), lithographer and map engraver, b. Naumburg near Cassel. Studied painting and the graphic arts at Cassel and Frankfurt. He became involved in the Revolution and had to flee, arriving in New York in 1849. Here he started a small business with a lithographic hand press. Since map-making in the U.S. was in rather a primitive state at the time, Bien offered his skill to the government, and the Secretary of War, Jefferson Davis, entrusted the preparation of some maps for the Pacific Railway survey to Bien. He proved so successful in this work that his general map of the territory between the Mississippi and the Pacific remained standard for twenty-five years. Practically all maps for geographical or geological publications issued by the government from this time onward to the end of the century were engraved and printed by Bien. During the Civil War, Bien did a valuable service by equipping a field map printing outfit for General Sherman on his march to the sea. He was a pioneer in establishing scientific standards in American cartography. (DAB.)

BINDER, HEINRICH (1829–?), journalist, b. Vienna. Took part in Revolution in Germany and fled first to Switzerland and France. In 1852 he came to the U.S. as a refugee. He was associated with various newspapers, at first in the East and then with the *Illinois Staatszeitung* and the *Westliche Post* in St. Louis. In 1870 he became editor of the Detroit *Abendpost* and in 1888 of *Puck*, a humorous and political weekly published in New York. (Huhn, I, 34.)

BLENKER, LUDWIG (July 31, 1812–Oct. 31, 1863), soldier, b. Worms. In 1832 he took part in the expedition of a Bavarian legion to Greece, then went into business as a wine merchant. In 1849 he commanded Hessian *Turner* in the fighting in the Palatinate and in Baden. He arrived in New York in 1850 where he worked for a business firm. In April, 1861, he organized the 8th New York Regiment and distinguished himself at the first battle of Bull Run. In 1862 he was relieved of his command. Blenker was a very courageous but also a vain and pompous man—the latter qualities proved his undoing. (Huhn, I, 36; Kaufmann, 483; Schem.)

BLOEDE, GUSTAV (Sept. 23, 1814–?), lawyer, physician, journalist, b. Dresden. Studied law in Leipzig and then practiced his profession in Dresden. He was a liberal and as such elected a member of the Dresden city council and also of the *Vorparlament* in Frankfurt. When Prussian troops occupied Dresden after the uprising in May, 1849, Bloede was arrested and condemned to ten years' imprisonment for treason. He escaped, however, and arrived in New York in 1850. He studied medicine and practiced for some years, but later became editor of the Republican New York *Demokrat*. His wife, Marie Antoinette Francisca, published a number of narrative poems and translations under the pen name of Marie Westland. Their home was the center of literary gatherings, frequented by such men as Stoddard, Stedman, Aldrich, and Bayard Taylor. Their daughter, Gertrude Bloede, gained considerable fame as an author and is listed in the DAB. (DAB; Schem.)

BOEBEL, HANS. Took part in Revolution. Founder member of Milwaukee *Turnverein* and *Bund freier Menschen*. Lieutenant colonel in the 26th Wisconsin Regiment which he commanded at the Battle of Gettysburg where he lost a leg and was forced to leave the service. Later he was elected city treasurer of Milwaukee. (Kaufmann, 484; Hense-Jensen.)

BOERNSTEIN, HEINRICH (1805–1892), journalist, actor, novelist, consul, b. Hamburg. Began study of medicine at Vienna, but became an actor, then editor of *Vorwaerts*, a German liberal paper in Paris. He went to Vienna when the Revolution broke out there, but was forced to flee when the movement was crushed. Early in 1849 he arrived in the U.S. and in March, 1850, became editor of the *Anzeiger des Westens* in St. Louis, developing it into a powerful Republican paper in the Midwest. He was very active in founding a reading club and organizing and directing a German theater in St. Louis. Boernstein was one of the leaders in organizing German military regiments in St. Louis and was made colonel of the second German Missouri Regiment. He took part in only the first engagements and then was sent by Lincoln as consul to Bremen. In 1862 he was recalled to resume the editorship of his paper for the purpose of holding the Missouri German Republicans in the administration camp instead of going over to the radicals. Francis P. Blair wrote on August 1, 1862: "Boernstein has acted most nobly and done glorious service since his return. I have no doubt that he has done more to reconcile the Germans to the Administration than any other man of that race is capable of doing in so short a time." Boernstein spent his last years in Vienna as theater director. He wrote a successful novel, *Geheimnisse von St. Louis*, and very interesting memoirs. (P, V, 182ff.; Boernstein; Carman, 199.)

BOGEN, LUDWIG (June 7, 1810–April 6, 1886), journalist, b. Odenwald. Studied law. Very active in liberal movements, he was elected member of the Frankfurt *Parlament* and became a political refugee, arriving in the U.S. in 1853. After various activities in the Middle West, he found his proper calling in 1864 as editor of the New Ulm *Post*. He conducted the paper in a liberal spirit and died while writing an editorial on the exploitation of the workers by the railroad magnates. (P, XV, 347f.)

BONDI, AUGUST (1833–1907), soldier, lawyer, b. Vienna. At the age of 15 he enlisted in the Vienna Academic Legion and also fought with Kossuth. He came to the U.S. in 1848 with his parents who settled in St. Louis. In 1815 he joined an expedition planned to liberate Cuba and, after its failure, returned to St. Louis. In 1856 he moved to Kansas where, because of his strong antislavery sentiments, he joined and fought with John Brown. At the outbreak of the Civil War, he enlisted in the Fifth Kansas Cavalry and served as first sergeant for Company K for more than three years. After the war he settled in Salina, Kans., as a successful lawyer and real estate dealer. He held various local offices and was one of the directors of the Kansas State Historical Society to which he presented a musket John Brown had given him. (UJE.)

BRENDEL, FRIEDRICH (Jan., 1820–?), physician, botanist, b. Erlangen, Bavaria. Studied medicine in Erlangen and held a post as assistant in a Bamberg hospital. His liberal views caused him to be discharged and he went to the U.S. in 1850. After a two years' stay in St. Louis, he settled in Peoria, Ill., as physician. He served as meteorological observer for the Smithsonian Institute and wrote a botanical book, *Flora Peoriana*. (Bess, 431.)

BRENTANO, LORENZ (Nov. 4, 1813–Sept. 17, 1891), lawyer, journalist, Congressman, b. Mannheim. Studied law and established himself as a lawyer. In 1845 he was elected member of the Baden diet representing the radical group, but in 1848 he did not participate in Hecker's and Struve's proclamation of a republic; however, Brentano, now member of the Frankfurt *Parlament*, defended the revolutionaries in their trial. During the 1849 Revolution, Brentano was made one of the ministers of the revolutionary government. He favored moderation and endeavored to prevent revolutionary excesses. Despite his very moderate attitude, the reactionary government following upon the Revolution made it impossible for him to remain in Germany, and he therefore emigrated to the U.S. in 1850. At first he edited a short-lived weekly political paper in Pottsville, Pa., and when this endeavor failed, he bought some land near Kalamazoo, Mich., where for nine years he made a precarious living as a farmer. He took no part in public life and his friends thought that he had died. In 1859 he gave up farming and went to Chicago, where he at first tried to establish a law practice and then found his proper niche as editor of the *Illinois Staatszeitung*. Under his sensible, forceful editorship, the paper became the leading Republican organ among the Germans of the Middle West. Through the sale of his land in Michigan, Brentano was enabled to buy a half partnership in the *Staatszeitung* when its value was not very great, and later the vastly increased circulation made him moderately wealthy. His able leadership attracted wide attention and brought him into political life: in 1862 he was elected to the Illinois State Legislature and in 1878 to Congress. (DAB.)

BRETHAUER, OTTO (1830–1882), journalist, b. Bavarian Franconia. Just after he had begun his university studies he became involved in the Revolution and had to flee. On his arrival in New York, the struggle for existence proved very difficult for the young man with no special training. After some time he secured a position on the New York *Abendzeitung* and developed a humorous Sunday section with considerable success. In 1858 he began the publication of the New York *Humorist*, which flourished until the difficult times of the Civil War arrived. Afterward he was employed by various papers and in 1880 he published a selection from his writings, *Aus meiner Mappe*—poems, satirical tales, and epigrams. Many of these show considerable wit and are still readable. (Zimmermann.)

BRICKEL, ANDREW. Came to the U.S. as a result of his participation in the Baden Revolution. Major of artillery in the Army of the Potomac. His battery had been organized in Buffalo and consisted mostly of Germans. He fought with distinction throughout the Civil War. (Kaufmann, 486.)

BROOKMAN, ANTON (Oct. 28, 1818–?), jeweler, b. Vienna. He was apprenticed to a goldsmith and then established his own business. He took part in the street fighting during the Revolution and was forced to flee. He arrived in the U.S. in 1849. He found employment in Newark, N. J., in a factory, then he started a jewelry business in Saginaw, Mich., and after a decade moved to Chicago. His flourishing business was destroyed by the great fire of 1871, whereupon he joined his son in his chemical factory. (Chicago, 16off.)

BUSH, ISIDOR (Jan. 15, 1822–Aug. 5, 1898), publisher, viticulturist, b. Prague. Trained as a printer in his father's plant in Vienna. Because of his liberal views he was forced to flee during the Revolution and came to New York where he founded the first American Jewish weekly. The paper lasted only three months and Bush moved to St. Louis where he established a successful wholesale grocery business. In 1861 he was appointed aide to General Frémont, serving with the rank of captain until 1862. In 1864 he was a delegate to the Missouri Constitutional Convention and served on the State Board of Immigration from 1865 to 1877. He later won wide recognition as a viticulturist and published a manual on grape-growing. He was very active in B'nai B'rith and other Jewish organizations. (UJE.)

BUTZ, CASPAR (Oct. 23, 1825–Oct. 19, 1885), merchant, politician, poet, b. Hagen, Westphalia. Apprenticed to a mercantile house. Through his writings and speeches he became so involved in the Revolution that when Prussian troops entered Westphalia he was forced to flee—disguised in women's clothes. He arrived in the U.S. in 1849, first settling in Detroit where he helped Esselen edit his *Atlantis*. In 1854 he went to Chicago, engaging in the hardware business, but the chief interests in his life were poetry and politics; he was a *Turner*, an anti-slavery man, and an ardent Republican. At the conference of German Republicans in Chicago in 1860 he was elected secretary and member of resolutions committee. He voted for Lincoln, but by 1864 he disagreed with Lincoln's policies and led the movement for the nomination of Frémont, chiefly by means of his *Monatshefte*. In 1872 he attended the convention of the Liberal Republicans. He was intransigent in politics, very active in journalism, and also one of the leading poets among the Forty-eighters. (AGR, XII, 6 and XIII, 1; Huhn, I, 38; DAG, XXXII, 21.)

CANISIUS, THEODORE (1827 or 1830–Dec. 4, 1885), journalist, consul, b. Prussia. Studied medicine and is said to have been involved in the Revolution. Came to the U.S. in the early fifties settling first in Edwardsville, Ill., then edited the *Freie Presse* in Alton in 1858, but sold it after the second issue. In 1859 he became editor of the Springfield *Illinois Staats-Anzeiger* and published the famous letter Lincoln addressed to him on the Massachusetts "Two-Year Amendment." On May 30, 1859, Lincoln and Canisius drew up a contract under which Lincoln bought the *Staats-Anzeiger* and granted Canisius the use of the property so long as it strongly supported the Republican party. On December 6, 1860, Lincoln wrote a supplementary endorsement certifying that Dr. Canisius had faithfully fulfilled the obligations of the contract and that Lincoln, for a valid consideration, conveyed the type, paper, and good will to him. Lincoln appointed Canisius consul in Vienna. He was removed from his post for indiscreet correspondence with Garibaldi relative to an offer of a commission in the Union army, but restored after about a month. Afterwards he filled consular posts in Gestemuende, Germany; Bristol, England; and Apia in Samoa. He is described as tall, handsome, with auburn hair and beard, a man of most courtly manner. He was a vigorous antislavery man and obviously a good friend of Abraham Lincoln. His biography of the President was published in Vienna in 1867 and reprinted several times in Germany. (Paul M. Angle, *New Papers and Letters of Lincoln*, Houghton Mifflin Co., 1930; Howard R. Marrow, "Lincoln's Offer of a Commission to Garibaldi," *Century Magazine*, Vol. 75, pp. 63–74; W. T. Norton, *Centennial History of Madison County, Illinois*, Chicago, 1912, I, 397.)

CLAUSSEN, HANS REIMER (Feb. 23, 1804–March 14, 1894), lawyer, farmer, legislator, b. Feddringen, Holstein. Studied law in Kiel and practiced in his home town. In 1848 he was chosen one of the five Schleswig-Holstein delegates to present the demands for a more liberal regime to the Danish king. Later he was elected to the Frankfurt *Parlament*. For his staunch liberalism he was banished and came to Davenport as a political refugee. He wasted no time in hopes for another European revolution, but determined to make America his home and in two years he was admitted to the bar in Davenport, Iowa. He served several terms in the state legislature as a member of the Republican party where he was influential in a number of important committees. As leader of the Davenport Republican Club he sponsored a set of resolutions on March 7, 1860, which rejected Edward Bates as Republican candidate and set forth some principles for which German voters should stand. These were widely circulated and led to the meeting of German Republicans in the *deutsches Haus* in Chicago that had such great influence on the Republican convention that nominated Abraham Lincoln. Claussen was one of the conservative and influential Forty-eighters. (AGR, X, 5; Herriot, 83.)

CONRAD, CONSTANTIN (Aug. 1, 1828–?), *Turner*, b. Renchen, Baden.

Apprenticed to a cooper, he later set out as a journeyman and wherever he stopped he associated with *Turner*. His enthusiasm for freedom led him to join the Baden Revolutionary army in 1848 and he took part also in the battles of 1849. He made his escape when the Prussians took Rastatt and moved into Switzerland with the defeated army under Sigel. He landed in New Orleans in 1849, but soon went to Cincinnati where he was one of the most enthusiastic members of the *Turnverein*. In 1858 he went to Pittsburgh where he became a teacher of gymnastics. He introduced gymnastic training for girls. (Huhn, II, 42; JDAT, II, 281.)

CORVIN, OTTO VON [WIERSBITZKI] (Oct. 12, 1812–March 2, 1886), soldier, correspondent, author, b. Gumbinnen. Trained in military academies in Potsdam and Berlin and served as officer in the Prussian army, 1830–1835. Took part with Hecker in the Baden Revolution, where he was in command of the fortress of Rastatt. He was taken prisoner and condemned to death, but the sentence was then reduced to six years of imprisonment, which he served in Bruchsal. In 1855 he went to London. In 1861 he arrived in the U.S. as war correspondent for the *Augsburger Allgemeine Zeitung* and London *Times*. He wrote very interesting and amusing articles. He was one of the many members on General Blenker's staff and through his army service secured American citizenship. In 1863 he submitted to President Lincoln a plan to enlist for the Union army 20,000 trained German soldiers, a project at first considered favorably, but then dropped because Corvin's attitude impressed Secretary Stanton as that of an adventurer. In 1867 he returned to Germany as correspondent for the New York *Times* and served as war correspondent during the Franco-Prussian War. He wrote numerous historical works with a radical slant, among others a violent attack on organized religion, often reprinted, called *Pfaffenspiegel*. He was a close friend of Prince Salm-Salm and his dashing wife; the lady's memoirs were written or edited by Corvin. He represents definitely the type of the adventurer. (P, XVII, 283f.; Kaufmann, 489f.)

DAENZER, CARL (June 15, 1818–?), journalist, b. Odenheim, Baden. Law student at Heidelberg and Freiburg. Took active part in Revolution and had to flee first to Switzerland and then, in 1854, to the U.S. where he settled in St. Louis. He became associate editor of the *Anzeiger des Westens* and in 1857 founded the *Westliche Post*. He sold this paper to Olshausen and Lischer and revived the defunct *Anzeiger des Westens* which he made an independent and forceful paper until 1898 when it was consolidated with the *Westliche Post*. He was one of the most vigorous Forty-eighter editors and had the distinction of serving as delegate from Missouri to the Republican Convention in Chicago in 1860. Mr. Daenzer returned to Germany in 1898. (Herriot, 69; P, XII, 198.)

DEGENER, EDUARD (Oct. 20, 1809–Sept. 11, 1890), banker, gentleman farmer, Congressman, b. Brunswick. Son of a wealthy banker, he was trained by private tutors and also received schooling in England. He took over his father's business and, though he moved in aristocratic circles, he definitely favored liberal, democratic ideas. He was thus elected to the Frankfurt *Vorparlament* and twice to the Dessau diet where he stood for republican proposals. With the coming of the reaction he emigrated in 1850 and first traveled over the United States from Maine to Texas. He selected as his place of residence a valley near New Braunfels, Texas, where he established himself as a gentleman farmer, though, of course, not with slave labor. With the outbreak of the Civil War a group of Germans who favored the Union cause formed a company and tried to get to Mexico in order to join the forces of the North by way of the sea; at the Nueces River they were overtaken by a force of Confederates and almost all of them were killed, including two of Degener's sons. He himself had remained on his farm and was put in prison for several months, until he was released on bail through the influence of Gustav Schleicher. After the war he was elected to two constitutional assemblies in Texas and also to Congress for two terms. Degener is exceptional among Forty-eighters both because he was a man of wealth and also because he settled in the South. (Ruetenik, 287f.; Kaufmann, 490; Schem.)

DENGLER, ADOLF (d. May 22, 1863), soldier (birthplace unknown). A cap-maker by profession, he became a distinguished fighter in the Baden Revolution, commanding the defense of Freiburg against the royal troops. Later he came to the U.S. and settled near Belleville, Ill., as a "Latin farmer." He was an intimate friend of Sigel's and in April, 1861, organized a company of young Germans from Belleville and with them joined Sigel's 3d Missouri Regiment. He fought at Carthage, Wilson's Creek, and Pea Ridge, and was promoted to the rank of colonel. He met his death in the great assault on Vicksburg. (Kaufmann, 491; Valentin.)

DETTWEILER, HERMANN I. (July 13, 1825–Sept. 11, 1878). Though enrolled as a dragoon in the Baden army, he joined the revolutionary forces in 1848 and after the battle of Waghaeusel he was forced to flee first to France and then to the U.S. On the outbreak of the Civil War he enlisted in the 6th Kentucky Regiment and rose to the rank of captain. He was badly wounded and forced to retire from active service. He was elected constable in the city of Louisville. (P, X, 272.)

DIETRICH, HENRY (1832–?). At the early age of 15 Dietrich fought on the barricades in Hesse-Kassel. In the U.S. Civil War he was a captain

FUNERAL OF GERMAN PATRIOTS AT COMFORT, TEXAS
AUGUST 20, 1865
From *Harper's Weekly*, January 20, 1866

in the 39th New York Regiment and fought with such distinction at Gettysburg that a granite monument was erected on the battle field to commemorate the fighting of his company. (Kaufmann, 492.)

DIETZ, JOHANN W. (June 27, 1835–?), printer, poet, b. Cologne. In the home of his father, editor of a liberal paper, young Dietz met Kinkel and other poets of the Revolution and was inspired by them with such a love for freedom that he emigrated in disgust with the reactionary regime at the age of nineteen, thus following in the footsteps of many fighters for freedom. He worked as a printer in New York and Burlington, Iowa, and then established his own printing establishment in Chicago. He was an enthusiastic *Turner* and member of the Republican party. He published a great deal of verse in glorification of freedom. (Chicago; Zimmermann.)

DIETZ, OSWALD. All that seems to be available on the life of this remarkable Forty-eighter is contained in a humorous sketch of refugee days of 1848 by Philipp Betz and a note in Kaufmann. The latter reports that Dietz, resident in Texas, was pressed into service by the Confederates despite his sympathy with the Union cause. He served as captain with the engineers and drew plans for the fortification of Galveston. Only in March, 1864, did he find an opportunity to desert and to fight with the Union army. He fell as an officer in the fighting around Petersburg, Va. (Kaufmann, 492; *Kalender*, 1887, 98ff.)

DIETZSCH, EMIL (April 7, 1829–Sept. 12, 1890), pharmacist, politician (birthplace unknown). Studied pharmacy in Munich. Involved in the Revolution, he suffered arrest repeatedly, fled to Switzerland and came in 1853 to the U.S. He went to Chicago and worked as apothecary. Was an enthusiastic leader in the formation of the Republican party. In 1865 he became a partner in a large drug firm, but in the Chicago fire he lost all his property. He then turned to politics and was elected to several posts, including coroner and deputy sheriff. Dietzsch published historical works and verse in humorous vein. (Zimmermann; DAG, XXXII, 28.)

DOEHN, RUDOLF (1821–1895), teacher, lecturer, b. Dresden. Came to the U.S. as a political refugee and served as teacher and lecturer in the *freie Gemeinde* in St. Louis. Doehn was a strong Union sympathizer and a leader in the movement in St. Louis that saved Missouri for the Union. (Kaufmann, 494.)

DOMSCHKE, BERNARD (d. May 5, 1869), b. Saxony. Studied theology and philosophy. Took part in Revolution and was forced to flee. Arrived in the U.S. in 1850 and at first was employed by the *Neu-England Zeitung* in Boston where he became closely associated with Karl Heinzen. With the latter he signed the "Louisville Platform." Later he edited a number of papers in Milwaukee with definite Republican leanings. He was an enthusiastic *Turner* and in 1866 was elected national president. Attended the conference of German Republicans in Chicago in 1860. On the outbreak of the Civil War he joined the 9th Wisconsin Regiment as captain. He was taken prisoner and languished almost two years in a Confederate prison in Richmond; this experience undermined his health and caused his death two years after the war. (Herriot, 77f.; Huhn, I, 33; Hense-Jensen; WMH, XXIX (1945–46), 319ff., 435ff.)

DORSCH, EDUARD (Jan. 10, 1822–Jan. 10, 1887), physician, poet, b. Wuerzburg, Bavaria. Studied medicine in Munich and Vienna. Involved in the Revolution, he came to the U.S. in 1849. At first he had a difficult struggle for existence in New York as a correspondent for various European papers. Then he moved to Monroe, Mich., where he established himself as a successful physician. He wrote articles and poems for the *Illinois Staatszeitung* of Chicago and became an ardent member of the Republican party, writing articles and addressing political meetings both in 1856 and 1860. In the latter year he was a state elector for Lincoln. He donated his library to the University of Michigan and his home for a library in Monroe. (Zimmermann; Schem; DAB; Russell.)

DOUAI, CARL DANIEL ADOLF (1819–1888), teacher, b. Altenburg, Germany. Studied at University of Leipzig, 1838–41; private tutor in Russia and student at Dorpath. Sentenced to several prison terms because of his revolutionary writings. Left Germany in 1852 and arrived in the U.S. in the same year, settling in New Braunfels, Texas, as a teacher. In 1853 was editor of the San Antonio *Zeitung* in which he advocated gradual abolition of slavery. In 1856 he was forced to leave Texas and went to Boston where he founded a school and a kindergarten. Because of a speech in commoration of Humboldt, which was allegedly atheistic, his school was wrecked. Collaborated on Heinzen's *Pionier*. In 1860 he went to New York as editor of the New York *Demokrat*. Founded his own school and was at the same time editor of *Arbeiter Union*, a socialistic paper. Douai was a prolific writer in diverse fields; thus he published in 1850 a philosophical work, *Die Gottesidee*, in 1859 a German grammar and a phonetic primer, in 1867 a series of readers for *Turner* schools and an outline of world history, in 1870 *The Kindergarten in Public Schools* and various other educational reports, collaborated with Shem on his *Conversations Lexicon*, and wrote also a novel,

Erzaehlungen am Kaemp-Feuer, as well as numerous short stories. He was a delegate from Massachusetts to the conference of German Republicans at the 1860 convention in Chicago, where he and Caspar Butz served as a committee to draw up the resolutions. Douai was a brilliant and courageous writer, unafraid of offending his readers' opinion, for example, by condemning the Franco-Prussian War. He has been called first popularizer of Marxian ideas in the U.S. (Schem; Herriot, 63f.; Ruetenik, 311f.; Hillquit; Commons.)

DREIHAUS, GEORG (d. 1870), laborer, b. Osnabrueck, Hannover. Served his compulsory year in the army. When the Revolution broke out he was recalled to the army in Duesseldorf, but he joined other revolutionists who refused to serve, turned their coats inside out, tore the insignia off their caps, and stuck their bayonets in the ground. He returned to his home, but was forced to escape disguised as a woman. Via Rotterdam he came to Philadelphia and found employment in a sugar refinery. His son Henry became a noted wrought-iron worker in Pennsylvania. (AGR, XII, 6.)

DRESEL, JULIUS (1816–Dec. 7, 1891), "Latin-farmer," b. Geisenheim, Rhineland. Studied history and literature at Heidelberg and then assisted his father, a prosperous wine merchant, in his business. His home was a hospitable one where liberal poets, such as Freiligrath and Herwegh, were frequent guests. He joined in the Revolution with enthusiasm and, exiled, settled in Texas. At first he experienced the hardships of adjusting himself to the life of a farmhand and then took over a small farm in a German settlement near New Braunfels where he found agreeable associates, such as Eduard Degener. On the outbreak of the Civil War, Dresel, known for his opposition to slavery, was seized by Confederates and taken to San Antonio in chains. Released after some time, he opened a business in San Antonio which barely supported him and his family. In 1869 his bitter luck changed when he inherited a vineyard in Sonoma, Calif. Dresel throughout many years published essays and poems in various journals; his sonnets deal frequently with the theme of *Heimweh.* (Zimmermann.)

DRESEL, [FRIEDRICH] OTTO (Sept. 21, 1824–Jan. 5, 1881), lawyer, legislator, b. Detmold. Studied law in Jena and served as minor official at the law court in Detmold. In 1848 he began writing for *Die Wage* and became the leader of the revolt in Lippe-Detmold that established popular government in the principality for some months. On the return of the reactionary government, he was charged with treason and condemned to two years of prison. However, he managed to escape to Bremen where a friendly sea captain hid him so successfully on board ship that the police did not find him even though they searched the vessel from top to bottom. He arrived in Baltimore in 1849 and then went to Massillon, Ohio, where he studied American law while he earned a meagre livelihood as night watchman and music teacher. In 1853 he established himself as a lawyer in Columbus and took a vigorous part in politics as a Democrat. Like most Forty-eighters, he deplored the institution of slavery, but he wished to see it abolished in a Constitutional manner. In 1860 he stumped for Douglas and, during the course of the war, frequently found himself the object of violent attacks. In 1861 Dresel was elected superintendent of schools and later a member of the Ohio legislature. Just as he had protested in Germany against the high-handed practices of the princes, Dresel in Columbus organized protest meetings against the excesses of the military. In 1864 he resigned his legislative post in disgust—a typical Forty-eighter attitude. Typical also was his interest in cultural matters: he served repeatedly on the school board; he organized the public library of Columbus; he was an accomplished violinist and repeatedly national president of the federated German singing societies; he wrote a number of novels and numerous poems. Regarding what later came to be called "the hyphen" he said in a speech in 1877 before the *Pionier Verein* in Cincinnati that the complete absorbtion of the German element in the U.S. was a "logical, physical, psychological, historical necessity." (P, XIII, 419ff., 482ff.; IX, 132ff.; Zimmermann.)

DULON, RUDOLF (1807–April 12, 1869), teacher, preacher, b. Stendal, Prussia. Studied theology in Halle and held several pastorates as a distinguished preacher. He published theological works in which he favored a free, unorthodox Christianity. He took part in the revolutionary movement, was discharged from his pastorate in Bremen, and, when the Prussian government demanded his extradition, he fled to the U.S. in 1853. He conducted a school in New York for ten years and also served as speaker of a *freie Gemeinde* where, however, he estranged his hearers by his hypercritical attitude. Later he was called to the German-American school in Rochester, N. Y. He was a progressive, if cantankerous, pedagog. (Schem; DPV, XI, 13.)

EICKHOFF, ANTON (Sept. 11, 1827–?, 1901), journalist, Congressman, b. Lippstadt, Westphalia. Trained as a teacher. Through his liberal articles he became involved in the Revolutionary movement and was pursued by the police and the courts. He came to the U.S. in 1848, landing in New Orleans. His first experiences in the new country were filled with hardships rather difficult for an idealistic young teacher. He worked, for example, as a roustabout on a Mississippi steamer. Later he was given a teaching position at St. Louis University and later founded the St. Louis *Zeitung*. The journal was not successful and Eickhoff became editor successively of six other papers in various parts of the country. Thus he gained a great deal of first-hand experience about American political life. Having moved to New York, he became influential in politics in the Democratic party and in 1861 was appointed by Governor Seymour as commissioner for supplies of the New York troops. In 1863 he was elected member of the New York legislature, but he declined a second term because he disliked the hurly-burly of politics. Ten years later he again ran for public office and was elected coroner and in 1876 member of Congress. After one term he retired to devote himself to literary work and in 1888 published an historical work on the Germans in the U.S., *In der neuen Heimat*. (Ruetenik, 447.)

EICKEMEYER, RUDOLF (Oct. 31, 1831–Jan. 25, 1895), inventor, manufacturer, b. Altenbamberg, Bavaria. At the age of seventeen, immediately after completing his studies at the Darmstadt Polytechnic Institute he took part in the Revolution and after its collapse came to New York in 1850. He found employment in the building of the Erie Railroad and in 1854 opened a machine shop in Yonkers. Here the main industry was hat-making and Eickemeyer made numerous inventions which revolutionized the industry throughout the world. His inventions in the field of electrical machinery were of greater importance and led to the establishment of a large electrical plant and laboratory, which was consolidated with the General Electric Company in 1892. He was the first employer of Charles P. Steinmetz. During the Civil War he converted his plant into a revolver factory and also served a thirty-day enlistment. He was active in civic affairs for decades as water commissioner and trustee of the school board. (DAB.)

EIFLER, KARL (Oct. 18, 1821–July 7, 1888), *Turner*, b. Goerlitz. As an ardent *Turner* he became involved in the Revolution and arrived as a refugee in the U.S. in 1849, where he immediately joined the New York *Turnverein* and was identified with it for the rest of his life as a teacher, business manager, and also as a national officer. He did much to promote day schools supported by *Turnvereine*. (JDAT, I, 95.)

EISENLOHR, GUSTAV WILHELM (Nov. 19, 1811–May 18, 1881), pastor, b. Loerrach, Baden. Studied theology in Halle and Heidelberg and served as pastor in Emmendingen. He fought in the Revolutionary army in 1848 and 1849 and was to be sentenced for treason but was freed on condition that he leave for America. He arrived in U.S. in 1850 and served as pastor in New Braunfels, Texas, and in Cincinnati. He published two volumes of verse as well as numerous poems in the

Protestantische Zeitblaetter which he edited for twenty years. He translated the poems of Petrarch. A liberal theologian and a man of parts. (Zimmermann; P, XIII, 77.)

ELSNER, HUGO VON, music teacher. Son of a Prussian officer trained as engineer. He took part in the Revolution and came to Bloomington, Ill., where he made his living as a music teacher, since he could not find employment in his proper profession. (DAG, July, 1904, p. 22.)

ENGELMANN, ADOLF (1825–?), b. Bacherach. As a child of nine he came to the U.S. with his noted father, Friedrich Engelmann, (cf. DAB), who was one of the "Latin farmers" in Belleville, Ill. Adolf Engelmann served as officer in the Mexican War and was severely wounded. In 1848 he went to Germany to help the Schleswig-Holsteiners in their fight against the Danes. On his return to the U.S. he took up farming again, but with the outbreak of the Civil War he became lieutenant colonel in the 43d Illinois Regiment in which numerous young Germans from Belleville had enlisted. When Colonel Raith fell at Shiloh, Engelmann was made his successor. He fought at Vicksburg and in the remainder of Grant's campaign in the West. He won particular distinction in the Red River campaign where he commanded a brigade under Friedrich Salomon. (Kaufmann, 495.)

ESSELEN, CHRISTIAN (1823–1859), journalist, b. Paderborn, Westphalia. Studied law in Freiburg, philosophy in Heidelberg, and medicine in Berlin; served a year in the army and advanced to rank of lieutenant. In 1848 he joined the fighters for freedom on the barricades in Berlin. In western Germany he played a leading role in the organization of revolutionary workers' clubs and was arrested, fled to Switzerland, returned for the 1849 uprising and again became a political refugee. He arrived in New York in 1852 and then went to Detroit where he founded his journal, *Atlantis*, decidedly one of the best publications issued by a Forty-eighter. With touching devotion he managed to issue almost nine volumes, supported by different sponsors in a half a dozen different cities, until in 1859 his health broke down and he died in great poverty. He had made a valiant attempt to furnish German-Americans with a sound monthly for the discussion of political, philosophical, and scientific problems, but it did not win readers beyond the circle of intellectuals. Esselen published numerous poems filled generally with a materialistic pessimism. (Schem; DAG, XII, 405ff.)

ESSIG, CHRISTIAN. In the Baden Revolution Essig served as Sigel's adjutant. On the outbreak of the Civil War he commanded a battery under Sigel in the fighting in Missouri with considerable distinction, as General Osterhaus attests. He died in the war by drowning in the Mississippi. (Kaufmann, 496.)

FABER, PAUL (1827–1891), tailor, hotel-owner, b. Bisserl, Luxemburg. Trained as a tailor's apprentice. Driven out by reaction and arrived in the U.S. in 1848. He was a member of Minnesota constitutional convention, 1857; member of legislature, 1869–70; founder member of library society in St. Paul. (St. Paul, 9.)

FAEHTZ, ERNST F. M. (May 17, 1823–April 23, 1882), teacher, soldier, b. Linz, Austria. Studied law in Vienna; served as officer in the Austrian army. He took part in Revolution in Austria and also in 1849 in Baden, and went as refugee to Switzerland, France, and later to England. But he returned to Germany when there appeared to be hope for a successful revolt in Schleswig. In 1850 he came to the U.S. where he became principal of a school in Elkton, Md. In the Civil War he rose to the post of lieutenant colonel in the 8th Maryland regiment. After the war he served as interpreter in the criminal court in Baltimore and later held several public offices in Washington. He showed great interest in various cultural enterprises. (P, XIV, 115; Cunz.)

FALLER, ALOYS (Jan. 7, 1812–Aug. 16, 1882), lawyer, b. Freiburg, Baden. Studied law in Goettingen, Giessen, and Heidelberg and started on a legal career. His participation in the Revolution drove him to the U.S. as a political refugee. He first went to Illinois, but then established himself as a notary and lawyer in New York. He devoted a great deal of his time and energy to the legal protective association for German immigrants. (P, XIV, 277.)

FEIN, GEORG (1803–Jan. 26, 1869), journalist, b. Braunschweig. Participated in *Hambacher Fest* (1832) and was forced into exile in Oslo, Strassburg, Paris, and Zurich, where he edited *Neue Zuercher Zeitung*. From 1845 to 1848 he lived in the U.S. and then returned to Europe to work for a free Germany, settling in Switzerland. He was especially active in organizing German workers' associations and stimulating cultural interests among the working classes. During his short stay in Baltimore in 1847 he organized the Concordia Club whose purpose was to provide a library and lectures for the Germans of the city. (Cunz; *Allgemeine deutsche Biographie;* Valentin.)

FIEDLER, ANTON B. (March 7, 1828–Jan. 13, 1897), businessman, b. Schlettau, Saxony. He entered his father's upholstery business. In 1849 he was arrested because he had marched with a Revolutionary procession. He served two years in prison and in 1852 he came to the U.S.

He first found employment in factories in a number of cities and then established an upholstery business in Chicago. Fiedler was an ardent *Turner* and musician, master of numerous instruments. (Chicago, 523.)

FINK, ALBERT (Oct. 27, 1827–April 3, 1897), engineer, b. Lauterbach. Graduated from Darmstadt *Polytechnikum* in 1848 and because of the triumph of the reactionary forces came to the U.S. in 1849. He entered the drafting office of the Baltimore and Ohio Railroad and soon was placed in charge of design and erection of bridges. He invented a bridge truss which bears his name. In 1857 he became construction engineer of the Louisville and Nashville Railroad. During the Civil War he was assigned to reconstruct the property of the railroad destroyed by the fighting forces, and in 1869 became vice-president and general superintendent. In his annual reports he analyzed and standardized railroad costs in such a thorough and scientific manner that he came to be regarded as the father of railway economics and statistics. (DAB.)

FLAD, HENRY (July 30, 1824–June 20, 1898), engineer, inventor, b. Rennhoff, Baden. Took the polytechnic course at Munich. Participated in the Revolution as captain of a company of engineers. He arrived in New York as a political refugee in 1849 and found employment as a draftsman in an architect's office. Later he secured a position as engineer in the construction of the New York and Erie Railroad. In the Civil War he enlisted in the Union army and served with distinction in the "Engineer Regiment of the West," passing through all grades from private to colonel. After the war he occupied high positions in the construction of the municipal water works and of "Eads Bridge." In 1877 he was elected first president of the St. Louis Board of Public Improvements and during fourteen years in this post took public works out of politics and placed it on a sound engineering basis. In 1890 he was appointed a member of the Mississippi River Commission, a post he held until his death. As an engineer Flad was remarkable for his bold inventions. (DAB.)

FREUDENBERG, CARL GOTTFRIED, soldier. At the age of fifteen he fought in the Baden Revolution. Served as colonel of the 52d New York Regiment and at the conclusion of the Civil War he joined the regular army as a captain in the 14th Infantry and fought in the Sioux War. He was discharged as lieutenant colonel in 1877. (Kaufmann, 500.)

FRICKE, HEINRICH C. (Aug. 1, 1815–?), businessman, b. Spring, near Hannover. He held several municipal offices in his home town and was engaged in the lumber business when the Revolution broke out. Fricke counseled moderation but presided at a meeting at which a reorganization of the local government along democratic lines was voted. With the arrival of the reaction he was forced to emigrate. In 1853 he arrived in Chicago, where he found employment as bookkeeper, then as postal official, and later established a drug business. He was active in various cultural societies. (Chicago, 154ff.)

FROEBEL, JULIUS (1805–1893), scientist, journalist, b. Griesheim. Nephew of the famous pedagog Froebel. He became professor of mineralogy in Zurich. He held strong liberal opinions and published a radical paper in Zurich. In 1846 he went to Dresden and in 1848 took part in the Revolution in Vienna. He was condemned to death, but, pardoned on condition that he leave the country, he came to the U.S. in 1850 and remained till 1857. On his return to Germany he wrote extensively for liberal papers and published a number of volumes on political questions. (Schem; Ernst Feuz, *Julius Froebel, seine politische Entwicklung, bis 1849*, Bern, 1932.)

FUESTER, ANTON (1808–March 12, 1881), teacher, b. Krain, Austria. Studied theology and occupied several clerical and teaching positions in Austria. With the outbreak of the Revolution he joined the Vienna Academic Legion as chaplain. Was arrested but managed to escape and arrived in New York in 1849. He founded a school together with Struve which declined in Civil War days. Then he was appointed to a position in the public schools which he occupied for twelve years. In 1876 he returned to Austria. (P, XIII, 72.)

GAMBS, JOHANNES (May, 1797–April 13, 1879), teacher, b. Strassburg. Professor of languages, *Gymnasium*, Buedingen. Retired because of his revolutionary activity. He arrived in the U.S. in 1857 and taught at Dulon's School in New York. He was a very active *Turner* and repeatedly a delegate to national meetings. He attended the conference of German Republicans at Chicago in 1860. Returned to Germany in 1862 where he remained active in the struggle for political freedom. On his death the outpouring of friends at his funeral caused the police of Frankfurt no little concern. (Herriot received this information from Gamb's grandson.) (Herriot, 65.)

GEBRAETZ, GEORG (Jan. 1, 1827–Oct. 6, 1881), stone mason, soldier, b. Pfortzheim, Baden. Took part in Baden Revolution, was imprisoned, and emigrated to the U.S., settling in Wisconsin as a stone mason. On the outbreak of the Civil War he volunteered as a private and rose to the rank of lieutenant. (P, XIII, 283.)

GEIWITZ, GEORG (d. 1890), painter and actor. Had taken part in the revolutionary street fighting in Dresden and came to Baltimore as a political refugee. He earned his living by painting church murals, stage scenery, and by acting in the German theatre. In the *Turnzeitung* of August 21, 1860, Geiwitz was attacked savagely for his activity in painting angels on church ceilings—something very distasteful to most Forty-eighters. (Cunz; A. E. Zucker, "The German Theater in Baltimore," *Germanic Review*, April, 1943, p. 131.)

GERHARDT, JOSEPH (May 25, 1817–Aug. 19, 1881), turner, innkeeper, soldier, b. Bonn. Studied at Bonn *Polytechnikum*. During the Revolution in Baden he was the leader of a battalion. He made his escape from the fortress Rastatt when it was taken by Prussian troops. After a short stay in Switzerland, he made his way to the U.S., where he first worked at various humble jobs and then conducted a hotel in Washington. At the outbreak of the Civil War he organized a company among the Washington *Turner*, the first completely organized volunteer company in the nation's capital. His military career was a distinguished one; he soon rose to the rank of colonel and at the close of the war was made brigadier by brevet. An ardent Republican, he was a delegate to the 1860 convention that nominated Lincoln. (Kaufmann, 502; P, XIII, 282.)

GIESLER-ANNEKE, MATHILDE FRANZISKA. *See* Anneke.

GILLIG, KARL EMIL (Feb. 14, 1831–May 26, 1884), innkeeper, b. Hesse-Darmstadt. Trained as mechanic. He was an enthusiastic *Turner*. At the age of nineteen he joined the Revolutionary army in Baden, and after the return of the reactionary government was forced to flee. He arrived in Milwaukee in 1850, worked first as a mechanic and later established an inn in Peoria, Ill., which became a favorite haunt for the German citizens. Gillig also provided a stage for amateur plays and was liberal in his support of the *Turnverein* and musical organizations. At the outbreak of the Civil War he joined the 8th Illinois Regiment. (JDAT, II, 187.)

GILSA, LEOPOLD VON, soldier. Served as officer in the Prussian army, but in 1848 fought with the patriots in Schleswig-Holstein against the Danes and was forced to flee to the U.S. in the early fifties. At first he earned a miserable livelihood as pianist in Bowery saloons and similar menial occupations. With the outbreak of the Civil War he became colonel of the 41st New York Regiment, made up entirely of Germans. He fought with distinction at Cross Keys, the second battle of Bull Run, Chancellorsville, Gettysburg, and Charleston. He was a brave and picturesque soldier and the subject of many anecdotes. For example, General Howard (through whose fault the Battle of Chancellorsville was lost) met von Gilsa on the field after this disaster and admonished him to trust in God. Thereupon our Forty-eighter shouted at the general in the German language such a choice selection of army epithets that Howard thought von Gilsa must have become insane. (Kaufmann, 503.)

GINDELE, JOHN G. (Jan. 30, 1814–?, 1872), architect, b. Ravensburg, Wuerttemberg. Studied architecture in Munich and held the post of municipal architect in Schweinfurt. He took an active part in the Revolution, raising a company of 500 fighting men. He was forced to flee and went first to Wisconsin and then settled in Chicago in 1852 where he found employment as a stone mason. By 1859 he was able to establish his own firm. For twelve years he served as chairman of the Illinois Board of Public Works and for two years as president of the Illinois-Michigan Canal Board; his name is connected with numerous public works in Chicago. He was also president of the Germania Male Chorus. (Chicago, 123.)

GIRSCH, FREDERICK (March 31, 1821–Dec. 18, 1895), bank-note engraver, b. Guedingen near Darmstadt. Studied art at the Royal Academy at Darmstadt, but was forced to go to Paris as a political refugee and in 1849 to New York. He found employment as engraver for the *Criminal Zeitung;* particularly noteworthy was his series of "Heroes of the Revolution." During the Civil War he was engaged by the government as engraver of bank notes, a task for which he was especially well fitted. He designed a ten-dollar note with "De Soto Discovering the Mississippi." He designed also a plate "The Legion of Honor" which Lincoln proposed to give to soldiers, but this plan was not carried out because of Lincoln's untimely death. (DAB.)

GOEGG, AMANDUS (April 7, 1820–?, 1897), publicist, b. Renchen, Baden. Served as finance minister of the Baden Republic with unselfish integrity; Valentin calls him one of the most sympathetic figures among the Baden revolutionaries. He went to London as political refugee and was active there in a revolutionary society—one of several, for the refugees were far from united on the manner in which a new revolution was to be launched. He came to the U.S. in 1852 for the purpose of collecting funds for his group; his mission failed. He lectured on socialism in the U.S. and in Australia. He founded a league for peace and freedom in Geneva in 1867. He was a lifelong contributor of articles to pacifistic and democratic papers. (Valentin; DPV, XVIII, 1ff.; DAG, XII, 475ff.)

GOEHLMANN, MARTIN G. (Jan. 12, 1809–Aug., 1885), tanner, b. Hadersleben, Schleswig. Learned the tanner's trade. Took part in the Schleswig-Holstein Revolution and was imprisoned for several years. He arrived in the U.S. in 1857, settling in Charlotte, Iowa. He established a flourishing business and was a highly respected member of the Davenport Society of Forty-eighters. (P, XVIII, 184.)

GOEPPER, WILHELM (Sept. 25, 1830–May 3, 1879), innkeeper, banker, b. Kork in Baden. While he was still a student at the *Gymnasium*, he joined the revolutionary movement in Baden and came to the U.S. in 1848 as a political refugee. He first worked at various jobs and then established a very successful restaurant in Louisville; he was also on the board of directors of a bank and of an insurance company, as well as of an orphan's home. (P, XI, 502.)

GOLDMARK, JOSEPH (1819–1880), physician, businessman, b. Warsaw. Studied medicine in Vienna and obtained a research post. He was a captain in the Vienna Academic Legion and a member of the Vienna *Reichstag*. Because of his leading role in many phases of the Revolution, he was marked for execution by the reactionary forces and was forced to flee. After a short stay in Switzerland he sailed for the U.S. in 1850. He first practiced as physician in Brooklyn and then established a factory for percussion caps, which he later supplied to the Union army. He is also noted for his discovery of amorphous sulphur. (Josephine Goldmark, *Pilgrims of '48*, Yale University Press, 1930.)

GRAF, KARL (July 3, 1828–Oct. 3, 1885), teacher, b. Kaiserslauten. Graduate of teachers' seminary and a teacher in his native town. Took part in the Revolution and was forced to flee. He came to Cincinnati in 1849 as a political refugee. At first he earned his living as a laborer, farmer, surveyor. Finally he secured a position as teacher in a public school and rose to the post of principal. He had the reputation of a thorough German schoolmaster. (P, XVII, 133.)

GREINER, LUDVIGH. Came to the U.S. as a political refugee after the Revolution. He was a leader of Germans in Newark in liberal movements; prime mover in protest meeting against the Kansas-Nebraska bill of 1854; member of committee for relief of families of Germans who had enlisted in the Union army. In 1860 he attended the conference of German Republicans in Chicago. (Herriot, 67f.)

GUELICH, THEODOR (Jan. 29, 1829–Jan. 23, 1893), journalist, *Turner*, lawyer, b. Schleswig. Studied at Stuttgart *Polytechnikum* and took part in the Baden Revolution; he was wounded and then took part in the

Schleswig-Holstein Revolution. He was taken prisoner and condemned to thirty years in the penitentiary, but escaped and came to the U.S. in 1851. In Davenport, Iowa, he founded the *Demokrat* and, together with Rudolph Reichmann, made it into a very influential organ. In 1856 he sold the paper to devote himself to legal practice, after 1861 in Burlington. He was one of the founders of the Davenport *Turnverein* in 1851 and served repeatedly in the city council. At the outbreak of the Civil War he was one of the first to volunteer and organized Company G of the First Iowa Volunteer Regiment. He founded the *Iowa Tribuene* in Burlington and, though himself practicing abstinence, fought vigorously against prohibition, as he considered it an infringement of personal liberty. He published considerable verse in various journals. (Richter, 483f.)

GUENTHER, JOHANN GEORG, physician, journalist. Served as member of Frankfurt *Parlament* and emigrated to the U.S. with the return of the reactionary government. Guenther had married the sister of Robert Blum. She founded a school while he practiced as physician in Milwaukee. He was also a collaborator with Domschke on the *Atlas*, a Republican paper; when the Milwaukee *Herold* grew out of this paper, Guenther was one of the editors who made the *Herold* an influential journal. In 1860 he had the distinction of serving as a member of the Wisconsin delegation to the Republican convention in Chicago. (Herriot, 76; Koss, 456, 458; Hense-Jensen.)

HAAS, EMIL, physician. Was an intimate friend of Sigel's and took part in the Baden Revolution. He served as regimental surgeon of the 5th Missouri Regiment and later, with the rank of major, as chief physician of the hospital in Boonville, Mo. (Kaufmann, 506.)

HAGEN, THEODOR (April 15, 1823–Dec. 27, 1871), author and musical critic, b. Hamburg. Studied music in Hamburg and Paris and served as music critic for a number of papers. Because of his part in the Revolution he had to flee and, after a stay in Switzerland and England, arrived in the U.S. in 1854. He founded a musical journal, the New York *Weekly Review*, which exerted a considerable influence on the development of music in America. He also wrote a number of novels and dramas. (Schem.)

HAIMBACH, PHILIPP (Sept. 12, 1827–Sept. 11, 1904), merchant, b. Mannheim. Was apprenticed to a merchant. At the age of twenty-one he fought with Sigel's corps and in 1851 came to the U.S. He secured a position with an import firm in Philadelphia, where he remained for the rest of his life. He contributed articles to socialistic and musical journals, wrote the libretto of an opera, and published a volume of verse. (DPV, V, 30ff.; Zimmermann.)

HAMM, THEODOR (1825–?), brewer, b. Baden. Butcher's apprentice. Fought with the revolutionary army in Baden, 1848–49. Arrived in U.S. in 1854. He was very active in furthering cultural activities among Germans in St. Paul. (St. Paul, 8.)

HAMMER, ADAM VON (Dec. 27, 1813–Aug. 4, 1878), physician, b. Mingolsheim, Baden. Took his medical degree at Heidelberg and entered upon practice of medicine. In 1848 he joined Hecker in the Baden Revolution and upon its suppression came with Hecker to the U.S., settling in St. Louis as physician in 1848. He returned to Europe in 1853 and studied in Paris and with Virchow in Wuerzburg. On his return to St. Louis he founded the Humboldt Institute in order to acquaint American doctors with the progress medical science had made in Europe. He served as a member of the Missouri delegation to the Republican convention in Chicago in 1860. During the period when Confederates threatened to seize the arsenal in St. Louis, Dr. Hammer armed and drilled his students in order to prevent this *coup*. With the outbreak of the Civil War he joined the 4th Missouri Infantry Regiment as lieutenant colonel and, after the three months' service, devoted himself to the organization of military hospitals for the remainder of the war. He had a very fiery and bellicose disposition and was involved in numerous controversies. He is described as having a long, sharp, thin nose and a pointed chin emphasized by chin whiskers. He returned to Germany in 1877. (Herriot, 70; P, X, 242ff.; Kaufmann, 506; Stevens, II, 430.)

HARTMANN, KARL (d. 1863), surgeon. He participated in the Revolution, was forced to come to the U.S., and established himself in Cleveland as a physician. On the outbreak of the Civil War, he became staff surgeon of the 107th Ohio Regiment. When in the Battle of Chancellorsville the attack of Jackson's army threw his regiment into confusion, Dr. Hartmann, sword in hand, made an effort to rally the troops and was killed by an enemy bullet. Kaufmann remarks that this is the only known case of a surgeon who on the occasion of greatest danger acted the part of an officer. On the soldiers' monument in Cleveland, Hartmann's head in bronze commemorates this Forty-eighter. (Kaufmann, 508.)

HASSAUREK, FRIEDRICH (Oct. 9, 1831–Oct. 3, 1885), editor, politician, and diplomat, b. Vienna. At the age of sixteen he joined the Vienna Student Legion and was twice wounded in fighting against regular troops. Arrived in the U.S. in 1849 and went to Cincinnati where he wrote for German newspapers and soon established his own radically socialist *Hochwaechter*. He studied law and became a successful criminal lawyer. A brilliant orator, he became the most active organizer of the Republican party in Ohio, displaying great courage in antislavery discussions. Once he put a revolver beside him on the speaker's table and threatened to shoot anyone who interfered with his meeting. Hassaurek attended the Republican convention in Chicago in 1860 as an Ohio delegate. Lincoln appointed him minister to Ecuador where he served with distinction. He returned to campaign for Lincoln in 1864 and in 1865 became editor of the Cincinnati *Volksblatt*, having shed much of his utopian radicalism. In 1872 he was a leader in the liberal Republican movement. He published in 1867 *Four Years among Spanish Americans*, also wrote a novel and a book of verse. Hassaurek was one of the youngest Forty-eighters, brilliant, witty, violently anticlerical, and one of the most effective leaders among the Germans in the Republican party. (DAB.)

HAUSEN, JULIUS H., physician, b. Vienna. Took part in the Viennese uprising then fled to the U.S. During the entire Civil War he served in the Army of the Potomac, first as a regimental and then as a brigade surgeon. (Kaufmann, 509.)

HAUSSNER, CHARLES FREDERICK (Oct. 2, 1825–Feb. 11, 1911), politician, b. Plauen, Saxony. Fought against Prussian troops in the Revolution and was forced to flee to Switzerland. He arrived in the U.S. on October 4, 1849, settling first in Wisconsin and after 1855 in Chicago. Worked as a traveling representative of various German publications. Assisted in founding the Chicago *Arbeiterverein* and *Turngemeinde*. Joined the Republican party early and supported Frémont in 1856. In 1858 he was elected clerk of North Town, Chicago, but because of bitter relations with factions in Springfield he was denied the office. Later Mayor John Wentworth appointed him clerk of the South Town Market. He attended the conference of German Republicans in Chicago in 1860. From 1866 to his death, he was engaged in the real estate business. (Herriot, 84.)

HECKER, FRIEDRICH (Sept. 28, 1811–March 21, 1881), soldier, farmer, b. Eichtersheim, Baden. Studied law at Heidelberg and Munich and practiced his profession. In 1842 he was elected a liberal member of the Chamber of Baden. He proposed a German republic in the Frankfurt *Vorparlament*. In Baden he fought for a republic, but his small force was defeated at Kandern, April 20, 1848. He left for the U.S. to raise funds for a second revolution. On learning of a renewed uprising he returned to Europe, but when he arrived at Strassburg he found that the Revolution had again been crushed. He returned to Belleville, Ill., where he had bought a farm. He gave great impetus to the *Turner* movement in America. An ardent Republican, he attended the conference of German Republicans at Chicago in 1860. On the outbreak of the Civil War Hecker, at the age of fifty, enlisted as a private, but soon was made colonel. He was a very forceful orator and the most picturesque figure of the Revolution. He never approved of Bismarck's *Reich.* (DAB.)

HEDDE, FRITZ (Sept. 11, 1818–March 5, 1908), journalist, legislator, b. Rendsburg, Schleswig-Holstein. Studied law at Kiel and established himself as a lawyer. He took a leading part in the Revolution, was forced into exile, and arrived in the U.S. in 1854. He went to Davenport, Iowa, where many of his compatriots had settled. In 1857 he led a group of pioneers to Nebraska where they founded Grand Island. At first he farmed and engaged in business, and then turned to journalism, founding the Grand Island *Independent.* He fought corruption and the railroad monopolies, and was elected to the city council as well as the territorial legislature. (DAG, IX, 5–7.)

HEINE, PETER BERNHARD WILHELM (Jan. 30, 1827–?, 1885), painter, author, soldier, consul, b. Dresden. Studied painting in Dresden and Paris. Took part in the street fighting in Dresden and was forced to flee. He arrived in the U.S. in 1851 and enlisted in the U.S. Navy and rose to the post of engineer. As master mate he took part in Admiral Perry's expedition to the Far East and spent considerable time in Japan. Later he went to Tripoli and Egypt, then to Singapore to join a German expedition. He piloted the first German vessel to reach Japan into the harbor of Yeddo (Tokyo). When the Civil War broke out, he returned to the U.S. and entered the engineering corps of the Army of the Potomac, advancing to a colonelcy in 1863 and the next year to the post of titular brigadier general. At the end of the war he was in command of the 103d New York Regiment. Later he served as consul in Paris and Liverpool, spending his last years in his native city, Dresden. He wrote a number of volumes on his travels, including *A Journey around the World to Japan, Japan and Its Inhabitants.* Among all the Forty-eighters he had perhaps the most picturesque and adventurous career. (P, XVII, 48; Kaufmann, 510.)

HEINZEN, KARL PETER (Feb. 22, 1809–Nov. 12, 1880), journalist, b. Grevenbroich, near Duesseldorf. From childhood an individualist, he was dismissed from the University of Bonn on account of a revolutionary speech. He enlisted in the Dutch army and was sent to Batavia.

On his return he served the required year in the Prussian army and then entered the civil service. He issued radical and satirical writings for four decades. In 1844 criminal proceedings were started against him and he fled to Switzerland. On the outbreak of the Revolution he returned and took an active part in Baden. He had to flee again and was later banished from Switzerland, arriving in the U.S. in 1850. The rest of his life story is contained chiefly in his editorship of the *Pionier*, an absolutely intransigent radical sheet written with a brutal mastery of invective and a narrow, dogmatic intolerance. But, he fought constantly for freedom as he saw it. (DAB; Wittke, A.C.)

HENNE, ROBERT (Aug. 18, 1822–May 16, 1885), *Turner*, soldier, b. Breslau. Apprenticed to a bookbinder and served in the Prussian army, 1845–46. In the fight for freedom in Schleswig-Holstein he organized the *Turner* in Kiel as a military company, and lost an arm in the fighting. He arrived in the U.S. in 1851 and settled in Davenport, Iowa, where he joined the *Turnverein* and conducted a hotel. At the outbreak of the Civil War he responded to Lincoln's call for volunteers by joining the First Iowa Regiment and later the 12th Missouri. At the battle of Pea Ridge, March 8, 1862, he lost a leg and was forced to retire from the army. For a while after his recovery he had a book and cigar store in Davenport, but finally was forced to live on his pension. (Huhn, II, 38; Kaufmann, 511.)

HERTLE, DANIEL (1824–185–), journalist, *Turner*, b. Bergzabern, Palatinate. Studied law. His participation in the Revolution, together with his liberal attitude moved the parents of his fiancée to break off his engagement to their daughter. This blow cast a shadow of melancholy over the sensitive man for the rest of his life. He arrived in the U.S. in 1850 and soon became a leading journalist, associated in turn with the Albany *Freie Blaetter*, the *Illinois Staatszeitung*, and the St. Louis *Westliche Post*. He was an ardent adherent of *Turner* ideals and it was he who served as president when the national organization in 1857 passed the resolution· "The *Turner* are prepared to fight slavery, nativism, or any other deprivation of rights because of color, religion, place of birth, or sex, since such attitudes are not compatible with a cosmopolitan *Weltanschauung*." Later he returned to Germany and accepted a position with a Mannheim paper, but he resigned soon because he could not join in the rejoicing over the new Kaiser. With a friend he set out on a tour of the Bavarian Alps and was never heard of again; it is thought that he drowned himself in the Chiemsee. (Huhn, I, 32f.)

HEXAMER, ADOLF (Jan. 10, 1824–Jan. 20, 1859), physician, b. Koblenz. Studied medicine in Heidelberg and entered the Prussian state service in Berlin. He took a leading part in collecting funds for the Revolution and was forced to flee the country. He settled in New York where he made a name for himself as a physician. He was the eldest of the four Hexamer brothers, all Forty-eighters. (DPV, XX, 26ff.)

HEXAMER, ERNST (May 29, 1827–Dec. 3, 1912), civil engineer, surveyor, b. Koblenz. Studied with his brother Wilhelm at Heidelberg and at the Karlsruhe *Polytechnikum*. He fought with Sigel's corps in the Baden Revolution and went as refugee first to Switzerland and then to the U.S. He found employment in New York as a designer of grave monuments and later as a surveyor. In 1856 he established himself as a civil engineer in Philadelphia. (DPV, XX, 26ff.)

HEXAMER, FRITZ M. (Jan. 21, 1832–May 29, 1910), botanist, b. Koblenz. The fourth of the Hexamer brothers joined Wilhelm and Ernst in the fighting in the Baden Revolution and was known as "Sigel's youngest soldier." He fled with his brothers to Switzerland and then to the U.S. Upon the fall of the republican government in Baden, the state seal was entrusted to Fritz Hexamer, who carried it out of the country in his boot. It is still a cherished memento of the Hexamer family in Philadelphia. Dr. F. M. Hexamer gained considerable reputation as a botanist and horticulturist. (DPV, XX, 26ff.)

HEXAMER, WILHELM (April 11, 1825–April 25, 1870), engineer, soldier, b. Koblenz. Studied in Heidelberg and at the Karlsruhe *Polytechnikum*. Participated in the Baden Revolution in Sigel's corps and took refuge in Switzerland and later in the U.S. He established himself as engineer in Hoboken, N. J., and was elected to the city council. At the outbreak of the Civil War he organized a company of artillery (A of New Jersey) consisting only of Germans. This battery gained considerable distinction at Antietam. Captain Hexamer's death was hastened by an injury sustained in the war. (Kaufmann, 512; DPV, XX, 26ff.)

HIELSCHER, THEODOR (Dec. 16, 1822–April 11, 1907), editor, teacher, b. near Breslau. Trained as a teacher in Berlin under the distinguished educator F. A. W. Diesterweg. When this liberal schoolman was dismissed, Hielscher took part in the Berlin uprising. On March 19, 1848, he commanded King Frederick William IV, "Remove your hat before these dead!" (the victims of the street fighting). The king complied. Hielscher arrived in the U.S. in 1851. About 1855 he became editor of the *Freie Presse* in Indianapolis. He was an ardent *Turner* and lived for a while in New Ulm. He returned to Indianapolis where he opened a private school. In 1860 Hielscher attended the conference of German Republicans at the Chicago convention. He published a number of revolutionary poems. (Herriot, 75; Valentin, II, 578; Zimmermann.)

HILLGAERTNER, GEORG (April, 1824–Oct. 23, 1865), journalist, lawyer, b. Frankenthal, Palatinate. Studied law and literature in Munich; settled as a lawyer in Heidelberg. Condemned to death as a participant in the Revolution, he was forced to flee. He accompanied the poet Kinkel to the U.S. for the purpose of raising funds for a second revolution. This was in 1852 and, while the tour proved abortive, it provided Hillgaertner with a valuable American experience. In 1853 he began to practice law in Chicago. He was associated with Georg Schneider in organizing the mass protest against the Kansas-Nebraska Bill. In 1854 he became editor of the *Illinois Staatszeitung* and later of the St. Louis *Westliche Post*. He was national president of the *Turner* in 1859. In 1864 he revived the *Neue Zeit* in St. Louis, but death took him within a year. Hillgaertner was one of the Forty-eighters who became impatient with Lincoln's conduct of the war and he worked for Frémont's nomination in 1864. A monument was erected to this idealistic and energetic editor in Bellefontaine Cemetery in St. Louis. Caspar Butz says of him that his story is just like that of many others: a German political refugee driven by bitter circumstances to the U.S. where he devoted his best years to the German press and died in poverty. (Butz in P, XIV, 468–470; Huhn, I, 33; Ruetenik, 318ff.; Schem.)

HOCHHEINER, HENRY (1818–1912), rabbi, b. Ansbach, Bavaria. Trained in theological studies. He became involved in the Revolution and fled to the U.S. in 1849. He became rabbi of the oldest Jewish congregation in Baltimore. With Benjamin Szold he collaborated on a revision of the prayer book. (UJE.)

HOFFBAUER, WILHELM (1812–?), physician, b. Nordhausen, Saxony. Received his M.D. from the University of Berlin. Very active in the Revolution and was a member of the extreme left in the Frankfurt *Parlament*. Fled to Switzerland and in 1850 to the U.S., settling in St. Louis and later in Dubuque, Iowa, where he remained until his death. Carl Schurz stopped with him on his visits to that city. He served as delegate to the conference of German Republicans in Chicago in 1860. (Herriot, 81.)

HOFFMANN, ERNST F., army engineer, b. Breslau. Fought in the Revolution in Schleswig-Holstein, then fought with the British in the Crimean War and with Garibaldi in Italy. The war against slavery induced him to come to the U.S. to join the forces of the North. He was chief of engineers of the 11th Army Corps and later in the same post with General Thomas's corps in Tennessee. He gained distinction for a number of exploits, among others, during the campaign in Tennessee, the reconstruction in the course of one night of a bridge destroyed by the enemy. Major Hoffmann served as army engineer in flood control work after the close of the War. (Kaufmann, 513.)

HOFMANN, LOUIS, soldier. Took part in the Revolution as an artillerist and came to the U.S. as a refugee. Chief of "Hofmann's Battery" which distinguished itself in the fighting in Missouri, at Pea Ridge, and at Vicksburg, where a monument was erected in its honor. (Kaufmann, 514.)

HOTTINGER, ANTON (Jan. 7, 1824–?), apothecary, politician, b. Waldshut, Baden. Apprenticed to an apothecary. He found employment in Switzerland, and on the outbreak of the Revolution he hurried to his native Baden to join Hecker's forces. On the defeat of the revolutionary army, he fled to Switzerland, but in 1849 he joined in the renewed fighting. He was forced into exile again at first to England and then, in 1851, to the U.S. He became a druggist's assistant in Pittsburgh, then entered a drug firm in Cincinnati, and in 1856 founded his own business in the completely German town of Guttenberg, Iowa, where he was three times elected mayor. Later he established himself as druggist in Chicago and twice served as alderman. He was an early and enthusiastic member of the new Republican party and an active opponent of corruption. (Chicago, 147.)

HUHN, HEINRICH (March 3, 1830–?), *Turner*, editor, soldier, b. Landau, Palatinate. Apprenticed to a bookbinder and traveled as journeyman through Germany, France, and England. Joined the *Turner* in Frankfurt in 1847 and took part in the Revolution in Baden. He arrived in the U.S. as a political refugee in 1849 and worked at his trade and also as a journalist. He also took a fling at play acting. In 1861 he joined the Union army, advancing to adjutant in the 108th Ohio Regiment. In 1862 he was taken prisoner during which time his health suffered considerably. For a year he was a reporter on the *Westliche Post* in St. Louis but joined the 104th Missouri Regiment in 1864, serving to the end of the war. After the war, he edited a paper in Washington, Mo., and founded a *Turnverein* there. He served a term in the Missouri state legislature and later as deputy collector of internal revenue. He held several journalistic positions and devoted many years to the furthering of the *Turner*, visiting every *Turnverein* in the U.S. in his capacity of national officer. Huhn wrote a great deal for *Turner* publications, among other items valuable biographical sketches of leading members. (Huhn, II, 45; Schem.)

JACOBI, ABRAHAM (May 6, 1830–July 10, 1919), physician, b. Hartum in Minden, Westphalia. Studied medicine in Greifswald and Bonn,

Because of his participation in the Revolution he was imprisoned, but escaped after two years, arriving in the U.S. in 1853. In New York he began his practice in the tenement section with fees of 25 or 50 cents. His publications in the field of pediatrics soon won him recognition, and in 1857 he was appointed lecturer at the College of Physicians and Surgeons, becoming in 1860, the first professor of children's diseases in this country. In 1892 he was offered a similar professorship at the University of Berlin, but as a firm Forty-eighter he declined. He and Carl Schurz were close friends and had adjoining summer homes at Lake George. He ranks high among medical scientists in this country and was the recipient of many honors here and abroad. (DAB.)

JACOBS, WILHELM HEINRICH (d. 1882), soldier, banker, b. Braunschweig. Arrived in the U.S. in 1850 as a political refugee. In the Civil War he served as colonel of the 26th Wisconsin Regiment. He was wounded at Chancellorsville but managed to return to his regiment in time to command it at Gettysburg. The unpleasant slanders concerning the action of German troops at Chancellorsville embittered Jacobs to such an extent that he resigned his commission in 1864. Jacobs was a prominent banker in Milwaukee and, himself a fine tenor, interested in furthering musical organizations. (Kaufmann, 515; Koss, 413ff.)

KALISCH, ISIDOR (Nov. 15, 1816–May 11, 1886), Reform rabbi, b. Posen, Prussia. Studied at Jewish institutions and at Berlin, Breslau, and Prague. His political writings in 1848 were condemned as seditious and he was forced to flee. He arrived in New York in 1849 and filled various pastorates; after 1875 he devoted himself to lecturing and writing theological works. His importance lies in the impetus he gave to Reform Judaism; with great idealism he worked for this cause in the belief that political and inward spiritual emancipation of the Jews would lead to universal brotherhood. (DAB.)

KAPFF, EDUARD and SIXTUS. Kaufmann reports that these brothers were Forty-eighters from Wuerttemberg who served as officers in the 7th New York Regiment, Eduard as colonel.

KAPP, FRIEDRICH (April 13, 1824–Oct. 27, 1884), lawyer, politician, author, b. Hamm, Westphalia. Studied law at Heidelberg and Berlin and practiced at Hamm. Took part in the Revolution as a journalist in Frankfurt. He was forced to flee to Paris. Returned to Germany on the renewed outbreak of the Revolution, but left immediately again for Paris, disillusioned by the lack of plan and organization. He arrived in the U.S. in 1850 and earned his living at various jobs until, with the attainment of citizenship in 1855, he founded in New York City a law firm with two other Forty-eighters, Franz Zitz and Julius Froebel. Kapp also was editor of a New York German-language paper and correspondent for the *Koelnische Zeitung*. He took great interest in American politics; in 1860 was New York State delegate to the Chicago convention, and played a leading role in organizing the preconvention conference at the *deutsches Haus*. He was a very active member of the new Republican party and highly influential in winning the support of German Americans for the Union cause. As a leading member of the philanthropical *Deutsche Gesellschaft*, he was appointed by the governor of New York as commissioner of immigration, serving from 1867 to 1870. He traveled widely and wrote on the condition of immigrants, arousing public opinion on the subject of their mistreatment and exploitation. Kapp's chief historical works are biographies of von Steuben and of de Kalb, an account of the early German settlers in New York, a history of the sale of soldiers by German princes, an account of Frederick the Great's relation to the U.S., and a two-volume collection of essays. He returned to Germany in 1870 and was elected to the *Reichstag* for three terms; as a Forty-eighter he rejoiced over the unification of Germany and supported the National Liberal party; he opposed Bismarck when the latter collaborated with the conservatives. He was a man of vast culture who wrote in elegant style with balance and humor; of his own works, for example, he remarked that in Germany he was regarded as an authority on America because no one had read his books. He was an exponent of the cosmopolitan spirit of his day, but he definitely found life in Germany more to his liking than in the U.S. He loathed the term applied to him, "a citizen of two worlds." As a lifelong fighter for freedom and humanity he stands in the very first rank of the Forty-eighters. (DAB; Lenel; Valentin; *Magazin*, I, 16ff.; Kaufmann, 517.)

KAUFMANN, SIGISMUND (Sept. 8, 1825–Aug. 17, 1889), journalist, *Turner*, lawyer, b. Frankfurt. As an enthusiastic *Turner* he was involved in the Revolution and, threatened with arrest, he fled to the U.S. in 1848. After considerable hardships he secured a post on the New York *Abendzeitung*. He was the first president of the New York *Sozialistischer Turnverein* and founded a *Turner* paper. He then took up the study of law and by dint of great energy attained a successful practice. He was one of the founders of the Republican party in New York and served as presidential elector in 1860. He also was president of the New York *Deutsche Gesellschaft*, an organization for the protection of immigrants. His interest in the *Turner* continued through the decades; in the eighties he was a frequent lecturer before the group. (Huhn, I, 28; JDAT, I, 32ff.)

KAUFMANN, THEODOR (Dec. 18, 1814–?), painter, soldier, b. Uelzen, Hannover. Studied painting in Duesseldorf and Munich and at first painted religious subjects, but dissatisfied with orthodoxy he studied science and in rationalistic spirit he composed eight etchings, "The Development of the Idea of God," published with explanatory text in 1850. In 1848 he became an ardent partisan of the Revolution and fought on the barricades in Dresden. On the suppression of the revolt by the Prussian army, Kaufmann fled to Switzerland, Belgium, and then to the U.S., arriving in New York in 1850. Here, supported by some American art lovers who appreciated his talent, he painted in oil his series of eight etchings depicting his conception of the deity; but a few days after their completion they were destroyed in a fire. Thereupon Kaufmann started a school for instruction in drawing in which Thomas Nast, the famous cartoonist, was his only pupil. After the financial failure of his school, Kaufmann eaked out a meagre existence as portrait painter and assistant in photographic studios—his hapless wanderings took him even to Cuba. On the outbreak of the Civil War he felt the call to aid in the fight against slavery and enlisted as a private, taking part in the naval expedition against Forts Hatteras and Clark, which were captured on August 28, 1861. Next he sought service under General Frémont because of the latter's radical attitude toward slavery. When Frémont was relieved of his command and there was little military action in Missouri, Kaufmann went to St. Louis to support the Union cause as a speaker and writer. A painting which he contributed to a bazaar for the benefit of wounded soldiers attracted such favorable attention that he received numerous orders and was enabled at the age of 48 to make a living by his profession. He produced numerous historical paintings, the most famous among them Admiral Farragut (with the subtitle, "Damn the Torpedoes, Go Ahead, Boys"), General Sherman, and two of Abraham Lincoln's assassination. (Kaufmann, 517f.; Ruetenik, 344, 485; Schem.)

KELLNER, GOTTLIEB THEODOR (Aug. 27, 1819–May 12, 1898), journalist, b. Kassel. Studied and then practiced law. On the outbreak of the Revolution he founded a social-democratic *Verein* in Kassel, which with affiliated groups soon attained a large membership and great influence. He was also very active in the spread of revolutionary publications and was elected member of the diet. When the notorious ministry of Hassenpflug returned to power, Kellner was imprisoned but he escaped through the courageous efforts of his wife on the very day he was condemned to life imprisonment. (The guard who aided in Kellner's escape was named Zinn—pewter—and when this sympathizer with the Revolution also escaped, the Duke offered a $300 reward for his capture. The word *Kellner* is German for waiter. A comedian perpetrated the following joke which the populace appreciated highly: he impersonated an innkeeper and said, "Now my Kellner has run away and taken with him $300 worth of Zinn." The Duke ordered the comedian imprisoned for his insolence!) Kellner's wife managed to join him in Belgium and from there they came to the U.S. in 1851. At first he supported himself by means of lectures and journalistic work in New York. In 1856 he found a permanent position of influential activity as editor of the Philadelphia *Demokrat*. This was a Democratic paper, and, unlike many other Forty-eighters, Kellner seems to have been less interested in politics than in social enterprises. In 1868, through the German Society of Philadelphia, he founded an evening school for adults which flourished to such an extent that it was taken over by the Philadelphia School Board. Like many other Forty-eighters he was an advocate of cultural endeavors for the workers; in this spirit he helped found a German theater in Philadelphia and gave his support to various musical organizations. (Ruetenik, 313ff.)

KIEFER, C. F. (Sept. 6, 1803–April 12, 1878), businessman, b. Emmendingen, Baden. Served in the Baden army. Became superintendent of a chemical factory. When the Revolution broke out, he was a leader in the Heidelberg deliberations and was elected to the *Vorparlament*. Later he organized a company of civilian guards in Baden and played a leading role in the revolutionary government. Forced to flee, he came to Philadelphia in 1849 where he became engaged in various business enterprises and was actively interested in the *freie Gemeinde* and numerous charitable organizations. (P, X, 74.)

KIEFER, HERMANN (Nov. 19, 1825–Oct. 11, 1911), physician, professor, consul, b. Sulzburg, Baden. Studied medicine at Heidelberg, Prague, and Vienna. Elected chairman of the Upper Rhine District of *Vaterlaendischer Verein*, chairman of the Freiburg Mass Meeting, and had a part in the battles of Philipsburg and Ubstadt. He was forced to flee and arrived in the U.S. in 1849, establishing himself in medical practice in Detroit. Joined Republican party on its organization in 1854, and attended the conference of German Republicans at the Chicago convention in 1860. He was Presidential elector of Michigan in 1872 and a delegate to the convention of 1876. He was U.S. consul to Stettin, 1883–85; regent of the University of Michigan, 1889–1901, and professor of medicine there, in 1902. His speeches and poems were published posthumously. Kiefer was a fine liberal, in Europe and in America, and one of the few Forty-eighters to obtain an important university professorship. (Herriot, 74; Kiefer.)

KINKEL, GOTTFRIED (Aug. 11, 1815–Nov. 13, 1882), poet, professor of art history, b. Oberkassel. He was Carl Schurz's professor in Bonn and, after imprisonment in Spandau for participating in the Revolution, he was freed by his devoted student. He then lived in England as a refugee and in 1851 came to the U.S. for a speaking tour with the purpose of raising funds to finance another revolution in Germany. He was received with great enthusiasm in numerous cities with large German populations as a hero of the Revolution and a brilliant orator, but the amount he was able to collect was disappointingly small. He soon returned to England and later held a professorship in Zurich.

KNAPP, FRIEDRICH (April 26, 1821–?), teacher, b. Degerschlacht, Wuerttemberg. Trained as a teacher and appointed to a position in Reutlingen, he sided with the Revolution and was hailed into court for treason. He therefore left, arriving in Baltimore in 1850 where he founded his long-lived "F. Knapp's German and English Institute" which had 700 pupils about 1860. (Cunz)

KOENIG, F. C. (d. 1877), businessman, b. Blieskassel, Palatinate. Fought in the Revolution and, after some years spent in France as a political refugee, came to the U.S. in 1855. He settled in Peoria, Ill., where he established a soap factory. (P, IX, 252.)

KOERNER, JOSEPH ALOYS (Aug. 2, 1805–Aug. 28, 1882), teacher, b. Cologne. Studied art in Duesseldorf and taught the subject. His participation in the Revolution forced him to flee to Switzerland and shortly afterward the Prussian government insisted that he be expelled. Consequently he left for the U.S. in 1850. In New York he went to the office of the *Evening Post* and tried, in imperfect English, to place an advertisement for pupils in drawing. William Cullen Bryant happened to pass by and recognized Koerner as the man in whose company he had some years previously viewed the work of the Duesseldorf painters. Bryant spoke to him in German and gave him various letters of introduction that ultimately led to Koerner's appointment as teacher in the public school system, a post that he occupied for twenty-six years. (P, XV, 91, 195, 293.)

KRAUS, ALBERT, chaplain. Though owner of a landed estate, he took part in the Revolution and came to the U.S. as a refugee. He served as chaplain of the 12th Missouri Regiment after his friends had founded a *freie Gemeinde* in order that this freethinker could be given the title "Reverend." It was his habit to go forward into the firing line in order to assist the wounded. (Kaufmann, 521.)

KREZ, KONRAD (April 27, 1828–March 9, 1897), lawyer, soldier, poet,

b. Landau, Palatinate. Studied law in Heidelberg and published a volume of poems. Fought in the Revolution in the Palatinate and Baden and was sentenced to death *in contumaciam*. He lived for some time as a refugee in Switzerland and France. He arrived in New York in 1851 and started a legal practice. In 1854 he settled in Sheboygan, Wis., where he remained until his departure for Milwaukee in 1885. His Civil War service as colonel of the 27th Wisconsin Regiment was so distinguished that he was awarded the brevet rank of brigadier general. For several terms he was member of the state assembly; from 1885 to 1889 he was collector of the port of Milwaukee on President Cleveland's appointment; and in 1892 he became city attorney of Milwaukee. Krez is considered the most gifted poet among the Forty-eighters and is particularly famous for his bitter and at the same time nostalgic poem, *An mein Vaterland* (1869). In this as well as in other lyrics he could give poignant expression to the suffering of the uprooted. (DAB.)

KRIEGE, HERMANN (July 20, 1820–March 31, 1850), journalist, labor leader, b. Lienen, Westphalia. Studied at the University of Leipzig and was forced to flee because of persecution on account of his liberal ideas. He arrived in the United States in 1845, but on the outbreak of the Revolution he returned to Germany to fight for freedom. Once more exiled, he settled in New York to edit the *Volkstribun*, an antislavery, prolabor paper with socialistic tendencies. Since he refused to accept the Marxian ideas of class struggle, "Jupiter Marx" read him out of the party along with his friend Wilhelm Weitling. Kriege died insane at the age of 31 and was buried, as he had requested, with an American flag draped about his chest. (Schem; Carl Wittke, Marx and Weitling.)

KROEGER, JACOB, pastor, farmer, b. Preetz, Holstein. While serving as pastor of the Lutheran church in Schwabstedt, he became involved in the Revolution and was forced to emigrate. He joined his older brother who had a farm near Davenport, Iowa, served for a period as pastor in Wheeling, W. Va., and then returned to the Iowa farm. He devoted himself also to the education of his son Adolph Ernst (1837–1882) who is listed in the DAB as a prominent journalist and a minor figure in the St. Louis philosophical movement. (Richter, 358; P, XIV, 243.)

KUDLICH, HANS (Oct. 23, 1823–Nov. 11, 1917), physician, author, b. Lobenstein, Silesia. The son of poor peasants, he went to the University of Vienna to study law. When the Revolution broke out, he joined the student legion and was severely wounded on March 13, 1848. He was elected to the *Reichstag* and proposed a bill to free the peasants from the last vestiges of serfdom. The bill passed and the Emperor signed it. With the coming of the reactionary government, Kudlich had to flee to escape death. He went at first to the Palatinate and Baden, where he again joined the revolutionary forces, and then to Switzerland. Here he studied medicine, taking his degree in 1853. When the Austrian government demanded his extradition, he went to the U.S., settling in Hoboken, N. J., as a very successful physician. Kudlich was sometimes called the Father of Hoboken because in the course of his long practice he had brought so many of its citizens into the world. He was also very outspoken in his desire to have the Negroes emancipated and at one of his lectures he was asked whether he would be willing to have his daughter marry a Negro; his reply was, "Certainly, provided the Negro were a decent person." In this respect Kudlich definitely went further than most Forty-eighters. In 1879, after amnesty had been declared, he went to Austria for a visit and received numerous ovations, particularly from grateful peasants. Up to his last years he followed political events in Austria and Germany and gave as his opinion that there was little hope for these countries so long as Hapsburgs and Hohenzollerns were the rulers. He published *Rueckblicke und Erinnerungen* (3 vols., Vienna, 1873), an account of his part in the Revolution of 1848. In 1942 a Nazi author, Bruno Hans Wittek, published an historical novel, *Sturm ueberm Acker*, with Kudlich as the chief character—it was propaganda for the peasants and carried an introduction by Konrad Henlein. In 1944 H. Krommer and P. Raimann published *Verlasst das alldeutsche Narrenschiff* (with the subtitle, *Hans Kudlichs politisches Testament*) in order to show that Kudlich had remained a democrat all his life and could not possibly have had any truck with a Nazi regime. (Valentin.)

LAMBACH, HEINRICH (July 7, 1815–?), surveyor, teacher, b. Essen. Trained as a surveyor, he was employed in railway construction work when the Revolution arrived. His participation forced him to leave the country as a political refugee. He went directly to Davenport, Iowa, and served as surveyor for several railroads, including the Union Pacific, up to the time that the driving of the golden nail marked the completion of this undertaking in 1869. After that he taught drawing in the Davenport public schools. He is described as a rugged, out-doors individual who enjoyed a fight and criticized what he considered to be wrong. His biographer says, "Even though he was not always right, his intentions were always the best." (Eiboeck.)

LEIST, FRIEDRICH, sculptor, b. Kassel. Trained as a sculptor in Kassel he was serving his obligatory year in the army of Hesse when the Revolution broke out. His liberal views brought him into conflict with his superiors and he escaped to America at the same time as Dr. Kellner.

He settled in Baltimore and was employed for forty years by the firm Bevan and Sons, dealers in marble monuments. While Leist never attained great fame as an artist, he took an interest in and gave elementary instruction to a poor farmer's son, William Henry Rinehart, Baltimore's best-known sculptor. (SHGM, XVI, 69.)

LESER, FRITZ (Feb. 1, 1837–?), *Turner*, banker, b. Lahr, Baden. Though very young at the time of the Revolution, he was so deeply imbued with liberal ideals that life under the reactionary regime became impossible for him and he left for the Land of Freedom at the age of sixteen. He arrived in the U.S. in 1853 and, after some time, settled in St. Louis where he joined the *Turnverein*. At the outbreak of the Civil War, he served as adjutant in the 17th Missouri, a *Turner* regiment. Disabled by an unfortunate accident, he was forced to quit the service. He accepted a post as cashier in a bank, at the same time continuing his ardent interest in the *Turner* organization, serving for a while as one of the national officers. In 1880 he moved to Philadelphia where he became a partner in a banking firm. (Huhn, II, 41.)

LEUCHTWEISS, AUGUST (Feb. 1, 1819–Oct. 8, 1875), businessman, b. Nauheim. Fought in the Revolution and came, after a short stay in France, to the U.S. as a political refugee. He settled in Cincinnati and established a successful brass foundry, the same business he had carried on in Germany. (P, VII, 385.)

LEUSSLER, ROBERT (1822–Aug. 6, 1873), b. Durlach. Took part in the Baden Revolution and was forced to leave Germany. He settled in St. Louis where his older brother August had gone earlier to escape military service and political repression. He served as private in the Second Infantry Regiment, Missouri Volunteers, Company F, under Colonel Boernstein. His brother was a member of the executive committee that organized the Home Guards and served as quartermaster of the First Regiment. (Rombauer; letter from Virginia Leussler Brown.)

LEXOW, FRIEDRICH (Jan. 29, 1827–Dec. 3, 1872), journalist, b. Toenning, Schleswig. In 1849 he established himself as a printer and editor of the liberal paper, *Das Volk*, in Rendsburg, but soon found himself accused of political crimes and condemned to eight years' imprisonment. He was pardoned after one year and left for the U.S., arriving in New York in 1852. Here he joined his cousin Rudolf Lexow in the publication of the *Belletristische Journal*, one of the longest-lived German journals in this country. Under his editorship the paper shifted its support to the Republican party. Lexow published a number of novels. His *Gedichte* (1872) contains a poem to Abraham Lincoln that is characterized by the freedom-loving spirit of the Forty-eighter. (P, V, 267ff.; Zimmermann; Schem.)

LIEBER, OSCAR MONTGOMERY (Sept. 8, 1830–June 27, 1862), geologist, b. Boston. Son of Francis Lieber, the noted political refugee of 1827, he went to Goettingen as a student and, imbued with a love of freedom, went to Berlin in March, 1848, and took part in the street fighting. Again in 1849, when only 18 years of age, he fought for three days on the barricades in Dresden. On his return to the U.S., Oscar Lieber settled in South Carolina and entered upon a very distinguished career as a geologist. To his father's dismay he accepted the regional views on slavery and states' rights. Francis Lieber's family became "a symbol of the Civil War" as his sons Hamilton and Norman fought in the Union army, while Oscar joined Wade Hampton's Legion in South Carolina. Oscar was mortally wounded in the battle of Williamsburg. He was a gallant but quite untypical Forty-eighter. (Frank Freidel, *Francis Lieber*, Louisiana State University Press, 1947; Appleton's Cyclopaedia of American Biography.)

LOEHR, FERDINAND VON (1817–Jan. 15, 1877), physician, journalist, b. Giessen. Studied medicine in Giessen and was serving as army surgeon in Hesse when the Revolution broke out. Despite his official post, and the fact that his family was extremely conservative, he joined the revolutionary army under Blenker and became a political refugee. In 1852 he settled in San Francisco as a physician, giving his services gratis to the German hospital, and at the same time serving as editor of the *California Demokrat*, which flourished for twenty-five years. On the occasion of his death the Oregon *Deutsche Zeitung* asked, "Will there ever again be such an energetic, capable group of Germans in this country as the Forty-eighters?" (P, VIII, 514, IX, 59.)

LOES, FRANZ E. (1809–May 21, 1883), bookkeeper, civil servant, b. Erfurt. He was a bookdealer in Leipzig at the time of the Revolution and, because of his participation, had to flee the country. He went to Philadelphia where he earned his living as a bookkeeper and then joined a publishing firm. On the outbreak of the Civil War he volunteered for three months' service. Later he served as statistician in the customs service. (P, XVI, 118.)

LOEWE AUS CALBE, WILHELM (Nov. 14, 1814–Nov. 3, 1886), physician, politician, b. Olvenstadt, near Magdeburg. Studied medicine at Halle and began medical practice. In 1848 he was elected member of the Frankfurt *Parlament*, representing the democratic left. He was chosen vice-president and, when the *Rumpf Parlament* went to Stuttgart, was made president. A tribunal condemned him to life imprisonment, but Loewe had meanwhile escaped to Switzerland. In 1853 he settled as a physician in New York, where he took a very active part in politics as a member of the Republican party. When in 1862 amnesty was declared for all German political "offenders" Loewe returned to Germany; here he once more entered upon a political career, serving in various legislative bodies, including the *Reichstag*. He was consistently associated with the liberal, progressive groups. (P, XVIII, 180f.; Valentin.)

LOHMANN, HEINRICH (Aug. 23, 1820–Dec. 25, 1889), cigar maker, *Turner*, soldier, b. Bremen. Became a *Turner* in Leipzig and fought on the barricades. He was forced to flee and arrived in Baltimore in 1849. He was one of the founders of the *Sozialistische Turnverein* and also conducted his own school of gymnastics. He was in business as a cigar maker. With the outbreak of the Civil War he joined the Maryland forces and fought through the entire war. Politically he was radical, a Spartan in his habits, and, like many Forty-eighters, an advocate of cremation. After the war he became a teacher in Knapp's German and English Institute. (JDAT, I, 96; Cunz.)

LOOS, ALEXANDER (Aug. 11, 1821–Sept. 15, 1877), teacher, author, b. Schlesien. Studied theology and philology in Breslau and in 1848 joined the "free" religious movement, serving as "speaker" of such a group. His liberal opinions caused his expulsion by the Prussian government and he came to the U.S. in 1852. He held various positions as language and music teacher in a number of cities and finally settled in Philadelphia as "speaker" of a *freie Gemeinde*. He translated Ludwig Buechner's *Materialism* and wrote extensively on his favorite subject of undogmatic religion. In 1876 he was secretary of the convention of the Free Religious Society held in Philadelphia. (DPV, XI, 35.)

LOOSE, HEINRICH (1810–1872), pastor, *Turner*, speaker of a *freie Gemeinde*, b. Stuttgart. Trained in theology and appointed as vicar, he broke with the dogmatic Protestant church and the free religious movement in Bavaria. When the Revolution broke out, he participated in the republican movement in Baden and was held in prison for a year and a half. He had begun his literary activity early with a novel and a volume of poems. In prison he wrote a history of the Baden Revolution. When he was freed, he left for the U.S. and established a school in Williamsburg, N. Y. He was called to Milwaukee as speaker of the *freie Gemeinde* and, together with August Willich, founded the *Soziale Turnverein*. It was Loose's thoughtful lectures that made the *Turnverein* the center of liberal and progressive Germans in Milwaukee.

He also edited for a while the *Humanist*, founded by E. Schroeter, and later the *Arbeiter*, a Socialist paper. Afflicted by numerous disappointments, he died in an institution for the insane. (Huhn, II, 26.)

LUCAS, JACOB (Nov. 9, 1825-?), teacher, journalist, b. Ginsheim, near Worms. Trained in teachers' seminary and became a teacher near Frankfurt. Because of his outspoken liberal opinions, he was discharged and arrived in the U.S. in 1851. He was an ardent *Turner* and a freethinker and was invited to the headship of the school conducted by the *Verein der freien Maenner* in St. Louis. He held this post for about a decade, serving at the same time as editor of the antislavery *Freie Blaetter*. From 1861 to 1869 he was editor of the Peoria *Deutsche Zeitung*. Lucas wrote a great many articles in the *Turnkalender*, emphasizing the high ideals of the *Turner*. (Huhn, II, 33.)

LUEDEKING, CARL (Nov. 5, 1819-?, 1885), speaker of a *freie Gemeinde*, b. Giessen. Studied philology, theology, and pedagogy. In 1848 he demanded the abolition of the state church and the founding of "free congregations." Naturally his liberal opinions brought on persecution by the police and he fled to the U.S. in 1851. In the following year the *freie Gemeinde* in St. Louis called him as speaker, a post which he held until his death. At the same time he conducted a liberal school and wrote widely for *Turner* publications. He published with an introduction eight speeches by the European revolutionary A. Ruge as well as numerous pamphlets favoring the emancipation of women and free thought in the spirit of Feuerbach. He served as American delegate to the congress of freethinkers in Naples in 1869. (Huhn, I, 29f.; Schem.)

MAAS, BENJAMIN (1822–Oct. 13, 1891), physician, b. Neustadt. Studied medicine at Heidelberg. On the outbreak of the Revolution he joined the fighting forces and after the defeat took refuge in Switzerland. He arrived in the U.S. in 1849, establishing himself as a physician in New York. An enthusiastic *Turner*, he was elected to the national executive committee. He published a brochure describing an ideal state on a socialistic basis. In 1850 he settled in New Orleans; one of the few Forty-eighters to go to the South, and became one of the leading physicians in that city. He was an outspoken antislavery man and during the Civil War met with considerable persecution, which, however, by no means changed his attitude. (Huhn, I, 28f.)

MAHLER, FRANZ (d. July 5, 1863), soldier. Though an officer in the Baden army, Mahler fought on the side of the Revolution and later came to the U.S. as a political refugee. He became colonel of the 75th Pennsylvania Regiment, which consisted entirely of Germans and took part in numerous battles—Cross Keys, the second battle of Bull Run, Chancellorsville, and Gettysburg. At the last-named engagement Colonel Mahler was shot off his horse while leading his regiment against the enemy, but he paid no attention to his wound and continued with the attack until a second bullet wounded him mortally. (Kaufmann, 530.)

MAERKLIN, EDUARD (Jan. 16, 1816–Feb. 20, 1892), pharmacist, poet, b. Calw, Wuerttemberg. Trained first as mechanic and then as pharmacist. Early in life he became an enthusiastic *Turner*. His participation in the Revolution brought him a prison term of a year and a half after which he departed for the U.S., settling in Milwaukee as a pharmacist. He also was secretary of the *Turnverein*. During the entire Civil War he was in the field as pharmacist with the 35th Wisconsin regiment; his deafness disbarred him from active duty. He published three volumes of poetry characterized by a virile quality and also some prose sketches of American life. His *Song of the German Cavalrymen* was a favorite among the soldiers under Sigel. (Huhn, I, 39; Zimmermann; Kaufmann, 531; Hense-Jensen.)

MAISCH, JOHN MICHAEL (Jan. 30, 1831–Sept. 10, 1893), pharmacist, b. Hanau. Received a good fundamental education in languages and science, but before he could begin study of his chosen field, pharmacy, he took part in the Baden Revolution and was forced to flee to America in his nineteenth year. He arrived without money or friends, but found employment in pharmacies in various cities. In Philadelphia he became associated with a manufacturing pharmacist and soon began to publish scientific articles. In 1863 he was placed in charge of the United States Army Laboratory in Philadelphia, in which medical supplies were made for the Union army. In 1866 he became professor in the Philadelphia College of Pharmacy and remained connected with that institution until his death. He was for 22 years editor of the *American Journal of Pharmacy*, for 28 years permanent secretary of the American Pharmaceutical Association, and internationally famous in his field. (DAB.)

MATZKA, GEORG (1825–June 22, 1883), musician, b. Coburg. As a mere boy he showed such great talent that the Prince of Coburg afforded him a musical education in Prague, after which he returned and became concert master in the Prince's orchestra. When in 1848 he joined in the revolutionary spirit, the Prince abruptly dismissed him and, after some time in England, he came to New York in 1853. He settled down to a musical career of thirty years as concert master and later conductor of the Philharmonic Orchestra. (P, XVI, 163.)

MAYERHOEFER, WILHELM (1814–Sept. 18, 1880), musician, b. Prague. Studied law in Prague and was appointed librarian of the Royal Library in Prague. His lifelong passion for music gradually drew him into this profession. A meeting with Mendelssohn in 1836 led to an enduring friendship, as a result of which Mayerhoefer was called to the Leipzig Conservatory in the middle forties as professor and organist. He played the organ at Mendelssohn's funeral. Becoming involved in the Revolution he arrived in New York in 1848 as a political refugee and established himself there as organist and music teacher; among his pupils was Theodore Thomas. In 1877 he was called to the Louisville Conservatory. He was the author of numerous compositions and a volume, *Organ Studies*. (P, XII, 280.)

MEININGER, KARL (Oct. 16, 1816–July 25, 1883), bookbinder, innkeeper, b. Dietz, Nassau. Followed his father in his business as bookbinder. He became an enthusiastic *Turner* and was involved in the Revolution. When the reaction came, he left for the U.S., landing in New Orleans and then settling as bookbinder in Cincinnati. He was deeply interested in the theater and, in order to make it possible for the Cincinnati troupe to play in the off-season, he built with all his savings a summer theater, unhappily destroyed by fire. Meininger then set up an inn and soon regained considerable prosperity, permitting him to encourage musical and other cultural activities. (P, XVI, 238ff.)

MERSEY (or Mercy), AUGUST, soldier. At the time of the Revolution Mersey was a lieutenant in the Baden army, but he joined the revolutionary forces and commanded the 3d Division of the Baden People's Army. In the Civil War he won distinction as colonel of the 9th Illinois Regiment. (Kaufmann, 531.)

METTERNICH, GERMAIN (April 10, 1811–May 13, 1862), soldier, b. Mainz. Though trained as an officer in the Austrian army, Metternich was a very active agitator and fought with Sigel in Baden. He was forced to flee, and in New York became one of the founders of the *Turnverein* and an exponent of its liberal principles. With the outbreak of the Civil War he became a lieutenant colonel in the 46th New York Regiment. He met with an accidental death near Savannah when a soldier stumbled and thrust his bayonet through Metternich's neck. (Kaufmann, 532; JDAT, III, 285; Valentin.)

MILLER, HEINRICH (Dec. 1, 1829–?), jeweler, b. Eppertshausen, Hesse. Apprenticed to a silversmith. He moved in liberal circles and joined the Offenbach *Turnverein* in 1848. He became involved in the Revolutionary movement and left for the U.S. in 1849. He settled in Louisville, Ky., where he established an engraving business. In 1850 he helped found the Louisville *Turngemeinde* and remained very active in the movement, frequently serving as a national official. He supported vigorously *Turner* ideals and progressive political movements. (Huhn, II, 41.)

MOHR, CHARLES THEODOR (Dec. 28, 1824–July 17, 1901), botanist, b. Esslingen, Wuerttemberg. Attended Stuttgart polytechnical school, specializing in botany and chemistry. In 1846 he went as botanist with an expedition to Dutch Guiana. On his return he became involved in the Revolution and came to the U.S. as a political refugee. He joined the gold rush, but was not successful. In 1852 he became a pharmacist in Louisville and in 1857 moved to Mobile, Ala., where he continued in the drug business until 1900. During the Civil War he tested in his laboratory many drugs brought from England by blockade runners for the Confederate army and he also manufactured drugs from local plants. He built up an herbarium of some 25,000 species for the University of Alabama, published widely in his field, and was a member of numerous scientific societies. (NCAB, XXVI, 406; DAB.)

MORWITZ, EDWARD (June 11, 1815–Dec. 13, 1893), physician, journalist, b. Danzig. Studied medicine at Halle, Leipzig, and Berlin, and began the practice of his profession. Because of his espousal of the Revolution, he was attacked by a royalist mob and forced to emigrate. He first went to England and then came to the U.S. in 1850, settling in Philadelphia. He took up the practice of medicine and established a dispensary for the poor. In 1855 he began the publication of a political weekly favoring the Democratic party, but when the Civil War broke out he strongly favored the Union and helped raise several German regiments. His interest in journalism widened and led to his organizing the Newspaper Union which furnished "patent insides" for hundreds of German and English papers throughout the country, leaving them to supply the local news on the outside pages. (DAB.)

MOSCHZISKER, FRANZ A. VON (d. 1880), physician, b. Lemberg, Galicia. Was graduated from the military academy in Vienna and served in the Austrian army. In 1848 he left the service to join the Hungarian revolutionaries and was taken prisoner. Through the influence of his family he was secretly freed and fled to London. He became professor of modern languages at King's College, London, and published an outline of German literature that is said to have won him praise from Carlyle. He studied medicine and came to the U.S. in 1852, establishing himself as a physician in Baltimore. During the Civil War he served of army hospitals in Washington, where he insisted on the necessity in establishing a special ophthamological hospital. (P, XII, 357.)

MUELLER, EDUARD (1803–Nov. 15, 1886), *Turner*, b. Mainz. Studied art in Munich and was an active *Turner*. He was exiled for seven years for participation in the *Hambacher Fest*, 1832. After his return to Germany he became leader of the *Turnverein* in Mainz. He was also on the editorial staff of the *Mainzer Zeitung* in 1848 and 1849 and was forced to flee because of his revolutionary activity. He arrived in New York in 1849 where he became gymnastics teacher of the New York *Turnverein*. In 1871 he accepted a similar post in Rochester, N. Y. He wrote numerous articles for the *Turnzeitung* and published a manual of gymnastics. In New York he continued to wear the Jahn costume and long locks. (P, XVIII, 181.)

MUELLER, JACOB (March, 1822–?), lawyer, lieutenant governor, consul, b. Alsenz, Palatinate. Had legal training; took part in the Revolution and was appointed by the provisional government of the Palatinate to a high civilian post. With the return of reaction, he was forced to flee and came to the U.S. in 1849, settling in Cleveland where he established himself as a lawyer. He joined the Republican party and at the outbreak of the Civil War he was instrumental in the organization of several German regiments in northern Ohio. He was known as a brilliant orator and had the distinction of serving as a member of the Ohio delegation to the Republican convention in Chicago in 1860. In 1871 he was elected Republican lieutenant governor of Ohio. He joined the liberal Republican group in 1872 and later worked for the election of Cleveland. In 1885 he was appointed consul general in Frankfurt. His memoirs, *Errinnerungen eines Achtundvierzigers*, is a fine source of information on the lives of these political refugees. (Herriot, 71; Huhn, I, 28; Ruetenik, 316; Schem.)

MUELLER, NIKOLAUS (Nov. 15, 1809–Aug. 15, 1875), poet, printer, b. Langenau, near Ulm. He was apprenticed to a printer and traveled widely as a journeyman, settling in Ulm as a printer. He published a volume of poems which received high praise from Uhland and other critics; it sold so well that he was able to undertake a journey to England where he studied the art of printing woodcuts. After a year's stay he went to Paris to improve further his skill as a printer. On his return to Germany he was associated with the Cotta publishing firm and attained a comfortable income, enabling him to found a printing house of his own. He joined in the Baden Revolution with enthusiasm and was elected to the constituent assembly. When the Prussian troops restored the reactionary government, he was forced to flee to Switzerland. From there he emigrated to New York, establishing himself once more as a printer. Thirty years after his first volume of poems, he published a second volume in New York in 1867, in addition to numerous poems printed in the New York *Staatszeitung;* freedom and love of nature are the chief motives in his verse. (Ruetenik, 304ff.; Schem; Zimmermann.)

MUELLER, WILHELM, teacher and author. Political refugee in Baltimore who taught for some time in the school of the *Turnverein*. He published verse in the *Turnkalender* and one volume of his *Radikale Schriften* appeared in Baltimore in 1852—"In both poetry and prose it preaches materialism and atheism in a manner as radical as it is primitive." (Cunz.)

MURER, JOHN (Aug. 1, 1827–?), carpenter, b. Erlendorf, Bavaria. Traveled widely as journeyman carpenter and in 1848 fought with Hecker in Baden. He arrived in the U.S. as a political refugee in 1854, found work in New York, then at the Sault St. Marie Canal, and finally settled in Buffalo, Iowa, where he was elected mayor three times and was active in various civic enterprises. His photograph, showing him with hammer and plane in his hands, no doubt indicates the pride he took in his calling. (Eiboeck, 485.)

NAST, THOMAS, Sr. (d. 1857), musician (birthplace unknown). While Nast was serving as trombone player in the 9th Bavarian Regiment band at Landau, the German Revolution approached and the musician, a quiet man of convictions, definitely did not hide his liberal sympathies. Thereupon the commandant advised him to leave for America, which Nast decided to do. His family preceded him, since he first enlisted on a French man-o'-war and later on an American vessel. In 1850 he arrived in New York to join his family and to make his living as a member of the Philharmonic Society and of the band in Burton's Theatre. He imbued his son with his enthusiasm for freedom and fighters for liberty (Kossuth, for example) and this son grew up to be the greatest artist working for the antislavery cause—Thomas Nast. (Albert Bigelow Paine, *Thomas Nast*, Harper's, 1904; DAB.)

NEUHAUS, RUDOLF, physician. Served as regimental physician with the Revolutionary army in Baden and later fled to the U.S. At the outbreak of the Civil War he joined Sigel's corps as medical officer. He was repeatedly wounded while coming to the aid of wounded soldiers on the battle field (as at Rappahannock and at the second battle of Bull Run), and was forced to retire from the army. (Kaufmann, 535.)

NEUSTAEDTER, J. ALBERT, engineer and soldier, b. Trier. Trained as artillery officer in the Prussian army, he fought with the revolutionary army in Baden and was in Rastatt when the fortress was surrendered to the Prussian troops. He escaped with Carl Schurz, and in 1851 he arrived in the U.S. In St. Louis he served as business manager of the *Anzeiger des Westens,* which Boernstein was developing into a vigorous Republican paper. In 1861 he organized a battery and, as its captain, took part in the early battles in Missouri. He fought under Lyon and Frémont and later served on Sherman's staff. He was considered one of the best artillery officers in the Cumberland army and took part in numerous battles. (Kaufmann, 536; Schurz.)

NIX, JACOB, soldier, *Turner,* b. Bingen. Served as captain in the Baden Revolution, fought in Algiers, probably with the Foreign Legion, and settled in the *Turner* community of New Ulm, Minn. In August, 1862, he was chosen to command the defense of this town against the Sioux Indians. (Kaufmann, 536; P, VIII, 423.)

OLSHAUSEN, THEODOR (June 19, 1802–March 31, 1869), lawyer, journalist, b. Glueckstadt, Holstein. Studied law and became an official in Kiel. Took part in the Revolution, was imprisoned, and then was forced to emigrate. He arrived in the U.S. in 1851. He edited the Davenport *Demokrat,* a Republican paper, and, after 1856, the *Westliche Post* in St. Louis. He was a very influential member of the Republican party. In 1860 he attended the conference of German Republicans at the convention in Chicago. On the outbreak of the Civil War, he helped organize home guards in St. Louis and did much to save Missouri for the Union. He returned to his native Holstein after the war. (Herriot, 82; Schem; Richter, 493ff.)

OSTERHAUS, PETER JOSEPH (Jan. 4, 1823–Jan. 2, 1917), soldier, consul, merchant, b. Coblenz. Studied at military academy in Berlin and became an officer in the Prussian reserves. He was enthusiastically on the side of the Revolution and was made commandant of Mannheim. In 1849 he came to the U.S. as a political refugee and settled in Belleville, Ill., and later moved to St. Louis where he became bookkeeper for a hardware firm. At the outbreak of the Civil War he volunteered as a private but rose rapidly in rank in as highly distinguished a military career as any Forty-eighter. (Cf. Chapter VII). He served as consul in Lyon, France, from 1866 to 1877. He then returned to St. Louis and engaged in the hardware business. In 1898 he was appointed consul in Mannheim and served until 1900, when he resigned. By special act of Congress he was appointed brigadier general on March 3, 1905. All reports on General Osterhaus stress his gallant and chivalrous character. (DAB.)

OTTENDORFER, OSWALD (Jan. 26, 1826–Dec. 15, 1900), journalist, b.

Zwittau, Austria. Studied law in Prague and Vienna. As a 22-year-old student he was enthusiastic for the overthrow of the reactionary regimes in Austria and Germany. At first he joined the student legion in Vienna, next he fought in Schleswig-Holstein, then he joined Robert Blum's battalion in Vienna, fought on the barricades in Dresden, and participated in the renewed attempt at revolution in Prague. He fled to Switzerland, and after two years of extremely adventurous life he arrived in New York in the spring of 1850. He found employment on the *Staatszeitung* whose owner, Jakob Uhl, died the next year. Uhl's daughter Anna had for some time been managing the business affairs of the paper and she continued in this capacity with Ottendorfer's assistance. Eight years later the two were married and under their guidance the New York *Staatszeitung* became the most widely read German daily in the U.S. Unlike most Forty-eighters, Ottendorfer was a Democrat and remained in this party despite violent attacks from other Forty-eighters. However, he was not a party hack, but independent. In 1860 he resigned as Presidential elector when the Charleston convention nominated Breckenridge. His influential paper became a strong supporter of the Union cause. After the war, Ottendorfer favored reconciliation; he opposed the administration's reconstruction policy. In 1871 he joined in the fight on the Tammany Ring and in the following year was elected on the Reform party ticket as alderman. (DAB.)

PABISCH, FRANZ JOSEPH (March 30, 1825–Oct. 2, 1879), priest, professor of church history, b. Zlabings, Austria. Studied philosophy and law in Vienna and at the outbreak of the Revolution joined the Academic Legion and fought on the barricades. Nevertheless, he was able to continue his studies and, turning to theology, he was ordained a priest in 1850. However the treatment accorded him by his superiors caused him to leave for the U.S. in 1851. After serving in some small parishes and later studying for four years in Rome, he accepted the post of professor of church history in a seminary, Mt. St. Mary's of the West, in Cincinnati. He published extensively on church history and church law. (P, XI, 411–420.)

PEISSNER, ELIAS (Sept. 5, 1825–May 2, 1863), teacher, soldier, b. Vilseck, Bavaria. Studied law in Munich. In 1848 the King's favorite, the dancer Lola Montez, was arousing popular opposition to the ruler. Though a Catholic, she was anti-Jesuit and did much to fight corruption on the part of clerical members of the government. It was probably this action that won her the devotion of liberty-loving, idealistic Peissner who openly espoused her side and accompanied her on her flight from Munich in 1848. This made it impossible for him to return to Munich and he came to the U.S. in 1849. He was appointed instructor in German and Latin at Union College, Schenectady, N. Y. He was a successful teacher and the author of a German grammar as well as a history of German literature. In 1861 he wrote *The American Question*, a spirited defense of the North. He attended the conference of German Republicans in the *deutsches Haus* in 1860. On the outbreak of the Civil War, he organized the Union College Zouaves and, as colonel of the 119th New York Infantry, fell at Chancellorsville. Schurz writes of him: "Colonel Peissner was a gentleman of the highest type of character, exquisite refinement, large knowledge, and excellent qualities as a soldier." (Herriot, 65ff.; Mo., XXXII (1940), 314ff.; Schurz.)

PELZ, EDUARD (Sept. 9, 1800–May 14, 1876), publicist, b. Penig, Saxony. As a bookdealer he carried on his business in Copenhagen, Breslau, St. Petersburg, and Leipzig. In Silesia his espousal of the weavers' revolt of 1844 brought him a prison term. In 1848 he was elected to the *Vorparlament* and in the same year edited a radical paper. He was forced to leave his native land and came to the U.S. in 1850. He supported himself as a publicist in New York and labored devotedly to improve the condition of immigrants. He spent his last years in Germany. (P, VIII, 213ff.)

PETERS, CHRISTIAN H. F. (Sept. 19, 1813–July 19, 1890), astronomer, b. Coldenbuettel, Schleswig. Studied mathematics and astronomy at Berlin and Goettingen. From 1838 to 1843 he was engaged on a survey of Mt. Etna and later was appointed director of the trigonometrical survey of Sicily. In 1848 he sided with the Sicilian revolutionists and was ordered to leave the country; but he returned and served as major of engineers in the Revolution. After the fall of Palermo he fled to France, and, after spending some time in Constantinople, he came to the U.S. in 1854 with letters of recommendations from Alexander von Humboldt. He obtained a position in the U.S. Coast Survey and in 1867 was appointed Litchfield Professor of Astronomy at Hamilton College in Clinton, N. Y., and director of the Litchfield Observatory. He took part in numerous astronomical expeditions, is credited with quite a number of discoveries, and prepared a critical edition of Ptolemy's *Almagest*, in which his knowledge of Arabic, Greek, Latin, Hebrew, Persian, and Turkish proved useful. (DAB.)

PETERSEN, LORENZ (July 29, 1794–Jan. 17, 1880), pastor, b. Hadersleben, Schleswig. Studied theology at Kiel and Goettingen and served as pastor in Hoptrup. With the outbreak of the Revolution he joined the fighting forces and was taken prisoner by the Danes. After serving a prison term, he came to the U.S. in 1854 and settled in Lowdon, Iowa, as pastor of a Lutheran church. (P, XII, 16.)

PFAENDER, WILHELM (July 6, 1823–?, 1905), *Turner*, farmer, soldier, politician, b. Heilbronn, Wuerttemberg. While an apprentice in a business house he became an enthusiastic *Turner* and was involved in the revolutionary movement. He came to the U.S. in 1848 and with Hecker he founded the Cincinnati *Turnverein* in 1848; in 1850 he was the chief founder of the *Turner* colony in New Ulm, Minn. In Chapter III there is an account of the political and war record of Pfaender, who exemplified the ideals of the *Turner* in distinguished fashion. (Huhn, II, 36.)

PILAT, IGNAZ ANTON (June 27, 1820–Sept. 17, 1870), landscape gardener, b. St. Agatha, Austria. Studied at the University of Vienna and the Imperial Botanical Gardens at Schoenbrunn. He received the important commission of laying out a park for Prince Metternich. Shortly afterward the Revolution broke out, and Pilat came to the U.S. in 1848. He spent his first years in the South, where he layed out the grounds of several estates. He then settled in New York. "His lasting memorial is his work on Central Park, where his experience and knowledge of plant materials, his cultivated taste, and his great zeal resulted in his successful interpretation of the plans of Frederick Law Olmsted and Calvert Vaux. He died at his home in New York City of consumption, thought to have resulted from his untiring devotion to the interests of the Central Park and the exposure consequent thereon." (DAB.)

PLESSNER, MICHAEL CARL THEODOR (1813–1894), physician, politician, b. Prussia. He studied medicine at Berlin and followed this profession in Berlin and Stettin. He took part in the Revolution and consequently came to the U.S. in 1849, settling in Saginaw, Mich. He immediately entered public affairs, serving as justice of the peace, superintendent of the poor house, president of the city board of education, and Presidential elector in 1868. He also attended the conference of German Republicans at the Chicago convention in 1860. After 45 years of medical practice in Saginaw he died in 1894. (Herriot, 74; Russell.)

POESCHE, THEODOR (March 23, 1826–Dec. 27, 1899), teacher, statistician, b. Merseburg, Saxony. Studied first theology, then philosophy at Halle. He was an enthusiastic orator and the leader of the revolt in Halle. When the brief uprising was put down, he made his escape, but was condemned to sixteen years imprisonment *in contumaciam*. He stayed in England with Arnold Ruge and other refugees until 1854 and then settled in Philadelphia as a teacher. Here he made the acquaintance of Charles Goepp and with him published *The New Rome*. Poesche had a great flair for statistics. His work in this field for the Internal

Revenue Bureau and the Census Bureau prompted the German ambassador to ask that he be given leave to go to Germany as advisor to the German government. In this capacity he conferred repeatedly with Bismarck. (DAG, XII, 496ff.)

POHLE, CARL ADOLF JULIUS (Oct. 19, 1813–Nov. 22, 1859), pastor, b. Bautzen, Silesia. Studied theology in Leipzig and served as pastor in his home town. In 1848 he courageously expressed his liberal opinion from the pulpit and was dismissed and persecuted by the government. He took refuge in the United States and served as pastor in Williamsburg, N. Y. He published verse. (Zimmermann.)

POSCHNER, FRIEDRICH, soldier. Though an officer in the Prussian army, he joined the Revolutionary forces and came to the U.S. after the movement failed. In the Civil War he served as colonel in the 47th Ohio Regiment. (Kaufmann, 539.)

PRAHL, CHARLES (1826–1904), jeweler, b. Alterslohe, Holstein. Learned trade of jeweler and watchmaker. In 1848 he took part in the Revolution and in 1853 came to New York as a political refugee and established himself in business there. At the time of the Civil War he moved to Staten Island, where he indulged his hobbies of the study of botany, as well as hunting and fishing. At the time of the draft riots in New York, when Negroes fled from the mobs for safety and took refuge in the woods of Staten Island, Prahl supplied them with food. (Schlegel, III, 81.)

PRANG, LOUIS (March 12, 1824–June 14, 1909), publisher, lithographer, b. Breslau, Apprenticed in his father's dyeing factory until he was eighteen; he then spent some years in further study of this trade and of printing in Switzerland, France, and Great Britain. Because of his liberal opinions, he was banned by the Prussian government in 1848, and fled to Bohemia, Switzerland, and in 1850 to the U.S. After several unsuccessful ventures, he started a lithographing firm in Boston in 1856 which proved very successful. He did much for the spread of knowledge of famous works of art by producing reproductions in color. The Oxford English Dictionary credits him with being the first to apply the term "chromos" to colored lithographs. He also published drawing books and school texts for art appreciation. His only daughter married the only son of Karl Heinzen. (DAB.)

PREETORIUS, EMIL (March 15, 1827–Nov. 19, 1905), journalist, legislator, b. Alzey, Rhenish Hesse. Studied law at Giessen and Heidelberg. His participation in the Revolution forced him to flee Germany, and he arrived in St. Louis in 1853. He engaged in business, but was attracted to politics. He became an enthusiastic member of the Republican party and campaigned vigorously for Lincoln. In the first critical months of the war he worked to raise German regiments and otherwise helped prevent the secession of Missouri. As a member of the legislature, 1862 to 1864, he advocated immediate emancipation of slaves. His journalistic career is chiefly associated with the *Westliche Post* of which he was editor for forty years; for some years after 1867 Carl Schurz was coeditor. Preetorius was independent in his editorial policies and one of the leading journalists among the Forty-eighters. (DAB.)

PUCHNER, RUDOLF (Jan. 24, 1829–?), merchant, b. Beutelsbach, Wuerttemberg. Enjoyed an excellent education and was about to enter a business career when involvement in the Revolution drove him to the U.S. He settled in New Holstein, Wis., where he established himself in business. He was an ardent *Turner* and published many poems in *Turner* publications. In 1887 he published also an epic poem *Aglaia*, dealing with the Spartacus revolt in ancient Rome. (Zimmermann.)

QUERNER, EMIL (April 10, 1829–?, 1886), physician, b. Eisenberg, Saxony. Studied medicine and became involved in the Revolution in 1848. He came to the U.S. in the fifties and established a very successful medical practice in Philadelphia. He published several popular medical books and a book of verse. (Zimmermann.)

RAMMING, HEINRICH, journalist, soldier. Trained as officer in the Austrian army, but took part in the Revolution and came to Davenport, Iowa, as a political refugee. He was associate editor of the *Demokrat* and evidently an influential Republican, since he presided at the March 7, 1860, meeting of the Davenport Republican Club and was a delegate to the conference of German Republicans in the *deutsches Haus* in Chicago. At the outbreak of the Civil War he enlisted in the Hecker *Jaeger* Regiment. When it was mustered out, he became colonel of the 3d Missouri Infantry Regiment. (Herriot, 81; Richter, 475, 477.)

RAPP, WILHELM (July 14, 1828–March 1, 1907), journalist, b. Leonberg, Wuerttemberg. Studied at Tuebingen. A keen advocate of freedom and humanity, he took part in Baden Revolution and was forced to flee to Switzerland. On a secret visit to Germany he was arrested and imprisoned for several years. In 1852 he arrived in the U.S. He became editor of the *Turnerzeitung* in Baltimore and an energetic agitator for the Republican party. He continued in this spirit as editor of the Baltimore *Wecker* and later with the *Illinois Staatszeitung* in Chicago, of which he became editor-in-chief in 1891, continuing as one of the most influential editors of a German daily in this country until his death. (DAB.)

RASTER, HERMANN (May 26, 1827–?, 1891), journalist, b. Zerbst. In order to prepare himself for a journalistic career, he studied history and literature at a number of universities. His first position was that of secretary of the diet in Dessau. When the Revolution came he agitated for it so violently in newspaper articles that with the arrival of the reaction he was arrested but freed after some time on condition that he emigrate. In July, 1851, he arrived in New York penniless and was forced to accept various types of menial employment. But some articles from his pen attracted attention and earned him the post of editor, first of the Buffalo *Demokrat* and then of the New York *Abendzeitung*. Though the latter paper was not a very important one, Raster's political influence increased notably during his 15 years of editorship. He served also as correspondent for a number of European papers and was a contributor to *Appleton's Encyclopaedia*. In 1867 he went to Chicago to become editor of the *Illinois Staatszeitung* and made this paper once more a very influential one. He was very active in Republican national politics and was appointed by President Grant collector of internal revenue for the Chicago district. (Schem; Ruetenik, 325f.; AGR, VI, 3.)

RAUCH, CHARLES (1812–?), innkeeper, b. Germany. Apprenticed to a tailor. Fought in Revolutionary army in 1849 and came to St. Paul, Minn., in 1852. He was the owner of a restaurant, "Apollo Hall." He was a member of the St. Paul city council, 1856, and state legislature, 1858. (St. Paul.)

REIBETANTZ, CARL JULIUS (1827–1894), journalist. While a medical student at Jena he became involved in the Revolution and later came to Baltimore as a political refugee. He joined the staff of the Baltimore *Correspondent* and occupied a post in this paper for thirty-five years. (Information from his granddaughter, Else Geiwitz.)

REICHARD, JOSEPH MARTIN (Sept., 1803–May 17, 1872), notary, lawyer, b. Rhenish-Palatinate. Studied in Heidelberg, Wuerzburg, and Erlangen. Established himself as notary in Kusel and gained public confidence to such a degree that in 1848 he became a leader in the organization of Willich's army and was elected member of the provisional government. He arrived in Philadelphia as a refugee, having lost all of his property. He achieved a certain prosperity and continued to devote himself to liberal and philanthropic causes, such as the propagation of *freie Gemeinden*, the German Society to aid destitute immigrants, and the erection of a German hospital in Philadelphia. (DPV, III, 18; Valentin.)

REICHARDT, FRIEDRICH (Nov. 20, 1820–April 9, 1876), tailor. Trained as a tailor. He took an active part in the Revolution and came to Cincinnati as a political refugee in 1849. He lived there for the rest of his life. He was a member of the *Pionier Verein*, an historical society. (P, VIII, 80.)

REICHMANN, RUDOLPH (March 15, 1821–March 30, 1908), journalist, farmer, b. Schleswig. Trained as a printer and ready to open shop, he was refused a license by the Danish king because of his political opinions; Reichmann ended the audience by walking out with his back to the king and disrespectfully flipping his coattails. This incident is typical of the man who later fought in the Revolution and, exiled to America, started a paper to fight for the new Republican party. On one occasion when a political mob threatened to attack his print shop Reichmann posted himself at a window with two rifles and thus held the attackers at a respectful distance. From earliest youth he had been an enthusiastic hunter, and this passion led him to take up land in Iowa and later in the territory of Washington. His farming brought him greater prosperity than his newspaper ventures. At the age of eighty he married for the second time. (Richter, 489–493.)

REVENTLOW, OTTO (1817–?), *Turner*, author, b. Seeland, Denmark. Studied philology in Copenhagen and developed a mnemonic system on which he lectured widely in Germany. He took part in the South German Revolution and came to the U.S. as a political refugee. For some years he was assistant editor of the *Turnzeitung*. In 1863 he returned to Germany. (Huhn, I, 31; Schem.)

RITTIG, JOHANN (March 26, 1829–?, 1885), journalist, actor, b. Prague. Studied law. Took part in the Revolution and was imprisoned, but escaped after three months. In 1851 he was in Nice, serving as secretary to the prominent German liberal in exile, Karl Vogt. The Austrian government condemned him to death *in contumaciam*. After Napoleon's *coup d'état*, he left for America and arrived in Cincinnati in 1852 where he founded *Der Unabhaengige*, a short-lived antislavery paper. Next he turned to the stage and appeared as actor in the German theaters of Cincinnati, Milwaukee, Chicago, St. Louis, and Louisville. From 1857 to 1861 he was coeditor of the New York *Staatszeitung*, then he founded the New York *Journal* and was engaged in a number of other journalistic undertakings. In 1874 he became editor of the Sunday edition of the New York *Staatszeitung*. He served as collaborator on Schem's *Deutsch-Amerikanisches Conversations Lexikon*. In 1884 he published a volume of sketches of metropolitan life, *Federzeichnungen aus dem amerikanischen Stadtleben*. (Huhn, I, 34; Schem.)

ROESER, CARL (d. Nov., 1897), journalist. As a political refugee he came to the U.S. and in 1853 founded in Manitowoc the *Wisconsin Demokrat*, opposed to slavery and very outspoken for liberal principles. He was one of the founders of the Republican party in Wisconsin in 1854 and was elected county clerk on the first Republican ticket. He had the distinction of serving as a member of the Wisconsin delegation to the Republican convention in Chicago in 1860. His paper supported Lincoln energetically and the President showed his gratitude by appointing Roeser clerk in the Treasury Department. (Herriot, 77; *History of Manitowoc County, Wisconsin*, I, 217ff.)

ROESER, OTTO, farmer, b. Halle. Studied law at Halle, became involved in the Revolution, and went into exile, settling in Saginaw, Mich., in 1850. He became a farmer and served as justice of the peace, never seeking admission to the bar. (Russell.)

ROESLER, GUSTAV ADOLF [AUS OELS] (Oct. 31, 1818–Aug. 7, 1855), journalist, teacher, b. Goerlitz, Silesia. Trained as teacher. He was elected to the Frankfurt *Parlament*, where he served with firm conviction as a representative of the left. In this assembly he was a striking figure and he was caricatured in humorous weeklies as the "canary bird" because he wore a bright yellow suit that fought with his fiery red beard. When the Prussian government later demanded his imprisonment, he escaped through a ruse carried out by his wife. He arrived in New York in 1850 where he made the acquaintance of a number of prominent men, among them William H. Seward. The latter recommended him for the post of editor of a Whig German paper in Quincy, Ill., and Roesler, who had taught in a private school, accepted. He is reported to have been one of the most polemic editors among the Forty-eighters. (P, VII, 19–20; Valentin; DAG, Oct., 1905, 65.)

ROESSLER, FRIEDRICH (March 23, 1815–Jan. 4, 1870), physician, b. Wuerttemberg. Studied medicine in Tuebingen and Heidelberg and was practicing his profession when he became involved in the Revolution. For two years he was imprisoned and then arrived in New York in 1853. He founded the first German private hospital and won wide acclaim as physician and man of science. (P, I, 360.)

ROGGENBUCKE, OSKAR VON (1811–Jan., 1883), soldier, farmer, b. Suhl, Thuringia. Attained the rank of major in the Prussian army, but in 1848 resigned his commission to join in the Revolution. He came to Texas in 1854 as a political refugee and settled, after a sojourn in New Braunfels, on a farm near Comfort, Texas, where he remained for the rest of his life. During the Civil War he showed his sympathies for the

Union side; his two sons joined a group of Germans who set out for Mexico with the intention of joining the Northern fighting forces, but both lost their lives before the troop reached Mexico. (P, XV, 335; Kaufmann, 543; Valentin.)

ROSA, RUDOLF VON, soldier, engineer, b. Silesia. A Silesian nobleman and officer in the engineering corps of the Prussian army. In 1848 he resigned his commission and fought in the Revolution. He fled to the U.S. and arrived in Washington in 1850 where he found employment in the coastal survey. In 1862 he organized the 46th (Frémont) New York Regiment and was severely wounded in the Peninsular Campaign, but returned to lead his regiment at Gettysburg. He later established himself as an engineer in New York. (Kaufmann, 543.)

ROSKOTEN, ROBERT (Feb. 5, 1816–May 8, 1897), physician, b. Duesseldorf. Studied medicine in Halle and Jena. As a member of a *Burschenschaft* he became involved in the Revolution and was forced to flee. He arrived in the U.S. in 1849, and became a leading physician in Peoria, Ill. On the outbreak of the Civil War he was one of the first doctors appointed by Lincoln to an examining board for army surgeons. He took part in the war and rose to the rank of brigade surgeon. In the Battle of Shiloh his horse was killed by a bullet and fell on Roskoten, causing internal injuries that ended his army career. He was the author of two historical dramas. (Bess.)

ROSSWOG, CONSTANTIN (Sept. 22, 1822–?), goldsmith, *Turner*, b. Endingen, Baden. Traveling as a journeyman goldsmith, he reached Vienna in 1848. He joined the Academic Legion in the Vienna street fighting and in 1849 served as lieutenant in the Baden revolutionary army. After the collapse of the Revolution he came to New York. There he was one of the founders of the *Sozialistische Turnverein*, and, while carrying on a successful jewelry business, retained a deep interest in the activities of the *Turner*. (Huhn, II, 44.)

ROTHACKER, WILHELM (1828–Nov. 25, 1859), journalist, *Turner*, b. Engen, Baden. Studied literature and aesthetics at Freiburg. Fought with the Baden Revolutionary army and during the siege of Rastatt issued a newspaper for the troops. He suffered a long imprisonment and escaped execution only by a daring flight. He arrived in the U.S. in 1850 and was employed on newspapers in Wheeling, W. Va., Pittsburgh, and Cincinnati. He founded his own paper, *Die Menschenrechte* (Human Rights) which lasted only half a year. Friends secured for him a post as teacher, but this work did not suit his disposition. Rothacker was an enthusiastic *Turner* and for a while edited the national organ of this group. His imprisonment had caused him to contract tuberculosis and he died in poverty at the age of 31. He was the typical impractical idealist. His posthumous writings, published in Cincinnati in 1860, contain enthusiastic verses in praise of freedom and an essay on Patrick Henry. (Huhn, I, 31; Zimmermann; JDAT, III, 178.)

ROTHE, EMIL (Sept. 23, 1826–April 27, 1895), journalist, lawyer, b. Guhrau, Silesia. Studied law in Breslau, Jena, Heidelberg, and Berlin. Took part in a revolt in Breslau and organized a company to take part in the Revolution in Berlin. Later he was forced to flee and arrived in New York in 1849. He tried his hand at farming and then founded the *Weltbuerger* in Watertown, Wis., and edited the paper for seventeen years. He also studied law and began to practice. In 1860 he was a delegate to the Democratic convention which nominated Douglas; out of opposition to the Know-Nothing movement he did not join the Republican party. In 1869 he became editor of the *Volksfreund* in Cincinnati and in 1872 turned again to the practice of law. He was an eloquent and popular speaker in the German language. (Schem; DAG, XI, 222ff.)

ROTTECK, CARL, journalist, politician. Took part in the Baden Revolution and arrived in the U.S. in the early fifties. Tried farming and then a shoe business—both without success. In 1857 he became editor of a Republican paper in Muscatine and a fiery opponent of Know-Nothingism, slavery, and the Massachusetts Two-Year Amendment. His outspoken views alienated many readers and in 1859 he moved his paper to Burlington, Iowa, and later to Keokuk. He attended the conference of German Republicans in Chicago in 1860 as one of the Iowa contingent. (Herriot, 81.)

RUDOLPH, JOSEPH (Feb. 5, 1825–?), businessman, b. Teplitz, Bohemia. Studied at the University of Prague and the Vienna *Polytechnikum*. During the Revolution he fought with the Vienna Academic Legion and was forced to leave for the U.S. as a political refugee in 1849. In Cincinnati he founded with Hassaurek the *Verein freier Maenner* and served as its secretary. After short sojourns in St. Louis and Dubuque, he opened a jewelry business in Chicago, in 1855. He lost everything in the Chicago fire and then started a furniture store which was sufficiently successful to permit him to retire in 1885. His memoirs, recounting vividly the economic difficulties of the immigrant, appeared in the DAG of 1907. (Chicago, 154.)

RUPPIUS, OTTO (Feb. 6, 1819–Jan. 25, 1864), journalist, novelist, b. Glauchau, Saxony. After a short term in the Prussian army and a few years' experience as a book dealer, he turned to writing as a profession. In 1848 he edited a revolutionary paper in Berlin, took part in the March Revolution, and was condemned to a term in prison. He managed to escape and arrived in the U.S. in the early fifties. He settled at first in Milwaukee, later in New York, St. Louis, and Chicago —everywhere engaged in journalism of belletristic nature. For a while he was a music teacher and conductor of an orchestra in Nashville, Tenn. After amnesty for political offenders had been declared in 1862, he returned to Germany. He ranks with Sealsfield and Gerstaecker as a writer of German novels with settings in the U.S. His best-known works are *Der Pedlar* and *Der Prairieteufel*. His *Karriere in Amerika* is full of amusing local color. (AGR, IX, 3; Schem.)

RUSCH, NICHOLAS (Feb. 16, 1822–Sept. 22, 1864), farmer, lieutenant governor, immigration commissioner, b. Marne, Holstein. Studied at University of Kiel. As a result of his revolutionary activities, he emigrated to the U.S. in 1847. He became a successful farmer near Davenport, Iowa, and a political leader in the Republican party. In 1859 he was elected state senator and in 1860 lieutenant governor. In 1860 he attended the conference of German Republicans at Chicago; the resolutions adopted at this meeting were largely based on ideas agitated by Rusch in resolutions previously passed by the Davenport Republican Club. He became immigration commissioner in New York in 1862. In 1863 he organized a labor corps of German immigrants who supplied the Union fleet on the Mississippi with fuel. While engaged in this work he died at Vicksburg. (Herriot, 82; Eiboeck, 417ff.)

RUTHS, PHILIPP (Dec. 9, 1828–Dec. 10, 1874), policeman, b. Zwingenberg, Hesse. Took part in the Revolution and came to the U.S. as a political refugee. He went directly to Cincinnati where he served for many years on the police force. He was also a member of the *Pionier Verein*. (P, VI, 414.)

SAHM, KARL (1821–Feb. 8, 1883), musician, b. Grumbach, Prussia. Studied music at the Paris Conservatory and elsewhere. His participation in the Revolution brought him to New York in 1853 as a political refugee. He became director of a number of musical organizations and the author of numerous compositions, among them cantatas as well as comic operas. At his funeral he was praised as "a man of freedom." (P, XV, 348ff.)

SALOMON, CARL EBERHARD (June, 1822–Feb. 8, 1881), surveyor, soldier, b. Halberstadt, Prussia. Trained as a surveyor. His love of freedom, nourished by his father who had fought in the War of Liberation against Napoleon, caused him to take part in the Revolution and brought him a sentence of two years' imprisonment. He escaped and came in 1849 to the U.S., establishing himself in St. Louis as a surveyor. Upon Lincoln's call for volunteers, Salomon organized the 3d Missouri Regiment and commanded it as colonel at Wilson's Creek and Pea Ridge. He further distinguished himself in 1864 in the Red River campaign, especially at Pine Bluff and Jenkins Ferry, where he served under his brother Friedrich S. Salomon. At the conclusion of the war, Salomon returned to his former occupation in St. Louis. He had been given the rank of brigadier general by brevet. (Kaufmann, 544f.; Ruetenik, 347; P, XII, 450; Schem.)

SALOMON, EDWARD (Aug. 11, 1828–?, 1908), lawyer, governor, b. Halberstadt, Prussia. Studied at the University of Berlin and became involved in the Revolution. In 1849 he arrived in Wisconsin, held positions as a teacher and surveyor, then studied law and began a successful practice in 1855. In 1861 he was elected lieutenant governor and, upon the death of Governor Harvey, became the wartime governor. He served with distinction: he organized fighting forces, sternly enforced the conscription law, saw to it that the Indian War originating in Minnesota did not touch Wisconsin, and made his appointments on the basis of merit. After the expiration of his term he continued his interest in the University of Wisconsin which he had kept open and otherwise favored during the war. In 1869 he moved to New York where he engaged in legal practice and took part in the civic reform movement, serving as chairman of the Committee of Seventy. (Kaufmann, 545; Ruetenik; Schem.)

SALOMON, FRIEDRICH S. (April 7, 1826–?, 1895), civil engineer, b. Halberstadt, Prussia. Trained as surveyor, he was engaged in the study of architecture in Berlin when he became involved in the Revolution and had to leave Germany. He settled in Manitowoc, Wis., where he first held the post of registrar of deeds and then was employed by a railway as civil engineer. In 1860 he moved to St. Louis and on the outbreak of the Civil War entered his brother's (Carl E. Salomon's) regiment as captain. On the expiration of the three months' service, his brother, Edward S. Salomon, then governor of Wisconsin, called upon him to organize the 9th Wisconsin Regiment. In the fighting against the Cherokee Indians he won such distinction that he was appointed brigadier general and as such he commanded the victorious Union troops at Helena, Ark., on the Mississippi on July 4, 1863. He took part in many other, minor, battles and at the end of the war was given the rank of major general by brevet. He died as a federal official in Salt Lake City. (Ruetenik; Kaufmann, 545; Schem.)

SANDER, ENNO (Feb. 27, 1822–Feb. 12, 1912), pharmacist. Studied in Berlin and Halle. Took part in the Revolution in Baden, where he served for a time as war minister. He was imprisoned for a term and arrived in St. Louis in 1853. He established himself as an apothecary and founded the American Pharmaceutical Society in 1858. In 1863 he founded the St. Louis College of Pharmacy. His vivid memoirs of the Revolution are published in the DAG, XIII, 309ff.

SCHADE, LOUIS (March 8, 1829–Feb. 25, 1903), journalist, lawyer, b. Berlin. Studied law in Berlin. In 1848 his participation in the Revolution forced him to flee and he came to the U.S. in 1851. He received a position as assistant librarian in the Smithsonian Institution in Washington and later posts in the census bureau and the State Department. From 1856 to 1858 he was engaged in journalism in Chicago and spent some time in Burlington, Iowa, where he was admitted to the bar. In 1859 he settled down in Washington as lawyer. A real Forty-eighter deed on the part of Schade was in 1865 his undertaking the defense of Captain Wirz, the superintendent of Andersonville Prison where many Union soldiers had suffered terribly; the manner in which Wirz was tried in the midst of aroused public opinion is now considered not to have been in conformity with justice, but Schade did all in his power to secure a fair trial for the hated man. (Schem, information from Miss Anita Schade.)

SCHIEFERDECKER, JULIUS (1801–Sept. 8, 1881), typesetter, b. Saxony. He worked for a few years in Paris, printing works of Greek literature. In 1848 he established himself as publisher, but soon became involved in the Revolution; his business was confiscated and he was to be imprisoned, but he managed to escape. In the U.S. he supported himself meagerly as a typesetter in a number of cities, finally in Milwaukee. He was almost fifty when he reached America, and probably for that reason never attained any success and died in poverty. (P, XIII, 326.)

SCHIEREN, JOHN NIKOLAUS (d. July 3, 1863), businessman, b. Aachen. The father of the noted inventor and leather manufacturer Charles A. Schieren. He brought his family to the U.S. in 1856 after he had been forced to flee Germany as a result of his participation in the Revolution. He was proprietor of a tobacco store in Brooklyn. (DAB; Schlegel, I, 130.)

SCHIMMELFENNIG [Schimmelpfennig], ALEXANDER (1824–Sept. 7, 1865), soldier, author, b. Prussia. Though trained as an officer in the Prussian army, he fought both in the Schleswig-Holstein and the Baden revolutions on the side of the liberals. He emigrated to the U.S., settling in

Philadelphia, and at first occupied himself with literary work, publishing, for example, in 1854 *The War between Russia and Turkey*. In the Civil War he had a very distinguished career at Bull Run, Gettysburg, Charleston, and elsewhere. Shortly after the conclusion of the war he died in Minersville, Pennsylvania. (Ruetenik, 351; Kaufmann, 549; Schurz.)

SCHLAEGER, EDUARD, journalist. Refugee who functioned as secretary of the Wheeling Congress in September, 1852. In 1854 he is reported as publisher of *Der Deutsch-Amerikaner*, a weekly in Chicago. Active in his opposition to the Kansas-Nebraska Bill, he called the protest meeting of March 16, 1854. In 1880 he was living in Berlin. The *Pionier* of 1876 contains an article from his pen on the Wheeling Congress. He belonged to the most radical group of Forty-eighters. (P, VIII, 90ff.; P, XII, 513.)

SCHLEICHER, KARL (1787–1882), soapmaker, hunter, b. Stuttgart. Took part in Napoleon's campaign in Russia as a noncommissioned officer of a Wuerttemberg regiment. In 1848 he was commander of the civilian guard in Stuttgart and planned to join the revolutionary forces, but was betrayed. Thus he was forced to come to the U.S. as a political refugee. He settled in Sauk City, Wis., where he made a miserable living at various callings. He was probably the oldest of the Forty-eighters. (P, XIV, 116.)

SCHLUND, FIDEL, soldier, b. Immenstadt, Bavaria. Member of the Bavarian Chamber and of the Frankfurt *Parlament*. He took part in the Baden Revolution and was imprisoned for a long period. He came to the U. S. as a political refugee and on the outbreak of the Civil War enlisted together with his four sons. (Kaufmann, 550.)

SCHMIDT, CARL WILHELM (d. 1886), lawyer, brewer, b. Palatinate. Studied law and functioned as notary. Took active part in the Revolution and was a member of the Palatinate defense committee. After the violent suppression of the movement, he fled to Switzerland and found himself condemned to death *in absentia*. In 1851 he came to the U.S. His property had been confiscated, but he started a brewery in Cleveland which he developed in the course of years into a flourishing business. (P, XVIII, 335.)

SCHMIDT, ERNST (March 2, 1830–Aug. 26, 1900), physician, politician, b. Ebern, Bavaria. Studied medicine in Wuerzburg, Zurich, Heidelberg, and Munich. At eighteen he took part in the Revolution, was ordered into exile, but influential relatives won him a pardon. At twenty-two he was appointed to the medical faculty at Wuerzburg, where he formed a lifelong friendship with the liberal scientist Rudolf Virchow. His "radical" past made it impossible for Schmidt to advance, and he emigrated to Chicago in 1857 where he soon established a good practice. However, his participation in the antislavery movement, particularly his speech at a memorial meeting for John Brown, lost him his respectable, paying patients. He therefore moved to St. Louis and on the outbreak of the war joined the 3d Missouri Regiment of Colonel Osterhaus. Exposure brought on a severe illness and permanent impairment of his hearing, and he returned to Chicago. Political conditions had changed—he was now honored for his attitude on slavery and was elected coroner. But he resigned when he learned what the corrupt politicians expected of him. On a trip to Germany he received the offer of a professorship, but declined because the freedom of America appealed to him more than dignity under reaction. In 1879 he ran for mayor of Chicago on the Socialist ticket. In the eighties he had the courage to organize a committee for the defense of the Haymarket Riot anarchists. Schmidt wrote considerable verse, among other items a good translation of Poe's *Raven*. (DAG, III, 12ff.; XXXII, 22f.)

SCHMITT, NIKOLAUS (d. 1870), businessman, journalist, b. Palatinate. Member of the Frankfurt *Parlament* and a fighter in the Palatinate Revolution. Came to Philadelphia as a political refugee and was in business for some time with his friend Joseph M. Reichard. In 1856 he was elected president of the German Frémont Club. He was influential in organizing the Republican party in Philadelphia and was president of the *freie Gemeinde* there, a society in which men and women were to enjoy equal rights in the furtherance of humanity and the fight against dogma and every sort of oppression. For some time he edited the Philadelphia daily, *Volksvertreter*. (DPV, III, 19; XI, 17; XXI, 19.)

SCHMOLZE, KARL HEINRICH (1823–1859), artist, caricaturist, b. Zweibruecken, Palatinate. Studied art in Metz and Munich. In 1848 he founded a radical weekly, *Leuchtkugeln*, and was imprisoned for his satirical drawings. When the citizens of Munich arose to drive out Lola Montez, they freed Schmolze and his fellow prisoners. Later he fought with Schimmelfennig in the Palatinate and was condemned to death but escaped. He came to Philadelphia in the early fifties and supported himself as an illustrator. Throughout his life he remained a hater of all forms of oppression. He also published verse, including some excellent sonnets. (*Magazin*, I, 37ff.)

SCHNAUFFER, CARL HEINRICH (July 4, 1823–Sept. 4, 1854), poet, soldier, editor, b. Heimsheim, Stuttgart. Studied at Heidelberg and was very much influenced by his association with Hecker and Struve. He fought in the Baden Revolution and was forced to flee to Switzerland. On the renewed outbreak of the fighting he returned to Germany and was taken prisoner. He escaped from prison under the guise of a locksmith and again took refuge in Switzerland. Later he went to England and in 1851 arrived in Baltimore. He identified himself with the *Turner* movement and founded the *Wecker*, a Republican, antislavery paper which stood for freedom, popular education, and general enlightenment. Though he died after a few years, his paper was continued by his wife, and for decades was the liberal German paper of Baltimore. He wrote beautiful poems in praise of liberty, and a drama on Charles I. In Germany he had been called the Tyrtaeus of the Baden Revolution and in the U.S. he became the most brilliant of the *Turner* poets. (DAB; Cunz.)

SCHNEIDER, GEORG (Dec. 13, 1823–Sept. 16, 1905), journalist, politician, b. Pirmasenz, Palatinate. After graduation from a *Gymnasium*, he turned to journalism. He took an active part in the Revolution as a journalist and organizer of armed groups to fight for a republican government. When Prussian troops suppressed the South German uprising, Schneider was condemned to death. However, he managed to escape and arrived in the U.S. in 1849. He founded the *Neue Zeit* in St. Louis, a paper of liberal, antislavery tendency in a slave state; in 1850 a fire destroyed the plant. In 1851 he was called to Chicago to take over the *Illinois Staatszeitung*. He transformed this conservative weekly into a daily and perhaps the most influential German newspaper in the politics of the fifties. Schneider, in addition to making his influence felt as an editor, played a very aggressive part in politics. On January 29, 1854, he called a public meeting to draft resolutions against the Kansas-Nebraska Bill and took a leading part in the anti-Douglas meeting (described in Chapter III). He was one of the leaders in organizing the Republican party in Illinois, and at the state convention in Bloomington in 1856 he proposed a plank condemning the Know-Nothing policy of discrimination against naturalized citizens. When opposition arose, Schneider appealed to Lincoln, who had appeared at the convention. The latter read the paragraph very carefully and then said: "Gentlemen, the resolution introduced by Mr. Schneider is nothing new. It is already contained in the Declaration of Independence, and you cannot form a new party on proscriptive principles." Schneider was a friend of Lincoln's, did much to win the German vote for him in 1860, and was sent by the President as consul to Elsinore with the special mission of influencing public opinion in the northern European countries in favor of the Union cause; he returned to the U.S. in 1862 after achieving considerable success. Lincoln appointed him collector of internal revenue for the Chicago district. After the conclusion of his term, Schneider devoted himself to banking. But he continued, in harmony with his opposition to slavery, his lifelong interest in other humanitarian causes. Next to Carl Schurz he was probably the foremost political leader among the Forty-eighters. (DAB; Herriot, 87; Chicago, 110ff.; DAG, XII, 516ff.; XXXII, 20.)

SCHOLER, JACOB (Jan. 30, 1807–July 19, 1885), editor, *Turner*, b. Karlsruhe. Trained as a printer. In 1830 he fought for the freedom of the Poles. On his return to Karlsruhe in 1848 he founded a revolutionary daily supporting the popular aims. When the Prussians entered the city, he was arrested, tried, and condemned to prison for two years. He arrived in the U.S. in 1854 and started a printshop. As an old *Turner* he immediately joined the New York *Turnverein*, serving as the printer of its publications. He brought with him from Europe the type he had employed in printing his revolutionary paper. Customs officials, sympathizing with the European revolutionaries, admitted the type duty free. (Huhn, II, 39; JDAT, III, 132.)

SCHOTT, CHARLES ANTHONY (Aug. 7, 1826–July 31, 1901), geodesist, magnetician, b. Mannheim. Studied civil engineering at Karlsruhe and served for a while in the Baden revolutionary army. He came to the U.S. in 1848 and soon obtained a post in the office of the United States Coast Survey. In 1855 he was made chief of the computing division and remained in this post for forty-five years. Schott wrote numerous scientific articles in the fields of astronomy, geodesy, magnetism, map projections, and tides. He was elected to numerous scientific societies and was awarded a prize by the French Academy of Sciences. (DAB.)

SCHRAIDT, KASPAR (March 26, 1823–Aug. 1, 1886), viticulturist, b. Germany. Trained as carpenter. As a result of his participation in the Revolution, he had to endure so much chicanery that he decided to go to America, arriving in the U.S. in 1852. He established himself in Put in Bay on Lake Erie and began to cultivate high-quality grapes on islands in the lake, a pioneer in this field. He founded the successful Put in Bay Wine Company and was chosen an officer of the American Vine Growers Association. (P, XVIII, 98.)

SCHROETER, EDUARD (June 11, 1811–?), speaker of a *freie Gemeinde*, b. Hannover. Studied theology in Jena and Goettingen but left the state church in 1845. He organized a "free congregation" in Worms, but because of his liberal views was ordered to leave Germany. In 1850 he arrived in the U.S. and accepted a call to Milwaukee as speaker of the *freie Gemeinde.* In 1853 he went to Sauk City, Wis., in a similar capacity. He published many essays in the *Freidenker* and similar radical publications. He also edited the freethinking *Humanist*, and through his efforts many *freie Gemeinden* were founded in Wisconsin. (Huhn, I, 30; Schem; DPV, XI, 10ff.)

SCHUENEMANN-POTT, FRIEDRICH (April 5, 1826–?, 1881), speaker of *freie Gemeinde*, b. Hamburg. Studied theology in Marburg and became interested in Feuerbach and Strauss. Became preacher of *freie Gemeinden*. Because of his activity in the Revolution he was imprisoned for treason and lese majesty. He was adopted by a Baron Pott whose name he joined to his own. After considerable persecution on account of his freethinking, he left for the U.S. in 1854. He became speaker of the *freie Gemeinde* in Philadelphia and editor for 21 years of *Blaetter fuer freies religioeses Leben.* He lectured all over the U.S. and was no doubt the leading spirit in the movement of freethinking religious groups among the Germans in this country. A lifelong fighter for freedom, he attended the conference of German Republicans in Chicago in 1860. (Herriot, 68; DPV, XI, 33–35.)

SCHULTZ, EDUARD, *Turner.* Fought in the Baden Revolution and came to the U.S. as a political refugee. He is remembered as the founder of the first *Turnverein* in Milwaukee, in March, 1850. (Hense-Jensen.)

SCHURZ, CARL (March 2, 1829–May 14, 1906), Minister to Spain, soldier, Senator, Secretary of the Interior, journalist, author, b. Liblar, near Cologne. Studied history in Bonn. Fought in the Baden Revolution and made a sensational escape from the fortress Rastatt. Freed the revolutionary poet Kinkel from prison. Refugee in England and came to the U.S. in 1852. Lived in Philadelphia and later in Watertown, Wis. Becoming prominent in Republican politics, he was chief of the Wisconsin delegation to the Republican convention in 1860 and was an influential speaker in the election campaign. Lincoln sent him as minister to Spain, but Schurz returned as soon as possible to fight in the Civil War. At the request of President Johnson he made a tour of the South and wrote a report on conditions there. For a year he was editor of the Detroit *Post* and then became part-owner with Preetorius of the St. Louis *Westliche Post.* In 1868 he was elected Senator from Missouri. In 1872 he was a leader among the Liberal Republicans. In 1877 he was appointed Secretary of the Interior in Hayes's cabinet. Later he served in an editorial capacity on the *Nation* and *Harper's Weekly.* He was president of the Civil Service Reform League. He wrote numerous noteworthy speeches, an essay on Lincoln, a life of Henry Clay, and his *Reminiscences* in three volumes. He was by far the most distinguished Forty-eighter. (DAB.)

SCHUSTER, CHRISTIAN F., musician, b. Mainz. For his part in the Revolution he was forced to emigrate. He was a master of many instruments and in New York became a member of the Germania Orchestra. He gave the first trombone solo heard in New York. Dr. Wesselhoeft, who had the famous Water Cure at Brattleboro, Vt., induced him to take charge of musical programs at the sanitarium. Mr. Schuster acquired many pupils for pipe organ, piano, and violin, and also served for 19 years as church organist. (Mary R. Cabot, *Annals of Brattleboro, Vt.*, II, 572.)

SEIFFERT, KARL (1818–1881), legislator, police judge, b. Hanau. Fought with the Hanau *Turner* in the Baden Revolution, fled to Switzerland, and arrived in the U.S. in 1850. He settled in Newark, N. J., served as secretary of the *Turnverein*, and helped found a German-English school. He was twice elected as a Democrat to the state legislature and also served as judge of the police court in Newark. (P, XIII, 153.)

SENGES, ADAM, soldier. While captain of artillery in the Baden army he went over to the revolutionary army with many of his comrades. He was taken prisoner and condemned to a long prison term which he spent with Otto von Corwin in Freiburg. In the U.S., he served as colonel of artillery in the Army of the Potomac and won considerable distinction in the bombardment of Fort Pulaski. (Kaufmann, 552.)

SERODINO, HERMANN FRANZ (Feb. 22, 1821–May 12, 1879), jeweler, b. Nordhausen, Thuringia. Skilled at his trade as a jeweler, he found a very good position in Berlin. But as a member of a singing society, he took the patriotic songs they sang seriously enough to fight on the barricades in 1848. Serodino was arrested as a traitor but escaped to St. Petersburg where, on the strength of recommendations from his Berlin employer, he found a good position. But the Prussian police demanded the extradition of revolutionaries even from far-off Russia; Serodino's employer heard of the intended arrest just in time to place the young man on a ship bound for Boston where he landed on August 9, 1849. Serodino then went to Cincinnati and established himself, after some initial hardships, as a very successful jeweler. He joined a musical society and continued to sing the songs of freedom in the land of liberty! (P, XI, 404.)

SIBER, EDUARD, soldier. Captain in the Prussian army, he resigned in order to fight for freedom in the Schleswig-Holstein army. After the conclusion of the fighting Siber went to Brazil where he was called to train the army of Dom Pedro. He arrived in the U.S. in 1861 and served as colonel of the 37th Ohio Regiment. He served until the fall of Vicksburg in July, 1863, when failing health forced him to retire. (Kaufmann, 553.)

SIGEL, ALBERT (Nov. 13, 1827–March 15, 1884), journalist, soldier, b. Sinsheim, near Heidelberg. Like his more famous brother Franz, he received a good education and took an active part in the Revolution. Taken prisoner, he was for a while incarcerated in Kitzlau. On the renewal of the Revolution in 1849 his brother forced the commander of the prison to release the prisoners and Albert Sigel joined the insurrectionary army. In 1853 he came to the U.S. and found employment as a journalist on a number of newspapers. On the outbreak of the Civil War he became a colonel of the 5th Regiment of the Missouri militia and fought throughout the war. Later he held a number of political posts, the last as adjutant general of Missouri. He published an historical reference work in 1854 and in 1863 *Gedichte*, poems that show considerable metrical skill suffused with gentle melancholy. (Zimmermann.)

SIGEL, FRANZ (Nov. 18, 1824–Aug. 21, 1902), soldier, journalist, b. Sinsheim, Baden. Graduated from the military academy in Karlsruhe and served as lieutenant in the army. His liberal political views brought about his resignation in 1847. In both insurrections in Baden he was one of the leading military commanders. Forced into exile, he spent two years in England and arrived in New York in 1852. He taught at first in Dr. Dulon's school in New York and later in another school in St. Louis, advancing to the post of director of the schools of that city. After his Civil War service (cf. Chapter VII), he edited the Baltimore *Wecker* for two years and then served in turn as pension agent, collector of internal revenue, and editor of the *Deutsches Volksblatt*. While his military career was not highly successful, Sigel deserves great credit for his prompt and ardent espousal of the Union cause, which helped enormously in bringing the large German population solidly behind the Union. He published his memoirs of 1848–49 and was a prominent lecturer. (DAB.)

SOLGER, REINHOLD (July 17, 1817–Jan. 11, 1866), author, politician, b. Stettin, Prussia. As a result of his boyhood experiences in a military academy Solger wrote later a very droll epic with a Prussian lieutenant as hero—of course a bitter satire on the military mind. He studied history in Halle and Greifswald in preparation for an academic career. But in 1848 he joined the revolutionary army in Baden and on its defeat had to flee to Switzerland. In 1853 he went to Boston, where his scholarship won him an invitation to deliver the Lowell Lectures at

Harvard in 1857 and 1859. He was an effective orator for the Republican cause in 1856 and 1860, and in the latter year attended the preconvention meeting of Republicans at the *deutsches Haus* in Chicago. Solger was probably the most gifted author among the Forty-eighters; he won prizes both for a poem in honor of Schiller at the centenary in 1859 and for a novel on German-American life. Lincoln appointed him assistant register of the treasury in recognition of his services to the Republican party. (DAB.)

SORGE, FRIEDRICH ADOLPH (Nov. 9, 1828–Oct. 26, 1906), labor leader, b. Bethau, Saxony. Trained at the institute of the philanthropist Francke at Halle. In 1848 he fought in the Baden Revolution and fled to Switzerland. In Geneva he met Liebknecht and other members of the German Workers' Educational Society. He was expelled from Switzerland and, after a stay in Belgium and London, where he met Karl Marx, he came to New York in 1852. He supported himself as a music teacher. In 1858 he joined the Communist Club and became the authoritative representative of Marx in America. He was, however, definitely not in sympathy with anarchical tendencies, but strove to unite the American labor movement with the Socialist party. He was for a time general secretary of the International Working-Men's Association, attended numerous international conventions, was very active in the Eight Hour League, and was the leading exponent of the German-American proletariat. In the history of American Socialism he played a considerable role. (DAB.)

STARKLOFF, HUGO (1830–?), physician, b. Stuttgart. Fought in the Baden Revolution and came to the U.S. in 1849, establishing himself as a physician in St. Louis. He was an enthusiastic *Turner* and was for many years national president of the organization. In the Civil War he underwent numerous hardships in Indian fighting and in the swamps of Louisiana as surgeon of the 12th Missouri Regiment. After the war he returned to his practice in St. Louis. (Huhn, I, 29; Kaufmann, 554.)

STEINWEDEL, WILHELM (Dec. 21, 1827–?), businessman, soldier, b. Hannover. Trained in a commercial school he went into the hardware business. In 1848 his enthusiasm for freedom led him to join the revolutionaries, but before he was imprisoned his father supplied him with funds to leave for the U.S. After visiting Niagara Falls he went to the Middle West and settled in Quincy, Ill., where he established a successful hardware business. On the outbreak of the Civil War he organized a company of volunteers and saw considerable fighting in Missouri. (DAG, April, 1905, 9ff.)

STENGEL, WILHELM (182[?]–1879), journalist, chaplain, painter, b. Ludwigsburg. Studied philology and painting. After participating in the Revolution, he settled in Louisville. He made his living as a journalist, as a drawing teacher, and as a portrait painter. At the outbreak of the Civil War he entered the 9th Ohio Regiment as chaplain and later took over the command of a company. After the war he served as editor of a number of papers in Cincinnati and St. Louis. He was also an enthusiastic *Turner*. (Huhn, I, 33.)

STOCKMANN, C. O. (d. 1873), physician, b. Thuringia. In 1848 he organized the revolt in Thuringia and captured an entire squadron of hussars together with their officers. But with the arrival of 80,000 Prussian troops in Thuringia the Revolution was suppressed and Stockmann sentenced to lifelong imprisonment. After seven years he was pardoned under condition that he leave the country. He arrived in the U.S. in 1855, settled in New Haven, Conn., and established a successful medical practice. (P, V, 250.)

STOECKEL, GUSTAVE (1819–1905), b. Palatinate. At the time of the Revolution he was principal of a *Gymnasium* at Landstuhl and his political activities forced him to flee. He arrived in New Haven in March, 1849, and began as a private teacher. He had come with a letter of introduction to members of the Battell family, and their support, together with Stoeckel's outstanding work, led to the establishment of the Battell Chapel Choir, the Yale Glee Club, the New Haven Symphony Orchestra, and the Yale School of Music. His genius for arousing interest in music led to his appointment as choirmaster at Yale in 1855; in 1864 he was awarded the honorary degree of Doctor of Music; and by 1890 the New England suspicion against music as an academic subject had been overcome to such an extent that the Yale Corporation made him professor with faculty status. (Marshall Bartholomew, "A Century of Music at Yale," *Yale Alumni Magazine*, December, 1948.)

STRAUBENMUELLER, JOHANN (May 11, 1814–?, 1897), teacher, *Turner*, poet, b. Gmuend, Wuerttemberg. Trained as a teacher and taught in a number of towns in Wuerttemberg. He early became a *Turner* and wrote some fine lyrics expressing *Turner* ideals. Because he was very active in 1848 and 1849 as political poet and agitator, he was accused of treason, deprived of his teaching position, but pardoned on condition that he emigrate. He arrived in Baltimore in 1854, teaching there and writing for the antislavery *Wecker*. Two days before the election of 1860 he was shot at by a proslavery sympathizer just as he entered the Republican party headquarters. In 1863 he accepted the post of principal of the *Freie deutsche Schule* in New York. He wrote *Pocahontas,* an epic on the founding of Virginia, and many lyrics for the *Turner*, among others a cycle of songs which were set to music for male chorus and solo parts and often rendered at *Turnfeste*. (Huhn, II, 27; Cunz; Zimmermann; JDAT, I, 179.)

STRAUCH, ADOLPH (Aug. 30, 1822–April 25, 1883), landscape gardener, b. Glatz, Silesia. Studied horticulture in Vienna. His participation in the Revolution drove him to England where he remained for some time. He left for the U.S. in 1852, went to Cincinnati, and established himself there as a very successful horticulturist, receiving many commissions to lay out estates. He was also landscape architect for Spring Grove Cemetery. He imported many varieties of European trees and was in various ways a pioneer in his field. (P, XV, 428ff., 489ff.; XVI, 39ff., 62ff.)

STRUVE, GUSTAV (Oct. 11, 1805–Aug. 21, 1870), author, soldier, b. Munich. Studied law in Heidelberg and Goettingen. Entered the state service, but through his radical writings came into conflict with the authorities. As 1848 approached, he agitated for a German republic and was instrumental in calling the meeting at Offenburg in which revolutionary demands were formulated. He was elected to the *Vorparlament*, but considering it too meek left this "debating society" to raise an armed band to cooperate with Hecker. He was defeated and exiled, but returned to become a leader in the establishment of the ephemeral republic in Baden. After its collapse, Struve was condemned to five years of penal servitude, but was freed by a mob. After spending some time in Switzerland and England, he came to the U.S. in 1851. He was invited by a wealthy brewer to live on his Staten Island estate for the purpose of writing a history of the world from a democratic point of view—the nine volumes are his *magnum opus*. His thesis was that tyranny is detrimental to economic and cultural progress. He was an ardent Republican, supported Lincoln, volunteered as a private in the Civil War, and advanced to the rank of captain, but left the service when an aristocrat was appointed his superior officer. Struve was a consistent fighter for freedom, but he was always cantankerous and his career was in toto, somewhat futile. (DAB.)

SZOLD, BENJAMIN (Nov. 15, 1829–July 31, 1902), rabbi, b. Nemiskert, Hungary. Studied at Vienna and became involved in the Revolution. He acted as private tutor and rabbi, among other places, in Stockholm. From Sweden he came in 1859 to Baltimore, where he served a congregation for over 30 years. During the Civil War he stood out boldly against slavery in the face of excited popular opinion. He was courageous, philanthropic, and a scholarly man of parts. When, on one occasion, Szold was unable to induce President Lincoln to pardon a deserter, he held the condemned man's hand while a firing squad ended his life. (DAB.)

TAFEL, GUSTAV, journalist, legislator, mayor, soldier, b. Stuttgart. Took part in the Baden Revolution and arrived in the U.S. in 1848. He was one of the founders of the Cincinnati *Turnverein* and for some years was city editor of the Cincinnati *Volksblatt*. He was the presiding officer of the Cincinnati *Turnverein* who, on the news of the fall of Ft. Sumter, called for volunteers for an entirely German regiment. It became the 9th Ohio Regiment with Robert McCook as colonel and later the 106th Ohio with Tafel as colonel. After the war Tafel served as a member of the Ohio Legislature and also as mayor of Cincinnati. (Kaufmann, 557; Wittke, "The Ninth Ohio Volunteers," *Ohio Archaeological and Historical Quarterly*, April, 1926, 1–18.)

TAFEL, LEONHARD (Feb. 6, 1800–?), teacher, preacher, b. Sulzbach, Wuerttemberg. Studied philology and theology in Tuebingen. He taught at a Stuttgart *Gymnasium*, but in 1824 he was sentenced to eighteen months in prison because of his incautiously expressed desire for a free and united Germany. He resumed his teaching career, but the authorities hampered him, particularly in 1848 and the following years, to such an extent that he left for the U.S. in 1853. He taught ancient languages in a number of cities. He was a member of the Swedenborgian Church and when he was seventy-two years old he was invited to become pastor of the small church of this denomination in New York. His list of publications includes thirty titles, among them a Bible translation and numerous language textbooks. He was the father of Gustav Tafel. (P, XII, 331.)

TAUSSIG, JAMES (Sept. 30, 1827–?), lawyer, b. Prague. Studied law in Prague but left the university in 1848 to join the Student Revolutionary Corps; he served throughout the siege and capture of Prague by Austrian forces. Forced to flee, he came to St. Louis late in 1848, took up the study of American law, and was licensed to practice in 1851. He became an ardent supporter of the Republican party. In 1862 he was sent by the radical Republican group as a committee of one to Lincoln to demand immediate freedom for the slaves. It is characteristic of the rapid march of events at the time that Lincoln told him such an act would be a suicidal move, and yet three months later the President announced the Emancipation Proclamation. Taussig declined political offices and continued in his legal practice until his retirement in 1891. (Hyde and Conart.)

THALMESSINGER, MEYER (June 23, 1829–April 26, 1906), businessman, banker, b. Pflaumloch, Bavaria. Trained as commercial apprentice in Fuerth. In 1847 he took part in the uprising in Ulm and was forced to flee the country. While in Paris he became involved in the February Revolution and arrived in New York as a political refugee in July, 1848. After various sorts of employment in a number of cities, he embarked in the mercantile stationery and printing business in New York and in the course of 31 years attained considerable success. In 1885 he was elected president of the Mechanics and Traders Bank. He was an ardent admirer of Lincoln, founder of the B'nai Brith Society, and widely engaged in civic and charitable enterprises. (Information from his granddaughter, Mrs. Theodore Schorske.)

THIEME, AUGUST (1822–Dec. 15, 1879), teacher, journalist, b. Leipzig. Studied theology and philology in Leipzig and taught for some time. An ardent partisan of the Revolution, he was elected in 1848 as successor to Robert Blum in the Frankfurt *Parlament*, where he represented the extreme left. He forced the prince of Reuss to grant a constitution, and for a while he was practical ruler of the small principality. When the reaction came, he fled to the U.S. in 1849. In Cleveland he founded the very influential *Waechter am Erie*. He was a *Turner* and valiantly upheld *Turner* ideals. He served as a member of the Ohio delegation to the Republican convention in Chicago in 1860. He was a lifelong fighter for freedom. (Herriot, 72; Huhn, I, 33; P, X, 370ff.; 486ff.)

TIEDEMANN, HEINRICH, physician, b. Heidelberg. Came to the U.S. in the thirties and settled in Dixon, Ill., where his son Fritz, later Carl Schurz's adjutant, was born. He returned to Germany in 1841 and in 1848 took part in the Baden Revolution. His brother, Gustav Nikolaus, was commander of the fortress Rastatt and was executed. Tiedemann married the sister of Hecker and returned to the U.S. with Hecker in 1848, settling in Philadelphia as a physician. Two of his sons were killed in the Civil War. He accompanied Kinkel on his lecture tour through the U.S. and served as treasurer for the "Revolution Fund." He was active in Republican politics in Philadelphia and also in many cultural enterprises. He was a close friend of Carl Schurz. (Ruetenik, 481; DPV, XVIII, 15.)

TRAU, JOHANN PHILIPP (Sept. 20, 1810–June 25, 1883), surgeon, b. Laumersheim, Rhenish Palatinate. Studied medicine in Heidelberg and Munich. Took part in the Palatinate Revolution as a surgeon in Blenker's corps. Fled to the U.S. and settled in Philadelphia, establishing a successful medical practice. He became an active member of the medical society as well as of numerous philanthropic organizations.

In the Civil War he served again as surgeon in Blenker's division. (Kaufmann, 556; P, XV, 333.)

TUERCKE, KARL AUGUST (Nov. 15, 1808–Jan. 29, 1886), pastor, b. Brandenburg, Prussia. First trained as a teacher and then as a liberal theologian at the University of Berlin. As a convinced liberal he preached funeral sermons for executed fighters for freedom in 1848 and 1849. This later resulted in considerable persecution from the reactionary authorities causing him to leave for the U.S. in 1858. He became pastor of a Lutheran church in Cincinnati, a post he held for 28 years. (P, XVII, 249ff.)

ULFFERS, HERMANN (1827–Nov. 24, 1879), engineer, soldier, b. Westphalia. Trained as a civil engineer. As a result of his participation in the Revolution he came to the U.S. in 1849. He worked at his profession, mostly for railroads in Indiana and for the geological survey in Illinois and Missouri. In 1861 he entered the Union army as engineer and was present at the battles of Pea Ridge, Corinth, Perryville, and Mumfreesboro. Sherman then called Ulffers to his staff with rank of lieutenant colonel, but shortly afterward he was taken prisoner and sent to Andersonville. His escape from this "hell" aroused public opinion, when, clad in rags and reduced to a skeleton, he reached the Union outposts. After he had recovered his health he reentered the army. After the war he served as army engineer until his death from tuberculosis. (Kaufmann, 558; P, XI, 395.)

ULKE, HENRY (Jan. 29, 1821–Feb. 17, 1910), painter, b. Frankenstein, Silesia. Studied art in Berlin. In 1848 he fought on the barricades in that city, was wounded, imprisoned, and later warned to leave Germany. He arrived in New York in 1852 and supported himself by means of drawings for *Harper's* and *Leslie's* weeklies. Becoming interested in the then new art of photography he opened a studio in Washington in 1860 and remained in that city for the rest of his life. He painted portraits of public figures of his day; his portrait of Grant hangs in the White House and his Beethoven in the National Gallery of Art. He was also a naturalist and collected 100,000 specimens of beetles which are now housed in the Carnegie Institute in Pittsburgh. His diary of the Berlin Revolution days is a valuable record; it is printed in AGR, August, 1946. (AGR, XI, 2.)

UNGER, PETER, journalist, teacher. Came to the U.S. after the Revolution of 1848 and was a journalist in Baltimore and teacher at Baltimore City College. He collaborated on Schem's German-American *Conversations Lexikon* and Rattermann's *Pionier*. (Cunz 272; P, III, 109 note.)

VALENTINY, KARL HEINRICH (1810–June 7, 1882), physician, b. Dortmund, Westphalia. Served as surgeon with the French army in Algiers, but returned to Germany in 1848 to join the fight for freedom. After the failure of the Revolution he was sought by the police, but managed to escape and reached the U.S. in 1850. He established himself as a successful physician in Brooklyn after many initial hardships. (P, XIV, 155.)

VETTE, WILHELM (1821–1884), journalist, b. Detmold. Studied in Leipzig, became involved in the Revolution, and came to the U.S. as a political refugee late in 1848. He first went to Detroit to edit the *Michigan Journal* and later to Milwaukee as editor of the *Banner*. When the paper failed, he became local editor of the *Herold*. Like many other Milwaukee Germans, he was a Democrat in politics. (P, XVII, 158.)

VIOLAND, ERNST (March, 1820–Dec. 18, 1875), lawyer, cigar maker, b. Lemberg. Though a member of an old Austrian family of Vienna, trained in a Jesuit College, and occupying a responsible legal post, he took part in the Revolution and was condemned to death. He escaped and arrived in the U.S. in 1849, settling in Peoria, Ill. He was noted as an able orator in the interest of liberal movements, as an enthusiastic *Turner*, and a supporter of cultural enterprises. Boernstein reports that Violand eaked out a meagre living as a cigar maker and retained his self-respect by refusing all aid from his friends, even honoraria for articles he wrote for Boernstein's *Anzeiger des Westens*. But in the course of time he managed to increase his business and even attained a comfortable prosperity. (JDAT, I, 187; Boernstein, II, 204f.)

VOGT, WILHELM (July 11, 1823–Nov. 16, 1871), jeweler, *Turner*, b. Hanau. Apprenticed to a goldsmith. An enthusiastic *Turner*—he won a first prize at a competition in Heilbronn—he was active in Revolutionary circles in Frankfurt. When he was about to be arrested, he decided to leave Germany. His friends gave him a farewell banquet at which Jahn read some verses dedicated to Vogt. He arrived in the U.S. in 1848, went into business as a jeweler, and helped found the Louisville, Ky., *Turnverein*. He also taught gymnastics in a private school. At a national *Turner* competition in Cincinnati in 1852 he won the first prize. During the Civil War he nursed wounded Union soldiers in Louisville. (Huhn, II, 31.)

VOLCK, ADELBERT JOHN (April 14, 1828–March 26, 1912), dentist, caricaturist, b. Augsburg. Studied in Nuernberg and Munich and participated in the Berlin Revolution. In 1849 he arrived in the U.S. as a penniless refugee and joined in the gold rush. He studied dentistry

SILVER TANKARD

CARTOON: PASSAGE THROUGH
BALTIMORE
From *Confederate War Etchings*, Baltimore

SILVER SHIELD

WORK OF ADELBERT JOHN
VOLCK

in Baltimore and became instructor in the Baltimore College of Dental Surgery, as well as a leading dentist in the city. He is one of the few Forty-eighters with Confederate sympathies and he gave expression to them in caricatures of Lincoln and other Union leaders that rivaled the cartoons of Thomas Nast on the Union side. He also did artistic work in bronze and silver. In 1861 he was incarcerated for allegedly sending medical supplies to the South. Volck was a man of spirit, progressive in his profession, and extremely versatile in the arts. (DAB; Cunz.)

VORTRIEDE, HEINRICH KARL JULIUS (Dec. 25, 1820–?, 1899), teacher, editor, b. Enger, Westphalia. Emigrated to the U.S. in 1850 because of his revolutionary activities in 1848. He taught in public schools of Dayton, Ohio, Louisville, Ky., and Toledo. From 1857 to 1872 he was editor of the *Telegraph* in Buffalo. He was active in local Buffalo and national Republican politics: In 1860 he attended the conference of German Republicans at Chicago, and in 1872 he was appointed by Governor Hoffmann as one of five commissioners to revise the city charter of Buffalo. Later he published the Toledo *Express* which he conducted until his death. (Herriot, 66f.)

WAGNER, PHILIPP (Jan. 23, 1811–?, 1895), lithographer, bookkeeper, customs official, b. Hesse. An associate of Struve and other liberals. When warned of police intentions to arrest him, he fled to Switzerland and France. He later returned to take part in the September insurrection in Frankfurt. Exiled again because he had urged action and violence, he arrived in the U.S. in 1849. He married the mother of his child after he had, from conviction, defied the marriage convention for three years. He worked as a lithographer and at various bookkeeping jobs. He was appointed customs official in 1861. He was active in the *deutsche Revolutionsverein* in Boston, but disapproved of the Wheeling Congress. In 1856 he joined the "North American Phalanx," but direct experience of life under socialism disillusioned him. Sigismund Kaufmann persuaded Wagner to speak in the 1860 campaign. Before and during the war he wrote for the Republican New York *Demokrat* and later published an autobiography. As customs official, Wagner saw much graft and became very critical of many aspects of U.S. life. In the late seventies he visited Germany for three months and there found social life richer than in the U.S. But he concludes: "The republic of the United States, despite its faults is the land of freedom and we must employ all our energy and intelligence to preserve and ennoble it, for its fall would be an irreplaceable loss for humanity." (*Ein Achtundvierziger*, Verlag Johannes Wagner, Brooklyn, 1882.)

WAGNER, WILHELM (Sept. 24, 1803–?, 1877), pastor and journalist, b. Duerkheim, Bavaria. Studied theology in Heidelberg and became pastor in Gersbach. He was not particularly active in the Revolution, but was denounced because of his liberal attitude and was condemned to prison; he fled to Switzerland and in 1851 arrived in the U.S. He was elected pastor of a Protestant church in Freeport, Ill., and in 1852 founded a Democratic paper. He continued in both occupations until his death. Wagner was a quiet, humble man, liberal in theology and politics, a *Turner* and a firm adherent of the Union cause. Published a volume of verse. (DAG, April 1904, 5–19.)

WANNER, GOTTLIEB (April 8, 1820–June 26, 1879), baker, *Turner*, b. Ludwigsburg, Wuerttemberg. He fought in the Baden Revolution and went as a refugee first to France and then, in 1850, to the U.S., where he settled in Cincinnati and gradually established a prosperous bakery business. He continued his *Turner* activities and participated in various progressive movements. (P, XI, 505.)

WAPPICH, LEOPOLD. Took part in the Baden Revolution and came to the U.S. as political refugee, living first in Buffalo and Keokuk, Iowa, and after 1860 in Peoria, Ill. He was distinguished by a good-natured eccentricity and was generally popular. (P, XVI, 288.)

WEBER, GUSTAV CARL ERICH (May 26, 1828–March 21, 1912), physician, consul, b. Bonn. Studied medicine at the University of Bonn. A fellow student of Carl Schurz, Weber also became involved in the Revolution and fled to the U.S. in 1849. He settled near St. Louis as a farmer, but like other Forty-eighters did not find this life so idyllic as he had expected. He therefore returned to Europe to finish his medical course in Vienna, Amsterdam, and Paris. Despite his earlier disappointments, he preferred America to Europe and returned to the U.S. in 1853, establishing himself as a physician in New York. In 1856 he accepted a call to the Cleveland Medical College. On the outbreak of the Civil War he was appointed by Governor Tod surgeon-general of Ohio in 1862 and later served as surgeon of the 129th Ohio until 1863. He organized the St. Vincent's Charity Hospital in Cleveland and also its medical college, where he was dean and professor of surgery. In 1897 President McKinley appointed him consul at Nuernberg. (DAB.)

WEBER, MAX (Aug. 24, 1824–?), soldier, hotel keeper, b. Baden. Although he was serving as an officer in the Baden army, he joined in the Revolution with enthusiasm. When this army was defeated, he had to flee and arrived in New York in 1850. He opened a hotel and proved very helpful to many fellow refugees. In 1861 he began his brilliant

Civil War career described in Chapter VII. After the war he was appointed collector of revenue of the port of New York. (Kaufmann, 561; Ruetenik, 359ff.; Schem.)

WEDEKIND, FRIEDRICH WILHELM (Feb. 21, 1816–Oct. 11, 1888), physician, b. Goettingen. While studying medicine at Goettingen, he became an active participant in the Republican Student Movement. He was imprisoned in the university jail (Karzer) for three days for "abuse and insult of the Royal Hannoverian Army." Undaunted, he continued in the revolutionary movement, propounding his democratic views in a newspaper which he issued together with his cousin, Eduard Wedekind, an alternate Hannoverian delegate to the Frankfurt *Parlament*. With the collapse of the Revolution he was forced to flee and landed in the U.S. in 1849. The opportunities of the West appealed to his adventurous spirit, and he made his way by foot, by horse, and by covered wagon to San Francisco, where he settled as a physician for the next fifteen years. He also won and lost a fortune in the gold rush. In 1864 he returned to Germany. He named his sons, born in Hannover, Benjamin Franklin and William Lincoln; the former became the famous dramatist, Frank Wedekind. Dr. Wedekind retained his American citizenship and continued publishing in the interest of liberalism. (AGR, XII, 6.)

WEIGEL, PHILIPP F. (1820–?), physician, b. Kandel, Palatinate. Studied medicine at Heidelberg where he was a friend of Hecker. Took an active part in the Revolution and arrived in the U.S. in 1850, settling in St. Louis as a physician. Later on he moved to Denver. He was an active *Turner* and wrote numerous satirical poems in freethinker spirit for *Turner* publications. (Huhn, I, 29.)

WEITLING, WILHELM (Oct. 5, 1808–Dec. 14, 1871), social reformer, labor leader, b. Magdeburg, Prussia. Trained as a tailor, he journeyed widely over Europe, agitating in the German workmen groups in Germany and abroad. His attitude is described as partly that of the old utopian critic of society and partly that of the modern aggressive reformer. In 1846 he was invited to New York by a group of German Free-Soilers to edit their *Volkstribun*. When 1848 arrived, Weitling hurried back to Germany, but the collapse of the Revolution forced him back to the U.S. in 1850. He refused to follow absolutely the Marxian dogma; because of his "warm brotherliness" and "meekness" Marx and Engels attacked Weitling as a reactionary and tried to undermine in every way his influence with the working classes. He and Weydemeyer were the most effective labor leaders among the Forty-eighters. (Schem; Wittke, Marx and Weitling.)

WESENDONCK, HUGO (April 24, 1817–?), businessman, b. Elberfeld. A lawyer by training, he practiced in Duesseldorf. He was elected to the Frankfurt *Parlament*, where he made the motion that all German armies be compelled to render an oath of allegiance to the *Parlament*. Owing to his participation in the rump *Parlament* in Stuttgart, he was charged with treason and, since he had escaped to New York, was condemned to death *in contumaciam*. He abandoned the law and founded the Germania Life Insurance Company which developed into a flourishing business with branches in a number of American cities as well as in Europe. (Lemke, 65ff.)

WEYDEMEYER [Weidemeyer or Wedemeyer], JOSEPH (1818–1866), journalist, utopian, soldier (birthplace unknown). Like Willich and Anneke he served as an officer in the Prussian army and also like these two he was discharged because of his revolutionary tendencies and activities. He became assistant editor of a liberal paper in Frankfurt and, of course, had to flee when the Revolution collapsed. In London he met Karl Marx and then, in 1851, he came to the U.S. He edited a short-lived monthly, *Die Revolution*, worked for a while as an engineer in Milwaukee, and then went to Chicago to publish *Die Stimme des Volkes*. Later he was associated with Weitling in his communistic *Republik der Arbeiter*. He attended the conference of German Republicans at Chicago in 1860. He served in the Civil War with considerable distinction as colonel of the 40th Missouri Regiment. After the war the citizens of St. Louis elected him comptroller, a post he was occupying when he died of cholera in 1866. (Herriot, 85; Huhn, I, 37; Kaufmann, 564; Karl Obermann, *Joseph Weydemeyer, Pioneer of American Socialism*, International Publishers, New York, 1947.)

WIEDINGER, BERNHARD MARIA (Aug. 15, 1826–Sept. 20, 1894), teacher, journalist, b. Engen, Baden. Studied in Heidelberg and fought in the Baden Revolution, sustaining a severe head wound. He was condemned to ten years of prison, but after one year managed to escape. He arrived in the U.S. in 1851 and became traveling salesman for a Philadelphia publisher. He was a vigorous opponent of slavery and as early as 1854 a campaign speaker for the Republican party. In Kansas he aided slaves to escape to free territory. He was a follower of John Brown and set out to join him at Harpers Ferry, but because of an accident arrived twelve hours late. In 1860 he founded an abolitionist paper in St. Joseph, Mo., but a mob destroyed his printshop. On the outbreak of the Civil War, he organized a company of one hundred men for the Hecker Regiment, but because of his defective eyesight his services were not accepted. He then opened a school in Chicago which flourished until failing health forced him to retire. He was one of the founders of the Chicago *Turnverein*. (Chicago, 152f.)

WIESNER, ADOLPH (1815–?), politician, b. Prague. Took part in the Revolution and sat as a delegate from Vienna in the left wing of the *Parlament* in Frankfurt. In 1849 he left Germany for Switzerland and in 1850 he came to Baltimore. He was prominent in the Baltimore *Turnverein* and for a time editor of the *Turnzeitung*. He was a courageous radical in politics and rendered great services to the Republican party in the slave state, Maryland. In 1860 he attended the conference of the German Republicans in Chicago. Shortly afterward he set out to return to Germany, but died en route. (Herriot, 67; P, III, 108; Cunz.)

WILHELMI, FRANZ, soldier. Came to the U.S. as a result of his participation in the Baden Revolution. In the Civil War he served as major in the 17th Missouri Regiment. (Kaufmann, 563.)

WILLICH, AUGUST (1810–Jan. 23, 1878), soldier, radical organizer, b. Posen. Trained in an aristocratic military school and served as captain of artillery in the Prussian army. Forced to resign from the army because of his revolutionary agitation, he learned the trade of carpenter. Associated with artisans and workers, he joined in the Baden Revolution under Hecker. He went to London as a refugee and lived there with a group of exiles, according to communistic principles. In 1853 he arrived in the U.S. and traveled widely through the states for the purpose of organizing political refugees for a military invasion of Germany in order to establish a republic. He also engaged in journalism. On the outbreak of the Civil War he helped organize in the course of a few hours the 9th Ohio Regiment (the first German regiment). His army career was brilliant. In 1870 he went to Germany, at the age of 60, to offer his services to the Prussian King, but was snubbed for his pains. He returned to the U.S. and spent his last years near Cincinnati in St. Mary's where a monument has been erected to him. Willich was a quixotic character, but utterly devoted to freedom and ever ready to lay down his life for the cause. He was widely beloved in *Turner* circles. Karl Marx ridiculed him, calling him a "communist with a heart"— which is exactly what Willich was. He also was the most dashing soldier among the Forty-eighters. (Huhn, I, 35; Kaufmann, 472ff.)

WITTICH, ALBERT (Nov. 2, 1823–June 3, 1877), butcher, b. Tuebingen, Wuerttemberg. He took part in the Baden Revolution and was forced to flee to the U.S. in 1848. He went directly to Cincinnati where after a number of years he was able to begin his own business and gradually became a prosperous butcher. He was a member of the *Pionier Verein*. (P, IX, 374.)

WOLFF, ALBERT (Sept. 26, 1825–?), journalist, politician, b. Braunschweig. Studied theology in Goettingen. In 1849 he took part in the revolutionary movement in Dresden, was taken prisoner and was given a ten years' sentence. In June, 1852, he was pardoned and came to the U.S. He went to St. Paul, Minn., where he at first found employment in a candy store and then turned to journalistic work on a number of papers, finally becoming editor of the *Volkszeitung*, a post he held for forty years. He took a very active part in politics. As early as 1855 he was elected a member of the legislature, served as immigration commissioner from 1864 to 1871, and in 1872 was a member of the St. Paul school board. In 1867 he published *Gedichte*, many of which deal with the Civil War in enthusiastic devotion to the Union cause. (Zimmermann.)

WRATISLAW, EDWARD C., soldier. Served as adjutant to General Mieroslawski in the Baden campaign. When the Revolution failed, he came to the U.S., and in the Civil War he served as lieutenant colonel of the 45th New York Regiment in Pope's campaign and at the second battle of Bull Run. (Kaufmann, 565.)

WUTSCHEL, FRANZ, soldier, b. Vienna. Fought on the barricades in Vienna, then came to the U.S. He served as colonel of the 8th New York Infantry Regiment. Because of indiscretion in the battle of Cross Keys, he was dismissed from the service—seemingly the only case of this kind among the Forty-eighters. (Kaufmann, 565.)

ZENTMAYER, JOSEPH (March 27, 1826–March 28, 1888), inventor and manufacturer of scientific instruments, b. Mannheim. Took part in the Baden Revolution and came to the U.S. as a political refugee in 1848. After employment in a number of cities, he set himself up as a maker of scientific instruments in Philadelphia, where he lived the rest of his life. His shop became the rendezvous of scientists. The microscopes he made were found to be superior to those imported from Europe and in the Civil War Zentmayer supplied most of those used in government hospitals. In 1865 he invented his famous photographic lens. His work received wide recognition in the U.S. and abroad. (DAB.)

ZERRAHN, CARL (July 28, 1826–Dec. 29, 1909), musician, b. Malchow. Studied music in Rostock. Involved in the Revolution, he had to flee and came to the U.S. in 1848. He was first flutist of the Germania Orchestra which gave concerts in various states of the Union. When the Boston Handel and Haydn Society, founded in 1815, decided in 1854 to select a professional conductor, Zerrahn was chosen. His success is shown by the fact that he held the post for forty-two years. In 1865 he conducted the Harvard symphony concerts and in 1872 the

Peace Jubilee in Boston where a chorus of 20,000 voices sang. For thirty-two years he directed the Worcester Music Festivals. He was one of the pioneers in American music. (DAB.)

ZIEGLER, KARL T. (1815–March 4, 1882), lawyer, b. Karlsruhe, Baden. He took an active part in the Baden Revolution, serving as civil commissioner in Karlsruhe. He was sentenced to ten years of imprisonment, but managed to escape to Switzerland and shortly afterward to the U.S. He settled in Newark, N. J. as a lawyer. (P, XIV, 36.)

ZIMMERMANN, JOHANN (June 24, 1820–Nov. 20, 1884), baker, b. Hesse. For his part in the Revolution he was forced to flee, arriving in the U.S. in 1848. He established himself as a successful baker in Cincinnati and continued in this business until his death. He was an enthusiastic *Turner* as well as a member of various musical organizations. He likewise took great interest in the work of the historical society, *der deutsche Pionier Verein*. (P, XVI, 527.)

ZITZ, FRANZ H., lawyer, b. Mainz. The "Nestor of the Mainz jurists," he was elected to the Frankfurt *Parlament*, became one of the leaders of the Revolution in Mainz, and commanded a corps of six hundred Palatinate troops in the field. With two fellow Forty-eighters he founded in New York the law firm, Zitz, Kapp, and Froebel. (*Magazin*, I, 22; Schurz.)

ZITZER, JOHANN (Feb. 20, 1826–Oct. 30, 1883), physician, b. Freiburg in Baden. Took part in the Baden Revolution and came to the U.S. in 1849, settling first in Carlisle, Pa. With the outbreak of the Civil War he became surgeon general of Pennsylvania. After the war he established himself in Baltimore as a very successful physician. (Kaufmann, 566; P, XVI, 326.)

INDEX

Frankfurt, ceremony in *Paulskirche* in honor of Schurz, 3

Frankfurt *Parlament*, congratulatory message sent by U. S., 4, 92; how revolutionary spark squandered and dissipated, 6 f.; petitions to, in behalf of religious freedom, 22; broadside on chief problem discussed, *text*, 83; American influences on thinking of, 155; president, 272; *see also* Revolutions of 1848

Franklin, Benjamin, 155

Freedom in America, 159, 161; *see also* Democracy

Free Press, Detroit, excerpts, 129, 135

Free-soil Party, 40, 179; *Turner* support of, 99

Freethinkers, 98; among Forty-eighters, 20; why they and the *Turner* had become: social and cultural life developed by, 55; schools, 55, 70; earliest societies founded, 55; feverish activity in Wisconsin, 56; service as chaplains in Civil War, 215; *see also* Religion

Freiligrath, poet, 171, 172

Frémont, John C., Presidential candidate, in 1856, 62; in 1864, 66, 115, 144 ff.; appeal to German voters, 128; unauthorized emancipation proclamations, 143, 144; Civil War command, 187, 189

Freudenberg, Carl Gottfried, 207, 294

Fricke, Heinrich C., 294

Friedrich, Wilhelm III, 21, 225

Friedrich, Wilhelm IV, 5, 225, 304

Froebel, Friedrich, 112, 178

Froebel, Julius, 46, 75, 112, 127; biography, 295

"Fruitlands," Concord, 15

Fuchshuber, Joseph A., 216

Fuess, Claude M., quoted, 240, 242, 243, 245, 246, 247

Fuester, Anton, 97, 295

Fugitive Slave Law, 38, 39

Gagern, General, 272

Gagern, Heinrich von, 272

Gambs, Johannes, 151, 295

Garibaldi, Giuseppi, 141, 210

Geary, John W., 192

Gebraetz, Georg, 295

Geiwitz, Else, 329

Geiwitz, Georg, 296

General Workingman's League, 179, 180

General Workmen's Convention, 179

Gebhardt, Joseph, 204, 271, 296

German-American Teachers Seminary, 57

German Democratic Association, 53

German-English Academy in Milwaukee, 57

German General Labor Union, 180

German language papers, *see* Newspapers

German Republican Central Committee of N. Y., 134

German Revolutionary League, 160, 166

Germans, number of distinguished men listed in *Dictionary of American Biography*, viii; Crefelders the earliest immigrants: ancestors of the "Pennsylvania Dutch," xi; Palatinate exodus: dates of persecution and of resulting flights, xi f.; always largest non-English speaking group in America, xii; type of success philosophy accepted by German historians, 3; little interest of early immigrants in U. S. politics, 22; "Latin farmers" of the thirties, 48; vast numbers of settlers attracted to Wisconsin, 53; early population and activities in Chicago, 61; relations between earlier immigrants (the "Grays") and Forty-eighters (the "Greens"), 62, 64, 113, 120, 168; leadership of the Forty-eighters, 67; types of immigrants during *Biedermeier* period, 111 ff.; political passivity and party affiliations of the pre-1848 immigrants, 111 ff., 120 (*see also* Politics); why pre-1848 immigrants not eager to follow "upstart" Forty-eighters, 119 f.; reaction to the Clayton Amendment, 125 f.; increasing importance accorded to German vote, 127, 128, 135 f.; extent of responsibility for Lincoln's election, 137 ff. (*see entries under* Lincoln, A.; Politics); states in which balance of power held, 135; contributed to defeat of Greeley, 150; question of their political ability, 156; factory conditions and low wages the chief reasons for emigration, 177 f.;

White, Andrew D., 122
Whitehead, Alfred, 24
Wiedinger, Bernhard Maria, 354
Wiesner, Adolph, 355
Wilhelmi, Franz, 207, 355
William I, 152, 170, 205
Willich, August von, 55, 130, 316; Civil War service, 108, 197, 199–201; biography, 198, 355; characteristics, 201
Willkie, Wendell L., quoted, 154
Wilson, James H., 210; on Hoffman, 211
Wisconsin, Germans in, 53–60; politics, 54 f.; *Turner* and Freethinkers' societies, 55 f.; education, 57 f.; 1860 vote analyzed, 139; bank note issues, 152
Wisconsin Banner, 54
Wisconsin Demokrat, 119
Wittich, Albert, 355
Wittig, L., 173
Wittke, Carl, quoted, 114, 120, 131
Wittmann, August, 58

Wolff, Albert, 46, 355
Woman suffrage, 34, 109, 154; career of Mathilde Franziska Anneke, 153
World Republic, radicals' plan for, 161 ff.; envisioned and started by Weitling, 180; Weydemeyer associated with, 354
World revolution, *see* Revolution, world
Wratislaw, Edward C., 208, 356
Wutschel, Franz, 207, 356

Y.M.C.A., adaptation of *Turner* idea, 110

Zeitung, Muscatine, 131
Zentmayer, Joseph, 356
Zerrahn, Carl, 356
Ziegler, Karl T., 357
Zimmermann, Johann, 357
Zipperlen, Adolf, 214
Zitz, Franz H., 357
Zitz, Kapp, and Froebel, 117, 308
Zitzer, Johann, 214, 357
Zuendt, Ernst Anton, 46